THE MARKET AND THE STATE

Books by the same author

The Effectiveness of Antitrust Policy Towards Horizontal Mergers, Ann Arbor, MI: UMI Press, 1983.

The Multinational Corporation in the 1980s (with Charles P. Kindleberger), Cambridge, MA: MIT Press, 1983.

The Convergence of International and Domestic Markets (with L. Sleuwaegen and H. Yamawaki), Amsterdam: North-Holland, 1989.

The Internationalization of US Markets (with M. Claudon), New York: New York University Press, 1989.

The Economics of Small Firms: A European Challenge (with Z. Acs), Boston: Kluwer Academic, forthcoming in 1990.

THE MARKET AND THE STATE

Government Policy Towards Business in Europe, Japan and the United States

David B. Audretsch

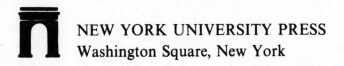 **NEW YORK UNIVERSITY PRESS**
Washington Square, New York

First published in the U.S.A. in 1989 by
NEW YORK UNIVERSITY PRESS
Washington Square
New York, NY 10003

Library of Congress Cataloging-in-Publication Data

Audretsch, David B.
    Market and the state: government policy towards business in
Europe, Japan, and the USA/David B. Audretsch.
        p.   cm.
    Bibliography: p.
    Includes index.
    ISBN 0–8147–1432–3
    1. Industry and state. 2. Competition, International. 3. United
States—Commercial policy. 4. Japan—Commercial policy.
5. European Economic Community countries—Commercial policy.
I. Title.
HD3611. A83 1989
338.9—dc20   89–12307
                                                       CIP

Printed in Great Britain

This book is dedicated to my wife, Joanne

CONTENTS

FIGURES

TABLES

PREFACE

This book is the culmination of over two years' research at the Wissenschafts-zentrum in West Berlin. While undertaking several research projects involving industrial organization and international competition, an important trend became apparent, namely that of an increasing integration of domestic with international markets. This has been true in Western Europe since the Second World War, whereas it has only recently become a major issue in the United States. As a result, public policies, which once may have been motivated out of purely domestic considerations, must now take into account the implications for international competitiveness. As the economies of Western Europe, Japan and the United States become increasingly interdependent, the domestic policies intervening in the economy are having an increased impact on global competition. The three instruments of intervention employed by these major industrialized countries are typically some variant of competition or antitrust policy, direct regulation or industrial policy, and international trade or commercial policy. The purpose of this book is to compare government policy towards business in Western Europe, Japan and the United States, analyze the impact and effectiveness, and assess the policies and the specific circumstances under which government intervention is most successful.

This book is divided into four major sections. Part I is an introduction to government intervention in the market. The other three sections each cover a substantive area of public policy towards business. Part II examines industrial policies – in particular antitrust and competition policies – which are oriented towards shaping market structure and business conduct; Part III considers direct regulation and industrial targeting; and Part IV examines the interaction between trade policy and domestic business. Within each section the three distinct approaches of Europe, Japan and the United States are compared.

I would like to thank a number of people who provided a significant amount of help and assistance in the development and preparation of the manuscript. Several of my colleagues here in Berlin were instrumental in forming and revising specific chapters. Zoltan Acs was very helpful in developing the ideas in Chapter 1 and Chapter 5. While many of these ideas have their origins in some of our joint work, which is referred to throughout these chapters, others are the fruit of numerous conversations that have taken place during the previous seven years. Much of the analysis in Chapter 4, Chapter 7 and Chapter 10 stems from my joint research work with Hideki Yamawaki. Without his influence and suggestions I would never have attempted to include much of the empirical analysis involving the response of the Japanese trade performance to industrial policy. Also, a substantial portion of the empirical analysis comes from or is developed in our joint papers which are referred to in these chapters. I would also like to thank participants in seminars at the New York University Business School, the Catholic University of Leuven, and the Institut für Weltwirtschaft in Kiel who provided numerous helpful comments concerning the analysis of Japanese industrial policy and trade performance. My colleague, George Bittling-mayer, was particularly helpful in discussing American antitrust with me. His influence, both in terms of written comments as well as informal discussion, is evident in Chapter 2. Joachim Schwalbach was particularly helpful in assisting me with the European data sources, particularly for competition policy and the exemptions of legalized cartels in West Germany, which are discussed in Chapter 6. Finally, some of the material in Chapter 5 was developed from joint work with Arthur G. Woolf of the University of Vermont.

Special thanks also go to Manfred Fleischer. Without his continuous presence and perseverance in providing support, both material and emotional, this book would not have been written. I am also grateful for the careful typing of parts of the manuscript by Marice Hartmann, Ilona Köhler, Christiane Loycke de Roux and Brigitte Schmidt. My debt to Linda von Chamier-Cieminski extends way beyond her typing the bulk of the manuscript. Not only did she practise her customary care and precision during the numerous revisions of the manuscript, but she also undertook painstaking editorial assistance in putting the book together. She went way beyond the call of duty in trying to help me produce a coherent and readable manuscript. The extent to which the resulting manuscript is comprehensible is in no small part attributable to Linda. Most amazingly, she exercised an uncanny degree of patience and goodwill throughout this endeavor, even under the pressure of impending deadlines. Finally, I especially thank my wife, Joanne, for not only helping with the proofreading and editing, but also for putting up with a husband who was too often absent in the evenings and on weekends during the first year of marriage in order to write this book.

ABBREVIATIONS

CAB	Civil Aeronautics Board (US)
COMPACT	Committee to Preserve American Color Television
CPI	Consumer Price Index
ECSC	European Coal and Steel Community
ECU	European Currency Unit
EEC	European Economic Community
EPA	Environmental Protection Agency (US)
ESPRIT	European Strategic Program for Research and Development in Information Technologies
EURATOM	Europäische Atomgemeinschaft (European Atomic Commission)
FCC	Federal Communications Commission (US)
FDA	Food and Drug Administration (US)
FEA	Federal Energy Administration (US)
FERC	Federal Energy Regulatory Commission (US)
FPC	Federal Power Commission, later FERC (US)
FTC	Federal Trade Commission (US)
GATT	General Agreement on Trade and Tariffs
ICC	Interstate Commerce Commission (US)
ITC	International Trade Commission (US)
MCF	thousand cubic feet
TCF	trillion cubic feet
MES	Minimum Efficient Scale
MITI	Ministry of International Trade and Industry (Japan)
NCRA	National Cooperation Research Act
NHTSA	National Highway Traffic Safety Administration (US)
OMA	Orderly Marketing Agreement
OSHA	Occupational Safety and Health Administration (US)
R&D	Research and Development
SIC	Standard Industrial Classification
TVA	Tennessee Valley Authority (US)
VRA	Voluntary Restraint Agreement

PART I

INTRODUCTION

1 · GOVERNMENT INTERVENTION IN THE MARKET: AN INTERNATIONAL PERSPECTIVE

INTERNATIONAL COMPETITIVENESS AND THE FAILURE OF MACROECONOMICS

Perhaps the hottest catchword in early 1987 in Washington DC, a city in which catchwords emerge only under the strictest conditions of competition, was 'international competitiveness'. Although Senator Bill Bradley had labelled it a 'mush word', by January of 1987 there were already eighteen reports undertaken by the US government to describe international competitiveness in detail, and by the spring 'competitiveness was rolling off the lips of everyone in Washington'.[1] That an issue such as international competitiveness had in a remarkably short time span ascended to a rank among the highest priorities in the nation's capital is not particularly unusual. By the summer of 1988 the Democratic Party had made the restoration of American competitiveness in international markets one of its major campaign goals.[2] Issues such as tax-incentive policies, anti-inflation programs, anti-poverty campaigns, among numerous others, had all enjoyed their shining moments of prestige in the limelight of American attention. What perhaps distinguishes the issue of international competitiveness from its predecessors is both the chronic nature of the problem and the consequences, which pose perhaps the most serious threat to the American way of life.

In an issue devoted to the question, 'Can America Compete?', *Business Week* concluded that the options facing the United States are either 'a surge in productivity – or a lasting decline'.[3] To the American public the crisis has been as difficult to recognize as it has been painful. During the first two decades following the Second World War:

> The U.S. was virtually unchallenged as industrial leader. Americans could make anything, and because their products were the best, they could sell whatever they made, both at home and abroad. But somewhere around 1973, the gravy train was derailed – and it has never really gotten back on track. It may have been a combination of things: Vietnam, the OPEC price shock, the inflation spiral. U.S. producers met fierce competition from foreign industries that churned out high-quality goods made by low-wage workers.[4]

The ascendency of 'international competitiveness into the limelight of the

American national agenda reflects a real economic transformation that has occurred among the leading developed nations. While the United States was clearly the economic leader during the first several decades following the Second World War, it no longer has a monopoly on either the frontier technology or the most highly skilled labour force. The consequences of this international economic restructuring have caused Rostow to conclude that 'The United States is entering a new political era, one in which it will be preoccupied by increased economic competition from abroad and will need better cooperation at home to deal with this challenge.'[5] According to Rostow, domestic competition is being replaced by global competition and, in turn, a new spirit of domestic cooperation must emerge to survive under the new order:

> The new question is whether the United States can so deploy its assets as to maintain its standard of life and avoid vicious mercantilist struggles in the face of competition from the Pacific basin and Latin America. The challenge has arisen because a major technological revolution was generated in the advanced industrial countries at just the time when the more advanced developing countries were mounting an educational revolution which is putting them in a position progressively to absorb and apply the new technologies.[6]

In this new awakening has come the concern that American business, especially in manufacturing industries, has not risen to the challenge posed by foreign competition during the last fifteen years. Rather, domestic producers have responded in a rather docile way, attempting more to ignore the inevitable than to implement the necessary changes to assure revitalization. The hope that foreign competition would somehow be unable to penetrate American markets could not be sustained. According to Abernathy et al. (1983, p. 9):

> This happy illusion lies shattered. Like a rich child away at school whose allowance – received weekly in the mail – has suddenly and mysteriously been cut off, all those who believed in the unquestioned primacy of American Manufacturing now find themselves abandoned by events. The harsh truth is that the industrial landscape in America is already littered with the remains of once-successful companies that could not adapt their strategic vision to altered conditions of competition.

The Reagan Administration's concern with international competitiveness has persisted from its earliest days in power, when tax concessions were hoped to induce a renaissance of American productivity growth, to the President's 1987 State of the Union Message, where Reagan placed a re-emergence of American superiority in manufacturing at the center of his new program, 'A Quest for Excellence'. Still, the balance on the current account has shifted from a surplus as recently as 1981 to a trade deficit in excess of $160 billion in 1985.[7] Recognition of the problem has not led to an automatic solution.

At the heart of the battle for global markets are the manufacturing industries. While the rate of growth in the United States has slowed, the

American economy has continued to expand throughout the 1980s. That is, while the annual percentage increase in real gross national product was nearly 3.5 percent between 1950 and 1960, and nearly 4 percent between 1960 and 1970, it decreased considerably to about 2.8 percent between 1970 and 1980, and even further to around 2.5 percent between 1980 and 1986.[8] Not only does Thurow suggest that America is 'losing the economic race',[9] but a number of economists and policymakers have expressed concern that what growth has been accomplished has emanated from the service sector and not from the manufacturing sector. In the face of high import penetration, plant closures and the displacement of jobs in the manufacturing sector by jobs in the service sector, Lee Iacocca, Chairman of Chrysler Corporation, warns: 'We can't afford to become a nation of video arcades, drive-in banks and McDonalds hamburger stands.'[10] In fact, employment in the American manufacturing sector fell from 40 percent of the total work force in 1959 to 27. 7 percent of the work force in 1984. At the same time the share of workers in the service sector rose from 40 percent in 1959 to 72. 3 percent in 1984.[11] Subsequently, as Thurow (1985, p. 23) observes: 'Today it's very hard to find an industrial corporation in America that isn't in really serious trouble basically because of trade problems. . . . The systematic erosion of our competitiveness comes from having lower rates of growth of manufacturing productivity year after year, as compared with the rest of the world.' And Kuttner, who asks, 'Must we lose the industrial world series?' speaks of the 'splendid illusion of the service economy vainly attempting to make up for the deficiencies of the manufacturing economy'.[12]

That the United States has only recently 'discovered' the significance of the issue of industrial competitiveness does not mean that the issue becomes less important to its major trading partners. In fact, the importance of maintaining or attaining the competitive advantage in global markets is at least as pressing today as it has been throughout the post-war period in Japan and Western Europe. As is discussed in subsequent chapters, success in foreign markets has played an important role in the strategy of countries such as Japan and West Germany and was instrumental in accomplishing the post-war 'economic miracles' that took place in both of these nations. The major difference between them and the United States is that America has only recently discovered what its major trading partners have been cognizant of since the end of the Second World War – namely, economic prosperity is bundled with international competitiveness. However, the concern about achieving international competitiveness looms large in Western Europe and Japan: 'The U.S. isn't the only country that can't seem to grow as fast as it used to. Japan, West Germany, and other leading industrial nations also have slipped from their robust growth rates of past years. . . . The result is that the so-called mature economies are now locked in a competitive struggle for each other's markets.'[13]

Perhaps not coincidentally, along with the deterioration of America's performance in international markets, has been the development of a crisis in macroeconomics. Where macroeconomics and macroeconomic policies could be generally relied upon to provide both an analysis and reasonable solution to the fundamental economic problems during the 1950s and 1960s, a vacuum emerged by the mid-1970s: macroeconomics could no longer be counted upon either to analyze the causes of the prevailing economic ills or suggest the appropriate remedies for correcting them. While aggregate demand management had adequately addressed problems such as recession and unemployment during the first two decades following the Second World War, it proved unable to grasp the underlying economic problems of the 1970s and 1980s. Thurow (1980, p. 24) was moved to write: 'At the end of the 1970s our political economy seems paralysed. The economy is stagnant, with a high level of inflation and unemployment. Fundamental problems exist but cannot be solved.' Not only could the received macroeconomic theory not adequately prescribe solutions to America's ills, but it also could not even explain the causes.

The failure of macroeconomics led to a revolution in economic thinking in the early 1980s, a renaissance of microeconomic ideas. Economists seemingly rediscovered the importance of economics at the market and firm levels. If the problems in individual markets could be better understood, it followed that the solutions appropriate for market-specific difficulties could then be provided. Above all, this revolution in economics was translated into the recognition of efficiency as a desired outcome of the market process. Thus, economic research allocated an increasing amount of energy and attention to the issue of what determines efficiency at the firm and market levels. This is reflected by the presence of only 27 articles in the field of macroeconomics among the 149 published in 1985 and 1986 by the *American Economic Review*, the profession's most prestigious journal.

While supply-side economics has its supporters and detractors, one aspect remains particularly decisive: supply-side economics is fundamentally a policy prescribing microeconomic solutions. While there are persuasive arguments that supply-side economics contributed little to improving America's deteriorating economy, its emergence reflected the need to turn towards microeconomic policies for both analyzing the contemporary problems and finding the answers. Thus, while *Business Week* writes that 'A new generation of economists is now focusing on ways to bridge the gap between the macroeconomic issues of saving and investment and the microproblems of productivity',[14] it would probably be more accurate to describe this as a retreat from the once seemingly infallible dictates of macroeconomics towards a revitalized microeconomic renaissance.

At the heart of the macroeconomic crisis was the premise that aggregate demand management offers little in terms of improving international competitiveness. The two traditional solutions – a devaluation of the US dollar and accelerated growth in major trading partners such as Japan and West Germany – are clearly inadequate measures for correcting a nearly $200 billion trade deficit. In fact, as the crash of the dollar during 1987 established, changing the dollar's value provides only superficial relief to the fundamental problems created by industries which cannot maintain viability in international markets. And, it seems equally futile to hope that faster economic growth in Western Europe and Japan would erode the American trade deficit. Although the ruling Liberal Democratic party in Japan announced a $34.5 billion plan to stimulate Japan's domestic economy, 'if US officials think this will make a big difference in Japan's trade balance anytime soon, they are sadly mistaken.'[15] Similarly, not only does West Germany resist efforts by the United States to coerce it into adapting a program of higher domestic growth, but it is clear that such higher growth would serve to reduce the US trade deficit only nominally.

MARKET FAILURE, GOVERNMENT INTERVENTION AND INDUSTRIAL POLICY

Until the late 1970s market failure was not acknowledged in the economic models of international trade. The conventional theories were built around the assumptions that perfect competition and constant returns to scale prevailed in every market. Such assumptions resulted in models where trade occurred only on the basis of comparative advantage. According to such models, trade would take place only to the extent that countries differ in tastes, technology or endowments of factors of production. While the Ricardian models emphasized technological differences as the primary determinant of trade, the Heckscher–Ohlin–Samuelson model emphasized differences in factor endowments.

Towards the end of the decade it became increasingly clear that the traditional models of trade, which had assumed away the possibility of market failure, no longer reflected the real world (Audretsch et al., forthcoming, a and b). The evidence mounted that market failure was a commonplace phenomenon in real world markets. That is, the two essential assumptions underlying the traditional trade models – that markets are perfectly competitive and that production is characterized by constant returns to scale – clearly did not represent a substantial number of industries. Most importantly, where these assumptions most obviously did not hold is in those industries in which trade plays the greatest role.

For example, there are substantial economies of scale in the production of aircraft, telecommunications equipment, semiconductors and pharmaceuticals, ensuring that the minimum efficient scale, or the maximum level of output required to attain minimum average cost, is sufficiently large that only several major firms can efficiently produce the product. A second source of scale economies occurs in the production of knowledge, which is a crucial input in high-technology industries. According to Krugman (1987, p. 137), 'Investment in knowledge inevitably has a fixed-cost aspect; once a firm has improved its product or technique, the unit cost of that improvement falls as more is produced. The result of these dynamic economies of scale must be a breakdown of perfect competition.'

The second source of market imperfection is externalities. The most obvious externality emanates from firms which innovate but are subsequently unable to appropriate fully the knowledge which they produced. Thus, external economies result from the inability of firms to completely appropriate the product from investment in R&D, which is the major input into producing knowledge (Acs and Audretsch, 1988). Finally, the learning curve, which implies that the marginal cost of production will tend to fall as output increases due to the gain in experience to the firm also implies that there will be substantial economies of scale and imperfect competition (Baldwin, 1988).

As a result of the disparity between the traditional trade models and real world markets, a marriage took place at the end of the 1970s between a handful of international trade economists and those who were experts at market failure and imperfect competition – the industrial organisation economists (Spence, 1976; Dixit and Stiglitz, 1977). The result of this collaboration was the development of economic models, such as those introduced by Krugman (1979), Dixit and Norman (1980), and Lancaster (1980), where imperfect competition and economies of scale led to 'arbitrary specialization by nations on products within monopolistically competitive industries' (Krugman, 1987, p. 133). Thus, increasing returns became a fundamental determinant of international trade. These models incorporating scale economies and imperfect competition provided a more accurate fit with the real world, since most trade is, in fact, in industries that are oligopolistic in the domestic market.

One of the implications of incorporating increasing returns to scale and imperfect competition into models of international trade is that firms which happen to be 'lucky' through product innovation and capture a large market share will be able to earn economic rents in that the rate of return will exceed the opportunity cost of employed resources. As a result, Krugman (1987, p. 131) observes that, 'These new models call into doubt the extent to which actual trade can be explained by comparative advantage; they also open the possibility that government intervention in trade via import restrictions, export subsidies, and so on may under some circumstances be in the national interest after all.' In fact, Brander and Spencer (1983; 1985) show that government policies, such as export subsidies and import restrictions can deter foreign firms from entering important domestic markets. Thus, interventionist policies by the government can mirror strategies that private firms implement, such as investment in R&D or excess capacity (Yamawaki and

Audretsch, 1988). Through pursuing such government policies, the market failure can be remedied, and one country can raise national output at the expense of its trading partners. This strategic trade policy argument concludes that government policy can influence the terms of oligopolistic competition and therefore shift the excess returns from foreign to domestic firms.

While Baldwin (1988, p. 209) suggests that, 'Essentially, targeting helps national firms grab as large a piece as possible of the international profit pie', it is clear that government intervention is not appropriate in every industry. Rather, the government policy should be targeted to those industries which are yielding the greatest externalities. In particular, industries in which knowledge and R&D play an important role are the most likely to generate such externalities. As Baldwin (1988, p. 208) implies, 'When an industry is marked by imperfect competition and scale economies, prices do not perfectly reflect tastes, technology and scarcity.... In such situations trade policy can take on a strategic role. Specifically, since governments have tools not available to firms, intervention can help firms commit to strategies that would not otherwise be profitable.'

One of the more prevalent economic myths in the United States is the notion that the absence of government intervention in the economy has been the historical norm. In fact, the government has played an enormous role in economic affairs and has maintained a substantial presence in the economy, especially since the early 1930s. However, to say that the American government has freely and extensively intervened in economic affairs is not to say that there has been an industrial policy in the sense of that which is implemented in Japan and Western Europe. Rather, US government intervention has been predominately a tool of macroeconomic policy and as an instrument to impose equity or redistribution. As will be seen shortly, none of these can be considered to be the essential aspects of industrial policy.

With the passage of the 1946 Full-Employment Act, the American Federal Government became, at least nominally, responsible for maintenance of full employment and economic growth. As discussed in the previous section, government intervention in the guise of aggregate demand management was certainly an accepted feature of the American economic landscape during the post-war period. But aggregate demand management, which proved to be so successful during its first two decades of implementation, failed with increasingly severe consequences to maintain economic prosperity during the last fifteen years. At the heart of the problem was the inadequacy of aggregate demand management to ensure market efficiency – especially in an international context. Ozaki (1984, p. 67) has observed that:

> American postwar economic policy has been based on the so-called 'neoclassical synthesis' – a doctrine that holds that a modern economy can be managed by a proper mix of monetary and fiscal policies generating sufficient aggregate demand for high employment without inflation, together with some government

regulations to alleviate negative externalities of private production, and product-specific protectionism here and there as politically necessary.... The trouble with the doctrine is that the Keynesian monetary-fiscal policy mix is primarily meant to cope with the problems of short-run business fluctuations by adjusting the level of aggregate demand. It is not well equipped to promote economic growth, a long-term process that requires close attention to the supply side of the equation.

The preoccupation of the supply-side policies that have accompanied the tenure of the Reagan Administration has been on the efficiency of firms and markets. While the policies have had an arguable amount of success, they represent a substantive change in focus – on the supply side of the economy rather than on the demand side. Seen through this lens, the underlying question accompanying most policies is now, 'What will be the impact on market efficiency?' Not coincidentally, this is the unifying issue that applies to the smorgasbord of policies which have recently been termed 'industrial policy'. Whatever form industrial policies in fact take on, they have in common the goal of improving the efficiency of certain industries or sectors. In this sense not only can the 'traditional' and obvious forms of government intervention such as subsidies and tax advantages be viewed as industrial policies, but also antitrust and competition policies, as well as decisions to regulate and deregulate entire industries.

An actual definition of industrial policy may be as difficult to formulate as it is prevalent in practice. As one US Supreme Court Justice expressed when trying to find a definition of pornography: 'You know it when you see it, but you can't define it', so it may be with industrial policy. According to Johnson (1984, p. 8):

> Industrial policy means the initiation and coordination of governmental activities to leverage upward the productivity and competitiveness of the whole economy and of particular industries in it. Above all, positive industrial policy means the infusion of goal-oriented, strategic thinking into public economic policy. . . . In more abstract terms, industrial policy is the logical outgrowth of the changing concept of comparative advantage.

Tyson and Zysman (1983) emphasize the distinction between sectorial policies and policies that apply across all sectors as being perhaps the most decisive criteria for what constitutes an industrial policy. While policies such as macroeconomic growth, unemployment, inflation, environmental quality and welfare programs generally touch all sectors of the economy, bona fide industrial policies are restricted to narrow sectors or industries. A second distinguishing feature is that industrial policy involves the application of 'market promotion' measures. Rather than aiming at improving aggregate economic conditions, market promotion policies are implemented to promote the efficiency in particular markets. Included as examples of market promotion policies are labor market policies, job relocation and retraining subsidies, incentive programs to increase the mobility of labor, capital market policies, government loan guarantees to small business and antitrust policies (Tyson and Zysman, 1983).

Grant (1982) points out that a central problem to identifying and assessing different industrial policy instruments is that the policies are generally distorted by the macroeconomic policies of a government, such as the exchange rate, tax rate, rate of growth in the money supply and the federal budget. Ozaki (1984, p. 48) considers industrial policy to include those government interventions which are undertaken with the objectives of

> accelerating the structural transformation of domestic industry in a desired direction, improving the international competitiveness of designated products, encouraging the development of new technologies, smoothing the phasing out of chronically depressed industries, assisting the rationalization and reorganization of a weakened industry that is judged to have a chance for recovery, and protecting domestic employment in a particular industry.

It is not surprising that Wildavsky (1984, p. 28) concludes that 'there is no such thing as not having an industrial policy. Action and inaction alike affect the condition of industry'. Thus, even the absence of a well-formulated program, such as has been practised in the United States, still constitutes a decision regarding industrial policy. According to Weil: 'We have an industrial policy in this country; the policy is that we do not want an industrial policy.'[16]

The goals and justifications for undertaking a positive industrial policy program are multifaceted. However, the fundamental goal is to restore, maintain or capture the global competitive advantage. This goal is a considerable claim in the face of the prevalent wisdom in international trade theory that trade patterns are determined on the basis of factor endowments. According to the Heckscher-Ohlin theory in international trade, the proportion of productive factors determines the trade structure. If there exists an abundance of physical capital relative to labor, a country will tend towards exportation of capital-intensive goods; an abundance of labor relative to physical capital leads to the exportation of labor-intensive goods (Stern, 1975; Stern and Maskus, 1981). Even when the Heckscher–Ohlin theory was extended by including human capital and R&D intensity as additional factors, the model remained static in the sense that it is only the endowments of those productive factors which determine trade flows. The implication being that there is virtually nothing a country can do to alter trade flows.

In hoping to change the trade flows and ultimately the competitive advantage, those proponents of industrial policies are essentially betting that the Heckscher–Ohlin theory does not actually hold in the real world. That is, the comparative advantage may in fact be endogenous to the policies of governments as well as firms. Porter, for example, has argued that 'factor endowments, which were at the heart of the traditional theory of comparative advantage, are less and less important in explaining competitiveness. Technological change and the globalisation of competition have both contributed to decoupling factor advantage from firm success, because firms can now substitute either factors and locations' (de Crombrugghe, 1987, p. 1).

In particular, factors such as the industry experience curve and learning curve tend to make international competitiveness an endogenous and not an exogenous phenomenon. According to the experience curve, average costs in an industry decline as the experience in producing that product increases. Porter (1979) attributes economies of scale, the capital–labor substitution and the gain in human capital by labor as the underlying factors for the experience curve. The existence of the experience curve creates a significant incentive to be the 'first-mover' in any given market, because the followers will presumably face substantial additional costs of entering. An entry barrier exists for followers because they have to compensate for their lack of experience in producing and marketing the product, while the incumbent faces lower costs which are attributable to the experience curve. Thus, by following policies which ensure that their firms and industries will be market leaders, governments can, perhaps, exploit the experience curve and influence the resulting patterns of global competitiveness. Gold (1986, p. 18) has similarly concluded that 'It is important to recognize that the concept of "comparative advantage", which implies an optimal division of production among countries, is not based solely on unchanging "natural endowments". On the contrary, relative competitiveness has been altered repeatedly by changing input requirements, technologies, production facilities, products, and transportation capabilities.'

Once it is recognized that international competitiveness is endogenous and not exogenous, it is natural to consider which government policies might best promote the competitive advantage. Only since 1980 have theoretical models been developed in economics which recognize that, in the presence of imperfect competition, government intervention results in the best outcome. For example, Brander and Spencer (1985) propose a model in which there is only one firm in the domestic and foreign countries that produces perfectly substitutable goods. Under the conditions of a Cournot–Nash equilibrium, they conclude that an export subsidy is optimal for competing in third-country markets. Similarly, Krugman (1984), using a model where there are increasing returns to scale, finds that protection of a domestic firm in one market actually bestows an advantage on the firm through a reduction in the marginal cost. And, Eaton and Grossman (1986) show that either trade policy or industrial policy can raise the welfare of the domestic country when the foreign country is also engaging in an industrial policy. Thus, Gold (1986, p. 21) has been moved to write: 'In the face of intensified improvement programs by producers and governments in many parts of the world, there is one most fundamental requirement of a program to restore the international competitivity of US industries. That need is to develop a more realistic, more constructive, and more forward-looking cooperative effort by industry and government.'

Bardach (1984) considers the instruments of industrial policy to include those means to coordinate commercial policy (foreign trade policy), antitrust policy and the actual channeling of funds into specific firms and industries. In particular, the ten major instruments of industrial policy include:

1. protectionism in the form of tariffs and non-tariff barriers;
2. export subsidies;
3. financial assistance to displaced workers in industries in the declining phase of the product life cycle;
4. subsidies and other support for R&D;
5. programs to improve the human capital and level of labor skills of the workforce;
6. antitrust policy and in particular those policies which are oriented towards restructuring industries;
7. support in developing the capital infrastructure essential to industrial development;
8. the provision of direct loans and loan guarantees to industry to share the risk;
9. tax policy oriented towards stimulating capital investment; and
10. the procurement policy of the government.

A glance at these ten items reveals that most of them are instruments of a supply-side oriented policy. This is not a coincidence. According to Johnson (1982, p. 11):

> By industrial policy I mean the government's explicit attempt to coordinate its own multifarious activities and expenditures and to reform them using as a basic criterion the achievement of dynamic comparative advantage for the American economy. Such an industrial policy would work on the supply side and would be long-term in outlook. It would seek to produce aggressive investment behavior by reducing risks, providing information, promoting R&D, removing irrational antitrust barriers and encouraging the appropriate education and re-education of the labor force.

Ozaki (1984) argues that the industrial policy implemented by a country cannot be separated from its history and culture. He points to the example of Japan, where a long tradition of excellence in bureaucracy has existed. Noting that, unlike in the United States, many of the most talented and able people in Japan enter the national civil service, Ozaki suggests that Japan's success with industrial policy has benefited from good working relationships between the bureaucracy and the parliament as well as between the bureaucracy and private business. Similarly, Ozaki notes that the group orientation in the Japanese culture is particularly conducive to promoting the success of industrial policies.

Streit (1984) has found that West Germany has also had a fairly long record of industrial policy. However, he argues that assistance has generally been more oriented towards conservation than towards modernization. He concludes that industrial policies in West Germany 'are easily overrated in terms of size and – like elsewhere – are based on very shaky analytical grounds which also prevent a conclusive assessment' (Streit, 1984, p. 14). In fact, the United States has also had historic bouts with direct intervention and industrial targeting. Examples include the Manhattan project, the Chrysler bailout, the TVA (Tennessee Valley Authority) and oil depreciation allowances. Still, the general resistance in America towards industry-promotion programs has been characterized as, 'How can bureaucrats tell, more accurately than private investors, which are the most promising firms or industries?'[17]

TECHNOLOGICAL CHANGE AND INTERNATIONAL COMPETITIVENESS

It is the particular relationship between the developed and developing nations, characterized by the product life cycle, which demonstrates the significance of technological change and innovation for determining the competitive advantage. The absence of a singular product concept in the market characterizes the introduction phase of the product life cycle. No unique product design dominates the industry, so firms must typically experiment with the design in short production runs and gauge the reaction and needs of consumers. Thus, firms rely more on a batch mode production of customized products rather than on continuous process manufacturing (Vernon, 1966). Wheelwright (1985) argues that market survival during this phase depends more upon developing and adapting technology than by offering the lowest-price product. Thus, the price-elasticity of demand tends to be relatively low because of (1) the absence of product standardization, causing significant technological product differentiation in the market, and (2) the lack of reliable product information and consumer experience (Wells, 1966).

Because of the typically short production runs required by constantly changing product design, the production process tends to be relatively labor-intensive, and to rely on relatively skilled workers, not only to operate general purpose machinery, but also to participate in modifying the product design and production process. Thus, the industry tends to be the least capital-intensive during the introduction stage.

As the industry evolves into the growth stage and towards maturity, the product becomes increasingly standardized. Vernon (1966, p. 196) notes that although product differentiation may still continue, and sometimes even intensify, leading to a proliferation of product variety, 'a growing acceptance of certain general standards seems to be typical'. Product standardization tends to raise price-elasticity of demand facing each firm. Because the rate of technological change typically slows, the potential for reducing average cost through the exploitation of scale economies increases. Thus, concern about searching for the optimal product concept and technology becomes replaced by a focus on minimizing production costs. As specialized replaces generalized machinery, manufacturing becomes a more continuous process and less batch-oriented. Hence, the production process becomes increasingly capital-intensive as the industry evolves over the life cycle, raising the capital–output ratio. Attaining the minimum efficient scale (MES) – the minimum level of output yielding the minimum average cost – requires increasing levels of output as the industry evolves towards maturity. Similarly, with the increased reliance on specialized machinery, skilled labor is no longer an essential ingredient. With product standardization, not only does the capital–labor ratio tend to rise, but unskilled labor is substituted for skilled labor (Vernon, 1966).

As the industry matures and evolves into the declining stage, the product concept approaches rigidity. According to Abernathy et al. (1983, p. 123), 'Competition proceeds along narrowing lines until, in a mature industry, the technological positions taken by the major producers are virtually indistinguishable.' During the latter phases, little technological distinction exists among producers as the product design becomes entrenched. The price-elasticity of demand rises as the focus of competition shifts towards price.

Despite the obvious qualification that no singular life cycle common among all manufacturing industries exists, there is concurrence that the basic concept of the life cycle is generally representative of the evolution of most industrial markets (Shepherd, 1979). As the industry evolves towards the mature stage of the life cycle, product standardization and consumer experience with the product bring about an increase in the price-elasticity of demand. According to Porter (1976), product standardization combined with a relatively high elasticity of demand are conducive to 'interindustry competition' – an increased significance in the element of price rivalry within the market. Thus, while foreign competition is generally reticent during the early stages of the life cycle, it typically becomes significant once maturity is attained. According to Vernon (1966), both imports and foreign direct investment become feasible by maturity. While empirical research indicates that industries which are technology- and skill-intensive (that is, still in the growth stage of the life cycle) tend to be net exporters, those industries that utilize unskilled labor and are not technology-intensive – the mature and declining industries – tend to be net importers (Audretsch, 1987a). With product standardization and a relatively fixed technology, the uncertainty regarding technological change decreases. The comparative advantage may switch from domestic to foreign firms, which enjoy lower import costs (Maskus, 1983).

Since the most developed countries, including the United States, Japan and those in the EEC (European Economic Community), cannot compete with the less developed countries for the advantage in industries which are in the mature and declining phases of the product life cycle, the importance of technological change and innovation activity in the industries that are new and growing is paramount. Piore and Sabel (1984), Abernathy *et al.* (1983), Reich (1983) and Wheelwright (1985) all argue that the key strategy for attaining the competitive advantage in global markets is to pursue a strategy of permanent innovation, which enables the firm to continuously maintain a position at the cutting edge of the product life cycle. Sveikauskas (1983) has found that it has been the high level of science and technology commanded by American industry, and not occupation skills or capital intensity, which have enabled the United States to capture the competitive advantage in certain key technology-intensive markets. In particular, the R&D intensity in the United States, along with the propensity to develop radical major innovations, has played a crucial role in its attainment of the competitive advantage in certain markets. Similarly, Hughes (1986) found that the export performance of the United Kingdom responds to domestic R&D expenditures. She finds that R&D is the most important input in determining the competitive advantage, while the effect of professional and technical staff on the export performance was rejected. However, the amount of skilled manual labor in the industry does have a positive and significant effect on the export performance in the United Kingdom.

As the importance of technological change to capturing the global competitive advantage has become more apparent, so have R&D expenditures become increasingly important: 'Industrial research has become the principal driving force behind the process of technological change.'[18] During the 1970s private R&D in the United States was stagnant. However, since 1980, there have been annual increases in the R&D expenditures in excess of 10 percent. Further, American companies have implemented mechanisms to attempt to protect valuable high-technology from being spread to competing foreign rivals.[19] Despite the surge in R&D spending in the United States, there is evidence that the period of neglect in the 1970s has proven to be costly and will continue to prove so. Griliches (1986), who used a newly available body of data on all of the major firms performing R&D in the United States, found that R&D contributes significantly to productivity growth. Further, the most important component of R&D has been that devoted towards basic research. He also found that privately financed R&D expenditures have a larger impact on productivity than do expenditures on R&D financed by the government. These results suggest that the recent productivity slowdown in the United States may be at least somewhat attributable to the slack in private R&D expenditures during the 1970s.

Another aspect of trying to stay at the cutting edge of the product life cycle involves the development and application of human capital and skilled workers. Kuttner laments: 'Ironically, as national concern grows about America's lagging productivity and competitiveness, the quality of the US force is declining. . . . In the debate about US global competitiveness, nearly everyone has concluded that a high-quality work force is our most important asset. Job upgrading and lifetime learning are new concepts for the American economy. But in a competitive global market, they are not merely quality-of-life issues but questions of economic survival.'[20] Not only do companies have to innovate to attain or maintain a competitive advantage, but they must also develop a workforce which is able to adapt with relative ease to new and continually changing technologies. Applications of advanced computer technologies in manufacturing industries, for example, require highly skilled workers who must be capable of mastering a multiplicity of functions, including materials handling, assembly, inventory control and testing. There is currently an evolving form of organization which 'will gradually replace the old system characterized by authoritarian management and an extreme division of labor epitomized by the assembly line. The new approach often entails socio-technical planning.'[21]

The pressing need for basic R&D, and the development of human capital and labor skills in order to promote industrial competitiveness, has been a significant ground given for implementing targeting programs. Tyson and Zysman (1983) argue that policies of government intervention can ultimately transform an industry facing a competitive disadvantage into a global leader through the development of technology and human capital. Combined with the concept of the experience curve, once a policy of targeting has been implemented, if the industry gains global dominance, it will be that much more difficult for foreign rivals to upseat it. They conclude: 'Seen in this light, the growing comparative advantage of Japan in many capital-intensive goods in the postwar period, and the declining share of US producers in the world markets for these goods, are the result of different national investment efforts influenced by different national policies' (Tyson and Zysman, 1983, p. 27). Not only has Japan followed such policies, but other countries, such as France, have recently begun to emphasize advanced science and technology in an attempt to attain competitive parity. In fact, the industrial policies throughout Europe are in some sense bringing those countries closer in line with the R&D patterns which have been experienced in the United States (Sveikauskas, 1983). And in the United States, there have been recent calls for life-long training and education programs.[22]

ANTITRUST, REGULATION, AND TRADE POLICY

Given the growing importance of international markets, along with the importance of becoming the leader in those markets, it is not surprising that all of the developed nations have resorted to trade protection in order to best exploit the gains accrued from the experience curve. However, like all types of government intervention, commercial policy can be classified according to type and purpose. That is, in the Great Depression, the United States resorted to imposing very severe trade barriers. This protectionist move, however, cannot be considered to be a type of industrial policy, because the goal was not so much to nurture particular industries as to maintain or support the level of aggregate demand in the overall economy. By contrast, Japan used selective protective instruments during the first several decades following the Second World War in an effort to promote these industries. That is, protection in the first example is not a case of industrial policy, while it is in the second one.

Along with the $32 billion US trade deficit for the second quarter of 1985 has come an intense demand for trade protection. In the face of displaced workers, plant closures and regional deterioration, imposition of trade protection measures seems like an effective and desirable solution. Thus, the US Congress has recently moved to impose trade restrictions in various forms, such as higher tariffs on imports, pressure on trading partners to acquiesce 'voluntary' export restraint agreements, and non-tariff barriers such as quotas and 'quality' restriction. Most recently proponents of such commercial policy measures have argued that 'America will become a service economy unless we protect threatened manufacturing industries from foreign competition' (Denzau, 1987, p. 14).

An interesting development within the last decade in the field of international economics has been the emergence of a new literature which has provided theoretical justifications for trade protection. This is a reversal of the standard conclusion of international trade models that universal free trade results in a *pareto optimal* solution for all participants in the global economy. However, this result applied only to a world in which markets could be characterized as being perfectly competitive and where governments do not intervene in domestic markets to promote the well-being of domestic firms and industries (Brander and Spencer, 1985). As Krugman (1984) shows, this result does not hold up in the presence of an oligopolistic international market structure. Under conditions of imperfect market structures, trade protection may actually be preferable to unhindered trade. In addition, arguments for protection have been made on the grounds that key technological sectors need to be promoted. It has been argued that through protection of industries such as electronics or robotics, subsequent growth and development, both within and outside of the sector, will be promoted because of benefits accrued from exploiting the experience curve (Boltho and Allsopp, 1987). Sharp (1987) has shown that arguments supporting protection of high technology sectors are valid only if there are externalities which cannot be incorporated into private transactions. This supports the claim of Borrus *et al.* (1986, p. 110) that such protection is appropriate in the electronics industry, because 'crucial innovation occurs at the level of the chip, and losing the ability to design systems can affect a wide range of industries'. Finally, in markets in which a slow adjustment to change occurs, temporary protection may be a second-best solution because the movement of resources is not instantaneous. In such cases, the cost of unemployment and displacement can be minimized.

In fact, the GATT (General Agreement on Trade and Tariffs) has provisions which sanction responses to the distorting measures of foreign trade. The preferred GATT procedure to foreign tariffs is to offer to undertake a multilateral tariff-reducing negotiation. Baldwin and Thompson (1984) conclude that this procedure has worked reasonably well. They also conclude, however, that there has been a breakdown of the so-called escape clauses (the safeguard provisions) of Article 19 of GATT, which allows import protection to be increased if it can be shown that the domestic industry has been injured because of increased imports. And, countries have been resorting to non-tariff restrictions with increasing frequency. Their observation is consistent with the findings of others that there has been an increasing trend in protection since the 1970s. Franko (1980) found that the trend in protection in Western Europe increased between 1974 and 1978, and Boltho and Allsopp (1987) conclude that protectionist policies have increased in the 1980s.

It appears that foreign trade policies have generally played three major roles. The first has been to influence domestic aggregate demand, which cannot be considered to be a part of industrial policy, except to the extent to which protection affects the performance of the domestic industries in the global market. The second role has been to protect declining industries or industries which would otherwise lose a considerable share of the domestic market to foreign firms. The third role has been to provide key technology and information industries with the opportunity to develop in order to exploit the experience curve.

The relationship between competition (antitrust) policy, and industrial policy has been an uneasy one in most developed countries. N. Owen (1983) argues that recent developments in US antitrust policy, particularly those aspects dealing with mergers, constitute a *de facto* industrial policy. Owen points out that while efficiency had not previously been considered to be a legal defense for mergers in American antitrust, the most recent evolution of policy has been towards allowing certain mergers on efficiency grounds. Probably more importantly, the 1982 and 1984 Merger Guidelines represent the attempts of the antitrust agencies to take a much more active role in 'shaping' industry structures, so that mergers that are more likely to bring efficiency gains and less likely to cause social losses due to collusion are permitted, while those less likely to result in efficiency gains but are more likely to promote collusion are not allowed. This represents a shift to where the antitrust agencies are taking a much more active role in promoting economic efficiency.

Historically, antitrust policy has been limited to negative sanctions in response to direct or alleged violations of the law. This has restricted the industrial policy component of antitrust to a subset of industries – those in which antitrust violations occur. B.M. Owen (1986, pp. 426–7) finds that

> it is anomalous that the powerful remedial tools of antitrust enforcement and trade sanctions should be applied negatively – that is, only in situations where someone is thought to have violated the law. There is no particular reason to suppose that the greatest potential gains from the application of economic analysis to industry structure should be found in industries where some colorable case of law violation can be found. Instead, the most important opportunities for beneficial intervention may be found in industries that are not themselves litigious.... There are significant interactions among the various trade, R&D, and antitrust policies employed by the government, and it makes little sense to try to wield them independently. The growing consensus that economic welfare is the most appropriate framework for such intervention, and the reforms leading to its adoption, may provide for the first time a basis for integrating these policy instruments.

As will be seen in Chapter 2, a new direction in American antitrust policy accompanied the eight-year tenure of President Reagan. Langenfeld and Scheffman (1988, p. 45) argue that much of this policy change was a response to the need to promote US international competitiveness: 'It has taken the combination of the election of Ronald Reagan and the burgeoning competitiveness "crisis" for competition policy to be redirected to provide a more hospitable environment for competition.'

It is clear that antitrust decisions affect the efficiency of an industry, both in an international and domestic context. In this sense, antitrust is perhaps the most widely used form of industrial policy which has been applied in the United States. The most recent concern about efficiency that has emerged in antitrust policy reflects the prevalent economic issue of the time – the need to promote international competitiveness. Thus, Owen (1986, p. 410) concludes that 'because the skills presently employed to make antitrust enforcement decisions are of a more general applicability, and because of the underlying evolution of confidence in the reliability of microeconomic analysis in policy making, it would be logical to expect a movement toward an integration of antitrust, trade, tax, and other policies affecting US industrial structure.'

In fact, there has already been considerable overlap between international trade policy and antitrust policy. Calvani (1985), who was acting chairman of the US Federal Trade Commission (FTC), one of the two major antitrust agencies in the United States, has observed that the presence of foreign competition may cause the Commission to allow a merger where it would otherwise be prohibited. The existence of international rivalry reduces the amount of actual market power which American firms can exercise.

The second way in which the two policies overlap is that firms sometimes file complaints charging dumping and other unfair trade practices by foreign competitors at the US International Trade Commission (ITC), in the hopes of obtaining trade protection, which would then increase the domestic firms' market power. There is obviously considerable interplay between these two functions. Calvani (1985, p. 15) writes of being 'troubled by the prospect of a firm using imports to justify a merger before my agency and then seeking to have them restricted by the International Trade Commission.'

The most recent bout with regulation in the United States has actually been to deregulate industries. While this may at first not sound like a policy of government intervention, the recent American deregulation movement can easily be seen as a form of industrial policy. Although a host of industries has been involved, including trucking, airlines, railroad, telecommunications, television, banking, natural gas, oil and securities markets, there was only minimal political resistance towards regulatory reform. The reason may be that the underlying motivation for deregulation was economic efficiency. The subsequent efficiency gains, which are discussed in Chapter 5, were spread throughout the economy, presumably contributing to the international competitiveness of various industries. Thus, the decision of a country to regulate, not to regulate or deregulate an industry has external effects which extend beyond the domestic economy. Where questions of equity and power may have played a relatively more important role in earlier periods, the goal of promoting economic efficiency seems closely related to the American deregulation movement.

THE EUROPEAN, JAPANESE AND AMERICAN EXPERIENCE

The experiences of government intervention in Europe, Japan and the United States offer a study in contrasts. For example, while the United States has tended to engage in a much more adversarial style of industrial policy, through its implementation by litigious means undertaken by the antitrust agencies and the trade policy agencies, such as the ITC, Japan has practised a much more positive and directive program, which emphasizes cooperation and minimizes dissension. Similarly, while countries in Europe have much more readily engaged in large, multi-country R&D projects, in an effort to develop new technologies, the United States has been much more reluctant to allow, let alone organize, joint R&D projects. Still, there are certain similarities that exist in the experiences with government intervention among Europe, Japan and the United States. Perhaps most notably is the recent emphasis towards efficiency. That is, the extent and form of government intervention is increasingly being dictated by what best promotes an efficient market performance. Perhaps it is the 'invisible hand' of the new global competition in most manufacturing markets that imposes this discipline upon government policies.

Towards the end of 1985 a merger wave struck Britain that involved high-technology industries. While the General Electric Company purchased another leading electronics company, Plessey Co., for $17 billion, 352 high-technology companies were acquired in the first three-quarters of 1985 for a total of $9 billion. Part of this merger trend was a response to a similar movement in the United States: 'You are seeing here much of what you have seen in the U.S.–a tendency toward bigger and stronger groupings.'[23] The Thatcher government generally favors these mergers, which hopefully make the firms involved stronger competitors in the international markets. This is particularly important, since the General Electric Company has not yet been able to penetrate the US market. Although the British Monopolies and Mergers Commission is examining the merger, as long as it does not result in a 'quasi-monopoly', the Thatcher government argues that the gains in international competitiveness more than offset the cost.

It is also clear that the domestic policies of one country are having a greater impact on the others. While at one time American antitrust decisions would have been seen even by major foreign trading partners as a purely domestic affair, this is no longer the case today. Thus, the deregulation movement in the late 1970s and early 1980s in the United States seems to be inevitably spreading to Europe, although with a different emphasis. If the US experiment with deregulation is proving to yield gains in economic efficiency, the European countries cannot afford to complacently continue their own policies of economic regulation. Thus, slightly over eleven years after the United States deregulated its securities market, the so-called 'Big Bang' in October 1986 marked the beginning of deregulation of the London securities markets. While deregulation in the United States led to an intense increase in competition, the final result was apparently lower rates for consumers and an explosion in new product forms. Based on the US experience, the British Exchequer and the Bank of England initiated deregulation of the London securities markets. As a result, there has been a vast increase in the participation of capital-laden foreign firms, particularly American and Japanese.[24]

The American experience with airline deregulation seems to be spreading to Europe. While Alfred E. Kahn, who was instrumental in promoting airline deregulation in the United States, argues that the American experience provides a 'lesson for Europe',[25] *The Economist* advocates that the EEC should break up the legalized airline cartels in Europe, 'but not the American way'.[26] In fact, the European Court of Justice ruled in May 1986, ten years after US deregulation was initiated, that national regulations which require government approval of fares based on airlines' price-fixing agreements are illegal under the free-trade statutes of the Treaty of Rome.[27] Still, the ruling allows routes between any two countries to be carved up between them on the condition that they evenly split them. National pride and other political obstacles present a challenge in deregulating the airline industry. There is an increasing feeling that 'a free market in air travel is what travelling taxpayers in Europe are calling for–and deserve.'[28] Ireland deregulated its airline industry in May 1986, leading to substantial savings within just several months. By December 1986 it was calculated that the consumer paid more than 50 percent less on a round-trip fare between Dublin and London.[29]

Telecommunications is another industry where Europe is likely to follow America's experiment in deregulation. While deregulation in the United States has led to a considerable amount of technological change and efficiency gains, European markets have become threatened by US firms. The fear is: 'If Europe doesn't move fast enough to satisfy demand for advanced services, and if costs there remain two or three times higher than in the U.S. and Japan, European companies could find themselves eating the dust of international rivals.'[30] The major problem confronting telecommunications deregulation is the vested interests in each country resisting change. Still, with passage of the British Telecommunication Acts of 1981 and 1984, which changed the status of British Telecom from a state corporation to a public limited company, there has been some deregulation. Although the telecommunications deregulation has been watched 'with some amazement' by the rest of Europe, it has had little effect outside of the United Kingdom (Müller, 1986).

It is not only the American deregulation movement that has had its effect on European countries, but the recent success of small entrepreneurial firms in high-technology industries in Japan and the United States has also had a similar impact on European policies. Servan-Schreiber (1968) was moved to warn Europeans about 'the American challenge' of monolithic multinational corporations, and encouraged the EEC to respond by creating European super-firms of its own. The more recent challenge, however, may be from small enterpreneurial firms which play key roles in developing new technologies. Piore and Sabel (1984) have argued that, through the application of 'flexible specialization' by small firms, a restructuring of manufacturing industries is taking place, enabling small firms to become increasingly persuasive. And there is strong evidence suggesting that small firms in the United States have expanded the greatest in the high-technology industries (Acs and Audretsch, 1987c).

In response to the 'new American challenge', European countries are implementing a host of programs to promote small firms, especially R&D undertaken by small firms. For example, since 1983, Britain's Business Expansion Scheme has granted $222 million supporting 1,200 new companies in high-technology areas. Similarly, since 1984 France has permitted tax write-offs to venture-capital funds, where a tax rate of 15 percent of income applies instead of the normal 65 percent.[31] A recent $45.5 million venture to manufacture sophisticated custom computer chips, European Silicon Structures (ES2), was recently formed. By 1989, European governments will have invested more than $10 million in grants and subsidies to promoting R&D in small firms developing new technologies.

Whether or not such interventionist policies will ultimately prove to be effective remains to be seen. One thing, however, is certain. Governments will continue to experiment with interventionist policies as the battle for global markets becomes increasingly intense. Those policies and approaches which are effective will most likely be copied by the other major industrial countries, although certainly in modified forms to fit each country's own historical and institutional framework. Paradoxically, even as the deregulation movement has been so successful in the United States, and is currently being copied in Europe, government interventionist programs will probably be on the rise and not on the decline. As was the lesson from deregulation, the ultimate judge of interventionist policies will be the extent to which they promote international competitiveness.

NOTES

1. *The Economist*, 31 January 1987, p. 32.
2. 'Dukakis: focus on future', *International Herald Tribune*, 22 July 1988, p. 1.
3. 'Can America compete?', *Business Week*, 27 April 1987 pp. 41–43.
4. *Ibid.*, p. 41.
5. W.W. Rostow, 'Here comes a new political chapter in America', *International Herald Tribune*, 2 January 1987.
6. *Ibid.*
7. *Economic Report of the President*, 1986.
8. *Economic Report of the President*, 1987.
9. Lester Thurow, 'Losing the economic race', *New York Review of Books*, September 1984, pp. 29–31.
10. 'US deindustrialization: the case against it', *Wall Street Journal*, 12 November 1986, p. 1.
11. *Economic Report of the President*, 1987.
12. R. Kuttner, 'Must we lose the industrial world series?', *Business Week*, 17 November 1986, p. 20.
13. 'No pain, no gain: how America can grow again', *Business Week*, 27 April 1987, pp. 64–5.
14. *Ibid.*
15. 'Japan's pump-priming wait too much for US exports', *Business Week*, 27 April 1987, p. 17.
16. Quoted in Johnson (1984, p. 8).
17. *Ibid.*
18. 'Now R&D is corporate America's answer to Japan Inc.', *Business Week*, 29 June 1986, pp. 78–9.
19. 'Main deals that won't give technology away', *Business Week*, 27 April 1987, pp. 58–9.
20. Robert Kuttner, 'The US can't compete without a top-notch work force', *Business Week*, 16 February 1987, p. 12.
21. 'Management discovers the human side of automation', *Business Week*, 29 September 1986, pp. 60–5.
22. 'America's R&D establishment is not just crying wolf', *Business Week*, 24 March 1986, p. 37.
23. 'British high tech wants to catch merger fever', *Business Week*, 16 December 1985, pp. 28–9.
24. William C. Freund, 'American lessons for London's big bang', *Wall Street Journal*, 27 October 1986; and 'As big bang looms, UK moves to adopt investor protections', *Wall Street Journal*, 8 October 1986, p. 1.

25. Alfred E. Kahn, 'American deregulation lessons for Europe', *Wall Street Journal*, 2 October 1986.
26. 'Europe's air cartel', *The Economist*, 1 November 1986, pp. 19–23.
27. 'Europe's airfare regulation is illegal, high court rules', *Wall Street Journal*, 1 May 1986.
28. 'Skyway robbery', *The Economist*, 1 November 1986, p. 14.
29. 'Irish airline's model for deregulation takes off', *Wall Street Journal*, 1 December 1986.
30. 'Can Europe untangle its telecommunications mess?', *Business Week*, 31 March 1986, pp. 46–8.
31. 'Europe learns to love the entrepreneur', *Business Week*, 26 May 1986, pp. 54–9.

PART II

INDUSTRIAL POLICIES TOWARDS MARKET STRUCTURE AND BUSINESS CONDUCT

2· THE ANTITRUST APPROACH IN THE UNITED STATES

While some type of competition policy is common in Europe, Japan and the United States, the role of antitrust policy has a unique position in America. The general approach towards industrial policy in Europe and Japan has been to build cooperative relationships between government and private enterprise, while, by contrast, the adversarial relationship between the public sector and private business in the United States is exemplified by American antitrust policy. That is, whereas cooperation has been the cornerstone of public policy in Europe and Japan, antitrust is the epitome of the adversarial relationship between government and private business in the United States. The purpose of this chapter is to examine the role of antitrust in the United States as an instrument of competition policy. We begin by considering the goals and objectives of US antitrust policy, followed by an examination of the major institutions facilitating antitrust. The policy approach towards collusion, dominant market power and monopoly, mergers and restrictive practices, including vertical restraints, is analyzed in the next section. Following this is an examination of historical and recent patterns of enforcement, followed by a discussion of contemporary trends in both the implementation of antitrust policy as well as the evolution in economic analysis. Finally, the chapter concludes with a general assessment of the current role of antitrust as competition policy in the United States.

ANTITRUST GOALS AND OBJECTIVES

Antitrust policy in the United States emanates from legislation enacted by the Congress. What are the basic goals underlying antitrust policy, and what did Congress have in mind when enacting the various antitrust statutes? These questions are as important as they are difficult to answer; without a clear conception of the purpose of the antitrust laws, it is impossible both to direct their implementation or to evaluate the social benefits from their enforcement.[1] Despite this importance, the objectives of antitrust have remained elusive and a source of controversy. F. M. Scherer (1977, p. 977), who served as Director of the Bureau of Economics at the US Federal Trade Commission (FTC), found Congressional intent 'muddled and often contradictory. I frequently felt that if we knew precisely where we're to go, we could proceed there in a more orderly fashion. But clear objectives were a luxury we seldom enjoyed, ambiguity was our guiding star.'

Despite, or because of, this confusion, considerable attention has been devoted to identifying the Congressional intent underlying US antitrust legislation. Interpretation of Congressional intent generally lies on a continuum, with three particular focal points.[2] At one extreme are economists, often associated with the 'Chicago Approach',[3] who interpret economic efficiency as the sole claim to antitrust enforcement. At the opposite extreme are economists who assign numerous non-economic and social goals to comprise the appropriate antitrust policy. Finally, between these two extremes lies the interpretation that antitrust should be oriented towards wealth redistribution as well as economic efficiency.

Posner (1976, p. 20) provides a characterization of the first group: 'although non economic objectives are frequently mentioned in the legislative histories, it seems that the dominant legislative intent has been to promote some approximation to the economist's idea of competition, viewed as a means toward the end of maximizing efficiency.' Bork (1966, p. 7), after reviewing the legislative history leading to the first antitrust statutes at the end of the nineteenth century, concurs with Posner's conclusion but disagrees that non-economic objectives were even a Congressional goal: 'My conclusion, drawn from the evidence in the Congressional Record is that Congress intended the courts to implement only that value we would today call consumer welfare. To put it another way, the policy the courts were intended to apply is the maximization of wealth or consumer want satisfaction.' According to this view, there exists just one equivocal goal of antitrust policy – the pursuit of economic efficiency. Thus, the extreme view characterized by Bork[4] and Posner concludes that (1) consumer welfare was the only major goal intended by the Congress in enacting the antitrust statutes, (2) consumer welfare is the only value that should therefore be pursued, and (3) most of antitrust's problems are the result of the erroneous pursual of goals other than economic efficiency (Bork, 1978, p. 310).

In the middle of the spectrum are economists who consider that one of the primary concerns of Congress should be the redistribution of wealth resulting from monopoly power. For example, Weiss (1974a, p. 35) argues: 'It seems doubtful whether Congress gave much, if any weight to allocative efficiency when formulating the antitrust laws, while the prevention of large capital gains to those who organized monopolistic cartels or mergers is probably a major concern of the public in its commitment to competition.' Perhaps acknowledging the fact that the concept of allocative efficiency was barely at the frontier of economic theory when Senator Sherman and his colleagues were engaged in debate, Weiss (1979, pp. 1104–5) concludes that 'it seems certain that Congress never thought in terms of the welfare triangle when it passed the antitrust laws and that the public and Congress do not concern themselves with it today.'

At the other end of the spectrum is the interpretation that broader, non-economic goals as well as economic ones motivated the Congress to enact the antitrust statutes. Mueller (1978, p. 18) characterizes this position: 'While Congress spoke much about broad economic, social and political consequences of economic power, when it wrote a statute to cope with these problems it applied an economic concept, the probable lessening of competition within particular geographic and product markets. It is important to keep in mind this distinction between the objectives of the act and the statutory language.' Certainly Mueller's interpretation of Congressional intent is consistent with Senator Sherman, who argued for passage of his 1890 bill, which became the first antitrust statute, because: 'If we will not endure a King as a political power we should not submit to an autocrat of trade with power to prevent competition and to fix the price of any commodity.'[5]

Thus, the goals of antitrust have been widely interpreted, varying from a relatively singular goal of economic efficiency and enhancement of consumer welfare, to a broad multidimensional goal. Recognition of this tension in the interpretation of the purpose of the antitrust laws explains a considerable amount of the ambiguity in their enforcement and the continuing debate among economists regarding the appropriate role of antitrust in the United States.

ANTITRUST INSTITUTIONS

The statute at the core of American antitrust, the Sherman Act, was passed by Congress in 1890 as a reaction to the predominant cartelization and centralization of market power prevailing in the United States at the end of the nineteenth century. The Sherman Act consisted of two main sections: the first prohibited all contracts, combinations, and conspiracies in restraint of trade; the second prohibited monopolization and attempts to monopolize. Specifically, Section 1 of the Sherman Act states:

Every contract, combination in the form of a trust or otherwise, or conspiracy, in restraint of trade or commerce among the several states, or with foreign nations, is hereby declared to be illegal. Every person who shall make any such contract or engage in any such combination or conspiracy, shall be deemed guilty of a misdemeanor.[6]

Section 2 of the Sherman Act states:

Every person who shall monopolize, or attempt to monopolize, or combine or conspire with any other person or persons, to monopolize any part of the trade or commerce among the several states, or with foreign nations, shall be deemed guilty of a misdemeanor.[7]

With passage of the Sherman Act came no new administrative agency set up to enforce the antitrust laws. Rather, enforcement lay within the jurisdiction of the US Department of Justice and the Federal Court System. However, the adequacy of both the stature and the 'zeal of the Attorney General in prosecuting those who violated it' (Areeda, 1974, p. 47) was considered dubious in the years following the passage of the Sherman Act. According to Kolko (1963), three different interest groups combined to support the establishment of an agency whose sole duty would be enforcement of the antitrust laws and preservation of 'fair' competition. The first group consisted of those generally hostile towards big business, such as farmers and small family-owned enterprises. The second group comprised people in big business who felt that some sort of protection from the volatility of market forces and cut-throat competition, in the form of government regulation, was required. The last was a group of intellectuals who argued that government should directly control and regulate large corporations.

To this end, Congress passed the Federal Trade Commission Act in 1914, which established the FTC as an independent (of the President) agency whose sole purpose was enforcement of the antitrust laws. The act itself was broadly written, instructing the newly formed Commission to disallow 'unfair methods of competition in commerce, and unfair or deceptive acts or practices in commerce'.[8] Additionally, in 1914 the Congress passed a second antitrust statute, the Clayton Act, which specifically outlawed certain business practices, including interlocking directorates (Section 8), price discrimination (Section 2) and tying contracts (Section 3).[9] Thus, the Sherman Act, the Federal Trade Commission Act and Clayton Act, with their subsequent amendments,[10] and the enforcement agencies consisting of the Antitrust Division of the Justice Department and the FTC combine to represent the institutions responsible for antitrust policy in the United States. However, the coverage of the laws and their enforcement is not evenly applied across the various markets in the economy. The major legal exemptions from antitrust include agriculture and fishing organizations, milk and other farm products, labor unions, public enterprises, regulated markets, baseball, newspaper joint-operating arrangements and export cartels.[11] Similarly, as a result of discretionary enforcement policy, many trades and services, urban services and national defense producers are, in effect, also exempt from antitrust (Shepherd, 1985).

Table 2.1 shows how antitrust has been allocated between the two enforcement agencies over the period 1963 to 1984 (Gallo and Bush, 1983). With the sole exception of 1981, the Antitrust Division of the Department of Justice has always initiated more cases per year than the FTC. Over the 22-year period, the Antitrust Division initiated an average of 41.7 cases per year, while the FTC initiated an average of 17.5 cases per year. As will be discussed later, this may reflect a difference in case selection between the two agencies; since 1950, the annual budget of the FTC has consistently been significantly larger than that of the Antitrust Division. For example, in 1960 the Antitrust

Table 2.1 US Antitrust Enforcement, 1963–1984[a]

Year of Initiation[b]	Number of DOJ Cases	Number of FTC Cases	Total Number of Federal Cases[c]
1963	26 (74%)	9 (26%)	35
1964	51 (81%)	12 (19%)	63
1965	29 (62%)	18 (38%)	47
1966	36 (65%)	19 (35%)	55
1967	34 (74%)	12 (26%)	46
1968	47 (76%)	15 (24%)	62
1969	43 (75%)	14 (25%)	57
1970	54 (83%)	11 (17%)	65
1971	43 (63%)	25 (37%)	68
1972	72 (82%)	16 (18%)	88
1973	47 (64%)	26 (36%)	73
1974	46 (70%)	20 (30%)	66
1975	39 (66%)	20 (34%)	59
1976	45 (65%)	24 (35%)	69
1977	40 (71%)	16 (29%)	56
1978	43 (75%)	14 (25%)	57
1979	33 (52%)	30 (48%)	63
1980	50 (64%)	28 (36%)	78
1981	18 (49%)	19 (51%)	37
1982	30 (75%)	10 (25%)	40
1983	52 (83%)	11 (17%)	63
1984	40 (73%)	15 (27%)	55
Total	918 (71%)	384 (29%)	1302

[a] DOJ refers to cases initiated by the Antitrust Division at the US Department of Justice.
FTC refers to cases initiated by the Federal Trade Commission. Percentages are listed in parentheses.
[b] Refers to the fiscal year.
[c] Excludes private antitrust cases.
Source: Gallo and Bush (1983).

Division had a total budget of $4 million and the FTC had a total budget of $7 million (Shepherd, 1985, p. 134). By 1983, the budgets of both agencies had been increased considerably, to $44 million at the Antitrust Division and $67 million at the FTC. This growth reflects the increase in antitrust enforcement that has taken place. In 1960, the Antitrust Division employed 290 staff attorneys devoted to antitrust enforcement. This number reached 476 in 1979 and, since then, has continued to decline to 338 in 1983, perhaps reflecting a de-emphasized role of antitrust policy in the most recent years (Shepherd, 1985, p. 134).

Besides the statutes enacted by both Congress and the implementation of policy by the enforcement agencies, there remains a third essential instrument of US antitrust policy – the courts. That is, the Congress passed relatively vague statutes into law, and instructed the FTC and the Justice Department to enforce those statutes, but their actual interpretation in actual cases is provided by the Federal Courts, and ultimately by the rulings of the US Supreme Court.[12] Thus, it is the Supreme Court's rulings on actual substantive antitrust cases that provide the third aspect of US antitrust enforcement.

POLICY TOWARDS COLLUSION

The first Supreme Court interpretation of the Sherman Act, which addressed the issue of antitrust policy towards price-fixing, was in 1897.[13] Eighteen railroads operating in the Midwest formally agreed upon the rates which each firm would charge for shipping certain commodities. After the US District Attorney alleged that such an agreement constituted a violation of the Sherman Act, the railroads argued that such agreements in their case did not, in fact, constitute a Sherman Act violation because they were required to ensure the stability of the industry. In the absence of such agreements, the carriers would be susceptible to cut-throat competition, and ultimately the consumers would suffer. The District Court judge[14] concurred with the defense and held that the price agreements did not, in fact, constitute a violation of the Sherman Act, because of their reasonableness: 'When contracts go to the extent only of preventing unhealthy competition, and yet at the same time furnish the public with adequate facilities at fixed and reasonable prices, and are made only for the purpose of averting personal ruin, the contract is lawful.'[15]

However, upon hearing the case, the Supreme Court overruled the district court, and asserted that the issue of reasonableness was beyond the concern of the Act. The Supreme Court reaffirmed this ruling one year later in the Joint Traffic Association case,[16] where several railroad companies had colluded to fix rates. Similarly, in another case, six midwestern and southern manufacturers of cast-iron pipe agreed to form a bidding cartel which restricted the bids on certain contracts and assigned exclusive markets to certain geographic areas. Presented with the defense that such agreements were requisite in an industry characterized by volatile orders, high fixed costs and relatively low marginal costs, and chronic excess capacity, the Court held that: 'It has been earnestly pressed upon us that the prices at which the cast-iron pipe was sold . . . were reasonable. . . . We do not think the issue an important one, because . . . we do not think that at common law there is any question of reasonableness open to the courts with reference to such a contract.'[17]

The '*per se*' rule against price-fixing was finally established in the 1927 Trenton Potteries Co. case.[18] Twenty-three manufacturers in the bathroom bowl market formed a trade association, and frequently published lists of standardized prices to which members were expected to adhere. Among other arguments, the defendants held that their agreements did not constitute a Sherman Act violation because of the failure of the agreements to be effectively implemented. That is, the defendants maintained that no violation should be found because they had not, in fact, succeeded in establishing a fixed price. With its ruling, the Supreme Court soundly established the precedent of an agreement to restrict prices, regardless of the outcome from that agreement, to constitute a *prima facia* violation of the Sherman Act:

> The aim and result of every price-fixing agreement, if effective, is the elimination of one form of competition. The power to fix prices, whether reasonably exercised or not, involves power to control the market and to fix arbitrary and unreasonable prices. The reasonable price fixed today may through economic and business changes become the unreasonable price of tomorrow. . . . Agreements which create such potential power may well be held to be in themselves unreasonable or unlawful restraints, without the necessity of minute inquiry whether a particular price is reasonable or unreasonable as fixed and without placing on the Government in enforcing the Sherman Law the burden of ascertaining from day to day whether it has become unreasonable through the mere variation of economic conditions.[19]

Included in the *per se* application of the law was not just price-fixing, but also agreements to restrict quantities,[20] to divide markets into exclusive territories, to allocate customers according to seller, to implement pricing formulas and to engage in concerted actions against firms deviating from industry-wide agreements. However, to say that certain agreements are in violation of the Sherman Act, and constitute a *per se* prohibition, is not equivalent to saying that all agreements between firms are either *per se* illegal or even illegal at all. Numerous agreements are made between or among firms which are held to be legal by the courts because they are ancillary in nature, or essential to normal business practices. As a general rule, the closer an agreement comes to affecting price, even indirectly, the more likely it will be held to be illegal. However, such rulings are more apt to invoke a rule-of-reason decision rather than a *per se* rule. That is, beyond agreements that directly affect price, or have a very apparent indirect effect, such as quantity restrictions, the court tends to use a rule-of-reason in determining whether or not the alleged agreement, in fact, constitutes a Sherman Act violation.

Thus, in the 1918 Chicago Board of Trade case, the Supreme Court ruled that the requirement forbidding Board members to engage in transactions during the hours when the Exchange was closed did not constitute a Sherman Act violation. Such agreements were interpreted as being ancillary by the Court:

> The legality of an agreement or regulation cannot be determined by so simple a test as whether it restrains competition. Every agreement concerning trade, every regulation of trade, restrains. The true test of legality is whether the restraint imposed is such as merely regulates and perhaps thereby promotes competition, or whether it is such as may suppress or even destroy competition. To determine that question the Court must ordinarily consider the facts

peculiar to the business to which the restraint is applied; . . . the nature of the restraint and its effect, actual or probable.[21]

In implementing the rule-of-reason in a case, the Supreme Court generally considers the effect that the agreement had, or potentially might have on price. For example, in the 1969 Container Corporation case,[22] eighteen companies, which accounted for 90 percent of the corrugated containers used in the Southeast, agreed to exchange information on prices quoted to certain customers. However, there were no agreements among firms concerning which price should be charged to customers. In reaching its decision, the Court examined the pattern of prices in the industry relative to long-term changes in demand and entry. Because the Court inferred that the agreements, although not restricting price or limiting quantity, had had the effect of preventing an inevitable price decline from actually declining further, it found the agreements to be in violation of the Sherman Act. In general, then, the closer an agreement comes to affecting the market price, the more likely that it will be found to constitute an antitrust violation. This stringent policy towards horizontal agreements, particularly those affecting market prices, which has continued to be vigorously enforced throughout the tenure of the Reagan Administration, is relatively unique among the developed nations. As will be seen in the following two chapters, both West Germany and Japan are considerably more lenient in allowing such agreements. In fact, West Germany goes so far as to allow cartels that set price.

POLICY TOWARDS MARKET DOMINANCE

Since actual text-book definitions of monopoly are virtually non-existent in major markets, with the exception of certain regulated industries, the most important issue is the manner in which US antitrust policy addresses market dominance. Market dominance is generally the result of two different market structures – an industry with a dominant firm (Weiss and Pascoe, 1984), or one with a relatively tight oligopoly. While a *per se* rule was developed with respect to price-fixing, as explained in the previous section, the law towards monopoly power took a different evolutionary course. Section 2 of the Sherman Act, which is the relevant statute, emphasizes 'monopolization' and 'attempt to monopolize', suggesting that possession of market dominance by itself does not, in fact, constitute an antitrust violation. Rather, according to the language of the Sherman Act, it is the pursuit of attaining such monopoly power that constitutes an antitrust violation. Thus, the central tension in the law and policy towards market power has been that entrenched monopoly, in the absence of any predatory conduct, has been beyond the reach of the law, while those trying to attain such status, and presumably not possessing such market dominance, have frequently been subjected to the scrutiny of the Sherman Act. This tension is enunciated by Galbraith (1967, pp. 187, 197), who charged that anti-monopoly policy 'exempts those who possess the market power and concentrates on those who would try to possess it', and therefore, 'defends and gives legitimacy to a charade'.

The law with respect to monopoly power was largely shaped in 1911, when the Supreme Court reached two decisions in the Standard Oil[23] and American Tobacco[24] cases. In both cases, the defendant had what could reasonably be considered to constitute a dominant market share of 90 percent. However, in both cases the Court ruled that mere size and dominant market share alone did not constitute an offense. Rather, it was the *intent* to monopolize, which the Court inferred from the defendants' predatory conduct towards rivals and potential rivals, combined with the dominant market share which constituted the Sherman Act violation. In particular, the Court pointed towards Standard Oil's reliance on extracting rebates from the railroads, which put its competitors at a cost disadvantage. Similarly, American Tobacco had excluded rivals from sources of supply, had purchased plants and subsequently closed them, presumably to preempt their use by competitors, and had engaged in predatory pricing.[25]

These two cases established the precedent of a rule-of-reason application of the law in the cases involving dominant firms. In order to find a violation the Court must be convinced of two aspects concerning the defendant. First, the firm must possess a dominant share of the market. Because both Standard Oil and American Tobacco had such large market shares, this aspect was not a focal point, and therefore no ruling was actually made in these two cases over what minimal market share actually constituted a dominant firm. Second, the firm must be found to have engaged in some type of exclusionary conduct which was judged by the Court to be 'unreasonable', as exemplified in the Standard Oil and American Tobacco cases. The necessity of both of these conditions to exist for the Court to reach a verdict against the defendant was evident in the 1920 US Steel case.[26] Although US Steel controlled over 90 percent of the market for steel mill products in 1901, when it was created by combining twelve firms which had been merged from about 180 independent companies, with more than 300 plants (Parsons and Ray, 1975), the Court found that it had not been engaged in any exclusionary conduct, as had Standard Oil and American Tobacco. In ruling that 'Size alone is not an offense', the precedent was established that, in the United States, monopoly, *per se*, is not illegal.

Although it was clearly enunciated that a rule-of-reason would apply to dominant market power by 1920, the issues of what market share constituted dominance and what conduct would be inferred as exclusionary has never been firmly established by the US courts. For example, in the Alcoa[27] and United Shoe Machinery[28] cases in 1948 and 1953 respectively, the Court ruled that as little as 40 percent constituted a dominant market share. However, by the time of the IBM[29] and Eastman Kodak[30] cases in the 1970s, it was clear that the courts had receded from defining such low market shares as constituting dominant market power. The Court also adapted a relatively narrow interpretation of what constitutes exclusionary conduct in the Alcoa and United Shoe Machinery cases. The Court inferred that Alcoa did, in fact, 'attempt' to monopolize and had engaged in exclusionary conduct because it had: (1) built capacity for production of aluminum ingots in anticipation of future demand, thereby discouraging new entrants; and (2) purchased large amounts of raw materials, such as bauxite, enabling it to control the inputs of any rivals or potential rivals.

Despite the interpretation by many critics that Alcoa's practices of building capacity in anticipation of future demand and wide purchases of inputs fall within the norm of 'reasonable' business conduct (Armentano, 1982), the Court ruled that this was sufficient evidence to infer intent and therefore, along with the large market share, constituted a violation of the Sherman Act. Although the Court asserted that, 'Congress . . . did not condone "good trusts" and condemn "bad" ones; it forbade all', it did not rule that possession of dominant market power constituted a *per se* violation of the Sherman Act: 'It does not follow because "Alcoa" had such a monopoly, that it "monopolized" the ingot market: it may not have achieved monopoly; monopoly may have been thrust upon it.'[31] However, the Court seemed to imply that, unless the firm could demonstrate that monopoly power was not 'thrust upon it' due to 'superior skill, foresight and industry' the Court would infer the existence of an intent to monopolize.

Similarly, in the United Shoe Machinery case, the Court was willing to infer firm conduct that was not overwhelmingly pernacious as constituting exclusionary behavior. United Shoe Machinery Corporation had (1) tied all repair work needed by its machines to rental of the machines, (2) leased rather than sold its machines, and (3) entered into multi-year terms for the leasing contracts. The Court ruled that all three of these combined to discourage new entry into the industry and, combined with a dominant market share, constituted a Sherman Act violation. The Court's ruling was consistent and reaffirmed the Alcoa precedent.

Since 1969 there has been a marked shift in US law towards dominant firms. In the IBM case, the Justice Department argued that IBM had maintained its market share of 70 percent through price discrimination which was effectively predatory pricing. IBM maintained that its market share was, in fact, less than 40 percent and declining; its market share was attributable to superior management and scale economies, the firm had been innovative in a market with complex products, and the business had not been particularly profitable (Fisher, McGowan and Greenwood, 1983; Fisher, McKie and Mancke, 1983). In ruling that IBM's conduct had been competitive and not exclusionary, the Court seemingly reversed the Alcoa and United Shoe precedents. Further, as the Eastman Kodak case verified, the Court requires considerably more evidence of pernacious exclusionary conduct today than it did in the immediate post-war period to infer intent to monopolize.

US antitrust policy towards market power in the form of oligopoly is, like that towards the dominant firm, not entirely fixed, and always subject to evolution and change from the courts. While Section 1 of the Sherman Act, and its interpretation by the Court, makes it clear that price agreements in an oligopolistic industry would be *per se* illegal, just as Section 2 makes it relatively apparent that predatory conduct by a firm with entrenched dominant market share would also be ruled illegal, the issue relevant to oligopoly is, 'What is the policy with respect to what apparently are tacit agreements?' Such tacit agreements, or rather the results of such alleged conduct, have been termed *conscious parallelism* by the Court. That is, where there is only circumstantial, indirect evidence that firms have colluded, either explicitly or through tacit understanding, neither the cases nor the law that has evolved for explicit collusion or for dominant firms is readily applicable. Yet, since industries with less-than-perfect competition are probably more typical than not in US manufacturing, this issue is perhaps more important than market dominance by a single firm.[32]

In one of the first cases, Interstate Circuit,[33] the manager of a chain of movie theatres sent the same letter to eight major movie distributors, requesting that they neither distribute their best movies to theatres charging low entrance fees (i.e., below that of Interstate's), nor show the films as part of a double feature. Subsequent to delivering the letter, first-run films were, in fact, no longer distributed by Interstate to such theatres. Noting the parallel conduct of each of the eight motion picture distributors, the Court ruled: 'It was enough that, knowing that concerned action was contemplated and invited, the distributors gave their adherence to the scheme and participated in it.'[34] Even in the absence of explicit proof that an agreement actually occurred among the distributors, the Court inferred the existence of concerted action and thus found the distributors in violation of Section 1 of the Sherman Act.

In the 1946 American Tobacco Co. decision,[35] the alleged parallel conduct was: (1) virtually identical prices over two decades charged by the three dominant firms in the industry, American Tobacco, Reynolds, and Ligett and Myers; (2) refusal of each firm to engage in the auctions for leaf tobacco unless all three firms were present; (3) bidding practices assuring that all three firms would pay the identical price for leaf tobacco; and (4) simultaneous price cuts in June 1931 when their market shares were falling and simultaneous price increases in December 1932 after fringe firms had been eliminated from the market. However, no evidence was offered suggesting any explicit agreement among the three firms. In ruling against the tobacco companies, the Court explained: 'No formal agreement is necessary to constitute an unlawful conspiracy. . . . Where the circumstances are such as to warrant a jury in finding that the conspirators had a unity of purpose or a common design and understanding, or a meeting of minds in an unlawful arrangement, the conclusion that a conspiracy is established is justified.'[36] A number of economists have interpreted the Tobacco decision as the strongest case for what has become known as *structural antitrust*. That is, public policy intervention is justified, solely on the grounds that the market structure of the industry has somehow deviated too far away from the competitive norm. The Tobacco decision seemed to imply that 'wholly tacit, nonaggressive oligopoly [was] fully within the reach of the conspiracy provisions of the Sherman Act' (Nicholls, 1949, p. 72).

However, a permanent structural antitrust policy in the United States did not emerge. In another case involving film theatres, several distributors simultaneously refused to allow a new movie theatre in the suburbs of Baltimore access to the best films. When no evidence establishing an explicit collusive agreement among the defendants was presented, the Court ruled, '. . . this Court has never held that proof of parallel business behavior conclusively establishes agreement or, phrased differently, that such behavior itself constitutes a Sherman Act offense. Circumstantial evidence of consciously parallel behavior may have made heavy inroads in the traditional judicial attitude toward conspiracy; but "conscious parallelism" has not yet read conspiracy out of the Sherman Act entirely.'[37]

In a case that the FTC initiated against Kellogg in the 1970s, there were again three dominant firms in the industry which were charged with *shared monopoly*.[38] The alleged conduct that the FTC argued constituted an illegal tacit conspiracy was: (1) parallel prices, initiated by Kellogg's price leadership, (2) refusal by Kellogg and General Mills to produce dried cereal for private-label brands, and (3) proliferation of brands. The FTC argued that the third point, brand proliferation, served as an entry deterrent by requiring potential entrants to produce an equal number of different types of the basic product. Although the circumstances between the Cereal case and the Tobacco case are remarkably similar, public policy has changed considerably in three decades; the FTC dropped the case in the early 1980s, reflecting the dismal chance it faced for obtaining a conviction.

The United States has historically been much more aggressive in pursuing an interventionist competition policy towards breaking up dominant market power than have Japan or the European countries. As will be seen in Chapters 2 and 3, neither Japan nor the European nations such as West Germany or the United Kingdom have aggressively attempted to deconcentrate domestic markets.

POLICY TOWARDS MERGERS

Although the Sherman Act was undoubtedly the first antimerger law in the United States, two early cases reaching the Supreme Court – Northern Securities[39] and Standard Oil – established that unless an acquisition created or enhanced an actual monopoly, mergers were beyond the reach of the

Sherman Act. The inability of the Sherman Act to control merger activity was evidenced by the great merger wave that occurred at the turn of the century.[40] In fact, as Bittlingmayer (1985) argues, Sherman Act enforcement may actually have been at least partially responsible for the turn-of-the-century merger wave.[41] As Stigler (1950, p. 23) concludes:

> The Sherman Law seems to have been the fundamental cause for the shifts from merger for monopoly to merger for oligopoly. Sometimes its workings were obvious, as when Standard Oil was dismembered and when the leading banking mergers were prevented from combining. More often, its workings have been more subtle: the ghost of Senator Sherman is an ex officio member of the board of directors of every large company.

And so, in 1914, responding to sentiment to arrest further industrial consolidation, Congress passed the Clayton Act.[42]

Despite the intention of Congress,[43] the original Section 7 of the Clayton Act, which was intended as an antimerger statute, included a fatal loophole – language stating that the Act applied only to stock acquisitions. Thus, the law could easily be circumvented through the acquisition of a firm's assets instead of its stock. It required over thirty-five years to close the loopholes that effectively emasculated the original antimerger statute. In 1950, Congress passed the Celler–Kefauver Amendment to the Clayton Act, which stated:

> That no corporation engaged in commerce shall acquire directly or indirectly, the whole or any part of the stock or other share capital, and no corporation subject to the jurisdiction of the Federal Trade Commission shall acquire the whole or any part of the assets of another corporation engaged also in commerce where in any line of commerce in any section of the country the effect of such acquisition may be substantially to lessen competition or tend to create monopoly.[44]

The emphasis of the language on the concepts of 'substantial lessening of competition' and 'tendency to create monopoly' demonstrated Congressional concern at preventing mergers that might lead to monopoly power at some time in the future, even if the acquisition, by itself, did not immediately create market power. However, as in the language of the Sherman Act, the construction of the amended Section 7 of the Clayton Act left a significant burden of policy towards mergers in the interpretation of the statute by the Court. The first decision by the Court, Brown Shoe in 1962,[45] provided a very narrow, virtually *per se* interpretation of the statute towards horizontal mergers. The leading national shoe manufacturer, Brown Shoe, with a market share of 4 percent had purchased Kinney Company, which had a market share of 0.5 percent. In the retail market, Brown ranked third and Kinney eighth, but the regional market shares resulting from the acquisition were as high as 57.7 percent. US antimerger law was strongly influenced by the Court's interpretation of the statute: 'We cannot avoid the mandate of Congress that tendencies toward concentration in industry are to be curbed in their incipiency.'[46] This ruling established the precedent whereby the possibility that monopoly power in its incipiency could result from the merger was sufficient to disallow the acquisition.

That virtually all horizontal mergers would be disallowed, except between quite small firms in a market, was established in the Von's Grocery case in 1966. Although Von's Grocery was the third largest supermarket in the Los Angeles market, and the acquired firm, Shopping Bag, was the sixth largest, the combined market share preceding the merger was only 8 percent, which was less than the leading firm's share. However, the Court did not allow the merger to stand, because it viewed the intent of Congress 'to prevent concentration in the American economy by keeping a large number of small competitors in business'.[47]

Subsequent to the Brown and Von's Grocery rulings, the strict interpretation of Section 7 has receded somewhat. This development has emanated from both judicial ruling[48] and from discretionary enforcement practices by the antitrust agencies. For example, the acquisition of Schlitz by Stroh's – both beer breweries – which created the third largest brewery, was allowed to pass unchallenged by the antitrust agencies. Similarly, in 1983–4, Republic Steel, which had the fourth-largest industry market share, merged with Jones & Laughlin, which had the third-highest market share. The combined market share of about 16 percent of the resulting firm was the second highest in the industry, just slightly less than the leading firm's (US Steel) market share of about 17 percent. US Steel subsequently purchased National Steel, increasing its market share by about 6 percent in points.[49] In fact, these acquisitions reflect the relaxed enforcement by the Reagan Administration towards mergers. In 1981, the Justice Department announced revised guidelines enabling more mergers to pass than would have previously been possible.[50] As a result, under the Reagan Administration's enforcement policies, mergers involving market shares of less than 15 percent will not be contested, and those in excess of 24 percent will be blocked. Mergers involving market shares between around 15 percent to 25 percent will be decided after consideration of market-specific characteristics.

US antitrust policy is much less defined with respect to vertical and conglomerate mergers than it is with respect to horizontal mergers. In the Brown Shoe case, the Court considered the possibility of foreclosing competition in the retail market, which might result if only Brown Shoes were carried by Kinney retailers, as sufficient grounds for disallowing the merger. In general, if the merging firm in the downstream market possesses a relatively large share of the market, a vertical acquisition may be contested on the grounds that it will result in the foreclosure of competition in the upstream market. However, there exists no clear precedence in the law regarding vertical mergers, so that antitrust policy in this sphere remains somewhat ambiguous.

Antitrust policy is similarly ambiguous with respect to conglomerate mergers. While no pure conglomerate acquisition case has ever reached the Supreme Court,[51] there are several important decisions involving product-extension, geographic-extension, and other 'near' conglomerate mergers. For example, in Consolidated Foods Corporation,[52] the Court did not allow a merger because of the potential for reciprocity which conceivably could result in market foreclosure. However, the ruling was never reinforced by further decisions outlawing such acquisitions.

In general, the Court has established through a series of precedent rulings, including Falstaff Brewing[53] and Ford Motor,[54] that product- and geographic-extension mergers might not be permitted when the case involved (1) a leading firm, (2) a fairly concentrated market, and (3) a potential or likely entrant. Typically, all three conditions must be met for the merger to be disallowed. For example, in the Proctor & Gamble case,[55] the defendant was the largest company in the household products industry and, by its own admission, was likely to enter the liquid bleach industry. It acquired the Chlorox Chemical Company, which dominated the liquid bleach industry with a market share of 55 percent which was as high as 71 percent in certain geographic markets. Because Proctor & Gamble was among the largest firms in the United States, a likely entrant into the liquid bleach industry, and acquired the leading firm in the industry, the Court did not allow the merger. The Court reasoned that had Proctor & Gamble either entered *de novo* or acquired a 'toe-hold' acquisition (a relatively small and insignificant firm), competition would have actually increased in the industry. However, to allow the merger would have meant the loss of a potential competitor as well as the entrenchment of the dominant firm.

Of all the antitrust statutes, enforcement of the antimerger laws has probably provided the greatest benefit to market competition (Audretsch, 1983b). However, the benefits from US antimerger policy probably do not lie with the direct result of the Court's decision on any particular case. Only about one-quarter of merger cases in which the acquisition is found to be illegal (or settled under a consent decree by the defendant) actually results in a substantial remedy where most of the acquired assets are divested and an independent firm once more re-established. Rather, the benefits accruing from antimerger enforcement are more likely to come from the deterrent effect – the number of mergers that were not undertaken as a result of merger activity.[56]

As Markham (1965, p. 166) summarizes, 'it is relevant to inquire into the effect Section 7 has had on the volume of mergers it presumably was designed to prohibit. In any society governed by law it is generally expected that the law's principal effect is to be found in its observance rather than its breach.' It has been estimated (Audretsch, 1987b) that US antitrust enforcement has deterred between nine and thirteen large mergers per case undertaken by the antitrust agencies. In comparing the gain per case in market competition with the costs of undertaking the case, antimerger enforcement in the United States has been apparently very successful (Audretsch, 1983a).

Along with the election of President Reagan in 1980 came a shift in merger policy. This is reflected both by the Justice Department's merger guidelines in 1982 and 1984 (see Scheffman and Spiller, 1987), along with a more lenient anti-merger policy which considers the efficiency gains from a merger as well as potential decreases in competition. According to Schmalensee (1987, p. 41), 'Most knowledgeable economists seem now to agree that the Department of Justice, the Federal Trade Commission, and the courts were excessively hostile to horizontal mergers in the 1960s.' The major change in the new merger guidelines and enforcement policies of the enforcement agencies is the approach to defining the relevant market. Essentially, under the new guidelines the market is defined as the smallest group of firms, measured either in terms of the geographic or product market, that could elevate current prices by at least 5 percent and sustain these elevated prices for at least one year (White, 1987; Fisher, 1987).

POLICY TOWARDS VERTICAL RESTRICTIONS

US antitrust policy towards vertical restrictions has been particularly controversial and has undergone significant developments in recent years. In particular, there are four major aspects of vertical restrictions – tying contracts, exclusive dealing, requirement contracts and what has become known as 'resale price maintenance'. A tying contract requires the buyer of a commodity or service also to buy another good, usually related, from the same seller. Exclusive dealing results from a contract specifying that a firm, generally a retailer, sell only products manufactured by a single firm. A requirements contract binds the firm purchasing a product to purchase all of its requirements for that product from the seller. Finally, resale price maintenance requires a firm, generally a retailer, to sell the product at a price specified by the manufacturer.

The relevant antitrust statute with respect to vertical restraints is Section 3 of the Clayton Act, which prohibits contracts imposing the condition that the purchaser (or lessee) 'shall not use or deal in the goods, . . . supplies, or other commodities of a competitor . . . of the lessor or seller' where the effect 'may be to substantially lessen competition or tend to create a monopoly'. The challenge to the Court was to construct coherent law from the vague language of the statute. The earliest decisions suggested that tying contracts or arrangements were virtually *per se* illegal. In a 1949 case, the Court ruled that 'tying agreements serve hardly any purpose beyond the suppression of competition'.[57] In an analogous case, where the producer of salt-dispensing machinery had tied purchases of the salt to the purchase of the machinery, the Court ruled that it is 'unreasonable, *per se*, to foreclose competitors from any substantial market'.[58] However, the Court also ruled that a tying contract was legal when it was needed to ensure the quality of the manufactured product.[59] But even in certain instances where quality assurance is not a significant issue, tying contracts may not be found to be illegal. Precedent cases have revealed that when the manufacturer's market share is insignificant or trivial, the Court will allow such contracts. This generally follows the reasoning that foreclosure of competitors in the market of the tied good is unlikely when the market share is not significant. In general, a tying contract will be found to be illegal if the market share of the manufacturer is anything but trivial.

The result of the earliest Court decisions regarding exclusive dealing and related vertical restrictions was that they were virtually *per se* illegal.[60] Although the Supreme Court recognised that vertical restrictions frequently inflicted no anti-competitive effect and, in fact, sometimes resulted in efficiency gains, the *per se* interpretation was defended on the grounds of administrative enforcement and sparing the courts from having to 'ramble through the wilds of economic theory'.[61] With the Schwinn case in 1967,[62] the Court ruled that territorial restrictions imposed by manufacturers on retailers constituted *per se* violations of the antitrust laws. However, with the GTE Sylvania, Inc. case,[63] the Court reversed its position, implying that such vertical restrictions would only be found to be illegal *per se* if the manufacturers possessed more than a trivial market share. In allowing GTE's geographic restrictions required of retailers of Sylvania television sets to specified store locations to stand, the Court indicated that when small market shares were involved, vertical restrictions were permissible. GTE had only 2 percent of the market at the time of the restrictions.

One industry that has been able to impose vertical territorial restrictions on retailers has been the soft drink market. Although the two leading firms, Coca-Cola and Pepsi-Cola, have market shares between 15 percent and 45 percent respectively, depending upon the geographical market, and the FTC ruled in 1978 that their requirements limiting the local areas in which their franchised dealers may sell the product,[64] a Congressionally approved antitrust exemption has enabled the practices to stand (Stern *et al.*, 1982).

As with other types of vertical restrictions, the Court's primary concern with requirements contracts has been the potential for market foreclosure. In one of the earliest cases, the Court ruled against a requirements contract because 'competition has been foreclosed in a substantial share of the line of commerce affected'.[65] In that case, the Standard Oil Company of California had required over 5,000 independent gasoline franchises of Standard to purchase only Standard's gasoline, batteries and tires, among other products. Because Standard had a market share of almost 7 percent, and the evidence indicated that at least some manufacturers of these products had been foreclosed, the Court found the contract to be illegal. However, as was made clear in another case where the defendant had a negligible market share of less than one percent, exclusive requirements contracts are not *per se* illegal.[66] Exclusive requirements, as with most of the other types of non-price vertical restrictions, will tend to be found illegal in situations involving manufacturers with a significant market share.

Resale price maintenance is a contract imposing a minimum permissible price at which the retailer can sell the product. Although the rule of reason has emerged with·respect to the non-price aspects of vertical restrictions, no analogous development has transpired for vertical price restrictions. The Court has consistently found resale price maintenance to be *per se* illegal. US policy towards vertical price-fixing was first established in the 1911 Dr Miles case,[67] in which the Court found that any vertical agreements between manufacturer and retailer were *per se* illegal. However, with passage of the 1937 Miller–Tydings Resale Price Maintenance Act, vertical price restraints were legalized and remained so until 1975. And, as evidenced by the recent Supreme Court ruling in Monsanto,[68] vertical price restraints are still considered to be *per se* illegal. Thus, although non-price and price restrictions are not significantly different in the view of economics, they are treated differently under the current US antitrust policy. In general, non-price vertical restrictions are subject to a rule of reason and will be found illegal where the manufacturer possesses more than a trivial share of the market. On the other hand, vertical price restrictions, or resale price maintenance, are still held by the courts to be *per se* illegal.

CONTEMPORARY STATE OF US ANTITRUST

There are two essential aspects to the contemporary state of antitrust policy in the United States. The first is the evolution of enforcement policy which has been directed by the Reagan Administration and its recent predecessors. As the record shows, although legal statutes may remain unchanged, and Supreme Court precedents may stand without reversal, policy can be vigorously shaped by the pattern of cases undertaken by the enforcement agencies. In this sense, US antitrust enforcement contains a large discretionary element. The second aspect is the evolution of economic ideas which may have at least some influence on the first aspect. Just as the prevailing economic wisdom about the appropriate stance towards antitrust differed in the 1960s and 1970s from the 1950s, the 1980s have seen a shift in economic thinking. Because the second aspect presumably has at least some influence on the first, the evolution and impact of economic ideas towards antitrust will be considered first.

Since the 1950s, two distinct schools of thought towards antitrust policy have evolved, and have been termed the 'Structuralist School' and the 'Chicago School' (Audretsch, 1988a). These two schools have advocated very different antitrust policies and exercised varying degrees of influence during the past three decades. In the last few years, two more extreme positions have evolved, both advocating the repeal of all the antitrust laws, but for very different reasons. In the 1950s and 1960s, the core of the Structuralist School was that market power *per se* is harmful and therefore should be illegal.[69] Thus, the antitrust laws were criticized for requiring exculsionary conduct to find a violation of the monopoly laws. Rather than the rule-of-reason application of the Sherman Act, Structuralists would have subsitituted a *per se* rule for the application of Section 2. Weiss (1979), for example, offered a pure Structuralist proposal: divestiture or dissolution for all dominant firms possessing a market share exceeding 50 percent. No exclusionary conduct would need to be established. According to the Structuralist vision, divestiture could effectively expand the number of competitors without sacrificing scale economies. Thus, Scherer (1977, p. 1,000) concludes: 'I believe there is persuasive evidence that in many situations substantial divestiture could be accomplished with little or no sacrifice of scale economies or other efficiencies.'

Since the 1960s, and particularly in the 1970s, the preoccupation with market structure evolved into a wider concern incorporating exclusionary conduct – business behavior that may create market power to realize economic rents. The question which Scherer (1977) characterizes as 'the jugular of structural antitrust' is how can supra-competitive prices be sustained over time in highly concentrated markets? The answer provided by the Structuralist School is exclusionary practices. The most onerous of these exclusionary practices is business conduct erecting barriers to entry. Structuralists have been particularly suspicious of conduct such as advertising, brand creation and all types of vertical restrictions, as practices potentially creating entry barriers.

The Chicago School, by contrast, argues that persistent market concentration is not at all synonymous with market power; rather, it indicates either that the market has been rendered concentrated by large scale economies, or that, through cost reductions and product improvements, some firms have been able to attain persistent economic profits. Most of the business conduct that the Structuralists condone as exclusionary, Chicago argues is precisely the opposite – namely, competitive. According to one of the most influential voices, Bork (1978, p. 196): 'All of the "artificial barriers" complained of in antitrust are, in fact, activities that create efficiency. . . . Bain mentions physical product differentiation as a barrier to entry, but I'm unable to understand from his writings or anybody else's, why it is not clearly a form of efficiency.' For example, Chicago generally considers advertising expenditures to be pro-competitive. Chicago argues that product differentiation, along with most other types of conduct classified as exclusionary by the Structuralist, to be the 'ghosts that inhibit antitrust theory. Until the concept of barriers to entry is thoroughly revised, it will remain impossible to make antitrust law more rational or indeed to restrain the growth of its irrational elements' (Bork, 1978, p. 310).

At the heart of the contemporary Structuralist School's view is the acknowledgement that effective market structure is endogenous to firm conduct through exclusionary practices. By contrast, the Chicago School considers market structure to be exogenous of conduct. Instead, the two sole determinants of market structure are scale economies and superior skill, foresight and management.

While these two views are, in general, supportive of the law towards price-fixing, there is considerable disagreement with respect to mergers and vertical restrictions. Chicago views enforcement of Section 7 of the Clayton Act as ranging from an unfortunate by-product of inadequately confronting collusion, to an outright inefficient policy (Posner, 1979). Bork (1978, p. 218) charges: 'The career of Section 7 of the Clayton Act, subsequent to its amendment in 1970, provides a fascinating example of the trends that have made large areas of modern antitrust a harmful policy. . . . It would be easy enough to parade the horrors of Clayton 7 case law in this field almost indefinitely.' The Structuralists, on the other hand, consider US antimerger policy as not only laudable, but perhaps the strongest, most decisive component of antitrust. They generally favor toughening Section 7. Shepherd (1982), for example, attributes merger policy in particular for not only preventing high levels of concentration but also for eroding them. While Chicago would only prevent mergers that directly lead to the creation of monopoly power, the Structuralists favor a relatively strict *per se* prohibition against horizontal acquisitions. According to Weiss (1974b, p. 232): 'Altogether, there is still plenty of reason to believe on both theoretical and empirical grounds that high concentration facilitates tacit or explicit collusion. To me this means that the present policy of prohibiting horizontal merger among viable firms whenever significant concentration is present or in prospect is well founded.'

While the Structuralists tend towards arguing that vertical restrictions should be subject to a *per se* application of the law (Comanor, 1968),[70] the Chicago School tends towards arguing that such restraints should be either *per se* legal, or at least considered with a rule of reason (Klein and Saft, 1985). The Structuralist recommendation for a *per se* application against vertical restraints rests on the argument that such restrictions can sometimes cause a reduction in economic welfare but can rarely cause significant increases in allocative efficiency. Chicago, on the other hand, argues that through reductions in transaction costs, vertical restrictions are frequently associated with efficiency gains.

More recently, two other views towards US antitrust policy have evolved, both of which advocate a dismantling of the antitrust laws, although for very different reasons (Audretsch, 1985b). One position is that antitrust policy in the United States should be abandoned precisely because of the implicit goal of competitive markets. It is argued that contemporary problems will not be solved simply by restructuring the economy towards more competitive markets. Thurow (1980, p. 146) reflects this view: 'The time has come to recognize that the antitrust approach has been a failure. . . . The attraction of the competitive ideals has faded.' Because antitrust policy is attributed with hindering, and in some cases actually causing, a deterioration in economic performance (Solow, 1984), it is argued that the need for US firms to maintain international competitiveness has rendered antitrust obsolete: 'If [the antitrust laws] do anything they only serve to hinder US competitors who might live by a code that their foreign competitors can ignore. . . . If we are to establish a competitive economy within a framework of international trade and international competition, it is time to recognize that the techniques of the nineteenth century are not applicable in getting ready for the twenty-first century' (Thurow, 1980, pp. 145–6). What is advocated is unequivocal. Public planning and direct regulation should replace the implicit solution of market competition inherent in antitrust: 'With the intellectual heartbeat of antitrust dead, regulation remains as the only alternative. Instead of creating competition, we get into the business of trying to control oligopolistic behavior' (Thurow, 1980, p. 127).

There is yet another emerging perspective towards US antitrust which also advocates abandoning government intervention under the guise of competition policy. While both the Structuralist and Chicago Schools are derived from the fundamental premise of the virtues and applicability of the neo-classical competitive model, their disagreements center upon which policies are in fact competitive and which are protectionist. In rejecting the validity and relevance of the perfect competition model, this alternative view is therefore not only rejecting the Structuralist but also the Chicago School. According to this perspective, the inherent flaw in the traditional model of competition, which is the cornerstone for policy advocated by both Structuralists and Chicagoans, is that it is not, in fact, concerned with competition. If an economic arrangement is not efficient, entry will ensure its extinction. Thus, all types of business arrangements, including price collusion, would be leagalized under this view. Rivalry among all firms in the economy would impose a competitive discipline, purging the market of all inefficient restrictions, but rewarding all efficient restraints (High, 1984–5; Armentano, 1982).[71]

The evolution of antitrust enforcement has generally followed the weight and importance of the various schools of thought towards antitrust. In the 1960s and 1970s, the Structuralist paradigm dominated economic thinking. The enforcement agencies generally reflected this in pursuing a relatively structuralist antitrust policy. Since the Chicago School has gained increasing influence in the 1980s, the Reagan Administration has implemented a much less interventionist policy towards structural market power. It cannot be easily ascertained whether the policy implemented is greatly influenced by the contemporary prevailing economic doctrine, but the two have tended to coincide. Still, the evolutionary trends are apparent enough for Mueller (1985, p. 1) to charge that contemporary US antitrust, 'if followed much further, is certain to produce a radical revision of antitrust enforcement, a *de facto* repeal of several sections of the antitrust laws'.

The shift in policy is perhaps best reflected by the reallocation of antitrust cases away from cases involving structural market power, notably monopolization and horizontal mergers, towards cases involving relatively simple price-fixing. For example, between 1965 and 1969, 65 (25 percent) of the total number of cases initiated by the Justice Department involved horizontal collusion, mostly price-fixing. In comparison, between 1980 and 1984, 446 (77 percent) of the total number of cases involved horizontal collusion (Gallo *et al.*, 1985). Even during 1970–74, only about 29 percent of the total number of cases were directed at horizontal collusion. Thus, along with the Reagan Administration has come an increase in the priority of price-fixing and other horizontal collusion cases.

A similar comparison reveals that the number and significance of enforcement resources allocated towards merger enforcement has diminished over time. Between 1965 and 1969, the Justice Department initiated 78 merger cases or 30 percent of the total number of cases. By contrast, between 1980 and 1984, only thirty-four merger cases were initiated, or about 6 percent of the total number of cases. In the earlier period, seventeen or about 7 percent of the total number of cases involved monopolization. Between 1970 and 1974, the allocation had risen to forty-two cases, or 12 percent of the total number of cases. However, during the most recent period, only ten monopolization cases were initiated, constituting less than 2 percent of the number of cases undertaken.

Not surprisingly, there were only two exclusive dealings and no tying arrangements cases initiated between 1980 and 1984. In the 1965–69 and 1970–74 periods there were 3 and 27 tying arrangements and 9 and 8 exclusive dealings cases, respectively, initiated.

Perhaps the shift in US antitrust policy has been most reflected by the shift in merger policy. In the 1950s and 1960s, virtually any horizontal merger that had more than a trivial effect on market concentration would be contested by the antitrust agencies. However, under contemporary antimerger policy, firms are allowed to divest themselves of some of their assets in the relevant submarket to compensate for an increase in the concentration level. Thus, in 1984, Texaco's purchase of Getty remained uncontested by the antitrust agencies. Recently, merger policy has been guided more by the hope of attaining increased economies of scale and scope through consolidation than by the concern for the consequences from increased market power. Thus, most recently the United States generally had adopted its least interventionist policy stance in post-war history.

ANTITRUST POLICY AND INTERNATIONAL COMPETITIVENESS

One of the main attacks levied against the structuralist approach to antitrust policy is that the policy retards efficiency gains and impedes US international competitiveness:

Consider now the implications of the structuralists' views for the treatment of innovation. The estimates of costs at the industry and firm levels were interpreted as evidence that larger firms generally did not have lower costs. Thus, firms were thought to grow for reasons other than that they were more innovative and efficient than their competitors. This belief was somewhat colored by what economists considered to be 'socially wasteful' innovations. For example, 25 years ago a successful new product was much more likely to be considered undesirable product differentiation, rather than creation of real economic value. And even 'true' innovations could be socially harmful if they could lead to market 'dominance'. (Langenfeld and Scheffman, 1988, p. 50)

As will be seen in Chapters 4 and 7, the Japanese have not only practised a more relaxed policy towards cartels, but they have also actively promoted cooperative ventures for R&D. Not only is this joint R&D among private firms aggressively encouraged by the Japanese Government, but it is frequently supported, at least in selected key industries, by public funding (Audretsch, 1988b and forthcoming b). The economic rationale for allowing cooperative R&D is that the results of R&D contain elements of a public good and involve an externality which is not likely to be completely appropriated by the firms undertaking the R&D (Link and Bauer, 1984). As will be shown in Chapter 7, cooperative R&D has played an important role in promoting the development of Japanese industries. By contrast, cooperative R&D ventures have been relatively rare in the United States. The major reason for this was that until very recently they were prohibited under the antitrust laws.

During the 1950s and 1960s the government brought a number of complaints against large successful firms on the grounds that their market power was the result of patented inventions. This policy accelerated in the 1970s, when the enforcement agencies became even less tolerant of patent licencing (Lipsky, 1982; Rule, 1986). Essentially, the Justice Department 'adopted a policy with restrictions in patent licensing such as division of territories, restrictions on a licensee's output, charging royalties on products or processes other than those explicitly covered by the patent, or requiring the licensee to also purchase unpatented inputs' (Langenfeld and Scheffman, 1988, p. 53). Of course, the licensing of patented inventions is an important vehicle for transferring technology between firms and encouraging the diffusion of innovations. Langenfeld and Scheffman (1988) argue that since patent licensing was inhibited by antitrust policy, innovation itself was reduced since there was less of an incentive for firms to innovate.

The structuralist approach to merger policy in the 1960s also applied to joint ventures. When the Pennsalt Chemicals Corporation and Olin Mathieson Company wanted to form a joint venture to produce sodium chlorate at Cavert City, Kentucky, in 1961, the Supreme Court sent the case back to District Court and ordered it to consider:

> the number and power of the competitors in the relevant market; the background of their growth; the power of the joint ventures; the relationship of their lines of commerce; the competition existing between them and the power of each in dealing with the competitors of the other; the setting in which the joint venture was created; the reasons and necessities for its existence; the joint venture's line of commerce and the relationship thereof to that of its parents; the adaptability of its line of commerce to non-competitive practices; the potential power of the joint venture in the relevant market; an appraisal of what the competition in the relevant market would have been if one of the joint ventures had entered it alone instead of through Penn-Olin; the effect, in the event of this occurrence, of the joint venture's potential competition; and such other factors as might indicate potential risk to competition in the relevant market.[72]

It should be observed that the Supreme Court paid little attention to any potential benefits emanating from technology transfer. That is, 'the key ingredient of most joint ventures – increased efficiency through the sharing of innovative technologies – was given a back seat to the potentially anticompetitive aspects of joint ventures' (Langenfeld and Scheffman, 1988, p. 74). Similarly, in the Brunswick[73] decision the FTC virtually ignored potential benefits from technology transfer and cited the loss of competition due to a joint venture involving a potential entrant.

Perhaps responding to the fact that the United States was virtually unique among the Western countries and Japan in not allowing most joint ventures and discouraging cooperative R&D, the US enforcement agencies altered their policies under the Reagan Administration. While all joint ventures must still be reported to the government prior to consummation, the enforcement agencies now consider the potential gains from innovation and efficiency as well as the anticompetitive effects. Thus, GM and Toyota were allowed to undertake a joint production venture that is equally owned by GM and Toyota.[74] The joint venture was originally limited to twelve years, but subsequent to private litigation initiated by Chrysler the duration of the agreement was reduced to eight years. According to Langenfeld and Scheffman (1988, p. 89), 'The efficiencies arising from the spreading of an innovative management and production system in GM–Toyota outweighed the concerns that a joint venture of two large competitors in a highly concentrated industry might lead to an anticompetitive effect. In essence, convincing substantial efficiencies were given more weight than speculative anticompetitive effects.'

While the more lenient policy towards joint ventures represented a change in the antitrust stance of the enforcement agencies with no alteration in one of the legal statutes, cooperative R&D among private firms was made legal through the National Cooperative Research Act (NCRA) of 1984.[75] Sentiment supporting the Act was so strong that no member of Congress voted against it. The NCRA codified a rule-of-reason approach to determining the legality of cooperative R&D. Joint R&D ventures are illegal under the NCRA only if there are anticompetitive effects, such as collusion. There is some evidence that private industry has responded to the different environment for undertaking joint R&D established by the NCRA. Within one year of its passage there were ninety cooperative R&D agreements registered with the enforcement agencies (Langenfeld and Scheffman, 1988).

In allowing joint ventures and cooperative R&D agreements the United States adopted a policy which has long been the practice of its major international competitors. This evolution in antitrust policy represents a change away from the Structuralist approach, which was concerned primarily with equity in domestic markets, to a concern with economic efficiency, which is the key determinant to international competitiveness. As Owen (1986) suggested for the recent developments in merger policy, this evolution in antitrust policy towards joint ventures and cooperative R&D reflects an approach that is more consistent with the industrial policy approaches taken in the European countries and Japan.

CONCLUSION

The antitrust experiment in the United States is unique among the developed nations in its tenacity and scope. That it has had a significant impact on US market structure is acknowledged by both its critics as well as its advocates. However, the nature of the effect, and therefore the appropriate role of antitrust policy in the future, is hotly contested. The Structuralist position is that an aggressive interventionist antitrust policy is required to ensure market competitiveness. Only through the spur of domestic competition, it is argued, will American firms ultimately be able to withstand the test of world competition. During the 1960s and early 1970s, antitrust policy reflected this view, and a relatively Structuralist policy was implemented.

More recently, however, the increased predominance and influence of the Chicago School has led to a considerable rethinking towards the appropriate role of antitrust. Much of this rethinking is apparently reflected in the Reagan Administration's antitrust policy. This position argues that a considerably less interventionist antitrust policy is appropriate to ensure maximum efficiency. It is argued that, other than price-fixing and horizontal mergers directly leading to monopoly power, firm rivalry will tend to ensure that only the most efficient economic arrangements will survive. By emphasizing the priority on scale and scope economies, US firms will be better equipped to compete in world markets. However, a counterview to both of these positions, which is gaining increased respectability and ascendence, is that the inherent goal of antitrust is misguided. Rather than try to impose domestic competition through market internvention by the government, it is argued, US firms would better benefit from direct planning and targeting by the government. Whether or not antitrust continues to serve as perhaps America's most resilient form of industrial policy hinges on this issue. If private firms, spurred only by domestic competition, continue to meet the challenge raised by their foreign counterparts, antitrust is likely to remain an essential, and perhaps the central, instrument of US industrial policy. If, however, US firms are unable to stay internationally competitive across a broad spectrum of industries, the American experiment with antitrust policy will likely become a historical anecdote.

NOTES

1. There is not universal agreement that the intent of Congress is relevant to the implementation of the antitrust laws. For example, according to Bittlingmayer (1986), 'It does not seem prudent to talk about the intentions of Congress since different congressmen no doubt had different ideas about what should actually be done about the trust problem, and since even individual congressmen contradicted themselves.'
2. Robert Bork (1966, p. 47) has warned that the construct of legislative intent must be applied with caution, 'if for no other reason than its inherent artificiality'.
3. For an explantion of the 'Chicago approach' see Audretsch (forthcoming a).
4. For a further enunciation of their position, see Bork (1978).
5. Statute 209 (1890), Section 1.
6. *Ibid.*
7. *Ibid.*, Section 2.
8. 38 Stat. 717 (1914), quote is from Section 5.
9. 38 Stat. 730 (1914).
10. In 1936, Section 2 of the Clayton Act was amended by the Robinson Patman Act (52 Stat. 446, 1936), to strengthen antitrust enforcement against price discrimination. The Act reads:

> It shall be unlawful for any person engaged in commerce in the course of such commerce to be a party to, or assist in, any transaction or sale, or contract to sell, which discriminates to his knowledge against competition of the purchaser, in that, any discount, rebate, allowance, or advertising service change is granted to the purchaser over and above any discount, rebate, allowance or advertising service, charge available at the time of such transaction to said competition in respect of a sale of goods of like grade, quality, and quantity; to sell, or contract to sell, goods in any part of the United States at prices lower than those exacted by said person elsewhere in the United States for the purpose of destroying competition, or eliminating a competitor in such part of the United States; or, to sell, or contract to sell, goods at unreasonably low prices for the purpose of destroying competition or eliminating a competitor.

11. Unions may legally seek to obtain identical contracts with every firm in a given industry if the unions are not conspiring with some firms to impose on competitors uncompetitive conditions. However, a consipiracy between a firm (or firms) and a union to impose such uncompetitive conditions on other firms constitutes a violation of the Sherman Act (*United Mine Workers* v. *Pennington*, 381 U.S. 657).

12. It should be noted that the FTC contains its own 'quasi-Judge', referred to as an 'administrative law judge'. While the hearing procedure and decision process is analogous to a court of law, it is, in fact, not a court of law. That is, a firm or the FTC staff can always, and in many cases do, appeal against the decision of an administrative law judge to the US Supreme Court.

13. *US* v. *Trans-Missouri Freight Association*, 166 US 290 (1897).

14. Under the US court system, a case involving federal law is first tried at a US District Court. Either party may appeal against the judge's verdict and the facts of the case are then argued in front of the US Court of Appeals. Cases reach the US Supreme Court following the decision of the Court to hear a case, presumably because the Court thinks that it involves an important point requiring Supreme Court interpretation. For a further description, see Neale (1970).

15. *US* v. *Trans-Missouri Freight Association, et al.*, 53 Fed. 440, 451 (1892).

16. *US* v. *Joint Traffic Association*, 171 US 505 (1898).

17. *Addyston Pipe & Steel Company et al.* v. *US*, 175 US 211 (1898).

18. *US* v. *Trenton Potteries Co. et al*, 273 US 392 (1927).

19. *Ibid.*

20. The *per se* application was extended to agreements to restrict quantities in *US* v. *Socony-Vacuum Oil Co. et al.*, 310 US 150 (1940).

21. *Board of Trade of the City of Chicago* v. *US*, 246 US 231 (1918).

22. *US* v. *Container Corporation of America et al.*, 393 US 333 (1969).

23. *US* v. *Standard Oil Co. of New Jersey et al.*, 221 US 1 (1911).

24. *US* v. *American Tobacco Co.*, 21 US 106 (1911).

25. A revisionist view suggesting that Standard Oil did not, in fact, engage in predatory pricing is presented by McGee (1958).

26. *US* v. *US Steel Corp.*, 251 US 417 (1920).

27. *US* v. *Aluminum Co. of America*, 148 F. 2cl 416 (1945). Note that in this case, the Second Circuit Court served as 'a court of last resort' (a substitute for the US Supreme Court), because several of the justices, who had previously worked with the prosecution, had to disqualify themselves, and the Supreme Court was unable to meet the necessary quorum of six justices to hear the case.

28. *US* v. *United Shoe Machinery Corporation*, 347 US 521 (1954).

29. *US* v. *International Business Machines Corporation*, 69 CIV 200, So. District of New York.

30. *Berkey Photo, Inc.* v. *Eastman Kodak Co.*, 603 F. 2cl 263, 2cl Cir. (1979).

31. *US* v. *Aluminum Co. of America*, 148 F. 2cl. 416 (1945).

32. For documentation of changes in market concentration, see Scherer (1979).

33. *Interstate Circuit Inc., et al.* v. *US*, 306 US 208 (1939).

34. *Ibid.*, p. 226.

35. *American Tobacco Co., et al.* v. *US*, 328 US 781 (1946).

36. *Ibid.*, pp. 809–10.

37. *Theatre Enterprises, Inc.* v. *Paramount Film Distributing Corp. et al.*, 346 US 537 (1954), pp. 540–1.

38. FTC complaint against Kellogg General Mills, General Foods, and Quaker Oats, Docket No. 8883, filed April 26, 1972. The Quaker Oats Company was subsequently dropped from the complaint.

39. 64 US Stat. at L. (1950), 1125.

40. For documentation of the great merger wave, see Nelson (1959).
41. 64 US Stat. at L. (1950), 1125.
42. Public Law No. 212, 38 US Stat. at. L. (1914).
43. For an analysis of Congressional intent underlying the Clayton Act, see Martin (1959).
44. 64 US Stat. at L. (1950), 1125.
45. *Brown Shoe Co.* v. *US*, 370 US 294 (1962).
46. *Ibid.*, p. 345.
47. *US* v. *Von's Grocery Co.*, 384 US 280 (1966).
48. For example, see *US* v. *General Dynamic Corp.*, 415 US 486 (1973).
49. The US Steel–National Steel merger was ultimately abandoned for reasons other than antitrust.
50. For a discussion and description of the merger guidelines under the Reagan Administration, see Fox (1982).
51. The one pure conglomerate case which the Supreme Court agreed to hear upon appeal, *US* v. *International Telephone and Telegraph*, 324 F. Supp. 19 (1970), was dropped by the Justice Department under pressure from the Nixon Administration in 1971 (see Mueller, 1983).
52. *FTC* v. *Consolidated Foods Corp.*, 380 US 592 (1965).
53. *US* v. *Falstaff Brewing Corp.*, 410 US 526 (1973).
54. *Ford Motor Co.* v. *US*, 405 US 562 (1972).
55. *FTC* v. *Proctor & Gamble Co.*, 386 US 568 (1967).
56. For an explanation of the deterrent effect, and how it is the result of the interaction among the existence of legal statutes, the establishment of clear precedent cases, and systematic enforcement, see Audretsch (1983b, 1985b).
57. *Standard Oil Co. of California et al.* v. *US*, 337 US 293 (1949), pp. 305–6.
58. *International Salt Co.* v. *US*, 332 US 392 (1947).
59. *US* v. *Herrold Electronics Corp.*, 363 US 567 (1961).
60. *US* v. *White Motor Co.*, 373 US 253 (1963); *US* v. *Topco Associates, Inc.*, 405 US 596 (1972), p. 610.
61. *US* v. *White Motor Co.*, 373 US 253 (1963).
62. *US* v. *Arnold Schwinn & Co. et al.*, 388 US 365 (1967).
63. *Continental TV Inc, et al.* v. *GTE Sylvania, Inc.*, 433 US 36 (1977).
64. FTC docket no. 8885.
65. *Standard Oil Co. of California et al.* v. *US*, 337 US 293 (1949), p. 314.
66. *Tampa Electric Co.* v. *Nashville Coal Co. et al.*, 365 US 320 (1961).
67. *Dr. Miles Medical Co.* v. *John D. Park and Sons Co.*, 220 US 373 (1911).
68. *Monsanto Co.* v. *Spray-Rite Service Corp.*, 1984–1 Trade Cas. (CCH), Sup. Ct. 1984.
69. For an excellent representation of the Structuralist School, see Kaysen and Turner (1959).
70. Comanor, 1968.
71. High (1984–5); Armentano (1982).
72. *US* v. *Penn-Olin Chem. Co.*, 389 US 308 (1967).
73. *Yamaha Motor Co.* v. *FTC*, 657 F.2d971 (2d Cir.1981).
74. 103 FTC 374 (1984).
75. 15 U.S.C. Secs. 4301–5 (Supp. II 1984).

3 · COMPETITION POLICY IN THE EUROPEAN ECONOMIC COMMUNITY

Competition policy in the European Economic Community (EEC) provides a strong contrast to the antitrust approach of the United States. There are some striking differences. While price-fixing and quantity agreements among US firms are *per se* illegal under the Sherman Act, collusion is legal under certain conditions in the EEC. In West Germany, legalized cartels have long been a fixture of the market structure in a number of industries. Similarly, policies towards dominant firms and mergers vary considerably between both sides of the Atlantic. The United States is unique in adapting a structuralist approach to monopoly power, under which firms have actually been dismembered and dissolved. By contrast, the approach under EEC competition policy has been more oriented towards eliminating the restrictive practices undertaken by such dominant firms. Similarly, EEC members have generally adapted much looser policy towards mergers, particularly horizontal acquisitions, in which all but the largest are generally allowed. This perhaps accounts for the biggest difference between EEC competition policy and American antitrust. Finally, there has been a concious effort by policymakers within the EEC to encourage cooperative enterprises in the belief that cooperative undertakings are conducive to innovation and technical change. It has been observed that 'the (EEC) Commission has always shown a favorable attitude towards R&D cooperation' (OECD, 1987, p. 239). By contrast, American antitrust has been characterized by the suspicion that such cooperation actually impedes innovation and technical change.

One of the challenges in characterizing competition policy in the EEC is that there are numerous competition policies, resulting in a matrix of complex levels of policy. That is, while an official competition policy of the European Community exists, each member country has its own independent set of competition policies. Thus, a certain tension exists between the overall competition policy set by the EEC, and the independent competition policies enacted by each member country. Still, the similarities between the various EEC members are much more striking than the dissimilarities. It is clear that competition policy in the EEC can be considered as an entity which is unique and singular, particularly when contrasted with the antitrust approach in the United States.

The second section of the chapter examines the competition policy adapted

by the EEC. In particular, the goals of EEC competition policy are considered along with the major enforcement and policy institutions. Specific policy
towards dominant firms, cartels and mergers is examined, along with an
investigation of the trends in concentration within the EEC. In the third
section, West German competition policy is explored. The statutes and
institutions implementing competition policy in the post-war period are
described, as is the specific policy towards monopoly, restraints-of-trade and
cartels. The various types of legal cartels, along with their frequency of
occurrence during the past thirty years, is also considered. Competition
policy in the United Kingdom is analyzed in the fourth section, with an
emphasis on public policy towards market power, restrictive practices and
mergers. After examining French competition policy in the fifth section,
conclusions are presented in the last section.

EEC COMPETITION POLICY

With Article 2 of the 1957 Treaty of Rome, which called for 'a harmonious
development of economic activities, a continuous and balanced expansion,
an increase in stability, an accelerated raising of the standard of living and
closer relations between the states belonging to it', the integration of economic interests in Europe was set as a goal. More specifically, Article 85 of the
Treaty of Rome explicitly forbids certain restrictive practices, thereby constituting the kernel of a European-wide competition policy. In general, EEC
competition policy bears a strong resemblance, at least in the legislative
statutes, to its counterpart on the other side of the Atlantic, American
antitrust. According to Jacquemin and de Jong (1977), the essential goal of
European competition policy is the diffusion of economic power and the
preservation of freedom for individuals. Thus, there is an *a priori* judgment
against the concentration of economic power, both in the form of large firms
and in the form of market concentration. In this sense, European competition policy, like American antitrust, is not apparently restricted to purely
economic considerations. Rather, political and social implications of market
structure and firm conduct play an essential role in the motivations underlying EEC competition policy:

> Our concern for the maintenance of effective competition extends beyond
> purely economic considerations. Competition is one of the foundations of an
> open society in which all member countries of the European Community have a
> substantial stake. . . . It is therefore necessary to weigh against the gains from
> industrial concentration the socio-political consequences of concentrations of
> private power, which could discredit property-owning democracy. (Cairncross,
> 1974, p. 143)

A secondary goal of European competition policy is the protection of the
'economic freedom of market participants'. In particular, EEC policy strives

to prevent predatory market conduct, such as boycotts, refusals to sell and discrimination, that would threaten the viability of small and medium firms. Finally, EEC competition policy includes allocative efficiency as an important goal.

> The Commission leaves little doubt that market competition is considered to be the best vehicle to realize the underlying values of European antitrust policy: Competition is the best stimulant of economic activity since it guarantees the widest possible freedom of action to all. An active competition policy makes it easier for the supply and demand structures continually to adjust to technological development. Through the interplay of decentralized decision-making machinery, competition enables enterprises continously to improve their efficiency which is the *sine qua non* for a steady improvement in the living standards. Such a policy encourages the best possible use of productive resources for the greatest possible benefit of the economy as a whole and for the benefit, in particular, of the consumer. (Commission of the European Communities, 1972, p. 143)

Articles 87, 88 and 89 enable the Commission's Council of Ministers to implement whatever regulations or directives which are deemed essential to carry out the competition policy mandated in Articles 85 and 86 of the Treaty of Rome. Regulation No. 17 of Article 85, which was passed in 1962, states that 'agreements between undertakings, decisions by associations of undertakings and concerted practices which may affect trade between Member States and which have as their object the prevention, restriction or distortion of competition within the Common Market shall be prohibited as imcompatible with the Common Market.' In particular, price-fixing is prohibited, while ancillary agreements are legal. In addition, Article 85, Section 1, prohibits restraints or division of output, the pooling of markets or sources of supply, and tying a purchase to some other condition which has 'no connection with the subject of such contracts' (Walsh and Paxton, 1975).

The EEC Commission is the enforcement agency of European Community competition policy. Competition policy hearings are undertaken under a secret procedure. Investigations are undertaken either in response to a complaint by an affected firm or party, or on the Commission's own initiative, in response to industry performance suggesting the presence of some deviation away from a competitive market process. In the investigation process, affected firms and governments are legally required to comply with all requests by the Commission for relevant evidence. In the course of the investigation, the Commission generally considers the opinion of the Consultative Committee on Cartels and Monopolies, which is represented by each EEC member country. If the Commission finds that an agreement between firms constitutes a restraint of trade, it can issue informal recommendations to the relevant firms or reach a formal decision making agreement illegal. If the Commission finds a violation of Article 85, the agreement is *per se* null and void, and the involved parties are liable for fines of up to 10 percent of sales. The option of appealing against the Commission's decision in the European Court of Justice applies in certain instances (George and Joll, 1975).

With respect to dominant market power, European competition policy differs somewhat from that of its American counterpart. Article 86 states that

> to the extent to which trade between any Member States may be affected thereby, action by one or more enterprises to take the improper advantage of a dominant position within the Common Market or within a substantial part of it shall be deemed to be incompatible with the Common Market and shall thereby be prohibited.[1]

Thus the attainment and possession of a dominant market position is not illegal under EEC law. However, the 'abuse' of a dominant position is illegal under EEC competition policy. Specific examples of abusive practices are clearly provided in Article 86. These include the direct or indirect imposition of any inequitable purchase or selling price or of any other inequitable trading conditions, the limitation of production, markets or technical development to the prejudice of consumers, the application to parties of transactions of unequal terms in respect of equivalent supplies, thereby placing them at a competitive disadvantage, and the subjecting of the conclusion of a contract to the acceptance by a party of additional supplies which, either by their nature or according to commercial usage, have no connection with the subject of such contract.

However, the statute does not clearly define what exactly constitutes a dominant firm, leaving the interpretation, instead, up to the Commission. The Commission has generally considered the market share, the technological predominance (patents and R&D), the dispersion of sales and geographic dimensions of the market, and the availability of obtaining capital from the international market.[2] Rather than a narrow focus on market structure characteristics, such as concentration, 'the ultimate test of a dominant position is the firm's ability to behave persistently in a manner which would be impossible in a competitive market, and not the structure of the market' (Jacquemin, 1975, p. 132).

Part of the tension in competition policy towards market dominance is that, to the extent to which European firms compete in world markets, a relatively high market share within the European market may be needed to attain the sufficient size enabling the minimum efficient scale level of output. That is, a firm may hold a dominant position within Europe, but may be very much under the force of competition from rivals in Japan and United States. While the goal of European competition policy is to maximize competition within Europe, the goal of European industrial policies is to promote firm size, thereby implicitly reducing the number of viable competitors, in an effort to promote the viability of European firms in competition with American and Japanese rivals. Thus, a likely conflict emerges between EEC competition policy and industrial policy. This conflict is examined in more detail in Chapter 6.

The interpretation by the Commission of 'abuse' of a dominant position has been quite broad: 'An improper exploitation of dominant position must be assumed when the dominant firm utilizes the opportunities resulting from its dominance to gain advantages it could not gain in the face of practicable and sufficiently effective competition' (Commission of the European Communities, 1966). For example, in one case the Commission decided that an exclusive dealing contract over a long period constituted an abuse or a dominant position.[3] Thus, it appears that the Commission has, in effect, interpreted Article 86 as prohibiting all firm conduct which would not occur in a market characterized by competition. Such conduct is defined as abusive and is therefore prohibited. Between the inception of Article 86 in 1971 and 1975, there were only four decisions prohibiting abuses, and one of the rulings was ultimately reversed by the European Court. In one case in 1982, for example, the Commission found that British Telecom, which operates the telecommunications systems in the United Kingdom, had engaged in practices constituting the abuse of a dominant position. British Telecom had not allowed private message-forwarding agencies the access to relay telex messages to and from other countries.[4] The Commission inferred that such conduct constituted an abuse in the form of creating a barrier to entry, and therefore was in violation of the competition laws.

Similarly, in a case in 1983, the Commission found that a manufacturer of benzoyl peroxide, AKZO, had engaged in pricing practices which constituted the abuse of a dominant position.[5] ECS, which had brought the complaint, produces a product which is used as a bleach in the flour milling industry and as a catalyst in the chemical industry. ECS accused AKZO of attempting to drive it out of the market through selective price decreases. The Commission, in reaching its decision, ordered AKZO to restore the prices to their original levels. Only in matching a price reduction already made by a competitor was AKZO allowed to reduce the price.

One of the major differences between antitrust policy in the United States and competition policy in the EEC is the absence of 'structuralist' remedies. While a number of major firms have been dismembered in the United States, including Standard Oil, American Tobacco and AT&T (see Chapter 2), there are no such structuralist remedies for dissolving dominant market power in the EEC. In some sense this reflects the greater emphasis of European competition policy on conduct and firm abuses, and the failure to consider the act of monopolizing as a violation of the competitive standards. Thus, the appropriate remedy consists typically of removing the obnoxious conduct and does not require dismembering existing enterprises. In contrast, US antitrust has historically had a more structuralist approach, whereby the kernel of monopoly power is considered to lie in an oligopolistic or monopolistic market structure. American antitrust has been more willing to consider the restructuring of firms as the appropriate remedy. Perhaps this discrepancy in approaches in some sense reflects the Europeans' greater concern with obtaining and preserving the scale economies which are pre-requisite to remaining viable in international competition. From this per-spective, the United States can afford a more structuralist approach to antitrust, since the minimum efficient scale level of output typically consti-tutes a considerably smaller percentage of the domestic market in the United States than in Europe (Scherer, 1973). Thus, while a number of American economists (Weiss, 1979; Scherer, 1977) have noted that divestiture and dismemberment would not adversely affect the productive efficiency of US dominant firms, the same might not hold for European firms.

Article 85 also places restrictions on agreements between firms, both horizontally and vertically. In particular, the statute makes all agreements, whether contractual or not, which restrict competition in trade between member countries, illegal. The Commission has interpreted this as a virtual *per se* prohibition of international cartels. Of the fifty-nine cartelization cases examined by the Commission between 1964 and 1974, only seven did not result in dissolution and a fine. And, virtually all of the thirty-two price-fixing cartels were found by the Commission to be illegal. In general, cartel agreements concerning price-fixing and quantity restrictions are rarely allow-ed (Jacquemin and de Jong, 1977). Thus with respect to price-fixing and quantity restrictions, EEC competition policy in practice closely resembles its counterpart in American antitrust. Even though such agreements are *per se* illegal in the United States, while a rule of reason is applied in the EEC, resulting in the possibility of legal exemptions, in practice the interpretation of the respective statutes concerning horizontal agreements closely affecting price are quite similar.

In a 1983 decision involving agreements on price-fixing and market-sharing in the cast iron and steel roll industry, the Commission found concerted practices had been undertaken which constituted a serious viola-tion of Section 1 of Article 85.[6] The case involved twenty-five producers of cast iron and cast steel rolls, including two trade associations and several countries, among them France and West Germany. Over the period 1968–80, the involved firms engaged in a system of exchanging quotations on prices prior to making price quotations in each other's home markets. In addition, price increases were agreed upon, as were several allocation systems. In reaching its decision, the Commission imposed a substantial fine on the involved parties.

Similarly, in a 1982 decision, again invoking Article 85, the Commission found that horizontal agreements between firms in the cigarette industry constituted an illegal price-fixing cartel.[7] After finding that firms in the industry had engaged in a scheme to fix cigarette prices in 1980, the Commission imposed a substantial fine on a number of cigarette firms, including the British American Tobacco Co., Philip Morris Holland, and R. J. Reynolds Tobacco.

However, the EEC is much more likely to allow agreements for joint sales agencies. Most of these legal cartel agreements involved only insignificant market shares. Similarly, small- and medium-sized firms are generally permitted to form cartels. As long as the combined market share of the firms forming the cartel does not exceed 10 percent of the market and total sales of the cartel remain under a ceiling equalling 150 million units of account, small- and medium-sized firm cartels are permitted.

The Commission has also reached several decisions – in the Dyestuffs Manufacturers, Pittsburgh Corning Europe, and Sugar Produces cases – suggesting that conscious parallelism, or concerted practices, will not be allowed by the Commission. While the Commission and the Court decided that all of these cases represented an illegal cartel, the inference was always based on the existence of conduct that would not normally be expected to be present in a competitive market (Jacquemin and de Jong, 1977).

Article 85 has also resulted in limiting the extent of vertical agreements between firms. A vertical agreement refers to agreements between firms at various stages of the production and distribution process. In general, exclusive dealing has not been allowed by the Commission. The Commission has generally taken the view that such contracts or agreements serve predominantly to create market power through erecting entry barriers. In a 1964 case, *Grundig* v. *Consten*, it was established that Grundig, which manufactured chemicals in West Germany, had given a French retailer, Consten, the exclusive rights in France. In addition, the retailers outside France were prohibited from shipping the product to France. In its ruling, the Commission found that the contract constituted an exclusive dealing agreement. The ruling was upheld by the Court in 1966.

However, under the present interpretation of Article 85, exclusive dealing contracts are not *per se* illegal. Only those contracts which were viewed as likely to create a barrier to entry are prohibited. Thus, in *S.T. M.* v. *M. B. U.*, the Court held that exclusive dealing contracts involving only a trivial share of the market are not illegal.

While in the United States resale price maintenance has been allowed only under certain conditions, it has generally been illegal in the EEC. However, manufacturers are not allowed to dictate from whom retailers can purchase. In the 1972 *W. E. A.* v. *Filipacchi Music S. A.* case, a company producing records in West Germany prohibited its dealers in France from shipping records to West Germany in an attempt to maintain a price differential of nearly 50 percent between the two markets (Jacquemin and de Jong, 1977). However, the Commission found such restrictions to be a violation of EEC competition laws.

Market (1975) has identified two major goals of EEC competition policy towards mergers. First, the EEC has attempted to facilitate the consolidation of small- and medium-sized firms in different countries by removing legal obstacles, thus making the requisite scale for efficiency considerations possible. Second, the EEC has acted to avoid the concentration of markets, which is explicitly stated in Article 3 of the EEC Treaty as an underlying goal of the European Community. It is clear, however, that both of these goals are not entirely mutually exclusive, and create a natural tension in EEC competition policy.

Rather than adapt a virtual *per se* prohibition of horizontal mergers, as had been the case in the United States until the 1980s, the Commission has developed the more lenient view of allowing the acquisition, unless it is clear that the merger would constitute the creation or entrenchment of monopoly power. The Commission has concluded that any acquisition or consolidation 'where a dominant enterprise strengthens its position through concentration to the point where, in violation of the concept on which the Treaty, and particularly 86(b), is based, it thereby creates a monopolistic situation which prevents competition from functioning, to the detriment of consumers, suppliers, and dealers'[8] constitutes a violation of EEC competition policy. However, the Commission explicitly acknowledged that such a violation would occur 'only in rare, exceptional cases'.

A major problem facing the Commission was the absence of a statute explicitly dealing with mergers. While Article 86 prohibits the abuse of a dominant position in either the more general market constituting the EEC or in any sub-market, this does not directly address the issue of mergers. Thus, while the Commission could find that any acquisition creating monopoly power or entrenching an existing dominant position constituted an abuse of a dominant position and therefore was in violation of Article 86, any mergers falling short of monopoly positions were essentially beyond the jurisdiction of the Commission. Responding to this statutory vacuum, in 1973 the Commission proposed a detailed method for regulating mergers and acquisitions. Essentially the Commission would be empowered to prevent mergers where the combined market share would exceed 25 percent of the relevant market and where the merger would enable the newly merged firm to effectively 'hinder effective competition in the Common Market or in a substantial part thereof'.

The leniency of the Commission towards horizontal mergers is evidenced by a 1982 decision, whereby the Commission approved the proposal by the two largest steel firms in Belgium, Cockerill SA, Liège, and Hainaut-Samber SA, Charleroi, to consolidate all of their assets in forming a new firm, Cockerill-Sambre SA.[9] The Commission referred to the increases in efficiency through rationalization and specialization in several product lines as grounds for permitting the merger. The combined firm constituted the eighth largest manufacturer in the EEC.

Table 3.1 shows the trends in the four- and twelve-firm concentration ratios between 1973 and 1981 for eight major manufacturing sectors in the EEC (including the first nine members). In fact, the trends in concentration have varied somewhat among the eight industrial sectors. In some sectors

Table 3.1 Concentration Trends in the European Community, 1973–1981

Sector	1973 CR$_4$	1973 CR$_{12}$	1974 CR$_4$	1974 CR$_{12}$	1975 CR$_4$	1975 CR$_{12}$	1976 CR$_4$	1976 CR$_{12}$	1977 CR$_4$	1977 CR$_{12}$	1978 CR$_4$	1978 CR$_{12}$	1979 CR$_4$	1979 CR$_{12}$	1980 CR$_4$	1980 CR$_{12}$	1981 CR$_4$	1981 CR$_{12}$
Food	33	54	34	53	34	52	32	50	31	49	29	46	28	46	30	51	25	43
Chemicals	25	57	27	58	27	58	30	59	33	61	30	58	34	62	33	61	31	56
Electrical engineering	38	66	43	69	44	67	42	66	42	69	44	65	46	68	41	64	43	68
Mechanical engineering	33	52	30	52	31	49	28	44	34	54	38	57	33	58	30	53	33	55
Metal industries	24	55	24	55	28	57	27	57	28	58	27	54	28	58	29	54	26	53
Transport equipment	34	69	35	70	38	68	36	65	39	69	40	71	41	74	42	74	44	75
Paper	47	73	47	72	46	71	43	68	53	77	51	73	50	74	48	75	45	75
Textile	53	80	48	78	50	79	39	65	45	74	43	70	49	78	43	70	42	70

Source: OECD (1982), *Competition Policy in the EEC.*

there has been a noticeable trend towards increasing concentration. For example, in the transportation equipment sector, the four-firm concentration ratio has risen from 34 percent in 1973 to 39 percent in 1977, and to 44 percent in 1981. However, in other sectors, there has been a noticeable decrease in the level of concentration. For example, in the food sector the four-firm concentration ratio in 1973 was 33 percent. In 1979, the concentration ratio had fallen to 28 percent, and by 1981 it was only 25 percent. Similarly, the four-firm concentration has fallen in the textile sector from 53 percent in 1973 to 45 percent in 1977, and finally to 42 percent in 1981. In certain industrial sectors there has not been a significant change in the level of concentration. While the four-firm concentration ratio in the mechanical engineering sector was 33 percent in 1973, 1979 and 1981, it remained between 24 and 29 percent over the period 1973 to 1981 in the metal industries sector.

There seems to be some relationship between acquisition activity and the trends in concentration. For example, the EEC (Commission of the European Communities, 1984) found that the greatest incidence of merger activity in the member countries was in the food sector, which, perhaps not coincidentally, also experienced a considerable rise in concentration (Table 3.1). The second highest incidence in acquisition activity occurred in the chemical sector, which also experienced a significant increase in concentration. On the other hand, the lowest acquisition rates were in the textile and paper sectors, which did not experience increases in concentration over this period. This might suggest that, regardless of the intention of EEC competition policy, the recent trends in concentration may be related to the inability of the EEC to implement a tighter control of mergers.

COMPETITION POLICY IN WEST GERMANY

The legal statute comprising the core of competition policy in West Germany is Section 22, which empowers the Cartel Office to prohibit abusive conduct by dominant firms, and Section 26, which prohibits discriminatory and exclusionary conduct by firms possessing dominant power. The underlying goal of the statutes is to check firms possessing monopoly power from engaging in abusive practices. In this sense the West German competition policy greatly resembles that of the EEC. Similarly, like the EEC policy, possession of monopoly power *per se* does not constitute a violation of competition policy. Rather it is the abuse of that power through exclusionary conduct, which would not be expected to occur under competitive conditions, which is prohibited under West German competition policy. The earliest interpretation of competition policy interpreted a dominant firm as one that was free from competition. More recently the definition of a dominant firm has evolved as one that possesses a dominant market position.

However, this does not preclude the existence of competition, at least from smaller firms or potential entrants into the market. In 1973, the law was amended to define a dominant firm as one possessing a superior market position in relation to its major rivals, and that 'regard shall be given to the firm's market share, financial strength, access to supply and sales markets, and interrelationships with other enterprises, and that legal and factual barriers to entry into the market shall be considered' (Monopolkommission, 1976, p. 84).

In fact, the conceptualization of market dominance in West Germany is considerably broader than its corresponding interpretation under the Sherman Act in the United States. While the American antitrust policy considers the extent of dominance in a single product or geographic market, the West German policy adapts a considerably broader stance in recognizing that monopoly power may be the result of the firm's position and conduct across a number of markets. That is, the general financial strength of the firm in question, along with the extent of vertical integration and diversification, is considered under German law, but not under US law. Similarly, the question of the applicability of Section 2 of the Sherman Act towards oligopolies has presented considerable difficulties, whereas the law in West Germany is much clearer. Once it has been established that an oligopolized industry has dominant power, each firm constituting the oligopoly is also considered to possess market power. That is, shared monopoly is incorporated into West German competition policy more easily than it is into American antitrust.

Like its American counterpart, the West German statute prohibits conduct that entrenches dominant power and explicitly authorizes the Cartel Office to prohibit conduct in which a dominant firm or oligopoly engages to expand its market power. However, also like its American counterpart, the statutes do not explicitly define what constitutes abuses of power; interpretation is up to the Federal Cartel Office. The Cartel Office has generally followed the precedent set by the EEC Commission in defining abuse as any market conduct that would not otherwise occur in a market characterized by competition. This essentially invokes a counter-factual test for abuse of a dominant position: What conduct would be expected from a firm in the absence of a dominant firm or oligopoly in the market? Such a test has been referred to as the so-called 'as-if-competition' test (Kellermann, 1968).

Abuse of a dominant position can be determined not only from the firm's alleged conduct in its primary market, but also from its practices in any market in which it has contact. In this sense, West German competition policy has a greater scope than does its American counterpart. Examples of conduct that have been interpreted as abuse include the charging of a price significantly in excess of costs, providing the customer with products of relatively inferior quality, and imposing disadvantageous restrictions on the sale of the product, such as a tying agreement. These three types of conduct represent potential losses to the consumers of the product. Additional sources of conduct that have been interpreted as abuse have a greater effect on the firm's rivals. For example, prices that are set too low can drive out competitors; extracting favorable prices of inputs, which are below those paid by competitors, can also adversely affect rivals. Similarly, engaging in exclusive dealing contracts and tying arrangements, along with reciprocity practices, are all examples of conduct that can be considered to affect adversely competitors through the erection of entry barriers.

Thus, West German competition policy towards market power, and dominant firms or oligopolies in particular, focuses more on the firm conduct and less on the market structure than does American antitrust policy. However, there are very few types of conduct which are interpreted as being illegal *per se*. Rather, each case is considered on its own merits, in the context of the firms actually involved. That is, certain types of conduct, which are considered to constitute an abuse of a dominant position for some firms, will not be considered to be abusive when undertaken by other ones. Not surprisingly, the remedies available under West German law reflect this preoccupation with firms' conduct, in that they enable the Federal Cartel Office to prohibit dominant firms from engaging in those practices that have been found to be abusive, but offer little in the way of a more structural solution. In principle, as well as in practice, this constitutes another significant difference between American antitrust and West German competition policy. While the Sherman Act enables the American antitrust agencies to restructure industries in certain instances, as has been the case in the tobacco and oil industries, West German law makes no provision for eliminating the structural problems associated with market power. Thus, by dismembering firms, US antitrust attempts to remedy the monopolized market by imposing a more competitive market structure, whereas West German policy replaces the unconstrained monopoly with a type of guidance from the government more closely resembling regulation. According to the Federal Cartel Office, the solution to the conclusion that an abuse of a dominant position has occurred leads to the result that 'the invisible hand of competition is replaced by the visible hand of state supervision'.[10]

For example, in 1982 five West German firms producing blood-clotting preparations were found to constitute an oligopoly which had engaged in abusive practices. The five firms accounted for 85 percent of the market, and the abusive conduct was in the form of excessive prices. It was estimated that, following the prohibition of charging such high prices, consumers would save between DM 60 and DM 70 million per year (OECD, 1982). Another example is the 1982 case against the pricing policies of gas stations along the West German autobahn. It was found that the prices for gasoline at such stations tended to be higher than at others. Thus, the government imposed a rule that the appropriate price to be charged was the average price charged by the five nearest accessible gas stations not located on the autobahn (OECD, 1982).

In 1984, the Federal Cartel Office found that two West German pharmaceutical companies had been charging prices considerably in excess of costs. The Cartel Office had determined that the sales revenue from an antidiabetic product, Euglucon N, greatly exceeded the associated costs. The Cartel Office required that the price be reduced by at least 37 percent (OECD, 1987).

West German competition policy also prohibits all horizontal cartels and agreements that restrict competition. However, the agriculture, transportation, banking, insurance and public utilities sectors are all exempt from the cartel laws. Further, the coal and steel industries are exempt according to provisions under the EEC Treaty. Thus, most West German steel companies participate in EEC-wide cartels, which are legal under EEC law.

In fact, Section 1 of the Law Against Restraints of Competition (*Gesetz gegen Wettbewerbsbeschränkungen*), which deals with cartäl agreements and cartel resolutions, explicitly states that 'agreements concluded between or among enterprises or associations of enterprises for a common purpose and resolutions of associations of enterprises are ineffective in so far as they are capable of influencing by restraining competition, production or market conditions regarding the trade in goods or commercial services' (Riesenkampff, 1977, p. 14).[11] However, West German law also allows for certain categories of legal cartels. In general, the types of cartels which are legal in West Germany can be divided into two groups – those affecting only foreign trade and those affecting the domestic market. By allowing a relatively large number of legal cartels, competition policy in West Germany more closely resembles the Fair Trade Laws of Japan, which are examined in Chapter 4, than US antitrust. As in Japan, all West German cartels must be registered with the cartel authority.

While Stocking and Watkins (1946, p. 3) observed that 'the term cartel was virtually unknown to the American language a generation ago', there were an estimated 300 cartels in German manufacturing industries at the turn of the century, 1,000 by 1922, and 2,500 by 1925 (Wagenführ, 1931). Although Cartel practices have been modified during the post Second World War period, there still remained more than 300 legal cartels in West Germany as of January 1987 (Audretsch, forthcoming a). As mandated by the West German competition law, the Federal Cartel Office has interpreted the fundamental premise of legalizing cartels to be 'the improvement in the economic well being of the participating firms as a result of the cartel contract in the form of higher efficiency and productivity.'[12] Further, these efficiency gains must be passed on to the consumer in the form of lower prices. Thus, Segelmann (1968, p. 155) observes that the West German competition laws permit such cartels 'only when it can be shown that cartelization measures lead to subsequent cost savings of sufficient quantity in the form of lower prices for the consumers... are cartels justified.'

The West German competition laws emanated from the strict prohibition of monopoly and cooperative agreements imposed by the Allies during the immediate Second World War occupation period.[13] Following a seven-year debate devoted to the question of how Germany could best adopt its own competition policy, the 'Laws Against Restraints of Competition' were passed by the Bundestag in July 1957 and went into effect in January of the following year. The drafters of the statutes deviated somewhat from the preoccupation with competition as an unequivocal goal generally attributed to the founders of the American Sherman Act. Rather, it was argued that 'competition is not in and of itself the goal, but rather the means for improving efficiency and technical progress', and that 'through certain necessary restrictions of competition inherent in rationalization agreements the premise for an increase in efficiency and an improvement in the satisfaction of consumer demands' can be met (Gabriel, 1971, p. 22). This, of course, represents a marked contrast to the US approach to competition and antitrust.

The officially stated purpose of allowing cartels is to promote increases in efficiency and productivity leading to reductions in cost, to facilitate technological change, as well as to reduce the risk involved in development, production and distribution.[14] It is argued that these should contribute to the general competitiveness of the domestic industry vis-à-vis rivals within and outside the European Community (Riffel, 1968, p. 7). While efficiency could normally be achieved without resorting to cartelization, cartel status would be granted if it were the only mechanism for attaining these goals. Thus, in enforcing the cartel statutes, the Federal Cartel Office ruled that, 'although competition serves as the best allocation mechanism, there are also certain markets in which, because of peculiar market conditions, this allocation mechanism only incompletely fulfils this role, so that rationalization through cooperation instead of free competition is preferable.'[15] The West German Government made it 'clear that the laws against restraints of competition are not against rationalization and cooperation based on efficiency';[16] it also excluded the possibility of cartelization involving only price agreements (Kramny, 1968). Along with the 'Guidelines for Cooperation', which were issued in the summer of 1962, came the relevance of the 'Gegenstandstheorie', where the cartel was permitted on the basis of the contents of the contract between the participating firms, and not on the basis of the 'Folgetheorie' or the economic consequences of the agreement (Riffel, 1968). Finally, the goal of legal cartelization has been to improve the conditions of the entire industry and not just of the participating firms (Gabriel, 1971, p. 29).

One type of cartel permitted in West Germany is the 'condition cartel' (Konditionenkartell). According to Section 2, these cartels allow

agreements entered for rationalization and standardization purposes and designed to provide for uniform application of general terms and conditions of

sale, to the extent such contracts do not regulate prices or price elements. . . .
Cartel agreements providing for uniform freight and delivery terms are also
covered . . . even though regulated freight costs will to some extent have an
effect on prices.

Condition cartels enable firms to jointly set the terms of sale. As Table 3.2
shows, they were the second most prevalent of the domestic cartels. While
there were sixty-one such cartels established under Section 2 between 1958
and 1963 (OECD, 1987), there were still fifty in effect as of 1983.

Section 3 provides for the existence of 'discount cartels' (*Rabattkartelle*) if
the discount is offered in return for 'real' considerations received from the
customer, namely that the discount represents remuneration for a 'genuine'
service rendered by the customer.[17] The Federal Cartel Office (*Bundeskartellamt*) has interpreted Section 2 as implying that a discount cartel is legal if the
discount is applied to encourage special services provided by the dealer.
However, if the discount is applied only to cover higher expenses incurred by
the dealer, such cartels are illegal. As Table 3.2 shows, there were only five
such cartels established under Section 3 which were still in effect as of
December 1983. Since 1958, thirty-two of these cartels had been established.

It is also possible to form a combined 'condition cartel' and 'discount
cartel'. While there had been fifteen combined cartels formed between 1958
and 1983, only four were still in effect by 1983.

A fourth type of legal cartel is a 'structural crisis cartel' (*Strukturkrisenkar-
tell*). According to Section 4:

> On application, the Cartel Authority may, in the event of a decline in sales
> caused by a protracted change in demand, grant permission for an agreement
> or resolution described in § 1 to enterprises engaged in the production,
> manufacture, processing or conversion, provided that the agreement or resolu-
> tion is necessary to bring about an appropriate adaptation of capacity to
> demand and that such arrangement considers the interests of the economy as a
> whole and the public interest.[18]

Only in the case of a long-term decline in demand can a structural crisis cartel
legally be established. The goal of such cartels is to enable the participating
firms to plan rationally how to implement an orderly adjustment process.
Further, the law allows structural crisis cartels to exist for a maximum of
three years. As Table 3.2 shows, between 1958 and 1983 only one was
actually established. This cartel consisted of twenty-eight West German
manufacturers of steel reinforcement fabric. The cartel accounted for over 90
percent of the market. Because the Federal Cartel Office found that demand
for steel reinforcement fabric had declined continuously over the previous
period, resulting in chronic excess capacity, the cartel was established to
enable the producers to manage a reduction in capacity. In fact, there is
evidence that by 1986, capacity in the industry had been reduced in accordance with the three-year plan (OECD, 1987).

Table 3.2 Legal Cartels in West Germany, 1973–83

Type	1973	1974	1975	1976	1977	1978	1979	1980	1983
Condition	42	42	43	44	44	44	45	43	50
Rebate	19	18	18	16	14	12	11	7	5
Condition and rebate	17	18	16	15	16	15	14	14	4
Crisis	0	0	0	0	0	0	0	0	1
Standardization	8	8	8	9	6	6	5	4	4
Rationalization	3	4	3	3	4	3	3	3	4
Rationalization with a price agreement	10	11	10	10	11	13	14	16	16
Specialization	25	27	30	28	26	30	29	28	22
Specialization with a price agreement	23	21	24	26	26	29	30	29	25
Cooperation	0	1	7	12	21	26	33	39	53
Export	64	66	64	62	58	58	59	60	52
Export with domestic effect	5	5	4	4	5	4	4	4	3
Import	0	0	0	0	0	0	0	0	—
Emergency	1	1	1	1	2	2	2	2	2
Total	217	222	228	230	233	242	249	249	241

Source: Official statistics of the OECD.

Three different types of 'rationalization cartels' (*Rationalisierungskartelle*) are permitted under West German law. Standardization cartels are designed to 'achieve a uniform application of norms, i.e., standard measures of size and quality of component parts and types.'[19] While there were ten standardization cartels established between 1958 and 1983, there were only four still effective by December 1983.

A second allowed type of rationalization cartel is referred to as a 'simple rationalization cartel' (*einfaches Rationalisierungskartell*). Agreements to avoid duplicate research between competing firms, to avoid excessive changes in programs, to stabilize excessive fluctuations in demand, to reduce inventory costs and to reduce transportation costs are all allowed under this category. While twenty such cartels were established under Section 5(2) between 1958 and 1983, there were only four still in existence by the end of 1983.

A third type of rationalization cartel allowed is the 'syndicate cartel'. These cartels 'may take the form of a price agreement or agreements relating to combined procurement or marketing/sales facilities (syndicates) serving all the participants. . . . Such cartels also require the permission by the cartel authority. Such consent must be applied for and will be granted only if it is shown that such cartels are the only means of achieving the objective of efficiency and that such cartels serve the general interest.'[20] The cartels typically establish price-fixing, production quotas, division of territories or allocation of orders agreements. Between 1958 and 1983, there were thirty-two cartels with a specific price agreement established. By 1983, there were still sixteen of these cartel agreements under Section 5(2) and (3) in effect.

'Specialization cartels' (*Spezialisierungskartelle*) typically involve agreements between the participating members to limit their commercial activities to a particular set of areas, while agreeing to restrain from participating in others. In a specialization cartel, each member often agrees to produce only specified product lines, and refrains from being involved in others. There were fifty-nine such cartels established under Section 5a(1) between 1958 and 1983, twenty-two of them were still in effect at year's end in 1983.

Certain specialization cartels involve a price agreement. Between 1958 and 1983, there were forty-seven such cartels, twenty-five of which still existed by 1983.

'Cooperation cartels' (*die Rationalisierung durch Kooperation*) refer to agreements among small- and medium-sized firms. The goal of this type of cartel is to improve the competitive position of the participating small- and medium-sized firms through such means as improving productivity, improving product quality, expanding the product line, reducing transportation costs, improving the efficiency of procurement and sales and marketing facilities, and by combining advertising services. These cartels do not typically involve price agreements, which are generally prohibited. However, if it can be demonstrated that price agreements are essential to remain viable, then they are allowed. In fact, if the cartel involves a price agreement, the combined market share of the participating firms cannot usually exceed 15 percent. Of the fifty-five cartels established under Section 5b(1) between 1958 and 1983, there were still fifty-three in existence by late 1983. Thus, 'cooperation cartels' constitute the most prevalent form of legalized cartelization in West Germany.

'Export cartels' (*Exportkartelle*) are defined as 'agreements and resolutions which serve to protect and promote export.'[21] In the *Ölfeldrohr* (Oil Field Pipes) case,[22] the German Federal Supreme Court in Civil Matters ruled that the cartel law applied only to domestic commerce. As a result, export cartels were viewed as extending beyond the jurisdiction of the Federal Cartel Office, and firms involved were no longer required to register the cartels. However, a 1980 amendment[23] to the law required firms engaged in export cartel activities to register the cartel with the Federal Cartel Office (Hölzer and Braun, 1982). Between 1958 and 1983, there were 107 'pure' export cartels established under Section 6(1). Of these, fifty-two were still in effect by the end of 1983. Similarly, there were eleven export cartels established which had a domestic effect between 1958 and 1983 under Section 6(2). Of these, there were only three still in existence by late 1983.

'Import cartels' (*Importkartelle*) are allowed with the goal of discouraging foreign sellers from charging monopolistic prices or where they 'unilaterally impose other unreasonable conditions of sale and enable domestic importers to restrict competition between or among them for the import of foreign goods in those cases where no or only insignificant competition exists between the foreign sellers.'[24] In fact, import cartels in West Germany have seldom occurred. Only two were formed between 1958 and 1983, and neither of these were still in existence as of 1983.

Finally, the statute contains a 'general exemption provision' (*Generalklausel*) which may be granted 'If there is imminent danger to the continued existence of the major portion of the enterprises within a particular business sector'. These cartels can be established when an industry is confronting an extraordinary circumstance. While four such cartels were established under Section 8 between 1958 and 1983, two were still remaining by late 1983.

Based on the legal cartels still in effect as of December 1986, the distribution of cartels across manufacturing industries is quite skewed. While cartels are permitted with the greatest frequency in industries within the stone and clay (73), food (29), textiles (21) and non-electrical machinery (23) sectors, many of the rationalization cartels were in the stone and clay sector and many of the specialization cartels involving price agreements were in the non-electrical machinery sector (Audretsch, forthcoming a). Interestingly, the distribution of cartels across German manufacturing industries in 1926 resembles that in 1986. The greatest frequency of cartels in 1926 occurred in the non-electrical machinery (147), food (170), textile (201) and steel (234) sectors (Enke, 1972). As has often been suggested with respect to illegal cartels in the United States (Scherer, 1980), the propensity to cartelize may be greater in industries that sell homogeneous products with high fixed costs.

In comparing changes in price and output between cartelized and non-cartelized products, a recent study (Audretsch, forthcoming a) shows that there does not appear to be compelling evidence that the legalized rationalization cartels in West Germany have contributed a great deal to productivity and efficiency improvements. On the contrary, the evidence suggests that prices are relatively higher, and output relatively less, as a result of cartelization. This would suggest that the American approach to a *per se* ban of cartels may, in fact, promote economic efficiency and technological change more than does the West German policy of allowing certain cartels to exist. And, as will be discussed in Chapter 4, there is little evidence suggesting that legalized cartels in Japan have led to an increase in consumer welfare.

The West German competition policy towards mergers has only evolved within the last fifteen years (Windblicher, 1980). Beginning in 1973, a series of amendments was introduced which placed constraints on the legality of mergers. Like its US counterpart, the law now requires that acquisitions beyond a minimum size level be reported to the Federal Cartel Office. If the Federal Cartel office expects that the merger will result in the creation of a dominant market position, or entrench an existing dominant market position, the merger will be prohibited. However, even under these conditions the firms involved still have the possibility of demonstrating that the merger will result in efficiency gains. And, if such gains in efficiency, presumably in the form of scale economies, significantly outweigh the anticompetitive effect, the merger will be permitted to stand. In this sense, the West German competition policy more closely resembles the EEC competition policy than the US antitrust approach. While American antitrust makes it possible to prevent mergers even when there is only the possibility of some future reduction in competition, West German competition policy allows mergers unless there is a clear reduction in competition, even after accounting for efficiency gains. Thus, US antitrust appears to be much stricter in its application than does West German merger policy.

Sections 23, 24, and 24a of the *Gesetz gegen Wettbewerbsbeschränkungen* of 1957, and amended in 1973, 1976 and 1980, require premerger notification, the reporting of consummated mergers, and provided the Federal Cartel Office with the power to prohibit anticompetitive mergers and to dissolve completed mergers (Windblicher, 1980). Like American antitrust decisions, the decisions of the Federal Cartel Office can be appealed to the appeals court[25] and ultimately to the highest court at the federal level.[26]

In 1973, there were only 34 notifications of mergers. However, this number rose to 294 in 1974, 445 in 1975, and peaked at 635 in 1980. In 1983 there were 506 merger notifications. Of these, 137 involved joint ventures. An additional 335 were classified by the Federal Cartel Office as horizontal, although 71 of these acquisitions had a product extension aspect. An additional 53 mergers involved vertical acquisitions, while 118 mergers involved conglomerate acquisitions. Thus, horizontal mergers tend to comprise a much greater proportion of acquisition activity in West Germany than they do in the United States. This may reflect the difference in the public policies towards horizontal mergers. While most horizontal mergers are permitted under West German law, very few have traditionally been allowed under American antitrust (Audretsch, 1987b)

This pattern in the distribution of mergers is generally consistent with the trend in merger activity in West Germany between 1973 and 1983. During this period there were 5,302 mergers reported. Of these, 3,506, or two thirds, involved horizontal acquisitions. While 957, or 27.3 percent, of the horizontal acquisitions involved some product extension aspect, almost three-fourths represented pure horizontal mergers. Only 17.6 percent of the total merger activity involved vertical acquisitions, while only 16.3 percent of the total merger activity involved conglomerate acquisitions. In Chapter 2, it was observed that conglomerate acquisitions are the most prevalent form of acquisition in the United States, followed by vertical mergers. Horizontal mergers have constituted only a relatively small proportion of the total number of acquisitions since passage of the 1950 Celler-Kefauver Amendment to the Clayton Act (Section 7). Thus, these differences in antitrust and competition policies with respect to mergers seem to account for the strikingly different patterns in merger activity between the two countries.

In 1984, there were six mergers that were prohibited in West Germany. For example, the Federal Cartel Office prohibited the proposed merger of the five leading cable manufacturers in Germany, including Philips, Siemens, AEG, Kabelmetal and SEL. The Federal Cartel office refused the merger on the grounds that it would have reinforced the market-dominating oligopoly in the cable market, created barriers to entry to other fiber-optics producers and impaired technological competition in the production of optical fibers. In another case, the Federal Cartel Office did not allow Touristik Union International to increase its share of ownership in a rival in the package tour market, Air-Conti Flugreisen GmbH, on the grounds that Touristik Union International would have obtained a dominating position as a result of the merger.

The Federal Cartel office also prohibited Klöckner-Werke AG from purchasing Seity Enzinger Noll Maschinenbau AG. Both companies are leading manufacturers of equipment used for filling glass bottles and cans with beverages. The merger would have resulted in a market share of 70 percent for Klöckner, which in the view of the Federal Cartel Office would have resulted in a market-dominating position, especially since the remaining competitors in the market were small firms with sales under DM 200 million.

COMPETITION POLICY IN THE UNITED KINGDOM

Like most of its European counterparts, competition policy in the United Kingdom is a post-Second World War phenomenon. The statutory basis for competition policy was established in several Acts of Parliament, including the Monopolies and Restrictive Practices (Inquiry and Control) Act of 1948, the Restrictive Trade Practices Act of 1956, the Resale Prices Act of 1964, the Restrictive Trade Practices Act of 1968 and the Fair Trading Act of 1973. Although restrictive practices and agreements between firms had actually been favored by the government during the 1920s and 1930s, as was the case in the United States during the Roosevelt era, this policy was reversed with the introduction of the 1944 White Paper 'Employment Policy' (George and Joll, 1975). Full employment and sustained high growth were the aims of the White Paper, and monopolistic practices were viewed as not being consistent with these goals. Thus, the 1948 Act established the Monopolies and Restrictive Practices Commission, with the stated task of holding investigations into anti-competitive behavior. However, while the Commission undertook a series of investigations, it had little authority to alter or restrain those practices. The 1948 Act did instruct the Board of Trade to notify the Monopolies Commission of enterprises involving firms which 'conduct their respective affairs so as to prevent or restrict competition in connection with the production or supply of goods of the description in question.'[27] However, such references were to be made only when the market share of the firms involved amounted to at least 33 percent. Still, the Board of Trade was able to make thirteen references involving alleged restrictive practices during the period 1948–56. In 1955, the Commission published a report, Collective Discrimination, containing a detailed study of exclusive dealing, collective boycotts, aggregated rebates and other prevalent discriminatory trade practices. The apparent result of this study was the passage of the 1956 Restrictive Trade Practices Act. Like the policy adapted by other EEC countries, the Act required the registration of cartels, or at least agreements incorporating 'the acceptance by two or more persons of restrictions relating to such things as prices to be charged, terms or conditions on which goods are to be supplied, processes of manufacture to be applied and persons and areas to be supplied.' While such agreements were originally kept by the Registrar of Restrictive Trading Agreement, in 1973 the Fair Trading Act established the Director General of Fair Trading, which was to be responsible for maintaining records on restrictive practices.

The 1956 Act is in stark contrast to section 1 of the Sherman Act, which holds combinations in restraint of trade to be per se illegal. Rather, the British approach is more similar to that towards cartels in West Germany, where a rule of reason is applied that requires an assessment of the social costs and benefits of the agreements.

In the 1956 Act, restrictive practices were stated to be contrary to economic welfare. However, there were seven exemptions explicitly listed in which restrictions would be permitted. The first involved protecting the public against injury in connection with the consumption, installation or use of the goods. The second involved restrictions in which their removal would prevent the public from benefiting from certain advantages emanating from the restrictions. The third applied to restrictions necessary to offset actions taken by another party. The fourth involves restrictions essential to negotiating 'fair terms' for the product. The fifth considers restrictions where their removal would have a detrimental effect on employment. The sixth exemption applies to restrictions in which their removal would lead to a decrease in exports. Finally, the seventh refers to restrictions required for the viability of any other legal restrictions. The Act made it clear that the burden of proof for the necessity of the restriction was on the firm.

Thus, the law in the United Kingdom towards restrictive practices varies considerably from that in the United States. While restrictive practices are generally *per se* illegal in the United States, they are permitted in the United Kingdom if they adhere to one of these seven categories. (In 1968, the Restrictive Trade Practices Act introduced an eighth exemption: Restrictions which do not restrict competition to any significant degree are also permitted.) The United Kingdom had adopted a rule-of-reason approach, where the American approach has been much more rigid. George and Joll (1975) note that this flexible approach 'has been criticised in this respect since it appears to invite balancing the advantages from a restriction against those from competition with no presumption in favor of either'.

Competition policy towards market power, and in particular monopoly and oligopoly, is dealt with in the Restrictive Practices Act of 1948, the Monopolies and Mergers Act of 1965 and the Fair Trading Act of 1973. Unlike the American antitrust laws, the UK statutes provide explicit criteria establishing the minimum market share needed to constitute a monopoly or oligopoly. While the Restrictive Practices Act considered a market share of 33 percent to constitute monopoly power, this was reduced to 25 percent by the Fair Trading Act in 1973. However, this critical market share is intended to constitute a necessary condition and not a sufficient condition for the possession of monopoly power (George and Joll, 1975). It was not until the 1973 Act that the Commission's mandate to protect the public interest was clearly defined. In particular, the Act listed five specific factors which should be considered by the Commission in controlling monopoly power. These included: (1) the maintenance and promotion of effective competition; (2) the promotion of consumer interests with respect to prices, quality and variety of goods offered; (3) the promotion, through competition, of reductions in costs and advancements in technological change; (4) a 'balanced' distribution of industry and employment; and (5) the promotion of the international competitiveness of goods produced in the United Kingdom.

The Monopoly Commission generally holds hearings consisting of two stages. The first is an investigative stage, in which the relevant facts and details involved in the case are brought to light. The second stage involves the Commission's assessment of those facts and its determination of the alleged monopoly's activities on the public interest. This results in the submission of a report to the government minister, who in turn must send the report before the Parliament. Most of the remedies involved tend to be oriented towards alleviating the anti-competitive conduct. In this sense, UK anti-monopoly policy more closely resembles its counterpart adopted by the EEC than the more structural approach followed in the United States.

An example of a recent monopoly case undertaken by the Monopolies and Mergers Commission involved the automobile parts industry in 1982. In this case the Monopolies and Mergers Commission found that a complex monopoly existed in the industry, on the grounds that twenty-two automobile manufacturers accounted for more than one-quarter of the automobile parts supplied in the United Kingdom. Further, these companies were involved in practices restricting competition by requiring their customers to engage in exclusive dealing contracts, where they agreed to acquire automobile parts exclusively from them. The Commission ruled that the complex monopoly operated against the public interest. The recommended remedy was that automobile manufacturers eliminate such exclusive dealing clauses from their contracts (OECD, 1983). In this particular case, the Minister for Consumer Affairs chose to follow the recommendation of the Monopolies and Mergers Commission, and subsequently passed a law prohibiting automobile manufacturers from imposing such exclusive dealing contracts on customers.

Merger policy in Great Britain is also covered by the Fair Trading Act of 1973. Under the Act, there are two essential criteria which explicitly state whether a proposed merger falls within the jurisdiction of the Act. These criteria involve the market share and the size of the firm, in terms of gross assets acquired. The market share criterion is one-quarter of the relevant market. In July 1984, the size criterion was increased from £15 million to £30 million.

In 1984, 259 mergers fell within the scope of the Fair Trading Act.[28] Of the three cases considered by the Monopolies and Mergers Commission, two were determined to be against the public interest. The first involved the acquisition of Steetley by Hepworth Ceramic Holdings. The Commission determined that the merger would have adverse effects on the public interest in the refractories market. Similarly, the consolidation between Buest, Keen and Nettlefolds, and AE was ruled by the Commission to be against the public interest on the grounds that the merger would result in a loss of competition in the UK engine parts market. Since both firms produce plain bearings and cylinder liners, the merger would result in a direct loss of competition, forcing consumers to turn to imports as an alternative. In both cases the Secretary of State accepted the recommendations of the Monopolies and Mergers Commission, and prohibited the mergers from taking place.

Table 3.3 Merger Activity in the United Kingdom, 1974–1984

	Proposals covered by Fair Trading Act (all cases)		Industrial and commercial
	Number	Assets acquired (£m)	Number
1974	141	7 621	85
1975	160	5 786	116
1976	163	4 123	133
1977	194	4 675	155
1978	229	11 999	202
1979	257	13 140	220
1980	182 (115)	22 289 (21 042)	141 (89)
1981	164 (105)	43 597 (42 537)	126 (79)
1982	190 (122)	25 939 (24 494)	143 (104)
1983	192 (129)	45 495 (44 275)	143 (104)
1984	259 (223)	80 688 (79 957)	200 (165)

Figures in brackets show the outcome if a £30 million assets criterion had been in operation throughout 1980, 1981, 1982, 1983 and 1984.
Source: OECD (1987).

Table 3.3 shows the extent of merger activity in the United Kingdom between 1974 and 1984. While the number of mergers covered by the Fair Trading Act increased by 83 percent between 1974 and 1984, it increased by more than one-third between 1983 and 1984. That is, merger activity, at least when considering acquisitions covered by the Fair Trading Act, has been increasing at a considerable rate. Even after adjusting the number of mergers by the £30 million asset criterion, there was a marked increased in merger activity during the last decade. This is also reflected by the increase in the value of assets acquired, from £7,621 million in 1974, to £22,289 million in 1980, and finally to £80,688 million in 1984. As with the number of mergers, even after adjusting the value of assets acquired by the £30 million asset criterion, the value of assets acquired has risen substantially over time.

Of the 259 mergers recorded in 1984, the greatest number (29) occurred in the distribution sector. These amounted to a value of £3,450 million in acquired assets, whereas the twenty-nine acquisitions in the banking and finance sector accounted for a value of £29,673 million in acquired assets. The largest mergers, in terms of acquired assets, tended to take place in the coal, oil and natural gas sector, where the nine acquisitions totalled £17,333 million in acquired assets, or an average of £1,926 million of assets per merger. The acquisitions in the banking and finance sector were considerably smaller, averaging £1,023 million of assets per merger. Within manufacturing, the greatest number of acquisitions were in the chemicals and man-made fibres industry with 21, while there were 14 in the metal processing industry, and 13 in the food, drink and tobacco industry. The least amount of merger activity in manufacturing was in the timber and wooden furniture industry and in the instrument industry, each with only two acquisitions. Similarly, there were only three mergers in the leather and clothing industry, and only four acquisitions in the textiles industry. The smallest mergers tended to occur in the instrument industry, where an average of £9 million of assets were acquired, and in the textiles industry, where an average of £18 million of assets were acquired per merger (OECD, 1987).

Despite the considerable difference in antitrust policy towards mergers between the United States and the United Kingdom, a comparison of the patterns in American merger activity across industries with those discussed above in Great Britain reveals a remarkable similarity. In both countries, acquisition activity tends to be high in the chemicals, metal processing and food industries, and low in the textiles, apparel, leather and wood industries, despite the presence of rather dissimilar anti-merger policies. Thus, it is not obvious that public policy towards mergers in either country greatly alters the distribution of mergers across sectors and industries.

However, examination of the types of mergers that have occurred in the United Kingdom suggests a striking dissimilarity between the composition of UK merger activity and of that in America. Between 1970 and 1974, nearly three-quarters of the mergers in the United Kingdom were horizontal, while only 5 percent were vertical and an additional 23 percent conglomerate. This trend has persisted fairly evenly throughout the 1970s and 1980s. The greatest deviations occurred in 1978 and 1979, when just over one-half of the recorded acquisitions were horizontal, while slightly over one-third involved conglomerate acquisitions (OECD, 1987). However, in 1983, 71 percent of the mergers were horizontal, as were 63 percent in 1984. Thus, as was discussed in Chapter 2, while American antitrust policy has tended to reduce greatly the number of horizontal acquisitions, in the United Kingdom horizontal mergers are still the predominant form of consolidation. Apparently US antitrust policy has had a stronger impact on the type of merger undertaken than has competition policy in the United Kingdom. Perhaps this disparity in merger patterns between the two countries reflects the intensity of enforcement undertaken by the responsible public policy agencies. In fact, anti-merger cases have not been undertaken with great frequency in Great Britain. In 1983, the Monopolies and Mergers Commission found in only three cases that a proposed merger would not be conducive to the public interest. Similarly, in 1984, the Monopolies and Mergers Commission found that in two cases the proposed acquisition would likely be harmful to the public interest.

COMPETITION POLICY IN FRANCE

In France, particular restrictive practices are considered to be illegal. These include refusals to sell, the imposition of price floors, price discrimination and other predatory pricing practices. When such restrictive practices are made by a single firm, they fall under the jurisdiction of the Directorate-General for Competition and Consumer Affairs. Active monitoring of markets and firms are made by the Directorate-General to enforce the restraints against restrictive practices. For example, in 1983, there were more than 700 such monitoring studies undertaken, which resulted in 80 summonses and 51 warnings (OECD, 1987).

When restrictive practices are undertaken jointly by a group of firms, they are referred to as 'collective restrictive practices' and come under the jurisdiction of the Minister for Economic Affairs. Such cases generally involve either cartels or else the abuse of a dominant position. There are two procedural mechanisms by which the legality of such collective restrictive practices are considered. The first is referred to as the 'normal procedure', according to which the minister reaches a decision only after receiving and considering the opinion of the Competition Commission. There were thirteen decisions made by the Minister for Economic and Financial Affairs between November 1982 and December 1983 under this normal procedure. The resulting fines amounted to FF 12,266,000 and included the pharmaceuticals, cosmetics, services, building materials, consumer goods and distribution sectors.

The second avenue for undertaking competition policy cases against collective restrictive practices is the so-called 'simplified procedure', whereby only the Chairman of the Competition Consultation is consulted before the Minister for Economic and Financial Affairs reaches a decision. The simplified procedure is generally followed for cases that are less complicated and of less significance. Between November 1982 and December 1983, for example, the Minister for Economic and Financial Affairs made five decisions under the simplified procedure.

A recent example of a case involving a collective restrictive practice is the 1984 case involving firms engaged in the distribution of perfume and cosmetics. Acting on the Commission's recommendation, the minister found that fifteen manufacturers had engaged in concerted action to prevent perfume sales from extending beyond the traditional distribution channels and agreed to boycott those retailers who offered discounts. As a result of this finding, the minister imposed fines on the trade organizations as well as on the fifteen manufacturers and required that new forms of distribution be permitted. Similarly, in 1984, the shoe manufacturers' trade association and two firms were fined for collectively organizing a boycott of a consumers' cooperative. The cooperative had been selling high-quality brand name shoes at prices below those normally charged (OECD, 1987).

The Directorate-General for Competition and Consumer Affairs also gives advice to firms seeking guidance in interpreting French competition policy. This is a feature that greatly distinguishes French competition policy from US antitrust enforcement. A common complaint of business in America is that a firm may have no way of unambiguously knowing the illegality of some action until it ends up in court. This is particularly true of proposed mergers, where the Directorate-General will allow an acquisition if: (1) the merger does not result in a substantial increase in market concentration, (2) the likely gains in efficiency would significantly exceed the losses due to decreased competition, and (3) the merging firms alter the acquisition in such a way as not to bring about a harm to the public interest.

There were two important merger cases in 1984. The first involved the proposed acquisition of Rohm and Hass France SA by the Duolite International Company in the ion exchange resins market. This proposed acquisition was of a horizontal nature, since all the firms involved manufactured similar products. Because the merged firm would have accounted for more than 80 percent of the market, the Commission ruled that it would result in a restraint on competition. However, the Commission also found that the proposed acquisition would result in sufficient gains in efficiency to more than offset the loss due to the restraint on competition. Thus, the minister approved the merger. The second case involved the carbon black market. Ashland Co., a major producer of carbon black, proposed an acquisition of the Cabot Co., which also was a significant producer of carbon black. (Carbon black is a product used to produce tires.) Because of the substantial increase in market concentration, leaving just two principal producers in the market, the Commission concluded that the merger would also result in a substantial restraint on competition. However, unlike the first case, the Commission found that the acquisition would contribute little towards improving economic efficiency or social benefit. Thus, since the subsequent social and economic gains from the merger could not be expected to compensate for the losses due to the restraint on competition, the Commission recommended against allowing the merger, and the minister refused to approve the acquisition.

The public policy towards mergers in France and the United States provides a strong contrast. While the French policy is essentially one which implements a rule of reason, where the costs and benefits of the proposed merger are considered, the United States has traditionally not taken into account the benefits in merger cases. Thus, while anti-competitive mergers are, in principle, never permitted in the United States, such acquisitions are legal in France if the corresponding benefits significantly outweigh the losses due to the reduction in competition.

CONCLUSION

Competition policy in the European Community provides a rather sharp contrast to antitrust enforcement in the United States. Perhaps the most salient difference is that cooperative undertakings are looked upon as being dubious, and are generally not permitted in America, while in the EEC, cooperation is accepted as being a much more integral and necessary feature of economic survival. This is, perhaps, attributable to the differences in market size between the member nations of the EEC and the United States. That is, while American companies can easily attain the minimum efficient scale level of output through domestic sales, this is often not the case in the smaller European countries. And, in industries in which R&D plays an integral role, it is crucial to achieve economies of scale in order to make adequate investment in R&D and technical innovation possible. Thus, while an implicit assumption underlying US antitrust is that innovation and technical progress are enhanced through competition and impeded by co-operative agreements (see Acs and Audretsch, 1986a, 1988), underlying competition policy in the EEC is a much stronger feeling that, in fact, cooperation is needed to enhance innovation and technical progress. Thus, competition policy is typically modified because

> although innovative efforts should be regarded as a normal part of the entrepreneurial spirit of individual undertakings, it cannot be denied that in many cases the synergy arising out of cooperation is necessary because it enables the partners to share the financial risks involved and, in particular, to bring together a wider range of intellectual and mental resources and experience, thus promoting the transfer of technology. In the absence of such cooperation, the innovation may not take place at all, or otherwise not as successfully or efficiently. Also, the present situation in the Community demands a more rapid and effective transformation of new ideas into marketable products and processes, which may be facilitated by joint efforts by several undertakings. (OECD, 1987, p. 239)

This attitude is reflected in the 1985 European Commission White Paper, 'Completing the Internal Market', which emphasizes the extent of cooperation among firms, something that is needed to improve the global competitiveness of European firms. This, perhaps, explains why EEC countries are willing to apply a rule of reason in cases where the Americans would clearly apply a *per se* rule. That is, under EEC competition policy, certain practices which have been determined to constitute a restraint of trade are permitted, as long as they show some promise of delivering greater efficiency gains in subsequent years. However, Jacquemin (1987, p. 27) warns against accepting this view too placidly:

> Net benefits from collusion, although real, are difficult to identify and to capture, from a private as well as from a public point of view. In situations of strategic interdependence and uncertainty, various forces within and between firms affect the ability and the interest of adopting and stabilizing collusive behavior. It follows that too much collusion can occur in domains where non-cooperative, non-collusive behavior would be more efficient.

The European experience where a rule of reason has been applied to areas such as cartels and restrictive practices, such as in Great Britain and West Germany, presents a contrast to the American policy of a *per se* ban against cartels and restrictive practices. Klein (1987, p. 6) argues that the US policy may, in fact, be preferable to that followed by some of the European countries:

> British experience under the RTPA (Restrictive Trade Practices Act) offers little support for arguments that a rule of reason is preferable to a *per se* ban on restrictive agreements. The rule of reason would probably require more resources, public and private, to administer, and at best might exchange one form of inconsistency for another. Proponents of the rule of reason argue that socially beneficial agreements are prevented by the *per se* ban. The British record raises questions about both the existence of beneficial agreements, and the ability of the courts to discover them. Finally, many of the social benefits claimed involve issues which can, have and should be addressed by policy makers, not the courts.

In fact, to the extent that smaller enterprises may be more efficient and responsible for generating innovations and technical change, as has been recently demonstrated through empirical evidence (Acs and Audretsch, 1987b, 1987c), such policies fostering cooperation may be misplaced in the 1980s. While EEC competition policy, although concerned about checking significant rises in concentration, encourages the cooperation among firms in certain cases, this may be, in fact, a policy that actually discourages innovation and technical change.

NOTES

1. Quoted from Jacquemin (1975).
2. This is evidenced in the 1972 Continental Car decision (Commission of the European Communities, 1972).
3. This occurred in the GEMA corporation case of 1971. The decision is discussed in Commission of the European Communities (1972).
4. Decision of 10 December 1982, OJL 360, 21 December 1982.
5. Decision of 29 July 1982, OJL 252, 13 August 1983.
6. Decision of 17 October 1983, OJL 317, 15 November 1983.
7. Decision of 15 July 1982, OJL 232, 6 August 1982.
8. Cited in Market (1975, p. 68).
9. Decision of 2.4.3.1982, Bull, EC3–1982, point 2.1.27.
10. *Tätigkeitsbericht des Bundeskartellamts für das Jahr 1967*, BTDR V/2841, p. 14.
11. The original version in German is, 'Verträge, die Unternehmen oder Vereinigungen von Unternehmen zu einem gemeinsamen Zweck schließen, und Beschlüsse von Vereinigungen von Unternehmen sind unwirksam, soweit sie geeignet sind, die Erzeugnisse oder die Marktverhältnisse für den Verkehr mit Waren oder gewerblichen Leistungen durch Beschränkung des Wettbewerbs zu beeinflussen' (Riesenkampff, 1977, p. 14).
12. Determination of the Federal Cartel Office, August 13 1965 ('Zementverkausstelle Niedersachsen'), Wu W/E, Bundeskartellamt.
13. The 'Dekartellisierungsgesetze' were in Mil. Reg. Law 56, U.S. 1947, in the American Sector; V.O. Nr. 78, 1947, in the British Sector; and V.O. Nr. 96, 1947, in the French Sector.

14. The goals of legalizing cartels are also identified in *Jahresbericht des Bundesverbandes der Deutschen Industrie*, 1964/1965 (p. 166), 1965/66 (p. 165), and 1966/1967 (p. 143).
15. Decision of the Federal Cartel Office, 29 November 1961 ('Süddeutsche Zementwerke'), Wu W/E, Bundeskartellamt, 421/422.
16. *Tätigkeitsbericht des Bundeskartellamtes*, 1962.
17. The original version in German is, 'Rabattkartelle sind zulässig, sofern der Rabatt das Entgelt für eine "echte" Leistung des Abnehmers darstellt' (Riesenkampff, 1977).
18. The original version in German is, 'Die Kartellbehörde kann im Falle eines auf nachhaltiger Änderung der Nachfrage beruhenden Absatzrückganges auf Antrag die Erlaubnis zu einem Vertrag oder Beschluß der in §1 bezeichneten Art für Unternehmen der Erzeugung, Herstellung, Bearbeitung oder Verarbeitung erteilen, wenn der Vertrag oder Beschluß notwendig ist, um eine planmäßige Anpassung der Kapazität an den Bedarf herbeizuführen und die Regelung unter Berücksichtigung der Gesamtwirtschaft und des Gemeinwohls erfolgt' (Riesenkampff, 1977).
19. The original version in German is, 'Vereinbarungen über die einheitliche Anwendung von Normen und Typen (§ 5, Abs. 1), die zu ihrer Wirksamkeit lediglich der Anmeldung beim BKA bedürfen (§ 9, Abs. 2), wobei die Stellungnahme eines Rationalisierungsverbandes beizufügen ist' (Riesenkampff, 1977, p. 28).
20. The original version in German is, 'Rationalisierungskartelle, die in Verbindung mit Preisabreden oder durch Bildung gemeinsamer Beschaffungs- oder Vertriebseinrichtungen (Syndikate) verwirklicht werden (§ 5, Abs. 3). Auch diese Kartelle bedürfen der Erlaubnis, die auf Antrag erteilt wird. Voraussetzung hierfür ist jedoch, daß der Rationalisierungszweck auf andere Weise nicht erreicht werden kann und die Rationalisierung im Interesse der Allgemeinheit erwünscht ist' (Riesenkampff, 1977, p. 30)
21. Decision of the German Federal Supreme Court in Civil Matters of 12 July 1973 – KRB 2/72, WUW/EBGH 1276, 1279 'Ölfeldrohre'.
22. The original version in German is, 'Verträge und Beschlüsse, die der Sicherung und Förderung der Ausfuhr dienen' (Riesenkampff, 1977, p. 36).
23. Gesetz gegen Wettbewerbsbeschränkungen, as amended by the Fourth Act to Amend the Act Against Restraints of Competition, 24 September 1980, BGBI.
24. The original version in German is, 'Diese Vorschrift ermöglicht es Importeuren, sofern zwischen den ausländischen Anbietern kein wesentlicher Wettbewerb besteht, ihrerseits dem Wettbewerb bei der Nachfrage nach Einfuhren zu beschränken' (Riesenkampff, 1977, p. 38).
25. The state court of appellate level is the Kammergericht.
26. The highest federal court is the Bundesgerichtshof.
27. Quoted from George and Joll (1975, p. 12).
28. This does not include newspaper mergers.

4 · FAIR TRADE IN JAPAN

On the surface, antitrust policy in Japan seems to strongly resemble its counterpart in the United States . The statutory laws prohibit roughly those practices prohibited in the United States, and might even appear to be stricter than their American counterparts. Further, the major enforcement agency in Japan, the Fair Trade Commission, bears a name suspiciously similar to that of its American counterpart, the Federal Trade Commission (FTC). However, the similarities do not hold beyond such superficial comparisons. In fact, while many hold US antitrust policy to be perhaps the strongest component of industrial policy in the United States, antitrust policy in Japan has typically been held subservient to the more general industrial policies directed by the Ministry of International Trade and Industry (MITI). Thus, rather than resulting in enforcement policies focusing on the maintenance of competitive markets, the most distinguishing feature of Japanese antitrust has been in the legally permitted exemptions from antitrust enforcement, generally in the form of legalized cartelization status. The immersion of Japanese antitrust policy in the larger sphere of industrial policy has moved Caves and Uekusa (1976, p. 522) to observe:

> What can be said about the service of Japanese industrial policy to the nation's economic interests and the lessons it conveys for other industrial countries? Japan's antimonopoly policy has been a hobbled and limited copy of that long used in the United States. Its enforcement has fallen far short of the US model, which itself hardly enjoys total adherence. The Japanese economy has borne significant costs in the form of allocative inefficiency and diversion of rivalry into costly non-price forms. We can detect no corresponding gains.

The purpose of this chapter is to examine Japanese antitrust policy, particularly in its context as one of the tools of industrial policy. In the next section, the historical development of the Antimonopoly Act of 1947, as well as the institution of antitrust in Japan, is examined. In this light, the specific statutes dealing with antitrust enforcement are examined as are the major institutions charged with the responsibility for enforcing those statutes. In the third section of the chapter, the actual record of enforcement is considered, and in the fourth section, the role of antitrust exemptions, and in particular of the legalized cartels is examined. While the fifth section explores the relationship between antitrust policy and the other major tools of industrial targeting, the sixth section provides a statistical evaluation of antitrust exemption as a tool of industrial policy, in terms of the relationship between legalized cartel status and subsequent trade performance. Finally, in the last section, it is concluded that the antitrust laws in Japan have not significantly promoted competition in domestic markets, nor has exemption from the laws, in the form of legalized cartelization status, resulted in a noticeably superior trade performance in subsequent years.

INSTITUTIONALIZATION OF JAPANESE ANTI-MONOPOLY LAWS

Antitrust policy in Japan came with the occupying American military forces in the wake of the Second World War. Prior to the US occupation, there was no antitrust legislation or policy in Japan. In fact, the Anti-Monopoly Law of 1947, which was patterned after the Sherman, Clayton and Federal Trade Commission Acts in the United States, was considerably more stringent than the US version. This statute provided the statutory basis of antitrust in Japan.

Prior to the Second World War, the most distinguishing feature of Japanese industrial organization was the presence of the *zaibatsu*. Zaibatsu organizations were family-dominated combinations, spanning manufacturing, trading, and financial services. According to Hadley (1970, p. 23), the goal of the *zaibatsu* combines was 'not high-market occupancy of a few related markets, but oligopolistic positions running the gamut of the modern sector of the economy'. In particular, four major *zaibatsu* combines comprised the 'big four'–Mitsui, Mitsubishi, Sumitomo and Yasuda. While the big four accounted for around one-fourth of the capital in Japan in 1946, the next six largest *zaibatsu* combines accounted for an additional 10 percent of the capital. Thus about one-third of the business capital was concentrated in the hands of the ten different combines right after the Second World War. And, the big four controlled nearly half of the financial markets, one-third of the heavy industry and over 10 percent of the light industry in 1946 (Hadley, 1970, p. 11). The largest of the *zaibatsu* firms, Mitsui, had considerable market share in coal, metals, mining, shipbuilding, aircraft, heavy and light electrical equipment, commercial banking, insurance and trade. The market share of Mitsui generally ranged between 10 and 20 percent. Behind each of the *zaibatsu* combines were the wealthiest families in Japan. A holding company, generally controlled by the wealthiest families, directed the *zaibatsu*. However, there was only minimal rivalry among the different *zaibatsu* combines, and restraint was more the rule than the exception: 'Historically, what inhibited competition . . . was not cultural values but the highly unusual situation of the oligopolists being the same oligopolists in market after market after market. The result was a live-and-let-live relationship among the great zaibatsu' (Hadley, 1970, p. 18). That the vast market power of the *zaibatsu* was not suspect within pre-Second World War Japan seems peculiar to contemporary scrutiny. However, as Hadley (1970, p. 10) explains: 'For many Meiji statesmen, and for statesmen in succeeding years, it has been difficult to distinguish between public and private interest. The combines' strength was regarded as national strength but their profits were seen as private property.'

From the beginning of the occupation period, General MacArthur was critical of the concentration of economic power. This became clear in one of the early directives from the General:

> Encouragement shall be given and favor shown to the development of organizations in labor, industry, and agriculture, organized on a democratic basis. Policies shall be favored which permit a wide distribution of income and of the ownership of the means of production and trade . . . . To this end it shall be the policy of the Supreme Commander . . . to favor a program of the large industrial and banking combinations which have exercised control of a great part of Japan's trade and industry.[1]

The actual intention of the Allies in pursuing a deconcentration policy has been contested. While some observers argue that such a policy was 'forced by the victors upon the defeated nation for the covert purpose of keeping down her economy in a weak condition', others defended the policy as the best method for ensuring competitive markets in the developing post-war economy:

> In calling for a competitive structure to replace concentrated business in Japan, the Allies were attempting to create a situation in which there would be reasonable opportunity for entry into the markets of the modern sector of the economy and in which ownership of the means of production in that sector would be widespread, rather than concentrated under the control of a handful of business families. They were in no sense proposing to atomize the Japanese industry along textbook lines. (Hadley, 1970, p. 11)

Under the Law for the Termination of Zaibatsu Family Control, 1,682 companies were involved, and 3,668 *zaibatsu* appointees were terminated. In particular, 294 subsidiaries of Mitsui were designated for dissolution, as were 241 from Mitsubishi, 166 from Sumitomo, and 60 from Yasunda, totalling 761 targeted subsidiaries among these four firms. An additional 436 subsidiaries were targeted for dissolution in an additional six firms, including Nissan, Asano, Furukawa, Okura, Nukajima and Normura. The Law for the Elimination of Excessive Concentrations of Economic Power (Deconcentration Law No. 207 of 1947) granted the legal authority to the Holding Company Liquidation Commission to reorganize the holding companies. The underlying intention of the law was to encourage entry by new firms into what had previously been highly concentrated markets.

According to Article 3 of the law:

> An excessive concentration of economic power shall be defined as any private enterprise conducted for profit, or combination of such enterprises, which by reason of its relative size in any time or the cumulative power of its position in many lines restricts competition or impairs the opportunity for others to engage in business independently, in any important segment of business.

And, Article 6 specified the criteria which were to be considered by the Holding Company Liquidation Commission in assembling the standards of what actually constituted 'an excessive concentration of economic power'. In particular, Article 6 emphasized: (1) market position, including the means by which that position was attained, such as internal growth or merger; (2) the number of subsidiaries; (3) the extent of vertical integration; and (4) the history of monopolistic practices associated with the firm. By 1950, nearly 4,800 firms had submitted some type of reorganization plan under the Enterprise Reconstruction and Reorganization Law .

In fact, the Japanese government provided considerable resistance to the Allies' efforts to impose antitrust legislation on the recovering nation: 'Virtually all Japanese government officials, with the exception of officials in the Fair Trade Commission, appear to believe that economies of scale continue indefinitely, a belief that stems partly from a lack of empirical work. . . . It also, however, reflects the difference brought about by the absence of an antitrust tradition' (Hadley, 1970, p. 109). The Fair Trade Commission is the major agency implementing antitrust policy in Japan. In fact, in contrast to the United States, all of the antitrust responsibilities are concentrated in one governmental agency in Japan. The Fair Trade Commission is an independent agency, consisting of five commissioners. It is independent in the sense that it has autonomous power to determine its own case selection.

The Anti-Monopoly Law of 1947 made illegal private monopolization along with unreasonable restraints of trade. In particular, monopolization, price-fixing, quantity-fixing, technological restrictions and participation in unauthorized cartels, either domestic or international, were explicitly made illegal. Section 1 of the Anti-Monopoly Law states the intended objectives:

> This Law, by prohibiting private monopolization, unreasonable restraints of trade and unfair methods of competition, by preventing excessive concentration of power over enterprises, and by excluding undue restriction of production, sale, price, technology, etc. through combinations and agreements etc. and all other unreasonable restraints of business activities, aims to promote free and fair competition, to stimulate the initiative of entrepreneurs, to encourage business activities of enterprises, to heighten the levels of employment and national income and, thereby, to promote the democratic and wholesome development of national economy as well as to assure the interest of the general consumer.

Some of these concepts were more precisely defined in Article 2:

- 'Competition' was defined to incorporate 'potential competition'.
- 'Monopolization' was defined as any conduct 'by which an entrepreneur, individually, or by combination, conspiracy or any other manner, excludes or controls the business activities of other entrepreneurs, thereby causing, contrary to the public interest, a substantial restraint of competition in any particular field or trade.'
- 'Unreasonable restraint of trade' was defined as 'business activities by which an entrepreneur by contract, agreement or any other manner, in conjunction with other entrepreneurs, mutually restricts . . . their activities.'
- 'Unfair methods of competition' were defined as 'unwarranted refusal to receive from or supply to other entrepreneurs, commodities, funds and other economic benefits', charging 'unduly discriminative prices', or 'unduly low prices', and 'inducing or coercing, unreasonably, customers of a competitor to deal with oneself by means of offering benefits or that of threatening disadvantages' (Hadley, 1970 pp. 121–2).

Caves and Uekusa (1975) point out one significant difference between the Anti-Monopoly Law of 1947 in Japan and the Sherman Act in the United States. While in Japan it is explicitly stated that it is illegal to attempt to monopolize or aggressively try to protect a monopoly position, but legal to possess a monopoly, the law is ambiguous on this last point in the United States. The antitrust statute concerning mergers in Japan is even stricter than Section 7 of the US Clayton Act. Mergers are prohibited where they 'may substantially restrain competition in any particular field of trade' or where 'unfair business practices have been employed'. All mergers and acquisitions are required to be filed at the Fair Trade Commission thirty days prior to the actual consolidation. When considering whether a proposed merger will 'substantially restrain competition', the Fair Trade Commission examines the market share of the combined firm, as well as the market shares of its major rivals. Additionally, industry-specific considerations play a major role, including the technological opportunity class of the industry, and the presence and intensity of foreign competition in the domestic market. Unlike the US example, there are no explicit merger guidelines involving critical levels of market share (OECD, 1972). However, one major difference between American and Japanese merger policy is that Article 15 of the Anti-Monopoly Law of 1947 permits the Fair Trade Commission to allow a merger if a convincing defense can be presented that the merger promotes the 'rationalization of production, supply, or management'. Under the Celler–Kefauver Amendment to Section 7 of the Clayton Act, increased efficiency has not been a legal defense for mergers in the United States.

Article 9 makes holding companies illegal, where a holding company is defined as 'a company whose principal business is to control, by holding stocks, the business activities of another company.' The principal business is defined as a stockholding in excess of 25 percent of assets. Similarly, Article

11 prohibits the intercorporate stockholding of non-financial companies, with the exceptions of extraordinary exemptions granted by the Fair Trade Commission for technological reasons. The Trade Association Law of 1948 restricted the legal activities of trade associations. As stated in the first article, the purpose of the statute was to 'define the legitimate scope of activities of trade associations and to provide for a system of their notification to the Fair Trade Commission.' While Article 4 listed the legitimate activities of a trade association as receiving and publishing voluntarily collected statistical data, the voluntary exchange of research, and the fostering of developing quality standards, Article 5 stated those activities prohibited, including restrictions on output, price-fixing, and the imposition of systems requiring the compulsory reporting of prices, orders, inventories, production, plant capacity, business accounts and facilities (Hadley, 1970).

In a 1953 notification by the Fair Trade Commission, the six categories of unfair business practices proscribed by the Anti-Monopoly Law of 1947 were modified to include boycotts and refusals to deal, price discrimination, unreasonably high or low prices intended to injure a competitor or as a coercive inducement of customers, exclusive dealing, vertical restrictive agreements including tying and resale price maintenance, and 'abuse of a dominant bargaining position' (Caves and Uekusa, 1975).

ENFORCEMENT RECORD

Like that in the United States, competition policy in Japan has undergone several distinguishing phases, representing a different emphasis in policy. Immediately following the Second World War, competition policy was largely inoperative. However, beginning in 1949, and lasting several years, the Fair Trade Commission undertook a series of cases involving trade associations and exclusive dealing arrangements. Between 1952 and 1962, along with the pressures to rationalize industries and promote concentration (see Chapters 7 and 10), antitrust policy fell out of favor, leading to a strong movement to dismantle, or at least weaken, the Anti-Monopoly Law. Not surprisingly, enforcement during this ten-year period was minimal, and the only cases actually undertaken involved flagrant violations of the cartel laws. However, in the early 1960s, the Fair Trade Commission began to receive more political and social support. Accordingly, antitrust enforcement became more aggressive, leading to a series of cases involving unfair business practices as well as price-fixing cases.

Between 1947 and 1971, there were 420 cases considered by the Fair Trade Commission of Japan involving either a price-fixing agreement or else some other type of collusive agreement. While 43 of these cases were brought up in 1970, an additional 32 were undertaken in 1971, and another 27 in 1978. Similarly, there were 61 unfair trade practices cases filed during this period, six involving resale price maintenance, only one involving tying arrangement, five involving refusals to deal, and five involving other unfair trade practices.

Between 1965 and 1973, there were 115 cartel violations found in the manufacturing sector, one in construction, and thirty in services, out of a total of 240 cartel violations. Of those found in manufacturing industries, 26, or 22.6 percent, occurred in the chemical industry, while 22, or 19.1 percent, were in the clay and stone products industry. Following these two industries came the pulp, paper and paper products industry, with thirteen violations, and the food processing industry, with twelve violations. Thus, most of the cartel violations tended to occur in just a few sectors of manufacturing. By contrast, there was only one violation in textiles, and only two in clothing and apparel, lumber and wood products, electrical machinery and general machinery (Ueno, 1980). Further, between 1965 and 1973, 73 of the illegal cartels involved the products of large firms, while 42 involved the products of small firms. While 95 illegal cartels were in producer goods industries, only 20 were in consumer goods industries. A bi-modal distribution of the illegal cartels, classified according to the four-firm concentration ratio level, emerges. There were thirteen illegal cartels in industries with concentration between 80 and 100 percent, and between 50 and 59 percent. An additional twelve violations occurred in industries with the four-firm concentration ratio ranging between zero and 19 percent. However, there was only one illegal cartel in industries with a concentration ratio between 60 and 69 percent, and only four in industries with a concentration ratio falling between 70 and 79 percent (Imai, 1980).

It was not until 1972 that the first significant case involving monopoly was filed. The case was brought against Toyo Seikan (Toyo Can Manufacturing Co.) for controlling competitors in the metal container industry. Toyo Seikan had a market share of nearly 60 percent and the Fair Trade Commission found that through interlocking directorates and shareholding, the company essentially controlled the decision making of four of its largest rivals, including the third, fourth, fifth and eighth largest firms in the market. Further, Toyo Seikan engaged in practices such as refusing to deal with packers who sought to start their own processes for manufacturing cans. In its determination of the case, the Fair Trade Commission prohibited the refusals to deal, did not grant approval to the pending merger between Toyo Seikan and the third largest company in the market, Hokkai, and prohibited restrictive arrangements which effectively limited Hokkai's freedom of action, as well as required Toyo Seikan to reduce its share of stock in Hokkai to 5 percent. However, as Caves and Uekusa (1976) observe, because of the circumstances which were particular to this case, the case is of questionable precedent value.

Merger policy became clearer in 1968 when the three largest paper companies announced their intention to consolidate. While the three producers accounted for around 60 percent of the newsprint capacity, the two largest steel firms, Yawata and Fumi, also announced their intention to merge. In fact, both mergers would have resulted in a market share exceeding the standard of 30 percent which had been established by the Fair Trade Commission as the criterion for disallowing the acquisition. While the Fair Trade Commission attempted to block the steel merger, MITI strongly supported the consolidation, forcing the Fair Trade Commission to ultimately approve the merger. However, the Fair Trade Commission was successful in blocking the paper consolidation.

Still, Japan has never approached a stringent merger policy even remotely resembling that undertaken in the United States. Between 1957 and 1961, there were roughly 500 merger applications and notifications filed at the Fair Trade Commission annually. Between 1962 and 1967, this number rose to around 800 applications annually, and following 1968, there were more than 1,000 applications annually. Since only one merger application was rejected in 1968, Japanese merger policy at best resembles a sieve (OECD, 1972). Caves and Uekusa (1975, p. 484) thus concluded: 'The Federal Trade Commission of Japan has made little headway in enforcing the merger and monopoly provisions of the acts.'

ANTITRUST EXEMPTIONS

A particular distinguishing feature of antitrust in Japan has been the existence of numerous cartels which have been legally permitted through the exemptions contained in the Anti-Monopoly Law of 1947. These exemptions enable industries to engage in joint actions that would otherwise not be permitted under Japanese law and certainly would constitute a violation of the American antitrust laws. In general the statutory exemptions tend to favor small business, industries and sectors targeted for industrial policy by MITI, and industries exposed to foreign competition. While a number of general exemptions for natural monopolies are actually contained in the Anti-Monopoly Law itself, including regulated industries and industrial property rights, resale price maintenance was allowed for copyrighted works and expanded in 1973 to include cosmetics, toothpaste, soaps, detergents and drugs.

In particular, two types of cartels are considered for antitrust exemption – 'depression cartels' and 'rationalization cartels'. The purpose of depression cartels is to facilitate the adjustment of firms in industries suffering from either insufficient demand or excess capacity. Article 24 of the Anti-Monopoly Law, which was passed in 1953, provided for the requisite legal approval of such cartels. This was reinforced by passage in 1978 of the Provisional Law on Measures for the Stabilization of Designated Depressed Industries, which enabled the depressed industries to apply for loan guarantees and tax credits. Upon expiration in 1983, the 1978 Act was replaced with a virtually identical statute. The government is able to designate an industry as a 'depressed industry' if such a designation has been requested by 66 percent of the firms in the industry. The appropriate ministry for that industry or sector is then responsible for forming a cartel and supervising the industry's development of a plan for eliminating the excess capacity. The plan must be either approved or rejected by the Fair Trade Commission. Under the Law, any new net investment can be made only with the approval of the appropriate government ministry. The Law specifies that production levels, but not prices, can be fixed. Further, firms in the industry are not compelled legally to participate in the cartel.

Table 4.1, which lists the cartel agreements exempted from the Anti-Monopoly Law by the Fair Trade Commission of Japan, shows that there were twenty-nine legal depression cartels between 1964 and 1972. While most of them occurred in the mid-1960s , including sixteen in 1966, nine were granted in 1972. Further, as Table 4.2 shows, there were 46 legal depressed industry cartels in the ten subsequent years. Thus, there is no evidence that the use of depression cartels has been declining over time. In fact, there were forty such depressed industry cartels between 1977 and 1982. Most recently, eight industries have been designated as depressed, including aluminum refining, chemical fertilizers, ferrosilicon manufacturing, open hearth and electric-furnace steelmaking, container board, shipbuilding, spinning and synthetic fibers. While petrochemicals was added to this list in 1982, ship-building was removed in 1983 (US International Trade Commission, 1983b). Yamamura (1982) has noted that the argument for using the depressed-industry cartels is to cushion the industry's profits in the presence of declining demand, thereby enabling a number of producers to survive, so that they will be viable suppliers once demand has returned to its normal level.

Under Article 24 of the Anti-Monopoly Law, firms have been allowed to form rationalization cartels in order to undertake joint actions to improve their industry's overall performance. While Nakazawa and Ukis (1987) observe that the term 'rationalization' is foggy in Japan, the essential feature is that the cartel is long term in nature. As Table 4.1 shows, there were considerably more rationalization cartels than depression cartels between 1964 and 1972. During this period there were 113 rationalization cartels established. Rationalization cartels generally undertake joint R&D, allocate product lines among the participating members, engage in joint purchases of raw materials and other inputs, share joint manufacturing facilities and engage in joint investment. For example, since the early 1950s, rationaliza-tion cartels in the steel industry have included plans, supervised by MITI, for joint expansion of industry capacity. Following the 1956 passage of the Ex-traordinary Measures Law for the Rehabilitation of the Machinery In-dustries, cartels have been formed establishing product standards, developing new products and assigning product lines. More recently, rationalization

Table 4.1 Cartel Agreements Exempted from the Anti-Monopoly Law by the Fair Trade Commission of Japan, by Year and Exempting Statute, 1964–1972

Statutory basis for exemption	1964	1965	1966	1967	1968	1969	1970	1971	1972
Depression cartels	2	2	16	1	0	0	0	0	9
Rationalization cartels	14	14	14	13	13	12	10	13	10
Export cartels	201	208	211	206	213	217	214	192	175
Import cartels	1	2	3	4	2	4	4	3	2
Cartels under Medium and Small Enterprises Organization Act	586	587	652	634	582	522	469	439	604
Cartels under Environment Sanitation Act	106	122	123	123	123	123	123	123	123
Cartels under Coastal Shipping Association Act	15	14	16	15	22	22	22	21	19
Cartels under other statutes	43	50	44	44	47	48	56	53	34
Total	970	999	1,079	1,040	1,003	948	898	844	976

Source: FTCJ, Staff Office, the Anti-Monopoly Act of Japan (1973), p. 27 (from Caves and Uekusa, 1975, p. 487).

Table 4.2 Number of Legal Cartels in Japan, by Types, 1973–1982

Type	1973	1974	1975	1976	1977	1978	1979	1980	1981	1982
Depressed industry	2	0	2	1	1	6	9	9	9	7
Rationalization	10	9	0	0	0	1	0	1	1	0
Export	179	136	105	95	82	72	70	66	62	59
Import	2	2	4	3	4	4	4	4	4	3
Small and medium business	607	591	511	395	279	290	274	267	268	290
Environmental hygiene	123	122	122	122	122	122	122	122	122	122
Machinery and electronics industry promotion	13	15	17	16	15	9	1	1	2	1
Fertilizer price stabilization	4	2	2	3	3	3	3	3	3	3
Export marine products promotion	7	7	8	8	8	8	8	7	7	7
Liquor tax preservation	4	4	0	0	0	0	0	0	0	0
Fishery production adjustment	7	7	7	7	7	6	5	5	4	4
Sugar price stabilization	0	0	0	0	1	0	0	0	0	0
Pearl culturing	7	6	6	0	0	0	0	0	0	0
Fishery reconstruction	0	0	0	0	1	9	5	1	2	3
Coastal shipping	14	7	4	4	5	5	5	5	5	6
Total	979	908	788	654	528	535	506	491	489	505

Source: Official Statistics of the Japanese Fair Trade Commission (from US International Trade Commission, 1983b, p. 116).

cartels in computers and semiconductors have engaged in joint R&D and divided up product lines in the area of computer peripherals (Magaziner and Hout 1980).

Like many of the West German legalized cartels, rationalization cartels in Japan are often formed to institute agreements on product standards and quality. However, these agreements sometimes go beyond product standards. For example, in a cartel which ended in November 1968, six members of the tire industry agreed not to produce white sidewall or deep-tread tires. In addition, the companies agreed to limit the mean life span of tires. Similarly, the Japanese Fair Trade Commission approved cartels for copper scrap and scrap iron in April 1955. While the scrap copper cartel lasted only two years, the scrap iron cartel lasted almost two decades. There were 87 members of the scrap iron cartel, which was formed to stabilize scrap iron prices. Nakazawa and Weiss (1988) conclude that the Japanese steel industry experienced higher prices than it would have otherwise as a result of the cartel.

As Table 4.2 shows, the use of rationalization cartels has subsided considerably during the last decade. While there were twenty-two such cartels established between 1973 and 1982, only three of them occurred after 1975.

Perhaps nowhere is the linkage between competition policy, industrial targeting and international trade policy more apparent than in the use of export cartels in Japan. The purpose of export cartels is apparently multidimensional – to exert pressure on foreign countries to eliminate or at least reduce import restrictions, to spread out the joint costs involved in marketing exports, to set product standards and to raise prices in foreign markets. In fact, Jacquemin *et al.* (1981) concluded that the major intention of the Japanese export cartels was to raise the price; this was verified in a study of over 80 export cartels in Japan in 1970, which found 62 of the cartels were formed to raise the price, six were formed to increase the volume of trade, five were formed to simplify import procedures in foreign markets and the remaining ten had other objectives for formation (Matsushita, 1979). Further, 27 of the 62 cartels formed to raise the price had the objective of avoiding dumping in foreign markets.

As Table 4.1 shows, there were 1,837 export cartels formed between 1964 and 1972. In 1965, such cartels accounted for 27.4 percent of all Japanese exports. By contrast, only 4.3 percent of US exports, less than 3 percent of West German exports and less than 5 percent of UK exports were covered by cartels. By 1970, Japanese cartels accounted for just under 19 percent of exports (Matsushita, 1979). As Table 4.2 shows, the number of export cartels declined considerably during the period 1973–82. In contrast to the previous ten years, there were only 926 such legal export cartels during this ten-year period. More significantly, the number has decreased in every year over this time span, so that by 1982 there were only 59 export cartels. Further, such cartels have constituted a decreased share of Japanese export activity since 1970.

By contrast, presumably the purpose of import cartels has been to protect the domestic firms from foreign competition. It is clear that such cartels have been implemented only in exceptional cases. While there were 26 import cartels between 1964 and 1972, there were 34 between 1973 and 1982. In 1983 there were only two import cartels, involving onions from Taiwan and woven silk from China (US International Trade Commission, 1983b).

It is clear from Tables 4.1 and 4.2 that the most prevalent form of legalized cartel is under the Cartel Under the Small and Medium Enterprise Organization Act. The number of such cartels ranged between 439 and 652 during the 1964–72 period, and between 267 and 607 during the 1973–82 period. These small- and medium-sized cartels are permitted in an effort to encourage the development of small business. Unlike the depressed industry and rationalization cartels, the small- and medium-business cartels are not industry-specific. Rather, these cartels tend to be regional in nature, and are allowed to exist for a long duration. In 1983, there were 260 small- and medium-sized business cartels, of which thirteen involved textiles and apparel. Other industries included stainless steel utensils, mosaic tiles, dyeing, polyethylene film, dinner-ware and carton boxes.

Environmental hygiene cartels also involve small- and medium-sized businesses and are also regional in nature. The stated purpose of these cartels is to improve sanitary conditions. In 1983, this included barber shops, beauty shops, beauty parlors, butchers, laundries, movie theatres and ice cream shops (US International Trade Commission, 1983b).

At one point MITI did have the power effectively to form cartels in an industry, even without a formal antitrust exemption. Through its administrative guidance (discussed in detail in Chapter 7), MITI could bring industry officials together with a stated goal to restrain output in an industry. In particular, MITI pursued such policies in depressed industries. These practices, however, have been curtailed since 1970. But, as occurred in the synthetic fiber industry in 1977, MITI can still resort to administrative guidance in organizing an orderly reduction of capacity in an industry. Following two Japanese court decisions in 1980, it became established that firms were under the jurisdiction of the Anti-Monopoly Law, even when acting under the auspices of MITI. Subsequently, the Fair Trade Commission issued guidelines announcing that administrative guidance impacting 'such market conditions as prices and quantities' would be in violation of the Anti-Monopoly Law and subject to antitrust enforcement (Porges, 1979).

In conclusion, the exempted cartels have played the greatest role in the textile products industry, where 78.1 percent of shipments came from legal cartels in 1960 and 69.1 percent in 1970. Similarly, 64.8 percent of the shipments in the apparel industry came from legal cartels in 1960 and 67 percent in 1970. Lumber and wood products experienced the greatest increase in cartel activity. In 1960, only 9.8 percent of shipments emanated from legal cartels. However, by 1970, nearly three-quarters of all shipments came from legal cartels. Industries with the least amount of cartel activity include food products, pulp, paper and paper products, leather and leather products, and stone, clay and glass.

Under the 1978 Provisional Law on Measures for the Stabilization of Designated Depressed Industries, the aluminum smelting industry was permitted to form a cartel under the auspices of MITI in an effort to reduce industry capacity. Under this cartel, capacity was targeted to be reduced by 50 percent.

ANTITRUST POLICY AND INDUSTRIAL TARGETING

A particularly distinguishing feature of government policy towards business in Japan is the practice of industrial targeting,[2] which is the focus of Chapter 7. As Pugel (1986) argues, much of the motivation underlying the Japanese experience with industrial policy emanates from the inheritance of a post-war economy dominated by what were essentially infant industries.[3] Further, as Sato (1986) emphasizes, all of Japan's industrial policy has resulted from its chronic scarcity of natural resources, resulting in a dependence upon exportation of manufactured goods to facilitate the importation of natural resources. That is, competition policy, or antitrust in Japan, has been only one part of the overall industrial policy of the country. Thus:

> Competition policy in Japan has been applied only as a facet – and not a major one – of a broader set of industrial policies. Yet those broader policies have existed not as a integrated whole – logically plotted to achieve coherent long-run objectives – but as a group of ad hoc measures and compromises arising out of political interaction between the business and government sectors. (Caves and Uekusa, 1976, p. 148).

A definite tension has developed between the traditional goals of antitrust and the model of competition, as patterned after the American example, and the Japanese concern for 'excessive competition'. In particular, MITI has had a chronic preoccupation with excessive competition, and with its supposed damage on industrial development in Japan. As Trezise and Suzuki (1976) have observed, antitrust was not a natural part of the political heritage of Japan. The principles of collective action and consensus are more familiar concepts in the Japanese heritage. According to Ueno (1980, p. 426): 'Oligopolistic systems, collusive actions, federations of the weak, and countervailing power all require collectivization of those with some common interest. Collective, organized group action is necessary in order to achieve objectives effectively.' Japan's reliance on such collective groups is further demonstrated by the vast number of enterprise associations, such as the Japan Iron and Steel Federation, the Japan Automobile Manufacturers' Association, the Japan Electrical Manufacturers' Association, the Japan Perfumers' Association, the Japan Machinery Federation and the Cement

Association. According to Ueno (1980, p. 427), 'These associations are called into question because they help to serve as a breeding ground for stagnant, collusive oligopoly systems and as an intervening instrument for cartel action and administered pricing'.

Such collective organizations are designed to curb the dislocation of humans that seem to be associated with 'excessive competition'. According to MITI:

> Such excessive competition has caused deterioration in the financial position of enterprises and obstructed the progress of rationalization. It is for these reasons that some measures were introduced to control competition: e.g., depression cartels, rationalization cartels, agreement among small firms and investment coordination. In the view of the Japanese authorities, the harmonious adjustment of the two objectives involved here – that of strengthening the competitive power of Japanese industry internationally, and that of maintaining effective competition in the Japanese market – would require an appropriate selection of policies for industrial coordination. (OECD, 1972, p. 57)

Thus, the Fair Trade Commission has frequently found itself at odds over the appropriate competition policy with MITI. Not only did MITI participate in efforts to overturn some of the attempts to expand the scope of competition policy in 1958 and 1963 (Trezise and Suzuki, 1976), but it sometimes worked deliberately to undermine the Fair Trade Commission's attempt to enforce the antitrust laws. In fact, while the Fair Trade Commission was pursuing competition policies, MITI was often pursuing policies fostering industrial concentration and cartelization. However, in the 1960s the Fair Trade Commission became somewhat more effective. In 1966, a joint memorandum of understanding was signed by MITI and the Fair Trade Commission, in which MITI agreed to avoid undermining the Anti-Monopoly Law. However, Caves and Uekusa (1976) still conclude that the conflict between the two agencies has been 'endemic' with the usual result of MITI gaining the upper hand over the Fair Trade Commission. The Fair Trade Commission has generally been unable to effectively counter the large cartels promoted by the MITI, demonstrating that, 'The Fair Trade Commission of Japan has suffered chronic weakness in its role as a law-enforcement agency dealing with ministries having general policymaking authority' (Caves and Uekusa, 1976, p. 151).

The overlap between industrial targeting and antitrust policy is perhaps the most obvious in the case of antitrust exemptions and the legal cartels. According to the US International Trade Commission (1983b, p. 115), 'Antitrust exemptions to to specific industries can be a form of targeting, because they may enable Japanese firms to make cost reductions that otherwise would not have been possible, thereby increasing their international competitiveness.' However, it is obvious that not all types of legalized cartels are a form of industrial targeting. For example, the environmental hygiene cartels and small- and medium-sized cartels, are generally a part of a policy to promote small business and are not confined to targeted industries. Similarly, while import cartels are generally formed to offset the market power of selling agencies in foreign controls, they have little relation to industrial targeting.

In order to examine the relationship between legalized cartel status and the other major targeting instruments, Table 4.3 relates the percentage of a sector's two-digit Standard Industrial Classification (SIC)[4] value-of-shipments emanating from legal cartels to various measures related to industrial targeting in Japan. The data have been aggregated from over 400 four-digit SIC industries to 18 two-digit SIC sectors for purposes of presentation. Thus, the sector experiencing the highest average rate of cartelization in 1970 was lumber, where nearly three-quarters of all sales came from legal cartels. Similarly, in the textiles and apparel sector, 69.1 percent of all sales came from legalized cartels. Other highly cartelized sectors include instruments and primary metals. By contrast, there were no legal cartels in the furniture, printing and petroleum sectors, and only a small amount in the paper and leather sectors.

The second column shows the average ratio of expenditures on R&D-to-sales. The sector with the greatest R&D intensity is electronics, where R&D expenditures amount to 3.38 percent of total sales. Other high R&D sectors include instruments, where the R&D-to-sales ratio is 2.80 percent, and chemicals, with 1.97 percent being allocated towards R&D. The sectors with the greatest extent of legalized cartels – lumber, and textiles and apparel – have relatively low R&D intensities (0.40 and 0.90 percent, respectively). However, instruments and primary metals, both of which had fairly extensive amounts of legalized cartels, are also relatively R&D intensive. By contrast, two of the sectors with the least extent of legalized cartels – printing, and petroleum – have quite low levels of R&D intensity; the other sector – furniture – actually had a relatively high level of R&D intensity.

A slightly different measure of the technical opportunity class of the sector is shown in the third column, which lists the percentage of the industry comprised of scientists. Thus, the industries in the chemical sector had an average of 4.48 percent of their employees as scientists, while the industries in the electronics sector had an average of 3.38 percent. By contrast, only 0.43 percent of the labor force consisted of scientists in the printing sector, and only 0.9 percent in the textiles and apparel sector. Thus, it appears that there was at least a slight tendency for the sectors which were granted the greatest extent of legalized cartel statutes to be in a relatively low technology opportunity class, both in terms of R&D intensity and the share of employment consisting of scientists.

The fourth column lists the total number of technological imports in 1969. As will be discussed in Chapter 7, through controlling the importation of foreign technology, MITI was able to exert considerable influence on the pattern of development in Japanese manufacturing industries. While the

Table 4.3 Legal Cartels and Industrial Targeting Instruments

Sector	% of sales from legal cartels	R&D/sales (%)	Scientists in labor force (%)	Total number of technological imports	Total technology payments (10 million yen)	Technology payments to US
Food	17.90	0.40	1.15	3.00	2.00	1.00
Textiles and apparel	69.10	0.90	0.90	28.00	36.00	18.00
Lumber	74.20	0.40	1.21	1.00	4.00	0.00
Furniture	0.00	1.60	1.53	31.00	23.00	12.00
Paper	8.50	0.40	1.05	14.00	27.00	23.00
Printing	0.00	0.20	0.43	0.00	0.00	0.00
Chemicals	22.70	1.97	4.48	242.59	903.50	518.97
Petroleum	0.00	0.30	1.91	51.00	174.00	139.00
Rubber	42.70	1.50	1.51	29.00	91.00	75.00
Leather	13.40	1.60	1.53	31.00	23.00	12.00
Stone, clay and glass	17.60	1.09	1.44	15.30	74.15	51.63
Primary metals	53.98	0.86	1.59	166.87	372.07	225.20
Fabricated metal products	19.90	0.60	1.61	42.00	19.00	17.00
Machinery (non-electrical)	27.50	1.60	2.02	148.00	816.00	491.00
Electronics	26.30	3.38	3.54	153.34	525.98	420.85
Transportation equipment	31.90	1.33	1.69	62.58	184.83	52.21
Instruments	55.60	2.80	2.82	71.00	63.00	35.00
Miscellaneous	6.50	1.60	1.53	31.00	23.00	12.00

Source: Audretsch and Yamawaki (1988).

greatest amounts of technological imports were permitted in the chemical sector, there was also a substantial number of foreign technological purchases in the non-electrical machinery, primary metals and electronics sectors. Of these four sectors only one of them, primary metals, had a relatively great extent of legal cartels. Further, those sectors which had a relatively high amount of legalized cartels were not apparently targeted for the importation of foreign technology. This pattern is validated by the fifth column, which shows the total technology payments. Again, the greatest amount of technological importation tended to occur in the chemical, non-electrical machinery, electronics and primary sectors, which, in general, were not highly cartelized. Finally, the last column lists the total payments for technology imported from the United States. With the exception of the primary metals sector, those sectors with a high share of legalized cartels tended not to be targeted for technological imports from the United States. Thus, it appears that legalized cartelization status was an industrial policy that served a somewhat different function from that filled by the control of technological imports.

To examine further the relationship between legalized cartel status and the other industrial targeting instruments, Table 4.4 shows the variation in industrial targeting instruments among industries with a low, moderate and high extent of legalized cartelization. A low extent of legalized cartelization is defined as the one-third of the sample of 233 industries with the least extent of legalized cartelization. Industries with a high extent of legalized cartelization are defined as the one-third of the sample of industries with the greatest extent of legalized cartelization status. Finally, industries with a moderate extent of legalized cartelization include the remaining one-third of the industries in the sample. For example, the average number of technological imports was 70.46 in manufacturing. However, in the sample of low-cartelized industries, the average number was slightly less, 64.31. The greatest number of technological imports occurred in the moderately cartelized industries, which had a mean value of 131.23. The lowest number of technological imports was in the highly cartelized industries, which had a mean value of just 15.85. Further, the hypothesis that the total number of technological imports is identical among industries with a low, moderate and high extent of legal cartelization is rejected at the 99 percent level of confidence. In fact, all of the variables shown in Table 4.4 exhibit a similar pattern, where the highest mean value of the variable occurs for the sample of moderately cartelized industries. Further, the low cartelized industries exhibit a higher mean value than the highly cartelized industries for every targeting variable shown. This again reinforces the conclusion that although the relationship between legal cartelization status and the other targeting variables is undoubtedly complex, there is little evidence suggesting that they served similar functions.

Table 4.4 The Variation in Industrial Targeting Instruments Among Industries with Low, Moderate and High Extent of Legal Cartelization (standard deviations in parentheses)[a]

Targeting instrument	Manufacturing mean	Low extent of legal cartelization	Moderate extent of legal cartelization	High extent of legal cartelization
Total number of technological imports	70.4639 (84.1051)	64.3147 (69.0810)	131.2308 (97.9938)	15.8462 (13.5954)*
Number of technological imports from US	32.5501 (43.9250)	27.6573 (28.2905)	63.4825 (57.3425)	6.5105 (7.5076)*
Total technology payments (10 million yen)	234.5012 (358.4996)	157.0210 (256.4077)	516.1958 (435.6652)	30.2867 (62.2375)*
Technology payments to US	146.6830 (219.2349)	84.1329 (126.9570)	334.9371 (267.6336)	20.9790 (39.7615)*
Number of companies introducing foreign technology	11.5897 (10.9706)	11.3566 (6.7713)	19.1958 (13.9412)	4.2168 (3.0814)*
R&D/Sales (%)	1.2629 (0.9776)	1.1308 (0.6353)	1.8154 (1.2877)	0.8427 (0.5624)
Scientists in labor force (%)	1.8088 (1.1202)	1.4225 (0.7070)	2.7494 (1.3458)	1.2546 (0.3472)

[a]Low extent of legal cartelization is defined as the one-third of the sample of 233 industries with the least extent of legal cartelization. Industries with a high extent of legal cartelization is defined as the one-third of the sample of industries with the greatest extent of legal cartelization. Industries with a moderate extent of legal cartelization include the remaining industries in the sample.
*Statistically significant rejection (at the 99% level of confidence) of the hypothesis that a given targeting instrument has identical mean values among industries with low, moderate, and high extent of legal cartelization.
Source: Audretsch and Yamawaki (1988).

AN EVALUATION OF ANTITRUST EXEMPTION ON TRADE PERFORMANCE

The export performance of Japanese manufacturing industries is one criterion which can be used to assess the effectiveness of industrial policy, especially prior to 1980. While such a criterion would not be appropriate for judging the public policies undertaken in other countries, particularly the United States, the goal of establishing viable export industries played a predominant role in the post-war Japanese economy (Sato, 1986). Thus, to analyze the relationship between legalized cartelization status and the 1977 bilateral trade performance with the United States, Table 4.5 lists the forty industries (four-digit SIC) which had the greatest extent of legal cartelization status in 1970. Four different measures of trade performance, along with the corresponding industry rankings in parentheses, are provided. The first column shows the 1977 Japanese import penetration ratio, defined as US imports from Japan, divided by the industry value-of-shipments, plus total imports minus total US exports. The ranking of the Japanese import penetration, in descending order, is given in parentheses. For example, of the high legally cartelized industries in Japan, the greatest import penetration occurred in the hardwood veneer and plywood market, where Japanese sales accounted for 4.43 percent of the total consumption in the United States, and in the apparel and accessories industry, where the Japanese import penetration ratio was 4.91 percent. However, only seven of the highly cartelized industries were among the 100 industries with the greatest import penetration ratio. Further, other highly cartelized industries had a relatively low import penetration ratio. In the particleboard industry the Japanese import penetration was zero, indicating the absence of Japanese exports to the United States. The Japanese import penetration ratio was similarly zero in logging camps and logging contractors, and special products from sawmills industries. The Japanese import penetration was also quite low in the mobile homes, sawmills and planing mills, automotive and apparel trimmings, and pleating and stitching industries.

The second column lists the US–Japanese bilateral trade balance ratio, defined as $TB = (X - M)/(X + M)$, where X represents the US exports to Japan in 1977, and M represents US imports from Japan in 1977. Thus, this measure weights net exports, $X - M$, by the total amount traded between the two countries, $X + M$. The identical variable, which was used by Pugel (1978) and Audretsch and Yamawaki (1986b), has the advantage of controlling implicitly for transportability, while still indicating the comparative advantage.[5] Thus, a relatively large, positive value of the bilateral trade balance ratio indicates that the United States tends to have the comparative advantage in the industry, while a relatively large, negative value of the bilateral trade balance ratio indicates that Japan tends to have the comparative advantage in the industry.[6] In some highly cartelized industries, such as particleboard, sawmills and planing mills, special product sawmills, and softwood veneer and plywood, the United States had a very strong comparative advantage. In other highly cartelized industries, however, such as wood pallets and skids, hardwood veneer and plywood, and waterproof outer garments, Japan has had a very strong comparative advantage. And, in still other industries, such as paddings and upholstery filling, and house furnishings, the bilateral trade balance ratio was near zero, indicating a relative equality in US–Japanese trade.

The fourth column lists the Japanese imports from the United States. While in some highly cartelized industries there was a very high value of imports from the United States, in still other industries US imports were non-existent. For example, the $832 million of imports from the United States in the logging camps and logging contractors' industry represented the largest import industry in Japan. Similarly, the $274 million of imports in the

FAIR TRADE IN JAPAN 107

sawmills and planing mills industry represented the fourth largest import industry in Japan. However, in the wood pallets and skids, mobile homes and nailed wood boxes industries there were virtually no imports from the United States.

The last column reveals the Japanese exports to the United States. Perhaps the most striking feature in Table 4.5 is the appearance of only one of the largest 100 Japanese export industries among the highly cartelized industries. The $76.9 million of goods in the hardwood veneer and plywood represented the 31st largest Japanese export industry, in terms of goods shipped to the United States; however, the next largest export industry was non-woven fabrics, which shipped only $14.9 million of goods, followed by apparel and accessories, which shipped $10.9 million of goods. On the other hand, numerous highly cartelized industries had little or no exports to the United States, including special product sawmills, logging camps and logging contractors, softwood veneer and plywood, and felt goods. Thus, whatever else it might have accomplished, it does not appear that legalized cartelization status resulted in creating high export industries (at least in terms of the United States) in Japan. This is particularly evidenced by the lack of high export industries among the highly cartelized industries.

In contrast, Table 4.6 lists the bilateral US–Japanese trade performance of the low cartelized industries in Japan. In general, the Japanese import penetration ratio in US markets listed in Table 4.6 do not appear to differ greatly from those listed in Table 4.5. While the import penetration ratio in the musical instruments industry of 7.27 percent was the tenth highest in manufacturing, and the import penetration of 5.99 percent in silverware and plated ware was the fourteenth highest, there were numerous low cartelized industries with very low import penetration ratios, including photoengraving, electrotyping and stereotyping, lithographic platemaking services, and paving mixtures and blocks.

Similarly, just as the United States tended to have a strong comparative advantage in certain low cartelization industries, including petroleum and coal products, paving mixtures and blocks, and asphalt felts and coatings, Japan apparently had a strong comparative advantage in other industries, such as engraving and plate printing, wood office furniture, and drapery hardware and blinds and shades. Still, in 28 of the 40 low cartelization industries, Japan held the comparative advantage, while the United States held the comparative advantage in the remaining 12 industries.

Japanese imports from the United States were particularly high in the petroleum refining industry, which imported $99.6 million of goods, and in the sporting and athletic goods industry, where $40.7 million of goods were purchased from the United States. Perhaps the most striking difference between Tables 4.5 and 4.6 is that, while only one Japanese export industry is included among the top 100 in Table 4.5, 6 are included in Table 4.6. For example, the $1 billion of goods in the sporting and athletic goods industries

Table 4.5 The Bilateral US–Japanese Trade Performance in Industries with a High Level of Legal Cartels in Japan

	Japanese penetration in US (%)	Bilateral trade balance ratio	Japanese imports from US ($100,000)	Japanese exports to US ($100,000)
Wood pallets and skids	0.10 (259)	−1.000 (418)	0.00 (418)	7.39 (301)
Nailed wood boxes	0.03 (317)	−0.908 (339)	0.04 (405)	0.75 (357)
Structural wood members	0.11 (256)	−0.877 (317)	0.56 (358)	8.55 (293)
Softwood veneer and plywood	0.00 (378)	0.910 (51)	11.29 (212)	0.53 (365)
Hardware veneer and plywood	4.43 (28)	−0.995 (409)	2.04 (304)	769.47 (31)
Wood kitchen cabinets	0.16 (243)	−0.926 (347)	1.04 (336)	27.23 (230)
Wood products	0.11 (254)	0.304 (118)	54.01 (123)	28.85 (225)
Particleboard	0.00 (422)	1.000 (7)	3.53 (288)	0.00 (428)
Prefabricated wood buildings	0.11 (255)	−0.877 (316)	1.36 (326)	20.63 (249)
Mobile homes	0.01 (347)	−1.000 (424)	0.00 (424)	3.27 (319)
Wood containers	0.04 (302)	−0.625 (240)	0.24 (388)	1.03 (351)
Special product sawmills	0.00 (418)	1.000 (4)	7.80 (242)	0.00 (424)
Hardwood dimension and flooring	0.18 (235)	−0.393 (202)	6.97 (253)	16.00 (263)
Millwork	0.10 (258)	−0.486 (216)	14.59 (201)	42.20 (203)
Sawmills and planing mills, general	0.01 (354)	0.992 (30)	2744.83 (4)	10.34 (288)
Logging camps and logging contractors	0.00 (391)	1.000 (16)	8311.87 (1)	0.41 (369)
Schiffli machine embroideries	0.01 (351)	−0.230 (184)	0.09 (395)	0.15 (381)
Apparel belts	0.84 (123)	−0.711 (258)	4.65 (276)	27.57 (229)
Automative and apparel trimmings	0.01 (349)	−0.406 (205)	0.87 (341)	2.05 (328)
Pleating and stitching	0.01 (350)	−0.230 (183)	0.37 (379)	0.59 (363)
Textile bags	0.03 (313)	−0.863 (311)	0.08 (397)	1.09 (347)
Leather and sheep-lined clothing	0.17 (238)	−0.168 (172)	5.80 (263)	8.15 (298)
Curtains and draperies	0.07 (279)	−0.989 (398)	0.04 (403)	7.23 (302)

Apparel and acessories	4.91 (22)	−0.970 (378)	1.64 (312)	109.30 (136)
Textile goods	0.70 (139)	−0.914 (342)	1.44 (322)	32.06 (219)
Cordage and twine	1.21 (90)	−0.944 (352)	1.46 (321)	50.72 (190)
Nonwoven fabrics	1.77 (67)	−0.411 (207)	62.22 (113)	149.04 (116)
Tire cord and fabric	0.11 (252)	−0.899 (336)	0.58 (356)	10.96 (284)
House furnishings	0.09 (269)	−0.026 (152)	18.82 (188)	19.85 (251)
Processed textile waste	0.29 (211)	−0.793 (285)	0.62 (353)	5.37 (310)
Paddings and upholstery filling	1.79 (65)	0.026 (145)	45.76 (130)	43.42 (201)
Lace goods	2.86 (46)	−0.966 (372)	0.27 (386)	15.30 (266)
Felt goods, except woven felts and hats	0.02 (329)	0.691 (88)	2.17 (300)	0.40 (370)
Thread mills	0.23 (225)	−0.837 (301)	1.08 (335)	12.16 (276)
Waterproof outer garments	1.09 (98)	−0.984 (395)	0.44 (372)	55.06 (182)
Robes and dressing gowns	0.35 (204)	−0.865 (312)	0.76 (346)	10.54 (287)
Costed fabrics, not rubberized	0.39 (195)	−0.574 (226)	10.52 (220)	38.94 (210)
Fur goods	0.05 (298)	0.901 (53)	36.71 (155)	1.92 (332)
Children's outerwear	0.86 (120)	−0.853 (306)	5.42 (267)	68.27 (162)
Children's coats suits	0.29 (209)	−0.935 (350)	0.18 (390)	5.45 (308)

[a]The industry rankings are listed in parentheses.
Source: Audretsch and Yamawaki (1988).

Table 4.6 The Bilateral US–Japanese Trade Performance in Industries with a Low Level of Legal Cartels in Japan

	Japanese penetration in US (%)	Bilateral trade balance ratio	Japanese imports from US ($100,000)	Japanese exports to US ($100,000)
Commercial printing, gravure	0.09 (263)	−0.199 (175)	6.38 (259)	9.55 (291)
Manifold business forms	0.03 (312)	−0.990 (400)	0.05 (401)	10.02 (289)
Greeting cards published	0.01 (344)	−0.343 (195)	0.61 (354)	1.24 (341)
Blankbooks and looseleaf binders	0.64 (143)	−0.949 (357)	1.93 (306)	73.74 (158)
Photoengraving	0.00 (379)	0.695 (87)	0.16 (393)	0.03 (397)
Electrotyping and stereotyping	0.00 (381)	0.695 (85)	0.01 (411)	0.00 (413)
Lithographic platemaking services	0.00 (380)	0.695 (86)	0.48 (364)	0.09 (388)
Petroleum refining	0.03 (319)	0.570 (98)	996.72 (12)	272.88 (80)
Paving mixtures and blocks	0.00 (426)	1.000 (11)	0.03 (410)	0.00 (426)
Asphalt felts and coatings	0.00 (425)	1.000 (10)	3.05 (292)	0.00 (420)
Lubricating oils and greases	0.01 (360)	0.734 (80)	5.87 (262)	0.90 (355)
Petroleum and coal products	0.00 (416)	1.000 (2)	200.73 (55)	0.00 (421)
Wood office furniture	0.06 (292)	−0.963 (369)	0.08 (398)	4.00 (314)
Metal office furniture	0.06 (284)	−0.664 (247)	1.84 (307)	9.12 (292)
Public building and related furniture	0.06 (288)	−0.899 (335)	0.27 (385)	5.14 (311)
Wood partitions and fixtures	0.06 (293)	−0.800 (288)	0.80 (343)	7.22 (303)
Metal partitions and fixtures	0.06 (287)	−0.145 (168)	6.36 (261)	8.51 (295)
Drapery hardware and blinds and shades	0.47 (182)	−0.964 (370)	0.59 (355)	31.91 (220)
Furniture and fixtures	0.06 (283)	−0.832 (299)	0.42 (373)	4.60 (312)
Household furniture	0.07 (282)	−0.613 (236)	0.47 (368)	1.97 (331)

Commercial printing, letterpress	0.09 (266)	−0.192 (174)	25.85 (169)	38.14 (211)
Wood household furniture	0.06 (286)	−0.795 (286)	3.09 (291)	27.09 (231)
Upholstered household furniture	0.06 (294)	−0.951 (238)	0.48 (366)	99.14 (252)
Metal household furniture	0.06 (290)	−0.751 (271)	1.21 (330)	8.53 (294)
Mattresses and bedsprings	0.08 (273)	−0.870 (314)	0.76 (347)	10.87 (285)
Wood TV and radio cabinets	0.07 (278)	0.812 (70)	9.18 (186)	1.99 (330)
Miscellaneous publishing	0.09 (265)	−0.185 (173)	1.34 (211)	16.48 (261)
Periodicals	0.02 (324)	0.133 (137)	7.57 (191)	13.46 (272)
Commercial printing, lithographic	0.07 (280)	−0.066 (160)	56.47 (119)	64.45 (168)
Engraving and plate printing	0.00 (382)	−1.000 (419)	0.00 (419)	0.04 (395)
Newspapers	0.00 (403)	0.757 (76)	0.67 (350)	0.09 (386)
Book publishing	0.39 (196)	−0.079 (161)	155.01 (64)	181.45 (106)
Lead pencils and art goods	1.48 (79)	−0.780 (277)	4.93 (270)	39.99 (207)
Musical instruments	7.27 (10)	−0.735 (268)	104.63 (83)	685.38 (33)
Games, toys, and children's vehicles	2.29 (55)	−0.917 (343)	29.50 (164)	680.56 (35)
Sporting and athletic goods	3.80 (34)	−0.439 (212)	407.33 (33)	1045.62 (21)
Pens and mechanical pencils	3.97 (31)	−0.433 (210)	95.36 (90)	241.14 (88)
Silverware and plated ware	5.99 (14)	0.945 (353)	9.36 (232)	331.28 (66)
Jewelers' materials and lapidary work	0.28 (213)	0.825 (67)	391.22 (34)	37.59 (212)
Dolls	1.28 (88)	−0.973 (381)	0.83 (342)	60.55 (176)

aThe industry rankings are listed in parentheses.
Source: Audretsch and Yamawaki (1988).

Table 4.7 The Bilateral US–Japanese Trade Performance and Legal Cartelization Status in Japanese Manufacturing

Sector	Number of industries	Percentage industry cartelized	Japanese import penetration in US (%)	Bilateral trade balance ratio	Japanese imports from US ($100,000)	Japanese exports to US ($100,000)
Food	46	17.9	0.06 (0.28)	0.563 (0.598)	655.11 (1268.19)	17.99 (49.99)
Tobacco	4	17.9	0.00 (0.00)	0.999 (0.008)	218.08 (160.52)	0.01 (0.01)
Textiles	28	69.1	0.88 (0.77)	−0.588 (0.556)	25.76 (25.10)	339.09 (445.15)
Apparel	31	69.1	0.41 (0.51)	−0.551 (0.529)	11.04 (12.42)	101.09 (118.03)
Lumber	16	74.2	0.18 (0.78)	0.264 (0.852)	2101.47 (2955.39)	36.93 (134.03)
Furniture	13	0.0	0.08 (0.08)	−0.752 (0.294)	2.09 (2.86)	15.26 (9.17)
Paper	17	8.5	0.06 (0.12)	0.170 (0.709)	160.69 (362.49)	16.05 (29.42)
Printing	14	0.0	0.09 (0.14)	0.093 (0.519)	32.69 (46.97)	40.06 (53.93)
Chemicals	28	22.7	0.42 (0.80)	0.406 (0.557)	694.43 (670.31)	337.55 (394.96)
Petroleum	5	0.0	0.03 (0.01)	0.591 (0.088)	938.88 (231.03)	256.75 (64.31)

Rubber	6	42.7	0.70 (0.56)	−0.488 (0.257)	321.70 (216.74)	948.38 (475.02)
Leather	9	13.4	0.70 (1.04)	−0.685 (0.281)	7.24 (12.36)	50.00 (68.76)
Stone clay and glass	27	17.6	0.64 (3.15)	−0.136 (0.554)	18.75 (32.06)	46.08 (95.86)
Primary metals	25	51.0	1.90 (2.14)	−0.401 (0.737)	102.62 (88.55)	7528.88 (10212.41)
Fabricated metal products	31	19.9	0.91 (1.58)	−0.720 (0.400)	45.17 (67.06)	337.75 (503.20)
Machinery (non-electrical)	44	27.5	1.48 (1.81)	−0.341 (0.400)	474.29 (814.39)	730.56 (698.93)
Electronics	37	26.3	3.65 (5.74)	−0.614 (0.442)	225.52 (249.58)	3024.88 (5470.16)
Transportation equipment	17	31.9	2.96 (3.68)	−0.593 (0.636)	655.7 (381.44)	21740.28 (22477.58)
Instruments	13	55.6	3.73 (3.43)	−0.181 (0.574)	671.43 (597.75)	2275.75 (2639.87)
Miscellaneous manufacturing	18	6.5	2.15 (1.88)	−0.363 (0.577)	110.05 (137.44)	404.47 (367.88)

which were shipped to the United States represented the twenty-first largest export industry in Japan. Similarly, Japanese exports to the United States were quite large in the musical instruments, games, toys and children's vehicles, and the silverware and plated ware industries.

Finally, the relationship between the extent of a sector which was subject to legalized cartelization status and the bilateral US–Japanese trade performance for two-digit manufacturing sectors is shown in Table 4.7. While two of the sectors subject to the greatest extent of legalized cartelization – lumber and apparel – had relatively low average import penetration ratios, the third sector – textiles – had a somewhat greater average import penetration ratio. Further, while the Japanese import penetration ratio in the United States was quite high in the non-electrical machinery and transportation equipment sectors, legalized cartelization apparently did not play a big role in these sectors. However, in the sector with the highest average import penetration ratio – instruments – over 55 percent of sales emanated from legal cartels.

Of the sectors in which the United States tended to have a strong comparative advantage, there was a relatively low extent of legalized cartel status in food, tobacco, paper, chemicals and petroleum. However, in the lumber sector, where the bilateral trade balance ratio of 0.264 indicates that the United States tended to have a relatively strong comparative advantage, nearly three-quarters of the industry sales came from legalized cartels.

The sixteen Japanese industries comprising the lumber sector also tended to have a relatively large value of imports from the United States. However, other high US-import sectors, including petroleum, chemicals, food and transportation equipment did not have a particularly high amount of legalized cartels in their sectors. Those sectors exhibiting the greatest amount of exports – transportation equipment, primary metals and instruments – had moderate amounts of legalized cartels, while those sectors with the greatest extent of legalized cartels tended to have a relatively low level of exports to the United States. Thus, the patterns observed in Tables 4.5, 4.6 and 4.7 tend to support the view that to the extent that the goal of providing legalized cartelization status was to promote the development of export performance, legalized cartelization status was not a strong success in Japan.

CONCLUSION

The role of antitrust in Japan is complex and serves functions that bear no similarities to its counterparts in Europe and the United States. In many ways, the role of antitrust in Japan reveals as much about the fundamental economic premises in that country as does antitrust in the United States and competition policy in Europe. That is, antitrust policy in the United States is based upon adversarial economic relationships. However, in Japan, the

adversarial approach has more often than not given way to one of cooperation and joint action. Similarly, while private antitrust suits are an important feature of US antitrust policy, in Japan they are a rarity. In fact, in Japan,
a plaintiff has never won a private antitrust suit. Perhaps, the most distinguishing feature of Japanese antitrust is its immersion in overall industrial
policy. That is, rather than viewing antitrust policy as a tool for ensuring
competitive markets, the more prevalent view has been to consider the anti-
monopoly laws as a means of achieving cooperation and centralization.

Caves and Uekusa (1975, p. 462) have thus concluded:

> The public policy environment surrounding Japanese industrial organization is
> far removed in both substance and procedure from that of the United States.
> Antitrust legislation following the American model was impressed upon
> Japan's statute books during the postwar occupation, but thereafter it was
> weakened by amendments and received only weak and partial enforcement.
> The Fair Trade Commission charged with enforcement has played a role
> subordinate to other governmental agencies, notably the Ministry of Interna-
> tional Trade and Industry, which have held sharply differing views on the means
> and ends of industrial policy.

That is, while MITI had been trying to promote centralization and
cooperation, the Fair Trade Commission was trying to implement policies of
decentralization and to discourage collusion. More often than not, it was
MITI that emerged as the victor. This tension has tended to place the Fair
Trade Commission, and antitrust policy in Japan, in a particularly un-
advantageous position. Few other developed countries have relegated competition policy to such a subservient position: 'In contrast to the UK
Monopolies Commission, which has been formally dependent on ministries
for enforcement action, the Fair Trade Commission of Japan has had to
operate behind the scene and enjoyed a few opportunities to mobilize public
opinion in support of its position' (Caves and Uekusa, 1975, p. 151).

One similarity between competition policy in Japan and West Germany is
that the policy of allowing legalized cartels does not seem to have benefited
the consumer in either country. As with the economic inefficiencies of the
West German cartels, there is little evidence that the Japanese cartels
promoted economic efficiency. Based on a detailed study of the legal cartels
of Japan, Nakazawa and Weiss (1987, pp. 10–11) have concluded: 'What did
Japan get from her cartels? In terms of direct effects, the answer is "surprisingly little". The depression cartels probably prevented a few bankruptcies and lots of price wars, but consumers lost something on the
latter. . . . We are convinced that if the U.S. were to adopt a cartel system, we
would soon have a badly malfunctioning economy.'

Still, the evidence suggests that antitrust is becoming an increasingly
important tool for influencing market structure in Japan. While the enforcement of the Anti-Monopoly Law has increased, both in terms of cases and
coverage, the reliance on exemptions from antitrust in the form of legalized

cartel status seems to be declining. Further, just as the United States has attempted to impose policy suggestions on Japan in the sphere of foreign trade and domestic macroeconomic policies, proposals have been made suggesting that the United States should seek to stimulate enforcement of Japan's Anti-Monopoly Act (First, 1986). Whether or not antitrust emerges as a more vital instrument for shaping competition within Japanese domestic markets probably depends greatly upon the direction of overall industrial policy in Japan.

NOTES

1. Quoted from Hadley (1970, p. 6).
2. As Pugel (1986) notes, the importance of industrial targeting has faded considerably in the last decade.
3. This interpretation of infant industries has been disputed by Pepper (1986).
4. For an explanation of the US Standard Industrial Classification (SIC) of manufacturing industries, see Audretsch and Woolf (1986) and Audretsch (1986).
5. As Pugel (1978) and Audretsch and Yamawaki (1988) note, this measure has the disadvantage of perhaps overstating the importance to the low balance of trade industries in which there is only little international trade.
6. It should be noted that the trade balance ratio is constrained to vary between positive one and negative one.

PART III

DIRECT REGULATION AND INDUSTRIAL TARGETING

5 · REGULATION AND DEREGULATION IN THE UNITED STATES

It is in the policies of direct regulation and industrial targeting that the US policy differs the most from that of Japan or the European nations. This may be due to the fact that following the Second World War, the United States was able to influence and shape the competition policies of Japan and West Germany, so that the laws and institutions implementing competition policy do not differ so greatly from those implementing antitrust policy in the United States. However, there was no such US influence in shaping the regulatory and industrial policies of Japan and West Germany. Thus, the United States has generally adopted a policy of economic regulation with a minimum of cooperation between the competing firms in an industry, while Japan, and to a lesser extent the European countries, have pursued policies fostering cooperation among economic agents, at least in targeted countries. While the United States offers an experience in economic regulation and deregulation, Japan and some of the West European countries offer experiences in targeting and industrial policies.

Direct regulation of US business by the government has resulted in an uneasy partnership between private enterprise and the state. This uneasy relationship has been more widespread and prevalent than might seem apparent given much of the current rhetoric in US political economy. Further, the proponents and detractors of public control have been composed of very different groups of people and economic interest groups during the last one hundred years. As a result, small firms and consumers generally advocated government control during the first regulatory movement towards the end of the last century; it was virtually the same groups who spearheaded the deregulation movement of the second half of the 1970s and first half of the 1980s. Similarly, while the large corporations, generally referred to as 'big business' in the popular press, strongly resisted regulation around the turn of the century, it was, at least in some cases, these same firms that made the strongest defense for continuing the regulatory regime during the past decade, thereby offering the greatest resistance to the deregulation movement. Regulation, as an institution, has served various interests at various times. The impact of government control of business on the economy should not be obscured by the rhetoric of the free market and unfettered competition; the significance of regulation is as substantial as it is pervasive.

Since the establishment of the Interstate Commerce Commission (ICC) in 1887 – which was charged with the responsibility of regulating interstate railroad commerce – government control of the utilities, transportation and communications industries was implemented. By the beginning of the 1960s, regulation had expanded to cover trucking, airlines, telecommunications, electricity, natural gas, oil, railroads, television and radio, banking and securities. During the 1960s, the scope of public control was further expanded to incorporate health and safety as well as environmental issues.

In this chapter, the forces underlying the regulation and deregulation movements are examined, along with the economic impact of regulation in many industries, and the early record of deregulation. The first section tackles the institutionalization of public control of business along with the regulation movement and the methods of regulation; in the second section the social and environmental regulation which developed in the 1960s and the deregulation movement of the late 1970s and 1980s will be discussed. An analysis of the economic effects of regulation, and subsequently deregulation in some cases, will then be presented for the railroad, trucking, airlines, securities, telecommunications, crude oil, natural gas and cable television industries. Finally, a conclusion and summary are presented in the last section.

THE INSTITUTIONALIZATION OF PUBLIC CONTROL

Probably the most transparent sign that the market was not, in fact, immune to state intervention came about with the 1877 Supreme Court decision in *Munn* v. *Illinois*.[1] During the years between 1850 and 1870, the transcontinental railroads and grain elevators possessed considerable market power with respect to their Midwestern customers, the farmers and small businesses. In response to the discriminatory prices commonly charged to Midwestern customers, farmers and small businesses combined to form what was known as the Granger movement and, subsequently, led to the populist movement. The unifying good of these movements was to restrain the market power being exercised by the railroad and grain elevator concerns (Abrams, 1970). Among other accomplishments, the populists managed to pressure a number of Midwestern states into enacting laws regulating interstate railroads and grain elevators. One grain elevator owner, Munn, brought a suit against the State of Illinois for enacting a law which enabled the state to control the rates charged by grain elevators and warehouses. When the Supreme Court agreed to hear the case, Munn charged that the statute violated the Fourteenth Amendment to the Constitution by effectively claiming a portion of his property in the form of foregone profits. The Court however, ruled that because the product was 'affected with the public interest', government regulation was constitutional. Because grain elevators provided a service essential to the community and had monopoly power, the Court asserted that it was 'affected with the public interest'.

A decade following the Munn decision, the populists succeeded in carrying the Court's ruling to its logical conclusion by pressuring Congress to enact the Interstate Commerce Act and establish the Interstate Commerce Commission (ICC), which was charged with regulating the interstate railroads. While the ICC was clearly a response to the demands of the populists, there is evidence that the railroad interests had essentially 'captured' the ICC by 1910. In fact, during its formative years, the ICC was more effective at preventing price competition than at fostering it (Mitnick, 1980). The ICC became, in effect, an instrument used by the railroads to eliminate sporadic outbreaks of cut-throat pricing, which they considered led to ruinous competition.

In fact, the institutionalization of government regulation seemed to present a solution to the contemporary corporation's greatest problem – the need for market stability. The corporation had emerged as the most efficient instrument of resource management during the American industrial revolution. If the application of British inventions had served as the catalyst for US industrialization, the revolution in management techniques – the modern corporate structure – enabled its implementation. According to Reich (1983, p. 26):

> Managerialism offered America a set of organizing principles at precisely the time when many Americans sensed a need for greater organization and these principles soon shaped every dominant American institution precisely as they helped those institutions become dominant. The logic of routine, large-scale manufacturing, first shaped its original business environment and then permeated the larger social environment.

Through the structure of the modern corporation, the new managerialism excelled at amassing large quantities of raw materials, labor and capital inputs, and at applying particular manufacturing processes, thereby achieving a very specific use of these resources. The leaps in productivity of US manufacturing during the late 1800s were the product of increased specialization.

The essence of the new managerialism was 'command and control of effort'. Labor was considered to be indistinguishable from all other inputs, as long as scientific management was able to extract a full day's worth of energy for a full day's pay (Wheelwright, 1985). As tasks became increasingly specialized, the skill level required of workers became less important. What mattered most under the mass-production regime was the consistency and reliability of each precise cog; what mattered least was the decision-making capability of each unit. However, the corporation did not prove capable of mastering the business environment sufficiently to ensure the viability of mass-production. While scientific management provided the means for controlling and assembling resources into specialized production processes, it had little to offer for controlling the external business environment. The stability, continuity and reliability that constituted the core of successful mass production failed to materialize at the market level. The American large corporation was threatened by market volatility.

Market volatility emanated from the relatively capital-intensive production process required of mass production. Attaining scale economies through specialization required historically unprecedented amounts of capital investment. Such investment was rendered particularly risky and vulnerable by two factors. The first was the dependence of profitability and survival upon the achievement of high levels of capacity utilization. Faced with industry excess capacity, firms resorted to 'cut-throat' pricing – dropping price below average total cost but above marginal cost – in an effort to maintain capacity utilization. Of course, such a policy pursued independently by each firm resulted in disaster for the entire industry. Scientific management, which could methodically squeeze out the highest levels of efficiency from scarce resources, was impotent in the face of such market volatility (Piore and Sabel, 1984).

The second risk associated with large-scale investment was its vulnerability to technological obsolescence. The viability of any one firm investing in mass production depended upon none of the other firms in the market making quantum-level technological advances. Thus, the corporation was rendered unstable due to its inability to control price through coordinating market output with its rivals and by the devastating effect of being technologically surpassed by rivals (Piore and Sabel, 1984, ch. 4).

Just as modern management had achieved the coordination of production within the firm, it analogously sought to extend that control to the external environment. The condemnation of business policies threatening stability – such as 'cut-throat pricing' – is reflected in the frontpiece of Eddy's (1912) *The New Competition*: 'Competition is War and War is Hell' (Eddy, 1912). Kolko (1963, pp. 30–1) quotes an early American Tobacco Company executive lamenting:

> Unrestricted competition had been tried out to a conclusion, with the result that the industrial fabric of the nation was confronted with an almost tragic condition of impending bankruptcy. Unrestricted competition had proven a deceptive mirage, and its victims were struggling on every hand to find some means of escape from the perils of their environment. In this trying situation, it was perfectly natural that the idea of rational cooperation in lieu of cut-throat competition should suggest itself.

The first attempts to achieve industry stabilization consisted of outright collusion – agreements either to fix price or to restrict output, enabling prices to be raised. Such agreements were often implemented under the direction of trade associations. For example, the Bessemer Pig Iron and the Bessemer Steel Associations were formed in the mid-1890s to restrict output and stabilize price among over 700 companies in the blast furnace, steel work and rolling mill industries. However, as the declining prices in 1894–5 of most steel goods indicated, such stabilization attempts proved ineffective (Reich, 1983).

Having failed at price-fixing, the corporations attempted to attain market stability through consolidation. The drive for stabilization through merger prevailed throughout the economy, culminating in the merger movement at the turn of the century. In 1895, only forty-three firms disappeared as a result of acquisition, representing a $41 million merger capitalization. Just three years later, mergers resulted in 303 firm disappearances, for a $651 million capitalization. However, consolidations typically fell short of achieving the desired goal. According to Kolko (1963, p. 27), 'The new mergers, with their size, efficiency, and capitalization were unable to stem the tide of competitive growth. Quite the contrary. They were more unlikely than not unable to compete successfully or hold on to their share of the market.' Although consolidation had succeeded in amassing large market shares, it had not succeeded in providing long-term industry stability.

As industries continued to find inadequate their attempts at coordination through collusion and consolidation, they increasingly turned to the federal government for help. Ultimately, the government accomplished what the industries could not – a stable environment for planning and coordinating investments among industry participants (Reich, 1983). Firms were besieged not only from increasing competition within the market, but also from the 'democratic ferment' that was nascent at the state level. Thus, Kolko (1963, p. 6) rejects the standard argument that the government intervention responded to the need to control monopoly power: 'Contrary to the consensus of historians, it was not the existence of monopoly that caused the federal government to intervene in the economy, but the lack of it.' He attributes the entire US progressive era as a movement to stabilize industry through government intervention.

Following the First World War, a network of government-managed advisory boards, trade associations and regulatory agencies was established, enabling companies and industries to coordinate investment and production, as well as pricing, both formally and informally. In this way, government regulation policy was an essential catalyst in the oligopolization of American manufacturing industries. Reich (1983) pronounces industry-wide cooperation as 'the rule' resulting from such government intervention. Woodrow Wilson enunciated this view earlier, by observing that the newly formed FTC 'has transformed the government of the United States from being an antagonist of business into being a friend of business' (Reich, 1983, p. 88).

In fact, the First World War solidified the partnership between government and the corporation as a 'working oligopoly', and marketing agreements were prevalent throughout US manufacturing industries. Herbert Hoover, just prior to his presidency, created the Division of Simplified

Practices within the Commerce Department's Bureau of Standards, which was charged with the responsibility of stabilizing production by eliminating 'wasteful competition'. Between 1921 and 1928, Hoover worked with over 900 trade associations, representing more than 7,000 firms, to stabilize output and prices (Reich, 1983). What is particularly significant is that Hoover's subsequent presidency has always been associated with a compelling devotion towards *laissez-faire*.

Thus, it was, at least partially, the failure of the corporation and scientific management to adequately manage the external market environment that led to the emergence of the regulatory state. Through intervention, the federal government provided the industry with the stability requisite for mass production. Based on the Munn ruling, and often responding to lobbying pressure from firms, electric and telephone utilities were regulated as well as interstate railroads. However, the Munn precedent dictated that government intervention was not, in fact, constitutional unless the regulated industry produced an essential product and monopoly power existed. This standard was virtually abandoned in the 1934 Nebbia case.[2] When Nebbia, who owned a grocery store in New York State, sold two quarts of milk for eighteen cents and included a free loaf of bread with the purchase as a promotional device, he was accused of violating a nine-cents-per-quart price minimum which had been established by the New York Milk Control Board. Referring to the Munn precedent, Nebbia's defense was that the retail milk industry was not monopolistic, but rather very competitive, and therefore could not be 'affected with the public interest'. The Court, in broadening the Munn ruling, found this argument to be irrelevant and upheld the state regulation as being constitutional. Thus, the principal emanating from Nebbia was that government regulation was constitutional and hence applicable in virtually every market.

Intervention by the state on behalf of producers, or consumers, wherever deemed appropriate, was validated with the Nebbia decision. Within the decade, the federal government established the Civil Aeronautics Board (CAB) to regulate the entry and pricing by airlines and extended the jurisdiction of the ICC to include trucking. The airline industry was regulated to prevent cut-throat competition in a fledgling industry (Keeler, 1981), while trucking was regulated to protect the profitability of railroads (Moore, 1976). Subsequently, economic regulation was applied to a host of industries, including natural gas, television, oil, cable television and securities.

It is probably not coincidental that the regulation movement, which lasted through 1970, coincided with the zenith of mass production in the United States. This was the world of counterveiling power, so aptly described by Galbraith (1967), where virtually every major institution in society acted to reinforce the stability needed for mass production. In fact, the unprecedented growth witnessed during this period has been attributed less to the outcome of technology than to the result of prevailing social and political forces working to provide the market stability required for the corporation to thrive (Piore and Sabel, 1984).

REGULATORY METHODS

Government regulation of business in the United States has generally been implemented through the establishment of regulatory boards and commissions. While the federal boards and commissions are authorized to oversee interstate commerce, their state counterparts regulate intra-state commerce. This has been the source of numerous administrative problems, particularly in the telecommunications industry, where one firm was subject to regulation at both the federal level, through the Federal Communications Commission (FCC), and similarly at the state level, through state regulatory boards. Commissions are generally headed by 5 to 8 people who, at the federal level, are appointed by the President and subsequently approved by Congress. For example, the ICC, which was established in 1887, consists of five members and a 1985 staff of 1,063 with a budget of about $60 million.[3] Similarly, the Federal Energy Regulatory Commission (FERC), established in 1934, has five commissioners, a staff of 1,707 people, and a budget of nearly $92 million. And the FCC, established in 1934, consists of a seven-person board, 1,975 staff members, and a budget of about $88 million in 1985. In general, commissioners are appointed because they have proved to be a valuable resource to the political party in power, and not because they have the knowledge, experience and technical expertise required for the position. Hence, they have been frequent targets for harsh criticism (Owen and Braeutigam, 1978).

The state commissions typically consist of 3 to 7 commissioners assisted by staffs of up to several hundred people, with an average 1985 budget of a little over $2 million. In thirty-eight of the states, the commissioners are appointed by the governor, in a manner analogous to their federal counterparts, but in the remaining twelve states the commissioners are elected.

At the heart of US government control of business is the method of 'rate-of-return' regulation. Under this method, the regulatory commission sets the rates at a level such that,

$$r = (R - C)/RB \tag{1}$$

where r is the targeted allowed rate of return of the regulated firm by the commission, R is the firm's total revenue, C is the firm's total cost, and RB is what has been termed as the rate base, or the valuation of the firm's capital (Schmalensee, 1979). More specifically, this has been operationalized by,

$$r = \frac{(P_i \times Q_i) - (p_j \times q_j - d - T)}{(p_k \times q_k) - D} \tag{2}$$

where P_i is the price of product i, Q_i is the quantity sold of product i, P_j is the cost of input j, q_j is the quantity of input j purchased, d is the annual depreciation of capital, T is the total amount of taxes paid, P_k is the price of capital of type k capital, q_k is the amount of k-type capital purchased and D is the accrued depreciation. In determining the rates to be allowed, the commission selects the level of P_i so that the firm earns a 'just and reasonable' return on its invested capital, which is measured by the commission as the original value of the capital (what the firm actually paid for it), adjusted for depreciation.

Regulatory commissions have generally attempted to set the targeted allowed rate of return, r, sufficiently high so that it attracts the efficient rate of new investment into the regulated firm. Even though the firm is regulated by the government, it still is owned by private individuals, and therefore must still attract capital from private sources. If the commission sets the allowed rate of return too low, that is, below the hypothetical market rate, the corresponding rates will subsequently also be too low, and chronic excess demand and inadequate capacity will result. However, if the commission sets the allowed rate of return too high, above the hypothetical market level, the corresponding rates will subsequently also be too high, and chronic excess capacity and inadequate demand will result.

Problems particular to rate-of-return regulation concern operating costs and valuing the rate base. By 'padding' its costs, a regulated firm can artificially inflate its costs, thus in reality realizing a rate of return in excess of that targeted by the commission. This is generally accommodated through accounting practices which measure costs beyond those actually accrued, shifting costs incurred by the firm from its non-regulated operations to its regulated operations,[4] and through X-inefficiency. That is, all operating costs, whether actually incurred out of necessity or out of waste, are deducted from the firm's revenues to calculate the allowed rate of return and corresponding rates.

The problem of how best to measure the regulated firm's capital investment, or rate base valuation, has plagued regulatory agencies since the turn of the century. In the 1898 *Smyth* v. *Ames* case,[5] the Court ruled that reproduction costs, rather than the original costs, should be used to measure the rate base. Whereas the original cost method uses the actual cost of the capital equipment to value the rate base, the reproduction method uses what it would cost to reproduce the identical machinery at a later year, presumably the year of the rate case. Because technological progress generally rendered older techniques and capital somewhat obsolete through the introduction of more efficient and less expensive technology, the reproduction method tended to overstate the actual cost of replacing capacity. However, with the 1944 *Hope Natural Gas* case,[6] the fair method value of rate base valuation was allowed, which enabled states to implement a weighted average of the original and reproduction cost methods (Cicchetti and Jurewitz, 1975; Trebbing, 1976).

Controversy has also surrounded the issue of the rate structure, or the relationship among the various rate classes for differing customer groups. While economic theory has gone a long way in advocating marginal cost pricing, price discrimination among the rate classes has played a significant role. Prior to the mid-1960s, commissions tended to implement either the declining-block tariff or the two-tier tariff for rate structures. The declining-block rate attempts to promote consumption by setting successively lower prices for increased levels of consumption. Since 1970, however, a number of applications of peak-load pricing, or marginal cost pricing applied to different time periods, has been implemented (Shepherd, 1983). In 1974, for example, the Wisconsin Public Service Commission ruled that utility rates were to be estimated on the basis of marginal cost, including a summer–winter level differential (Weiss, 1981). By 1986, a number of other states had adapted similar peak-load pricing schemes for utility rate structures.

The scope of regulation was greatly expanded during the 1960s to cover social and environmental issues. The Food and Drug Administration (FDA), established in 1906, was charged with controlling the safety of food, drugs and cosmetics, and in 1962, the effectiveness of drugs. The Environmental Protection Agency (EPA) was established in 1963, but continually strengthened and expanded over the following decade; it was charged with regulating air, water and noise pollution. In 1980, the FDA had a budget of $324.2 million, and the EPA had a budget of $420.0 million. In 1970, the National Highway Traffic Safety Administration (NHTSA) was established and charged with the regulation of automobile safety and, in 1975, also the regulation of automobile fuel economy. In 1971, the Occupational Safety and Health Administration (OSHA) was established, which has the responsibility of regulating industrial safety and health. In 1972, the Consumer Product Safety Commission was established to regulate the safety of consumer products, and in 1973 and in 1978, two separate commissions were established to oversee safety and health in mining, especially in coal mining.

The goal of the Occupational Safety and Health Act of 1970 was 'to assure so far as possible every working man and woman in the nation safe and healthy working conditions.'[7] Enacted into law to mitigate the 'on-the-job health and safety crisis',[8] it was predicted that by 1980, injuries would have fallen by about half. However, in the fifteen-year period since its establishment, OSHA has not had an appreciable impact on reducing the number of industrial accidents in the United States (Nichols and Zeckhauser, 1981). OSHA quickly became notorious for imposing unmanageable rules and regulations upon private firms. As an example, Nichols and Zeckhauser (1981, p. 203) point out the absurdity of the 140 standards set by OSHA requiring the use of ladders, and the 'meticulous requirements governing the height and coloration of fire extinguishers, or the requirements that life jackets be worn when crossing empty creek beds'.

THE DEREGULATION MOVEMENT

In the early 1970s, regulation in the United States seemed to be gaining momentum and showed no signs of retreating. For example, the number of pages of federal regulations in the Federal Register proliferated from 2,599 in 1936 to 65,603 in 1977, with the number increasing by 300 percent during the 1970s (Breyer, 1982). Similarly, the number of permanent full-time positions in the regulatory agencies increased from 28,000 in 1970 to 81,000 in 1979, and the federal regulatory budgets rose by more than 600 percent during the decade (Wallace and Penoyer, 1978). MacAvoy (1979) estimated that while in 1965, 8.5 percent of the US gross national product was produced in regulated industries, 23.7 percent of GNP in 1975 was produced in regulated industries.The growing momentum of regulation seemed inevitable, even in the early 1970s. Olson (1982, p. 74) prophesized this inevitability in his book, *The Rise and Decline of Nations*, by predicting that 'stable societies with unchanged boundaries tend to accumulate more collusions and organizations for collective action over time . . . [and] the accumulation of distributional coalitions increases the complexity of regulation [and] the role of government' (1982, p. 74). According to Olson, the special interest groups fostering government protection and regulation should become more numerous and increasingly entrenched over time, with no tendency towards dissolution. Lee and Orr (1980) concluded that regulation would continue to prevail in the trucking industry, even though 'consumers would gain more from deregulation than the trucking industry would lose. . . . This gain, even if consumers could be made aware of it, is spread over so many individuals that it provides no effective motive for organizing politically' (1980, p. 116). Lee and Orr suggested that the trucking industry illustrated 'the survival power of policies that induce inefficiency while simultaneously preserving concentrated benefits' by exerting political pressure against any possible deregulation movement: 'The greater the inefficiency of ICC regulation, the larger the loss of the trucking industry from deregulation, and the more we can expect the firms to mobilize against deregulation' (1980, p. 116). Ironically, Lee and Orr's paper was published the same year that the Motor Carrier Act of 1980 was enacted into law by Congress, dramatically reducing price and entry restrictions in the trucking industry.

Why had Olson, Lee and Orr, as well as most American economists, failed to see the brewing clouds of change, which ultimately worked to affect deregulation in numerous industries? What was the catalyst working to eliminate government policies which had been so effective in creating and maintaining large economic rents to powerful special interest groups? Certainly the trucking firms and organized labor, the Teamsters, were vehement opponents of the 1980 bill and had not experienced a significant erosion of their political power; the bill was passed despite their power. This seeming impotence of a vital special interest coalition was no fluke: special interest groups were also defeated in a host of other industries. Thus, the American deregulation movement of 1975–85 seemed to catch most observers by surprise.[9]

Although the criticisms of regulation seemed to expand in number and intensity through the 1970s, it is unlikely that they alone were the catalyst for the deregulation movement. Some of the criticism was directed at the aggregate waste of resources resulting from regulation, ranging from $3 billion to $6 billion annually for only the direct costs to $60–70 billion annually when including the indirect costs (MacAvoy, 1979). Examining a sample of forty-eight companies, which accounted for almost 80 percent of non-agricultural sales, the Business Round Table estimated that the firms spent $2.6 billion to comply with federal regulations (Breyer, 1982). And the chairman of the Federal Paperwork Commission estimated compliance to be in excess of $200 billion per year (Anderson & Co., 1979). Similarly, the 1960s and 1970s witnessed the increasing output of academic studies identifying efficiency losses in specific industries as a result of government regulation.[10] Still, as Stigler (1982) has observed, it is doubtful that the force of academic criticism alone could be sufficient to ignite a policy reversal.

A perhaps more significant catalyst for the deregulation movement was that the rigidities that had maintained a fixed market environment for so long under the regulatory regime had, in turn, created the conditions for its demise. As the inefficiencies resulting from government protection and oligopoly drove up costs, in the manner observed by the academic studies cited above, entry became increasingly attactive.That is, potential entrants considered the economic rents that could be earned if a lower cost firm were permitted to enter the industry. As the actual regulated industry costs rose over time, compared to what costs would have been had entry been allowed, the potential gain to new entrants correspondingly increased. In fact, a coalition was formed of economic agents who had much to gain from deregulation – potential entrants, along with the various consumer groups that had identified the potential gains to consumers from deregulation. Starting with deregulation of the securities market in 1975 and the airlines in 1978, the movement quickly spread to trucking in 1980 and crude oil in 1981, then to natural gas, cable television and telecommunications in the early 1980s.

THE RECORD OF REGULATION AND DEREGULATION

Although the forces and causes of the regulation and deregulation movements have been examined, their actual effects in particular industries have not yet been considered. Thus, in this section the record of regulation and deregulation in nine industries is examined.

Trucking and railroads

The railroad and trucking industries represent the bulk of the ground transportation sector. As previously mentioned, the ICC had little power over controlling the railroads within the first three decades of its establishment. It was not until the 1920s that the ICC finally attained the requisite legal status to enforce rate reductions (Kolko, 1965). The most significant aspect of ICC regulation was the use of 'value-of-service' regulation, whereas the rate structure imposed on the carriers reflected the value of the commodity shipped, regardless of the marginal cost incurred from shipping that commodity. Since manufactured goods typically had a higher value per ton than did bulk agricultural or mining goods, the rate set for manufactured goods would typically exceed the equivalent for bulk commodities for a given route and weight, even though the marginal costs of shipping that product were roughly equivalent. Thus, the railroads did not practise the much hated price discrimination with respect to individuals or geographic areas; rather, commodity price discrimination was built into the rate structures. At the time of its inception, commodity price discrimination was perhaps a sensible rate structure. It simultaneously appeased the populists, who were able to ship their products at roughly marginal cost, and enabled the carriers to cover the high fixed costs associated with rail transport from the large differential between price and marginal cost on manufactured and other high value products (Friedlaender, 1971).

During its first two decades, government regulation worked well enough to maintain the railroad industry as one of the most profitable in the United States (Kolko, 1965). However, with the advent of the truck as a viable mode for shipping, the prosperity of the railroads began to erode. In fact, the entry of trucks into the shipping industry proved particularly problematical to the railroads, because trucking companies tended to enter markets where the potential profit was the highest – namely, those high-value commodity markets where the regulated ICC rate structures had set the rates considerably above the marginal cost of shipping the product. Thus, the railroads were faced with erosion of their high-value traffic by trucks, leaving the railroads with excess capacity and an inability to cover the fixed costs of service.

With the drastic reductions in demand for shipping services that accompanied the Great Depression in the 1930s, the 'railroad problem' was significantly aggravated. While demand for shipping services was declining during the early 1930s, the number of new entrants into the trucking industry was growing by leaps and bounds. Displaced farmers and bankrupt shopkeepers could always take their truck and become a trucker, having failed at all else. The solution to the railroad industry was clear – extend the jurisdiction of regulation to incorporate trucking as well as railroads. Since the trucking interests were generally dispersed and disorganized, and the railroad interests were very well organized and experienced from the previous four decades of undertaking collective action, it was not surprising that Congress was persuaded to extend regulation to trucking with the Motor Carrier Act of 1935.

ICC regulation quickly provided the newly created trucking industry with the means for effectively colluding on price and restricting entry, the two crucial market structure variables that are needed for successfully maintaining economic rents. By essentially delegating the job of ratemaking to the rate bureaus, which were associations of private carriers operating under a grant of antitrust immunity provided by the Reed–Bullwinkle Act, the ICC provided the means for price collusion among trucking firms (Keeler, 1983). Similarly, by requiring a 'Certificate of Need' for every route, the Commission restricted entry into the industry as well as into individual markets. This government-enforced entry barrier eliminated the threat of potential price cutting by new firms and, since only a limited number of firms served any given route, virtually textbook cartel coalitions could be formed and maintained.

Extending ICC regulation to cover trucking (and the waterways in 1940) did not prove to be the panacea for the railroad problem. Narrowly interpreting the 1887 ICC Act, which instructed that regulated rates be 'just and reasonable', the Commission generally tried to maintain parity between rail and trucking rates for a given commodity on any particular route. However, because the railroads had a clear service disadvantage vis-à-vis their trucking competitors, parity rates led to a shift in traffic away from the railroads and to the truckers. The service advantages that trucking firms were able to offer included faster delivery, dock-to-dock delivery and better quality handling resulting from the smaller loads. Thus, the ICC rate structure between the two modes of shipping tended to cause a reallocation of traffic from the railroads to trucks, even at relatively long hauls (those exceeding 200 miles), where it has been estimated that the marginal cost of rail transportation is less than that of trucking (Friedlaender et al., 1980; Wyckoff and Maister, 1975).

Allocational distortion was not the only economic cost incurred from regulation of ground transportation. The particular route and commodity restrictions also led to considerable inefficiencies. Moore (1974) reports that 62 percent of truckers were limited to special commodities, of which 40 percent were restricted to a single commodity or commodity class, while 88 percent were restricted to fewer than six commodities. Such carrier restrictions imposed costs on the carriers and were inefficient because they led to empty backhauls and excess capacity. Route restrictions also led to circuitous and wasteful shipping lanes. For example, a carrier operating between New York and Montreal was required to detour 200 miles by way of Reading, Pennsylvania. Similarly, a trucker shipping between Salt Lake City and the Pacific Northwest region was allowed to carry cargo eastward but not westward (Adams, 1958).

Harbeson (1971) estimated the 1963 welfare loss due to railroad regulation by the ICC to be between $0.9 billion and $1.1 billion, or between 12 and 32 percent of total freight revenue. Similarly, Friendlaender (1971) estimated the 1969 welfare loss to be between $2.7 billion and $4.2 billion, or between 24 and 36 percent of the total freight revenue. Between 1962 and 1978, the average return on investment in the railroads was only 2.42 percent and the service was continually eroding (Winston, 1985). In light of the industry's dismal performance and ever-deteriorating economic problems which were clearly apparent with the bankruptcy of the Penn Central Railroad, the Railroad Revitalization and Regulatory Reform Act of 1976 was passed, enabling the carriers some rate flexibility and to abandon certain unprofitable routes and services. The major deregulation of railroads occurred with passage of the Staggers Rail Act 1980, enabling rates to become virtually unregulated and subjecting the rate bureaus to the scrutiny of antitrust enforcement. The railroads responded by quickly adjusting prices and services, resulting in marked increases in efficiency and profits. Railroad deregulation was almost complete by 1984, as the carriers tended towards shipping particular commodities, such as coal, ores and chemicals (Shepherd, 1985). Between 1975 and 1982, freight rates charged by the railroads decreased an average of 7 percent and average compensation decreased by 11 percent (Moore, 1985). There has also been a significant consolidation of assets in the industry. In 1978, the largest five class 1 line-haul railroads – Conrail Burlington-Northern, Southern Pacific, Union Pacific, Atchison, and Topeka & Santa Fe – accounted for 43.9 percent of the $20 billion of operating revenues in the industry. By 1984, the largest five carriers – CSX Corp (formed in 1979), Conrail Norfolk-Southern (formed in 1982), Union Pacific Group (formed in 1982), and Burlington-Northern – combined to account for 84.7 percent of the $30 billion of operating revenues in the industry. Thus, it is apparent how consolidation and merger have played an important role in restructuring the post-deregulation industry.

Under regulation, the trucking firms and the Teamsters Union had generally thrived. During the 1970s, the return on equity averaged 21.2 percent for the major trucking firms, compared to an average of 12.9 percent for all industries (Breyer, 1982, p. 228). Moore (1978) identified the market value of all certificates of need to be in the neighborhood of $26 billion, reflecting the economic rents accrued to the industry. And Rose (1985) estimated that regulations bestowed upon the existing firms an economic rent of between 8 and 19 percent which was divided between the owners and the Teamsters.

However, the ICC began to relax its policies in 1978, and with the Motor Carrier Act (1980) the trucking industry was effectively deregulated. Virtually unlimited entry was allowed (although gradually) along with unrestricted pricing. Almost immediately, 18,000 new operators were granted operating rights, and not unexpectedly the value of the existing certificates of need fell drastically. In 1980, for example, trucking firms wrote off more than $100 million as losses due to the decline in the value of the certificates. As a result of deregulation, rates fell by an average of 25 percent between 1975 and 1982 (Moore, 1985). Similarly, in the state of Florida, rates were found to have been reduced by an average of 14 percent within two years of deregulation (Blair et al., 1986).

While some of the efficiency gains subsequent to deregulation in the trucking industry can be attributed to increased route flexibility, decreases in labor costs have also played a significant role. Under regulation, it was estimated that Teamster union members earned between 30 and 45 percent more than did their counterparts in the unregulated trucking sector. Between 1977 and 1982, after deregulation, labour costs fell by an average of 14 percent for all workers, in part due to the large influx of new workers. The reduction in labour costs was even sharper for drivers and helpers – 21 percent. The downward pressure on wages is reflected in the 1985–7 three-year contract signed by the Teamsters union, limiting their wage increase to an average of 3.6 percent per year, which is, in fact, the first wage increase for Teamsters in the trucking industry since 1981. Labour concessions cover the virtual elimination of automatic cost-of-living pay increases, a reduction in the starting salary for new employees by nearly one-third and about an 8 percent reduction in salary for temporary workers.[11]

Whereas deregulation in the railroad industry also led to an increase in market concentration, no corresponding trend in concentration has occurred in the trucking industry. In 1978, the largest four carriers – Roadway Express, Yellow Freight, Ryder and Consolidated Freight – accounted for 10.5 percent of the $27 billion of operating revenues. The largest one hundred carriers accounted for 51.7 percent of the market in 1978. However, in 1983, the increase in market share of the largest four firms was only 2.6 percent and the share of the market accounted for by the largest one hundred firms had fallen to 48.6 percent (Bailey, 1985).

Airlines

Because the mandate for airline regulation resulted from Congress's concern to impose controls on excessive competition that was threatening safety and resulting in bankruptcy, the CAB was granted considerable powers to restrain competitive conduct (Richmond, 1961). Not only was the Board given the power to require airlines to conform to prices fixed by the CAB, but the statute instructed the CAB to allow entry only if an applicant could prove that it was 'fit, willing and able' and when service was 'required by the public convenience and necessity'. Apparently, the CAB never found any applicants worthy of these standards. Although the industry grew from $476 million in 1938, when the CAB was established by Congress under the Civil Aeronautics Act, to over $8 billion by 1977 (Breyer, 1982), no new trunk carriers were allowed to enter the interstate market between 1938 and 1978 (Keeler, 1981).[12] Entry was limited to eight supplemental carriers, which provided charter services following the Second World War, to fourteen local-service carriers, also shortly after the War, and to commuter carriers (Breyer, 1982).

This lack of entry was not due to a shortage of applicants. Between 1950 and 1974 the CAB was petitioned by seventy-nine applicants for entry; none were approved. The CAB was equally stingy in allowing the 'grandfathered' existing trunk carriers to enter new routes; fewer than 10 percent of such applications were approved between 1965 and 1977, and only 4 percent between 1969 and 1974 (Meyer et al., 1981).

In interpreting its mandate, the CAB placed a high priority on ensuring the viability and stability of the existing carriers. In 1974, 90 percent of all scheduled service was provided by the ten trunk carriers, with nine local-service carriers providing 8 percent. If stability of market share were a major goal, CAB regulation would be judged as having been remarkably successful. In 1938, United had a market share of 22.9 percent. In 1972, after its merger with Capital, United still claimed 22 percent of the market. Despite the 238-fold growth of the industry, the market share of the four leading firms – United, American, Eastern and TWA – fell only to 68.9 percent by 1950 and to 60 percent by 1972 from 82.5 percent in 1938 (Breyer, 1982).

As a result of the CAB's emphasis on stability, over 90 percent of all city-pair markets were non-competitive by 1940 (Eads, 1975). Since its mandate also required 'competition to the extent necessary to assure the sound development of an air-transportation system properly adapted to the needs of the foreign and domestic commerce of the United States, of the Postal Services and of the National Defense',[13] the CAB injected an element of competition by approving the expansion and entry of existing carriers into new city-pair markets. By 1970, as a result of this policy 4 city-pair markets had only one effective competitor, 90 markets had two effective competitors, 38 markets had three effective competitors, and 3 markets had four or more effective competitors (Eads, 1975).

The CAB's control over non-price competition, principally in the form of product quality, was not symmetric with its power over entry and price. The Board sought to standardize each class and maintain clear distinctions between the service classes. However, because of the absence of statutory authority, the CAB lacked the same precise controls with respect to standardizing the product as it held for price and entry. Thus, an airline's strategy under regulation towards product quality and non-price competition was elevated to a role of primacy. There were essentially three types of product strategy pursued by the airlines, all effectively contributing to product destandardization: (1) expansion of schedules and capacity, (2) equipment modernization, and (3) service enhancement. The particular deployment of these three types of strategies was largely influenced by market structure, the extent of competition, and the type of route (e.g., long or short haul, large or small city-pair, and whether entry had been permitted by the CAB).[14]

The most significant dimension of non-price competition occurred in aircraft scheduling. While the CAB preempted price-competition, and in some cases retarded or hindered service enhancement competition through its rulings to preserve the distinction between classes,[15] it had virtually no legal authority to intervene in flight frequencies. The major competitive tool of the airlines thus became the scheduling of an increasingly large number of flights. The carriers on any given city-pair route would tend to engage in such types of non-price competition, raising costs and driving down the earned rate of return below the CAB's target of 12 percent (Breyer, 1982). The Board would typically authorize whatever fare increase was required to attain the targeted rate of return, assuming an elasticity of demand of 0.7. However, the increase in rates generally led to a decline in the quantity demanded, and subsequent increases in non-price competition by the carriers in an effort to maintain market share. But, the increased expenditures on non-price competition only further reduced profitability, leading again to further CAB-approved rate increases.

As a result of the carriers' fixation on non-price competition, it was clear that the industry 'suffered from an excessive attention to service rivalry' (Eads, 1975, p. 53). One study in the 1960s estimated the 'excessive' service competition resulting from CAB regulation to be $84 million per year, or an escalation in costs of 12 percent (Richmond, 1961). However, it was clearly in the interests of each airline to continue with its strategy of non-price competition, even at the expense of short-term profits. As a representative of TWA testified during the CAB's Domestic Passenger Fare Investigation, 'a carrier attempting unilaterally to restrain capacity will suffer substantial losses.'[16] Any single carrier abstaining from non-price competition would subsequently lose market share, and, in the long run, profits to its more opportunistic rivals.

Not surprisingly, actual firm profitability was almost always below the CAB's targeted rate of return (Moore, 1985). Comparisons between the unregulated intrastate airlines in Texas and California and the regulated interstate carriers for comparable routes revealed the burden imposed by regulation. Keeler (1981) found that the unregulated interstate airlines proved to be more profitable than their regulated interstate counterparts by offering lower prices for a comparable distance, thereby achieving higher load factors and lower costs-per-passenger. Thus, while the trunk carriers generally earned less than 6 percent return on after tax equity, the intrastate carrier Air California averaged a 24 percent return between 1972 and 1974.

Although the Airline Deregulation Act[17] became law in October 1978, the exact date of airline deregulation is difficult to identify. Beginning with the New York–West Coast routes, 'super saver' discounts for advance purchases were permitted by the Board as early as the spring of 1977. Subsequently, the CAB administered the deregulation process in such a way that by the fall of 1978, carriers were able to set fares from 10 percent above to 50 percent below the CAB's former fixed price. Following passage of the 1978 Bill, deregulation proceeded along five phases. First, unused routes by the existing carriers were awarded on a first-come basis. Second, entry was encouraged by eliminating the need to prove public convenience and necessity. Between 1979 and 1981, each carrier was allowed to enter one market per year and to protect one of its existing markets from entry by another carrier. Third, entry restrictions were dismantled in 1981. Fourth, rate controls were phased out in 1982. Finally, the CAB itself went out of existence on 1 January 1985 (Graham *et al.*, 1983).

The carrier reaction to the removal of entry restrictions was anything but cautious: 'When the lid came off the cookie jar some companies thought it was alright to get a belly ache' (Leonard, 1983, p. 454). The first new entrants, in 1978, were former intrastate carriers, Southwest, PSA and Air Florida. Two former charter carriers, Capital and World Airways, also entered the interstate market in 1979, followed by New York Air in 1980, People Express, MUSE Air, Pacific Southwest and Jet America in 1981, and Northeastern, Pacific East and Hawaii Express in 1982 (Moore, 1985). In 1976 there were only 33 certified carriers; by 1985 the number had increased to around 100. In fact, had there been no bankruptcies or exits, there would have been 170 scheduled carriers by 1985 (Moore, 1985; James, 1985).

The established carriers had the greatest difficulties adjusting to deregulation. While service enhancement and escalation of flight frequency had been the most important strategic tools for the airlines under regulation, they became increasingly less important and ineffective following deregulation. With the new airlines entering the major markets, the status quo firms generally followed a strategy of abandoning the less lucrative small city routes in favor of the denser, long-haul markets. Within the first six months of the 1978 Act, thirty-five cities were dropped by the trunk carriers, and an additional forty were abandoned the following year (Leonard, 1983). Using a sample of different city-pair distances and densities, Moore (1985) found that between 1976 and 1983, 59 percent of the long-haul markets experienced a net gain in the number of carriers, while only 11 percent had a net loss.

A new dimension of airline strategy since deregulation has been the development of mechanisms for separating travellers according to their time and service valuations. Essentially, the price/product strategy of carriers has tended to be influenced by five factors: (1) the distance of the city-pair market; (2) the market density; (3) the existence of entrants and whether such entrants are new firms, the largest existing carriers, or medium-sized existing carriers; (4) the type of passengers travelling; and (5) the extent of competition on the route. Although there has been a proliferation of service types available to customers, as Bailey (1985) predicted, a standard prototype of basic service at a relatively low price has emerged as the predominant choice by consumers. According to Moore (1985, p. 15): 'It should be recognized that passengers have chosen the lower quality service with the lower rates over the higher quality and higher fares'. Responding to an overall ticket price increase of just 57 percent between 1978 and 1984, which was actually two percentage points less than the increase in the consumer price index, total passenger traffic increased by 64 percent (James, 1985). Most notable has been the advent of discounting. While the average price of a full fare ticket rose by 127 percent between 1978 and 1984, the average price of discounted tickets increased by only 68 percent. Because only one-third of all passengers flew with discount fares prior to deregulation, whereas 80 percent used them in 1984, the average price paid in real terms actually fell (Moore, 1985).

Price competition has tended to be intenser in those markets where a new carrier has entered. Perhaps the classic prototype of a new carrier is People Express, which started in April 1981 with three used Boeing 737s, connecting Newark with Buffalo, Columbus and Norfolk. By providing the minimal amount of service and adapting a type of marginal-cost pricing system that required passengers to pay for all additional services, such as $3.00 for each piece of baggage and $0.50 for coffee and soft drinks, People achieved rapid growth through offering very low rates. Within three years it had expanded to 22 cities, using 46 planes and a staff of 2,300 personnel (Moore, 1985, p. 32). People grew so fast that by 1986, it was the fifth largest carrier, using 80 aircraft.[18] However, it was purchased by Texas Air in the fall of 1986.[19]

Along with deregulation has come a literal race in the airline industry to reduce costs. Between 1977 and 1984, airline spending on passenger service per passenger mile had decreased by 14 percent in real terms, reflecting a decrease in service amenities. The nominal increase in total food costs of 40 percent was significantly less than the CPI increase of 62 percent, reflecting a real decrease of 35 percent, despite a 44 percent increase in passenger-miles (Bailey, 1985). In 1982 the average pilot at People Express earned $30,000, while the average unionized pilot made $60,000. United paid an average wage of $102,000, and $152,000 to fly a Boeing 747 to Hawaii (Moore, 1985). As a result of its wage and productivity policies, People Express had a cost of 6.66 cents per seat-mile in 1982, compared with 8.11 cents at Eastern and 8.63 cents at TWA.[20] Bailey (1985) compared the cost structure of a new entrant – Southwest – with that of an established carrier – United. United's cost per flight crew was more than three times higher than Southwestern's. The cost of the aircraft, fuel and servicing fees was about 30 percent higher for United than for Southwest. And United incurred passenger specific costs almost three times higher than Southwest's. Overall, the fully allocated costs per passenger were $24 for Southwest and $58 for United.

Because of the economies rendered from establishing a hub-and-spoke system, several economists have predicted that the current wave of airline mergers will continue until there remain only between six and eight carriers (Keeler and Abrahams, 1981, and Leonard, 1983). According to the president of Northwest: 'It is inevitable that the industry is going to wind up with a handful of carriers and then a number of specialists operating at the bottom of the structure.'[21] After purchasing Eastern, New York Air and controlling 78 percent of Continental, Texas Air has emerged as the largest firm in the industry, with a market share of 15.3 percent in 1985 and $0.8 billion more in revenue than its closest rival, American.[22]

Securities and brokerage

The securities and brokerage markets have been regulated since passage of the Securities Act of 1933. The essential economic feature of the Act was that commissions for brokerage services on the New York Stock Exchange were fixed by the Securities and Exchange Commission, and the number of members on the Exchange was limited to a fixed number of 'seats' (West and Tinic, 1971). The New York Stock Exchange had consisted of 1,366 seats, which, until deregulation, could be purchased and sold, but the total number remained fixed. Prior to December 1968, the commissions earned per share, or as a percentage of the value of the security, were directly related to the price of the stock but independent of the number of shares involved in the transaction. Since the costs of a transaction are inversely related to the number of shares involved, this resulted in a discriminatory rate structure, and rendered large orders significantly more profitable than smaller orders (Stoll, 1981). In December of 1968, a rate structure allowing volume discounts was introduced which had a negative, although not substantial, effect on the profits earned from the large volume sales.

As a result of the bias towards greater profitability from volume sales, which was built into the rate structure, firms started competing for large, institutional customers. Since rate competition was prohibited by the Commission, firms resorted to non-price competition, largely in the form of supplying information, research and other ancillary services (Mann, 1975). This led to a cycle, similar to that in the airline industry, of increases in the fixed rates resulting from rising costs. Thus, like the response to regulation in the airline industry, non-price competition in the securities industry kept rates of return from being other than mediocre.

In May 1976 the ability of the Securities and Exchange Commission to set fixed commissions was eliminated by Congress. Between April 1975, prior to deregulation, and December 1978, commissions as a percentage of the value of the order fell between 0.43 to 0.84 percent for institutional investors (Stoll,

1979). Along with deregulation in the securities industry has come an unbundling of the ancillary services from the execution and trading services. Certain firms have become known as research 'boutiques', offering a variety of relatively high-priced research and information services. Other brokerage firms have established niches as discount brokers, offering only the minimal execution and trading services, but providing the customer with no advice or other ancillary services (Stoll, 1981).

There has been an apparent increase in concentration among brokerage firms corresponding to deregulation. In 1972 the largest four firms had a market share of 18.6 percent. This had risen to about 25 percent by 1982.

Telecommunications

There were apparently two motivations underlying passage of the 1934 Communications Act, which established the Federal Communications Commission (FCC) to regulate interstate telecommunications. First, it was recognized that local service, and presumably long-distance service, constituted a natural monopoly, where duplication of services by competing companies would result in a waste of resources and higher costs per customer. Second, a national goal was to provide service at such a favorable rate that everyone in the country could practically be guaranteed access to the system (Noll, 1983). As the Bell System grew to be the largest non-financial corporation in the world, so did the complexity of regulating a multiproduct firm, where only several of the components involved a natural monopoly. Prior to deregulation, the Bell System consisted of AT&T, which managed the long-distance network through its longline department and controlled all but two of the twenty-three Bell Operating Companies which provided much of the intrastate and regional service (Breyer, 1982). The major manufacturer of telecommunications equipment, Western Electric, was also owned by Bell, as was the major telecommunications research center, Bell Laboratories. By 1978, the Bell System had net assets of about $100 billion and annual revenues of about $40 billion. Employing approximately one million people, Bell accounted for nearly 84 percent of domestic telephone operating revenues and spent over $750 million on basic research and development (Breyer, 1982).

Because the intrastate rate structures were set by state regulatory commissions, while the interstate, long-line tariff structure was established by the FCC, peculiar, though understandable, discrimination resulted in the overall rate structure. Namely, the rates on long-distance interstate transmissions tended to be set above marginal cost, while the intrastate calls were set much closer to marginal cost. This cross-subsidization resulted, in part, from the problem of allocating the joint costs incurred from use of the equipment and other fixed capital by both long-distance and local users. While the state public service commissions generally perceived their goal as trying to minimize the rates charged to consumers, the FCC was much more sensitive to Bell's need to cover all costs. Thus, it became politically more expedient to compensate for the relatively low local rates by raising the rates on long-distance calls. Further, technological progress tended to be greater for long-distance transmissions, enabling long-distance costs to be reduced significantly, some of which were essentially captured through a reduction of local rates.[23] Such price discrimination and the cross-subsidization of local users by the long-distance users was observed by FCC Commissioner Nicholas Johnson: 'During the time of actual use, subscriber plant is used only four percent of the time for interstate calls, roughly twelve percent of the cost is to be borne by the interstate system . . . . Basically, what we are doing is subsidizing the costs of local service with Bell's excess profits from long-distance service.'[24] Thus, in 1977, AT&T paid the operating companies almost $4 billion for the use of fixed capital including telephone terminals, local switching equipment, local lines, land and buildings (Breyer, 1982). However, AT&T maintained that the payment constituted 20 percent of the intrastate costs, even though long-distance calls account for considerably less than 20 percent of the total time.

With the advent of new technologies, such as microwave and satellite, came a new demand for entry into the long-distance telecommunications market. The first entry was allowed in 1959, with the FCC's Above 890 ruling,[25] enabling other firms to use microwave frequencies above 890 megacycles, particularly for companies that wanted to build their own microwave system (Sirbu, 1982). The more important ruling occurred in 1969 when the FCC allowed Microwave Communications, Inc. to construct a $600,000 microwave service connecting Chicago with nine other cities, thereby directly competing with AT&T.[26] Subsequent to the MCI decision, thirty-seven firms proposed to build 1,713 stations. The FCC tried to channel the new entrants into specialized services, whereby they would attract new customers, rather than preempt existing ones from AT&T.

However, entry posed a problem to the regulatory structure. Even though the long-distance lines were no longer considered to be a natural monopoly, Bell's operations in the natural monopoly aspect of the market – the local lines – were inseparably intertwined with the long-lines aspects because of the problem of joint costs and cross-subsidization. Thus, new entrants found it particularly attractive to enter the long-distance market, since AT&T's rates tended to significantly exceed the marginal cost of transmission (Evans, 1983). Whatever the motive, the total deregulation process of long-lines telecommunications began in 1974 with the filing of an antitrust suit against AT&T by the Department of Justice. Upon the suit's settlement in 1982, AT&T agreed to divest itself of its twenty-two operating companies (the local aspects) along with the dissolution of Western Electric, although AT&T still owned and operated plants producing equipment. Essentially, the settlement separated the natural monopoly aspect of telecommunications, which consisted of the local operations, from the remainder of the industry. Following the settlement, AT&T operated only in the potentially competitive sphere of the industry, while the local operations were still regulated.

With deregulation has come the entry of new long-distance signal carriers, which are guaranteed equal access to the local lines. Thus, consumers are free to choose between MCI or GTE Sprint, as well as AT&T for long-distance service. However, entry into telecommunications has not yet resulted in a competitive industry. As of 1984, AT&T still claimed a market share of 95 percent (Shepherd, 1985). Deregulation has exerted a downward pressure on costs, particularly wages. Between January 1982 and January 1984 there was a decrease of 6 percent in AT&T's labor force (Bailey, 1985). Employment at the regional operating companies was similarly reduced by more than 27 percent. And in the middle of 1984, AT&T imposed a freeze on the salary structure of all of its managers, affecting over 110,000 employees. In October 1986, AT&T was still trying to reduce its labor force by around 25,000 employees.[27]

The price effects of deregulation are most apparent in the market for telephone switching equipment. In 1983, AT&T had a market share for PBXs of just under 30 percent, compared to about 18 percent for Northern Telecom and 17 percent for Rolm (which was purchased by IBM in 1985). Prices had dropped by around 50 percent compared to their level several years earlier (Bailey, 1985).

Petroleum

Unlike the other regulated industries, there have been no restrictions on entry into the petroleum industry. Because of a peculiarity of American Law of Capture, the industry experienced considerable economic volatility almost from its inception. The Law of Capture states that, in the event that an oil reservoir is shared between two or more adjacent lots of land, there is no rule regulating its recovery; the producer who pumps the most reaps the greatest claim. Thus, the incentives were clear – when in doubt, pump as much oil, as fast as possible (Montgomery, 1981). The rule of capture led to chronic excess capacity and low prices. The perceived solution was state-level regulation. Through the establishment of 'pro-rationing systems', the regulatory commissions allocated what they considered the demand to be at an acceptable price among existing producers. However, by maintaining a relatively attractive price, entry was induced, leading to reductions in the quantity allocated to each seller or producer, until many producers were operating at sub-optimal levels of output and at excessively high levels of average cost. To maintain producer solvency, or in some cases prosperity, the regulatory boards would then seek to reduce production further to induce a market price increase, which only further exacerbated the problem (Montgomery, 1981).

At least somewhat as a result of pro-rationing and the resulting high price levels, oil imports continued to increase in the United States, until President Eisenhower imposed 'voluntary' oil import quotas in 1959. Thus government regulation, in the form of the pro-rationing system, combined with the preemption of import competition, led to production inefficiency and considerable excess capacity.

Because demand grew along with the economy, the import quotas were no longer in effect by 1970. But price controls were imposed in August of 1971 by President Nixon as part of his Economic Stabilization Program. While this price ceiling was part of an overall program to alleviate inflationary pressures in the United States, the Arab oil embargo in the fall of 1973 elevated the oil industry to a particular status. Because the market price of crude oil had jumped from about $3 per barrel in 1973 to $13 per barrel by December 1975, the Federal Energy Administration (FEA) implemented a two-tier pricing system. The price of 'old' oil, which was defined as oil produced in a quantity not exceeding its 1972 level for any given specific location, could not exceed the posted field price for 15 May 1973, plus $1.35 per barrel. The price of 'new' oil, which was defined as petroleum produced either in excess of its 1972 level from an existing well, or else oil recovered from a new well, was exempt from price controls (Montgomery, 1981).

While the price controls were implemented to suppress the prices of refined products for consumers, a critical problem arose as the differential between the restricted price of old oil and the market price of new and imported oil grew. Namely, those refiners which had access to the old crude oil enjoyed considerably lower costs than those refiners who purchased mainly new and imported oil. Since the refiners with access to low-priced crude oil tended to be the large vertically integrated oil companies, while the small, independent refiners faced considerably higher input prices, political pressure was placed on the government to offset the cost disadvantage of the refiners purchasing higher-priced oil. This resulted in the implementation of an 'entitlement' system. Under this system, it was illegal to refine the old oil, which was subject to price controls, without possessing a government issued entitlement. Each refiner was issued a number of entitlements, which allowed them to refine the same proportion of total output using old oil, as was produced in the entire country. Thus, in December 1974, 40 percent of the US refined oil came from possessing old oil. Thus, each refiner received a number of entitlements enabling him to process 40 percent of his output from old oil. Since, in fact, not all refiners had equal access to old oil, this resulted in a market for entitlements, whereby refiners processing mainly new and imported oil sold their entitlements to refiners processing mainly old oil. The price of an entitlement on the market generally compensated the high-priced oil refiners for the higher costs incurred. For example, in September 1975, the price of old oil was approximately $5, while the price of new oil and imported oil was about $12.50 (Montgomery, 1981). Since the market price of an entitlement was about $7.50, the refiners of high-priced oil were compensated.

Throughout the 1970s the system of price controls and entitlements became increasingly complicated, and ultimately consisted of three tiers. The economic effects of the system were generally to encourage consumption of petroleum products by restricting the market price to below the world price, and discourage production and discovery of new sources. In April 1979, President Carter initiated a policy of decontrol. Complete decontrol was finalized in January 1981 with the inauguration of President Reagan. Subsequently, US domestic crude oil prices have corresponded with the world market.

Natural gas

The natural gas industry consists of three parts – production and exploration, transmission and distribution to consumers. In 1938 the Congress passed the Natural Gas Act,[28] establishing the regulation of the interstate transmission of natural gas by the Federal Power Commission (FPC, subsequently the Federal Energy Regulatory Commission (FERC)). Prior to 1954, the FPC restricted its regulation only to integrated companies (i.e., those involved in production and transmission). However, in the *Phillips Petroleum Company* v. *Wisconsin et al.* case,[29] the Supreme Court ruled that, even though production of natural gas was exempt from federal regulation, the sales of natural gas to a pipeline for interstate transmission was under the jurisdiction of the FPC. Thus, the FPC was instructed to regulate the price of natural gas sold for resale in the interstate market.

As a result of the Phillips decision, the FPC had to consider the appropriate price to fix for over 11,000 rate schedules and more than 33,000 supplements from almost 3,400 independent producers. Faced with a mountain of impending rate cases, the Commission estimated that its 1960 caseload would not be completed until the year 2043 (Braeutigam, 1981). Thus, in an attempt to ease the implementation of regulation, the FPC decided to apply one standard set of regulations to each of twenty-three different geographic areas in the United States.[30] Since part of the mandate underlying regulation was to redistribute economic rents from the producers to the consumers, the FPC imposed a two-tier price system of regulation, beginning with the Permian Basin in New Mexico and Texas. Under the two-tier system, the price of old gas was determined from cost data from the producers in the area. The price of new gas was determined from the cost of exploration and drilling for new gas. The two-tier system was an attempt to prevent large economic rents accruing to the producers, yet to provide an economic incentive for further exploration, discovery and production of new gas.

However, even the area ratemaking proved to be unmanageable for efficient regulation, and in June 1974, the FPC imposed a singular national rate for old gas, defined as natural gas from wells completed after 1972. The major effect of the FPC imposition was to induce significant shortages of natural gas in certain sections of the country. As the price of oil drastically rose in the 1970s, the demand for substitutes, including natural gas, similarly increased. The sharp rise in demand was reflected in the price of intrastate sales, which were not subject to FPC regulation, as the average price nearly doubled between 1966 and 1972. However, under the FPC regulation, the interstate price of natural gas did not increase along with the rise in demand. Thus, in 1966, the average price for gas sold on the intrastate market was $0.168 per thousand cubic feet (MCF), and $0.185 per MCF in the interstate market, for a difference of about $0.017 per MCF. By 1975, this differential had increased to $0.20, as the intrastate gas was selling for an average of $0.60 MCF and the interstate gas was selling for $0.40 MCF (Braeutigam, 1981). Producers responded by reallocating their contracts and sales, as well as future commitments from the less profitable interstate market, to the more profitable intrastate market. Between 1965 and 1967, there was an average of about fourteen trillion cubic feet (TCF) of natural gas added to interstate reserves per year. Between 1970 and 1974, this fell to an annual average addition of less than one TCF. However, the additions to the intrastate reserves actually increased between the two periods (Breyer, 1982). Not surprisingly, there was a shortage in the interstate market, rising from 0.1 TCF in 1970 to 4.0 TCF in 1977 (US Federal Energy Administration, 1975). MacAvoy and Pindyck (1975) estimated that the economic efficiency loss from natural gas regulation was $2.5 billion in 1978.

As a result of the general economic disarray caused by regulation in the petroleum industry, President Carter signed the Natural Gas Policy Act of 1978,[31] leading to the gradual deregulation of the industry. As in the oil industry, the decline in all energy prices mitigated many of the problems anticipated to accompany deregulation, so that in the 1980s, both prices have declined and the shortage problems have virtually disappeared.

Cable television

Because of the historical policy of the Federal Communications Commission (FCC), established in 1934 to regulate broadcasting over wire and airwaves, a serious undersupply of the radio spectrum was allocated to television broadcasting, which resulted in a limitation of three or four viewable channels in most cities (Fisher, 1985). Not surprisingly, the three major television broadcasting networks which subsequently evolved, ABC, NBC and CBS, enjoyed economic rents reflecting the lack of competition in the market (Nelson and Noll, 1985). As cable television became technologically feasible in the early 1960s, it represented a very real potential threat to the networks by being able to import signals from distant 'independent' broadcasters offering a contrast in programming to that of the three networks. Confronting the likely loss in advertising revenues that would accompany a loss in market share (because independent broadcasters would much more likely be imported than network affiliates offering network programs), the networks united to pressure the FCC to restrict the spread and freedom of cable television and contested the constitutionality of distant-signal importation on the grounds that it infringed on the copyright of the producers of programs (Owen, 1981).

Responding to pressure from the networks, the FCC in 1966 'froze' the use of cable systems to their status quo conditions in the top one hundred markets, prohibiting the importation of additional signals. However, as the potential gain to be reaped from introducing a new cable system, or from expanding an existing one, increased, pressure mounted in favor of deregulation from potential entrants. In 1972, the FCC adopted a compromise approach, liberalizing the importation of distinct signals, but only to a limited extent (MacAvoy, 1977). And, since the beginning of 1979, signal importation has been virtually totally deregulated, leading both to an expanded variety of programs available to viewers along with an erosion of the profitability of the networks (US Federal Communications Commission, 1979). By 1986, some Americans subscribing to cable television could choose from among as many as one hundred stations.[32]

CONCLUSION

It would be erroneous to consider the regulation and deregulation movements in the United States as being polar economic and political phenomena. Although the regulation movement naturally required a significantly increased presence of government control in markets, just as the deregulation movement was a catalyst for the exit of government control, both movements may have emanated from similar political and economic forces. Namely, when technology and scale economics rendered large enterprises exploiting mass production as being the most efficient, regulation was used to enable the stability and viability of large corporations. However, with the evolution of technology and a shift in the economic environment no longer providing large corporations automatically with efficiency advantages,[33] deregulation has provided an environment facilitating entry and promoting only the most innovative and economical firms.[34] That is, while the role of government towards business was exceedingly different in the regulation and deregulation movements, perhaps the policy of each period was the appropriate one to enable maximum efficiency. Thus, as technology and economic environments changed, so did the necessary government policy required to maximize economic growth.

From examining the different industries subjected to economic regulation, several similar patterns emerge. First, perhaps the ultimate failure of regulation in the United States was not due to any particular bad will or ineptitude but rather an inherent flaw in the nature of regulation: namely, the inability of the regulators to completely control the market and firm environment. Thus, in several regulated industries, such as airlines and securities, price and entry were strictly controlled by the regulatory agencies, but non-price competition was not. The motive to maximize profits led firms to engage in non-price rivalry, leading to a continual escalation of costs and subsequent rate increases. In other industries, such as petroleum and natural gas, applying the traditional rate-of-return regulation to achieve the goal of economic rent redistribution and control led to perverse economic incentives, distorted allocations and chronic shortages. The incentive to enter an industry where price is set above marginal cost, combined with the regulatory agencies' inability to limit entry, led to continual entry and chronic excess capacity and inefficiency in the crude oil market in the 1950s; so too did the inability of the FERC to regulate intrastate prices lead to chronic shortages in the interstate natural gas markets in the 1970s. This liability of regulation moved Breyer (1982, p. 218) to write: 'This strategy did not work, but not because of any mistake in economic principle. Rather, it failed because of the regulatory problems that typically accompany standard setting – problems that were aggravated by a high degree of competitiveness and the lack of legal authority allowing control.'

Thus, it is not surprising that the general assessment of US deregulation has been positive. Along with deregulation have come gains in allocative efficiency, such as in the natural gas and trucking industries, where those consumers most valuing the product can pay the marginal cost of obtaining it. Similarly, with the elimination of price rigidity and entry restrictions has come an increase in productive efficiency, as unproductive costs are being eliminated. For example, since fewer services and a lower price seem to be superior to the majority of American airline travelers than the combination of more services and higher rates, which occurred under regulation, the public is presumably better served by deregulation. Thus, Bailey (1985, p. 37) has observed:

Perhaps the chief benefit of deregulation is that it has increased efficiency substantially. Regulated thinking had the regulators not the consumers as the most important customer. There was little incentive to plan or to pinpoint the sources of markets that were successful and those that were failures, nor to keep costs under control and be responsive to consumer desires. In contrast, deregulation is leading to a substantially more efficient industry, one in which cross-subsidy is absent, a diversity of price/service options are present, and cost-minimizing behavior is prevalent, both in delivery systems and in other operating costs.... Companies are finding that they must be driven by market opportunities and financial needs, not by regulatory considerations.

However, despite enjoying a generally positive assessment, the virtues of deregulation have recently been called into question. For example, the advent of spoke-and-hub systems among the various airline firms has led to considerable consolidation in the industry, causing questions about the viability of the competitiveness of the industry. Alfred Kahn, the former chairman of the CAB and 'father' of airline deregulation, now considers that the industry may be 'evolving into an uncomfortably tight oligopoly'.[35] Thus, there is a new questioning of the success of deregulation and some calls for re-regulation of the airline industry.[36] Similarly, AT&T's sluggish profits, causing its stock to drop by 11 percent from 25 to 22.25 in the first quarter of 1986, along with its inability to expand into the information market, has called the wisdom of telecommunications deregulation into question.[37]

Still, the American experiment with deregulation has been sufficiently compelling for calls to be made for a concomitant movement in Europe. Thus, the European Commission (EC) has proposed to the European Parliament a Europe-wide TV standard, moving in the direction of television deregulation.[38] Because it would impose only a 15 percent limit on advertising, which is higher than the current limits in most European nations, the proposal is a step towards deregulation. The European Community is similarly moving towards deregulation in the airline industry. According to Kahn, 'If and as the Common Market moves in the direction of emulating the American experience, it opens up the fascinating possibility of an exchange of freer trading opportunities between these two huge markets.'[39] And, in a direct replication of America's experience in the securities market, the London securities markets were deregulated on 27 October 1986, in what has been called 'London's Big Bang'.[40]

Perhaps the most interesting aspect about the American deregulation movement was the almost unanimous support that emerged in the 1970s which was not monopolised by either major political party. Just as Presidents Eisenhower, Kennedy, Johnson and Nixon all played a significant role in expanding and entrenching the regulatory network, Presidents Ford, Carter and Reagan all moved towards deregulation. Thus, the current move towards deregulation, which is seemingly pervasive in the 1980s, could feasibly change directions along with the political and economic forces. This, apparently, has been the historical pattern of government regulation and deregulation in the United States.

NOTES

1. *Munn* v. *Illinois*, 94 US 113, 1877.
2. *Nebbia* v. *New York*, 291 US 502, 1934.
3. Budget of the United States, 1984.

4. For example, prior to deregulation, while the transmission of signals by AT&T was regulated, its production of telecommunications equipment was unregulated.
5. *Smyth* v. *Ames* 315 US 586, 1898.
6. *Federal Power Commission* v. *Hope Natural Gas*, 320 US 591 (1944).
7. Occupational Safety and Health Act (OSHAct) of 1970, Section 2(b).
8. House Education and Labor Committee report on the OSH Act reprinted in Bureau of National Affairs (BNA), the Job Safety and Health Act of 1970 (Bureau of National Affairs, Washington DC, 1971), p. 152.
9. For an analysis of the deregulation movement, see Audretsch and Woolf (1987).
10. Early analyses of the effects of airline regulation are provided by Caves (1962), and Douglas and Miller (1974). Early analyses of the impact of brokerage regulation are provided by Baxter (1970), Friend and Blume (1972), and Mann (1975).
11. Reported in the Wall Street Journal, April 1985.
12. A trunk carrier refers to an airline that serves a national or inter-regional market.
13. 72 Statute 770, 49 USC, 1302 (d).
14. For an extensive discussion of airline non-price competition, see Caves (1962), and Douglas and Miller (1974).
15. For example, upon entering the transcontinental market, United's strategy for capturing market share from the two existing carriers, American and TWA, was to offer a seating configuration of relatively low density on its DC–4 coach service. Although United petitioned for low-density seating on the grounds of safety, its request was denied by the Board, citing that it would discriminate against first-class passengers by blurring the service differentials (Board Order Serial No. E-7126, 3 February 1953).
16. CAB General Passenger Fare Investigation, Docket No. 8008, pp. 5596–5601, 1974.
17. The Airline Deregulation Act of 1978, Public Law No. 95504, 92 Statute 1705, 1978.
18. 'Losses triple at people', *International Herald Tribune*, 2 May 1986, p. 13.
19. 'Airline in flux', *Business Week*, 10 March 1986, pp. 49–56.
20. *Ibid.*
21. *Ibid.*
22. 'Eastern airlines reports 2d. consecutive loss', *International Herald Tribune*, 1 May 1986.
23. See dissenting opinion of FCC Commissioner N. Johnson, FCC Docket No. 18866, 26 FCC 2d 247, 1970, p. 262.
24. See concurring opinion of FCC Commissioner N. Johnson, FCC Docket No. 16258, 9 FCC 2d 30, 1967, p. 129.
25. In the Matter of Allocation of Frequencies in the Bands above 890 MC, 27 FCC 359, 1959.
26. In Re-Applications of Microwave Communications, Inc., 18 FCC 2d 953, 1969.
27. 'AT&T offers severance pay to some middle managers', *Wall Street Journal*, 16 October 1986, p. 3.
28. Natural Gas Act, 52 Statute 821, 1938.
29. *Phillips Petroleum Company* v. *Wisconsin et al.*, 342 U.S. 672, 1954.
30. This was approved by the Supreme Court in Permian Basin Area Rate Cases, 390 U.S. 747, 1968.
31. Natural Gas Policy Act, para. 121, public law No. 95–621, 92 Statute 335, 1978.
32. 'Prime time regulation', *International Herald Tribune*, 1 May 1986.
33. For a discussion of the restructuring of the economy, see Piore and Sabel (1984), Reich (1983), Shepherd (1982), and Acs and Audretsch (1987b).

34. For further discussion see Abernathy *et al.* (1983), Wheelwright (1985), and Friedman (1983).
35. 'US airline industry's consolidation spurs questions on competition at hub airports', *Wall Street Journal*, 9 September 1986, p. 7.
36. 'Deregulation: an air race nobody wins', *International Herald Tribune*, 21 January 1986, p. 4.
37. 'Why AT&T isn't clicking', *Business Week*, 10 May 1986, pp. 78–82, and 'High-Tech Headache', *Business Week*, 10 May 1986, p. 83.
38. 'Prime time regulation', *Wall Street Journal*, 1 May 1986, p. 7.
39. 'American deregulation lessons for Europe', *Wall Street Journal*, 2 October 1986, p. 6.
40. 'American lessons for London's big bang', *Wall Street Journal*, 27 October 1986, p. 8.

6 · INDUSTRIAL POLICY IN THE EUROPEAN ECONOMIC COMMUNITY

While competition policy in the European Economic Community (Common Market) resembles antitrust enforcement in the United States and Fair Trade Policy in Japan, at least in the guiding principles, the industrial targeting approach of the EEC countries has no clear analogous institution in America. Four elements distinguish European industrial policy from any similar policy in the United States. First, the policies are the result of coordinated government planning. Second, productive resources are deployed. Third, those productive resources are channelled into selected industries. Finally, the underlying goal of the policies is to bestow the domestic firms with a competitive superior position in the global market (US International Trade Commission, 1984).

Like the case of EEC competition policy, industrial targeting in the EEC is complex because of the overlap between the policies of individual countries and those of the EEC policies as a whole. In fact, based on the fundamental treaty establishing the Community, the EEC administers and regulates industrial policy instruments within the member countries. In particular, the EEC has the statutory authority to either approve or disapprove of particular targeting practices implemented by any particular member country, if such policies distort competition within the Community.

Two types or groups of industries have tended to be the recipients of industrial targeting in the EEC. The first group comprises traditional industries now in the mature or declining phase of the industry life cycle (Audretsch, 1987a). These industries include steel, coal, shipbuilding, textiles, apparel and automobiles. The EEC policies in general have been oriented towards facilitating an orderly reduction of capacity. In the second group of industries, those which have been the recipients of industrial targeting, are new- and high-technology industries, such as aircraft, computers, telecommunications equipment and robotics. Industrial targeting has been implemented here for the purpose of trying to compensate for an otherwise deficient amount of R&D, with the hopes of restoring technological parity with the United States and Japan (Geroski and Jacquemin, 1985).

Policies targeted towards this second group of industries have been termed as comprising 'technology policy'. According to Corsten (1987, p. 155). 'The objective pursued by technology policy is the generation and dissemination of technologies, where technologies are understood as being the material and immaterial results of technical knowledge in the form of technical processes and products. If technology policy is viewed in terms of a sequence of stages, two distinct stages are discernible: the generation stage and the dissemination stage. The dissemination stage can be further split into the innovation stage and the broad application stage.' The goal of these technology policies is generally to strengthen the international competitiveness of the domestic industry.

Tax policies, financial assistance, and science and technology policies are three major types of instruments used in industrial targeting. While the majority of the EEC member countries do not use tax policies for specific industrial targeting, the French, British and West German governments stand in the minority with their deployment of tax policy as a tool for encouraging R&D in selective industries. Forms of financial assistance used to implement industrial targeting include subsidized loans, loan guarantees and grants. Such financial assistance is typically targeted in one of two ways: either at firms in declining industries or else at the promotion of small- and medium-sized firms.

The exact financial instruments used to target resources in selected industries vary, however, among countries. For example, while the French government implements policies through direct control over the banking system, which was nationalized in 1981, West Germany has emphasized grants and the United Kingdom has subsidized loans to businesses. France provides a slightly different example of industrial policy because of the extent to which industries and the banks have been nationalized. That is, while industrial policy in West Germany and the United Kingdom must be implemented through the use of indirect measures such as financial subsidies and tax incentives, the French government can allocate funds to selected industries directly from the federal budget.

The second section of this chapter examines the major industrial policy instruments which have been applied within the EEC at the EEC level. In particular, the EEC institutions created to implement industrial policy are considered. The third section explores the relationship between industrial targeting and competition policy in the EEC. The two policies often create conflicts which consequently provide a source of tension between EEC countries as well as within the boundaries of individual nations. The industrial policies of West Germany are considered in the fourth section, and the experience of industrial targeting in the United Kingdom is examined in the fifth section. Finally, after contrasting the French approach of nationalization and its implications for industrial policy in the sixth section, conclusions and a summary are provided in the final section.

INDUSTRIAL POLICY INSTRUMENTS IN THE EUROPEAN ECONOMIC COMMUNITY

Certain industrial targeting instruments for EEC member countries were approved with ratification of the 1951 Paris Treaty, which granted substantial power to the European Coal and Steel Community (ECSC), and the 1957 Treaty of Rome, which provided a mandate to the EEC to intervene in the agricultural sector of the member countries. However, there was no such mandate established for industrial policy in the manufacturing sector. The Treaty of Rome, however, did entrust the EEC with the regulation, administration and development of the industrial base of the Common Market, and the EEC has since adapted a number of industrial policy instruments with the goal of developing specified targeted industries. The use and deployment of these instruments are generally treaty-based.

While a common EEC industrial policy has been implemented for the coal and steel sectors, no such unified targeting has been achieved for industrial markets outside of these sectors. There are several reasons why. First, there is considerable disagreement concerning both the use and extent of a common industrial policy among the members: 'They agree on common EEC strategies only when it is in their own interest to do so and are generally unwilling to relinquish even a little control over their own industrial structure and policy to the EEC' (US International Trade Commission, 1984, p. 19). Second, as will be discussed in the following section, industrial policy is contradictory to the commitment to free trade within the EEC – a commitment inherent in the Treaty of Rome. While Article 93 requires approval by the Commission of all member governments' proposals to implement industrial policies, the Commission has generally ruled that when such targeting is in violation of the EEC competition policy it cannot be approved. Third, because the Treaty of Rome did not specifically provide a mandate for industrial policy in the manufacturing sector, the institutions of the Community are restricted in the manner in which they can implement programs of cooperation among member nations. Thus, the predominant influence from the Community on industrial policy is mostly through treaty agreements. Fourth, as will be discussed in Chapter 9, the presence of trade barriers, both tariff and non-tariff, within EEC trade, has a detrimental impact on cooperation between member nations. Fifth, funding for such industrial policies at the Community level is scarce. Finally, because a consensus among all members is required for matters of policy, including Community-wide industrial targeting, implementation is difficult.

Having qualified the extent to which a common EEC industrial policy is actually carried out, it must be said that industrial policy is alive and well, or at least a significant part of the policy landscape. The major targeting instruments used include subsidized loans and grants, as well as Community competition policy, control of the Common External Tariff and foreign trade policy (both of which are discussed in Chapter 9). A diverse system of subsidized loans, loan guarantees and grants has been applied in channeling funds to targeted industries.

The European Regional Development Fund is one of the EEC institutions facilitating industrial targeting based on subsidized loans and grants. Established in 1975, the Fund is managed by the Commission and provides grant aid to member states. In particular, grants tend to be approved for investment projects, especially for those involving the economic development of a member country's infrastructure. Assistance from the European Regional Development Fund is typically only granted as a complement to existing investment already occurring within the member country. Four conditions must be met in order to be eligible for assistance. First, the aid has to be applied to a project already receiving assistance from the member government. Second, at least ten new jobs must be created after applying for assistance. Third, there is a ceiling of 50,000 ECUs (European Currency Units)[1] for the amount of assistance. Finally, the investment must be completed before the Commission receives the application for aid. In 1982, there was a total amount of just over 2 billion ECUs, or around $2 billion, in aid allocated among 3,277 investment projects.

Another EEC institution responsible for providing subsidized loans and grants is the European Investment Bank. Since its inception in 1969, the European Investment Bank has increasingly resorted to loans made through intermediary institutions, better known as 'global loans'. These intermediary institutions, which include commercial banks, regional development agencies, government agencies and other public authorities are responsible for processing applicants. The interest rates are of a fixed nature, and the intermediary institutions bear the ultimate responsibility for repaying the loan. The share of global loans has risen from just over 10 percent between 1969 to 1974, to just over one-quarter in 1978, and finally to more than one-half since 1980 (Pinder, 1986).

An important aspect of the global loans process is that many are made to relatively small enterprises. Since 1982, more than four-fifths of sub-loans granted by intermediaries (between 25,000 and 7.5 million ECUs) were made to firms with fewer than 200 employees. Further, 60 percent of such loan recipients had fewer than 50 employees. As Pinder (1986) notes, this asymmetry in favor of small firms emphasizes the importance now being placed on developing the viability of small enterprises.

Between 1969 and 1979, nearly one-fifth of all global loans by the European Investment Bank was allocated to the metal working and mechanical engineering industry, and nearly 18 percent to the food industry. By contrast, only 3.1 percent of the funds was targeted to motor vehicles and transportation equipment, and 2.6 percent to the glass and ceramics industry. However, by the first half of the 1980s the composition of global loans by the European Investment Bank had changed somewhat. The industry subject to the most intensive targeting was motor vehicles and transportation equipment, which received nearly one-fifth of all global loans between 1980 and 1984. Funds for the metal working and mechanical engineering industry were reduced to 16.1 percent of the budget, and targeting for the food industry fell to less than 15 percent. Textiles and leather, paper pulp and printing, rubber and plastic, and woodworking all received less than 5 percent of the allocation of global loans between 1980 and 1984.

The virtue of targeting the funds to small- and medium-sized firms was thought to be the inherent diversity of such an approach. Not only were smaller enterprises unlikely to become dependent upon the aid for survival, but it was not likely that they would come to 'dominate communities and offer restricted employment choice' (Pinder, 1986, p. 176).

The allocation of global loans among the member countries has not been even. Between 1969 and 1979, Italy received over one-half of the loans, while the United Kingdom was given 12.6 percent and France 14.3 percent. The smallest recipients were Ireland with 4.7 percent, Belgium with 4.7 percent, Denmark with 5.8 percent, and West Germany with 6.9 percent.

In 1979, the Commission founded the New Community Instrument, established to provide the European Investment Bank with new resources. The New Community Instrument enables the Bank to borrow in international capital markets. Between 1979 and 1982, there were over 2 billion ECUs in loans financed this way.

It has been estimated that in 1979, approximately 40,000 jobs were either created or preserved in the EEC as a result of targeting from European Investment Bank funds. By 1982, the number of affected employees was estimated at 93,000. And, an estimate for the employment effect for 1990 is 246,000 jobs created or preserved (Pinder, 1986).

The EEC also provides funds to support cooperative R&D, particularly in the coal, steel, textiles, footwear, data processing, information technologies, biotechnology, nuclear and solar energy, nuclear fusion and telecommunications industries. Typically these research programs are implemented by the Commission which then, after a selection process, awards contracts to firms and research institutions of member countries.

Part of the motive for EEC R&D efforts may stem from the concern that member countries are not investing enough in R&D and in promoting innovation and technical change. In 1980, the EEC spent only 600 million ECUs ($588 million) on R&D, which was a substantial increase from the 70 million ECUs ($83.5 million) spent in 1974. This, however, does not represent a particularly large share of the total R&D undertaken in the EEC. In 1982, the EEC's contribution amounted to just 2 percent of the total R&D expenditures by the member states. However, over the period of 1975 to 1981, expenditures by EEC institutions on R&D increased at an annual average growth rate of nearly 19 percent, while the equivalent increase in the member countries was 12.5 percent.

The Commission's attitude towards funding cooperative R&D projects is clear from the three main priorities to promote industrial competitiveness. The first of these priorities focuses on developing standards to promote an EEC-wide market and move away from the segregated national markets. Second, the EEC seeks to spur innovation and modernization in traditional manufacturing industries through the application of new technologies, such as lasers, new materials and computerized applications for manufacturing. Finally, the EEC seeks to promote new technologies, such as information technology, biotechnology, and robotics. The sentiment of the EEC is clear: 'The Commission feels that if the EEC is to keep up with its foreign competitors, it must coordinate the national research programs and collaborate in joint efforts to master basic technologies, such as microelectronics, especially integrated circuits; software engineering; office automation; computer translation system; and industrial robots' (US International Trade Commission, 1984, p. 35).

Geroski and Jacquemin (1985) argue that such concerted industrial policy towards R&D within Europe is essential to reducing the barriers between the most efficient national firms and to expanding the relevant markets from being domestic to becoming essentially European in nature. They argue, therefore, that such industrial policies are particularly important for high-technology industries like semiconductors, and attribute the discouraging performance to an inadequate investment in R&D. Thus, EEC-wide industrial policies, in their view, should be undertaken to compensate for the tendency to under-invest in R&D.

Probably the most apparent example of the cooperative R&D approach within the EEC is the European Strategic Program for Research and Development in Information Technologies – ESPRIT. The ESPRIT program, which was developed in conjunction with the member states, has the goal of enabling firms in the information technology industries to attain global competitiveness. The ESPRIT program began in 1983 and, following a one-year initial pilot program, began the first five-year phase of the current ten-year program. There are five areas in which R&D has been targeted, including advanced microelectronics, software technology, advanced information processing, office automation and computer-integrated manufacturing.[2]

The Eurolaser is the largest EUREKA project. About $200 million of public funds have supported the Eurolaser project, compared with an average subsidy of $50 million for each EUREKA project (Klodt, 1987).

As Geroski and Jacquemin (1985) note, much of the rationale underlying the ESPRIT program emanates from the deteriorating performance of European firms in information technology products. while the trade balance for the EEC nations stood at a surplus of $1.17 billion for information technology products in 1975, by 1980 it had reversed to a $5 billion deficit, and to a $10 billion deficit in 1982. While nearly four-fifths of all personal computers purchased in EEC member nations are purchased from the United States, more than nine out of ten video recorders purchased were manufactured in Japan. Similarly, European-based integrated circuit manufacturers account for only about one-third of the EEC market and only slightly more than 10 percent of the global market.[3]

The ESPRIT program was established to help European firms and nations achieve technological parity with their rivals in the United States and Japan. Between 1984 and 1988, ESPRIT had a budget of 750 million ECUs from the European Community (Klodt, 1987). By emphasizing projects involving joint R&D efforts across firms and nations, the EEC is attempting to promote 'cross-frontier industrial R&D collaboration betwen member firms and research centers enabling them to benefit from a large common reservoir of knowledge that cannot be duplicated at the national level' (US International Trade Commission, 1984, p. 37). In addition, the EEC hopes that ESPRIT will generate a set of common standards for information technology along with a unified Community market for products emerging from information technology. Finally, the EEC is hoping to gain economies in R&D expenditures through avoiding wasteful duplication of national R&D expenditures.

The pilot phase of ESPRIT, which occurred in 1983, used 11.55 million ECUs ($10.23 million) of funds from the EEC. These funds covered one-half of the R&D costs of the projects. Of the thirty-eight projects undertaken, the largest, with a budget of 3.1 million ECUs, was devoted to the development of a portable common tool environment for software technology. The second largest project had a budget of 2.5 million ECUs used for high level computer-aided design for interactive layout and design. Other major projects affected by the pilot phase of ESPRIT included multimedia user interface at the office workstation for office automation, and design rules for computer-integrated manufacturing systems (Commission of the European Communities, 1982).

Under the first five-year phase of ESPRIT, which lasted between 1984 and 1988, the EEC paid $650 million towards the total cost of $1.3 billion. The total budget of ESPRIT represents around 6 percent of the total R&D expenditures currently being undertaken by the member states in information technologies. There are two major types of projects being undertaken in the program. Type A projects involve R&D on a large scale and require substantial resources and infrastructure. Around three-quarters of ESPRIT's budget has been allocated towards such large-scale Type A projects. By contrast, small-scale R&D activities, which focus on flexible infrastructure and emphasize small units rather than a systems approach are categorized into Type B projects. While the Commission is constrained to paying not more than one-half of the costs of a research project for the Type A projects, the Commission can exceed this amount for Type B projects.

Around one-quarter of the ESPRIT budget is allocated towards Type B Projects.

The ESPRIT program is not unique. In 1982, the EEC instituted a similar research program in biotechnology. As for information technologies, the goal of the biotechnology program is to encourage industrial competitivenss within the EEC. Between 1981 and 1983, the Commission allocated $7 million on food production research, and between 1983 and 1985, $6 million was contributed to other industrial products, with a special emphasis on pharmaceuticals.

The EEC is also sponsoring joint projects in energy, spanning conventional and nuclear sources. Under the EURATOM treaty, the Commission can make loans that enhance the Community's independence from oil imports through the promotion of nuclear energy. Based on Article 4, which states that 'the Commission has the responsibility of promoting and facilitating nuclear research in the member states and of complementing them by research and training programs undertaken by the EEC' (Commission of the European Communities, 1983, p. 9), between 1979 and 1982 the Commission channelled $784 million of loans from EURATOM into projects.

INDUSTRIAL TARGETING AND EEC COMPETITION POLICY

There is an inherent conflict regarding the definition of the goals of industrial targeting. The situation is often such that the goals of the Community as a whole are in conflict with the goals of several member countries' individual needs and goals. While the intrinsic goal of competition policy is to ensure competition among many producers, the underlying premise of industrial targeting is to preempt such rivalry and, instead, to foster cooperative agreements. Thus, on the one hand, competition policy is oriented towards creating conditions which instill as much competition among firms as possible, while on the other hand, industrial policy is oriented towards creating conditions conducive to cooperation and mutual enterprise. The EEC has acknowledged an increased tension between industrial targeting policies, or state aid, on the one hand, and the goals of EEC competition policy on the other:

> The pressure on Member States to grant State aids, and on the Commission in assessing the proposals submitted to it for their compatibility with the market increased markedly . . . reflects falling production, rising unemployment, increasingly fierce international competition for market shares and a growth of protectionist forms and pressures. State aids may contribute to engendering economic growth, the development, the amelioration of social conditions resulting from economic changes, and to improvement of the employment situation in a particular country. State aids can also be used as a form of

protectionism, to benefit national producers, to give them competitive advantages, to avoid necessary structural adaptation: in short, to transfer difficulties onto competitors in other states.[4]

In fact Article 92 of the EEC Treaty granted the Commission the power of either approving or rejecting aid from any member state targeted towards any particular industry. In accordance with Article 92, the Commission has developed a procedure for considering the appropriateness of targeting by member countries. In principle, the Commission takes a rather dim view of targeting practices and other forms of state aid, and has warned of 'the dangers posed by the growth of what might be regarded as an aid mentality, i.e. the danger that firms when they get into difficulties turn immediately to the State for assistance rather than rely on their own resources and efforts to overcome their difficulties' (Commission of the European Communities, 1983, p. 110).

Under EEC law, any member country wishing to target a particular industry as being a recipient for state aid must first receive the approval of the Commission. In reaching its decision the Commission in turn considers three aspects. The first is that the aid promotes the interest of the community as a whole and not just the individual interests of the member state: 'The promotion of such a national interest is not enough to justify the Commission exercising its discretionary powers under Article 92(3) EEC' (Commission of the European Communities, 1983, p. 110). Second, the requested aid is essential to ensure the development of the industry. If there is some other manner in which the industry can follow an equivalent course of development, without being subjected to targeting, the proposal will be rejected by the Commission. Third, the burdens which the particular form of targeting inflict on the other members of the Community, in terms of intensity, duration and the degree of distortion of competition, must be offset by the benefits accruing from the state intervention.

Since 1970, there has been a substantial increase in the number of applications to the Commission from member states pursuing some form of targeting through state aid. In 1970, the Commission received twenty-one petitions for targeting. In fifteen of these cases, the Commission approved the request; in one case the Commission reached a negative decision in rejecting the proposal; and in the remaining six cases the member states withdrew the application after it had become apparent that their application would be rejected. The number of applications for approval of industrial targeting increased to 35 in 1972, 45 in 1975, 112 in 1977, 133 in 1979, and 233 in 1982. In the following year, the number of applications for state aid fell somewhat to 174. Still, between 1970 and 1982 the number of applications for approval by the Commission of member country targeting practices increased more than tenfold. The proportion of applications approved by the Commission has not followed any apparent trend. In 1970, more than 70 percent of the petitions were approved. In 1974, the proportion fell to 57 percent but subsequently rose to nearly 90 percent in 1977. But by 1979, only 59 percent of the applications were approved by the Commission, and in 1982 only 45 percent of the petitions were granted approval.

Based on the increased numbers of applications for EEC permission to engage in industrial targeting, it is not surprising that the Commission has warned of

> a marked increase in the degree of intervention in industry by Member States. Governments have not only been providing State aid in order to encourage the recipient firms to carry out a specific project which would contribute to some objective for the industry or the region, but have also come to guarantee some firms' very existence . . . . The consequence is that Governments frequently step in to provide rescue aid on a selective basis, in order to provide urgent refinancing for firms whose capital base has been eroded by several years of poor results.[5]

Of course, the natural result of such intervention is that through preserving the natural capacity of such firms, the presence of inefficient producers and the existence of excess capacity in certain industries is encouraged. The Commission recognizes the danger in continually propping up such firms through targeting practices:

> There is often a serious danger of distortion of competition in such operations, not only because of the intensity of the aid, but also because of the industrial consequences of the rescue. If no rescue operation were mounted, the production capacity of the firm involved would be withdrawn from the market or would be substantially reduced if, following liquidation, the business was taken over in a reorganized form by another company.[6]

The ECSC Treaty makes provision for state intervention in the steel industry at the Community level. There have been two major goals of intervention. The first has been to try to place limitations on the amount of production, through both mandatory and voluntary quotas, which is facilitated by exchanging price information. The second has been to promote the restructuring of the steel industry, principally through encouraging technical progress and modernization of plant and equipment. The code for aids to the steel industry, which was first put into effect in 1980 and then again in the following year, requires that all recipients of targeting in the industry be undertaking programs to restructure in such a way as to reduce the amount of total capacity and simultaneously alter the remaining capacity to make it internationally competitive.

In an effort to implement this policy, the Commission reached nine decisions on steel aids in June of 1983.[7] Through these decisions, which affected each of the member states, the Commission sought to bring about an orderly reduction of capacity between 1980 and 1985 of at least 26.7 million tons of hot-rolled products. In 1980, hot-rolled steel production in terms of the amount produced and the percentage share of EEC capacity is shown in Table 6.1. Belgium, Denmark, Ireland, Luxembourg and the

Table 6.1 Steel Production in the European Community, 1980

	Amount produced (tons)	EEC capacity (%)
West Germany	53,117,000	32.0
Italy	36,294,000	21.5
France	26,869,000	51.9
United Kingdom	22,840,000	13.5

Netherlands all contributed less than 10 percent of total EEC hot-rolled steel products. The plan called for the largest percentage reductions in capacity to be met by the United Kingdom (nearly 20 percent), France (nearly 20 percent) and Belgium (19.4 percent), while West Germany reduced its capacity only by 11.3 percent.

Five principal forms of targeting were employed by the member states in implementing the state aid in the steel industry. The first involved grants, including interest relief grants, from the member state to private companies. Based on the aid payments authorized by the Commission prior to July 1983 in the first and second aids codes, this was the predominant form of targeting the steel industry in West Germany and Italy. Nearly 80 percent of West German intervention in the steel industry was in the form of grants, compared with about 16 percent of all EEC state aid. The most predominant form of targeting in the steel industry was the use of participatory loans. Participatory loans accounted for slightly more than 60 percent of state aid funds for the EEC countries. In particular, virtually all of the targeting by the United Kingdom, and the preponderance of targeting funds by France, were in this form. While the conversion of debt into capital was a form of targeting used solely by Belgium, reduced interest rate loans appeared as a more prevalent form of targeting in the Italian steel industry. Finally, market rates loans and guarantees were a fairly significant instrument for targeting, particularly by France and Belgium. Thus, each country tended to adapt the form of targeting for the steel industry which was presumably the most appropriate for itself, as what was appropriate and suitable for one nation was clearly not advantageous to its neighbor.

Shipbuilding is another major industry in which the EEC has approved massive state interventions on behalf of industrial development. In April 1981, the Fifth Directive on aid to shipbuilding was adopted,[8] based on Articles 92 (3) (d) and 113 of the EEC Treaty. The purpose of the Directive was to encourage the restructuring of the shipbuilding industry, which had simultaneously suffered from chronic excess capacity and a deterioration in international competitiveness. After this Directive expired at the end of 1982, the policies were extended into future years. In particular, state intervention in the industry was approved for the Netherlands, West Germany, the United Kingdom, France and Italy.

For the Netherlands, the Commission approved the intervention by the state in the form of grants with a ceiling rate of 10.5 percent, along with specific investment aid for modernizing certain shipyards. Subsequent approval enabled the Netherlands to extend this form of targeting with a ceiling rate of between 3 and 8 percent. The Commission permitted West Germany to make an effective subsidy of 5 percent, through the application of grants and financing arrangements. This was renewed in subsequent years. Similarly, the Commission permitted the United Kingdom to provide grants of 18 percent to its shipbuilders. In France, a production subsidy was approved which was the equivalent of 20 percent of the contract price for ships produced by the largest shipbuilding yards and 10 percent of contract price for the ships constructed in the smaller yards. Finally, Italy was permitted to provide production aid ranging from 26 percent for the big yards to 8.5 percent for the smallest yards.

A third industry subject to EEC industrial targeting and state intervention is textiles. While the 1982 EEC bilateral textile agreements resulted in extensions of import protection in the textile and clothing industries, the EEC policy goal has been to reduce the extent of excess capacity and to prevent member states from adapting so-called 'beggar-thy-neighbor' policies. Belgium is one of the countries with the greatest reliance on industrial targeting in textiles. In particular, the Commission has allowed the Belgian government to make loans for investment facilitating restructuring that cover a maximum of one-half of the total costs for a period not to exceed ten years. Similarly, a ceiling rate of seven percentage points on interest subsidies for a five-year period was approved. France is another country resorting to a significant amount of targeting in the textile industry. Under Article 93 (2) the French government petitioned to channel FF 2,000 million to the textile and clothing industry in the form of relief of social security costs. However, when the Commission ruled that the French policy was inconsistent with the goals of the Community, and therefore rejected the proposal,[9] the French government chose to continue the targeting policy. Subsequently, in 1983, the Commission brought a case against France[10] on the grounds that it had not lived up to a fundamental obligation under the EEC Treaty. When the Court upheld the Commission's charge, France restrained from its targeting practices. However, the Commission responded by allowing France to channel aid to the industry,[11] as long as not more than FF 1,200 million of aid to the textile and clothing industry was spent in 1984. Finally, the extent of the aid could not exceed one-quarter of all investment costs, and the social security contributions could not exceed a ceiling rate of 10 percent.

INDUSTRIAL POLICY IN WEST GERMANY

One of the striking differences between industrial policy in West Germany and in Japan is that in the case of West Germany, industrial policy played only a minor role prior to the mid-1960s and subsequently became more important, whereas in Japan, industrial policy played the most significant role prior to the mid-1960s. That is, when industrial targeting was the most dormant in West Germany, it was the most pronounced in Japan. And, when interventionist policies were the strongest in Japan, they were the least important in West Germany. Industrial policy in West Germany has grown out of the government's participation under the Stability and Growth Act of 1966, and in discussions with business executives and union leaders concerning the importance of chanelling resources into high-technology industries and away from the more traditional sectors of the economy. In response, the West German government became involved in supporting R&D efforts. Even by 1974, slightly more than 1 percent of West German civilian R&D was financed by the government, which made it the most active interventionist R&D policy in Western Europe. Responding to the technology gap with the United States, the West German government chose to target R&D in computers and aircraft, and these two industries were the recipients of nearly 7 percent of the subsidies to industry.

At the same time, government subsidies have played an important role in several industries in the declining stage of the life cycle. The coal mining industry received nearly one-fifth of all total subsidies to industry in 1972; shipbuilding was also heavily subsidized.

Another unique feature of industrial policy in West Germany is the numerous institutions involved in forming and implementing policy. In fact, industrial policy is generally formulated and implemented through a maze of eight major institutions. The Ministry of Finance, although predominantly oriented towards the implementation of macroeconomic issues such as tax policy and public finance, yields authority with respect to state-owned firms. The Ministry of Finance approves the allocation of the budget towards various programs, and thus has the power either to increase or constrain targeting policies. The Ministry of Economic Affairs, although historically responsible for international relations, has more recently been concerned with policy towards industries experiencing chronic structural decline. In general, the Ministry of Economic Affairs attempts to apply limited subsidies in bringing about an orderly restructuring of the industry. By contrast, the Ministry for Research and Technology is concerned with new and growing industries. Among its responsibilities is the coordination of the R&D programs undertaken by the various government agencies. In particular, the Ministry for Research and Technology has been responsible for subsidies in the computers, micro-processors, aerospace and nuclear energy industries. Thus, while the Ministry of Economic Affairs is charged with guiding the declining industries, the Ministry for Research and Technology is responsible for industries in the earliest stages of the product life cycle.

Although it is not oriented towards any particlar industries *per se*, the Ministry for Regional and Urban Affairs is charged with dispensing regional aid. Still, to the extent to which particular industries are associated with certain regions, the Ministry for Regional and Urban Affairs is a participant in West German industrial policy. The Ministry of Transport applies subsidies and other financial assistance to transportation industries including the railways, commercial air and shipping. Like the Ministry for Economic Affairs, the Ministry of Transport is concerned with managing the decline of traditional industries. Because of its control over monetary and exchange rate policy, which affect the international competitiveness of certain key industries, the Bundesbank can be considered to play a role in West German industrial policy formulation and implementation. In addition to these ministries, two other institutions contribute to the process of industrial policy in West Germany. The trade unions and employers' federations, and the five economic research institutes, which are sponsored by the Ministry for Economic Affairs, both play a significant role in the industrial policy landscape.

In applying industrial policy, the West German government has generally striven to select industries that need assistance in either maintaining the current level of output or in adjusting to new conditions in the industry. Second, industries are typically selected on the basis of the expected increases in productivity and growth resulting from government aid. Third, government intervention is only applied in situations where there is a public interest, and in the absence of government targeting, this public need could not be met. Fourth, the form of government aid should be oriented towards improving the underlying economic structure of the firm and not merely providing an alleviation of the symptomatic problems. Fifth, policies have to be consistent with EEC policy. Finally, government targeting can only be applied for a finite duration. That is, public intervention should be extraordinary case and not the rule in an industry.

Although tax policy in West Germany is more typically oriented to developments in particular regions rather than selected industries, in certain instances it has been used as an instrument for industrial policy. In particular, the coal, shipbuilding and steel industries have greatly benefited from tax advantages. Tax benefits usually take on two forms, either tax credits or else a special depreciation allowance. In the 1980s, the distribution of tax benefits has remained quite stable across different sectors of the economy. The largest tax benefits in industry in 1984 were for the steel industry, which took advantage of DM 100 million in tax benefits. While DM 126 million in tax benefits were applied to the mining sector, DM 148 million in tax benefits were applied for promoting innovation, and an additional DM 99 million in tax benefits were granted for energy and raw material supply. By contrast, DM 275 million in tax benefits were granted to the agriculture and forestry sector (Federal Republic of Germany, 1986).

A more direct tool for implementing industrial policy in West Germany is financial assistance. Financial assistance typically takes the form of grants, government guarantees of loans or loans bearing an interest rate below that of the going market rate. The loans are generally implemented through the Bundesbank and the other major banks, such as the Deutsche Bank, Dresdner Bank and Commerzbank. It is then left up to the commercial banks to select the recipients of the loans as well as to bear the risks. Between 1981 and 1984, the amount of financial assistance from the West German government targeted at specific industries has remained fairly constant at around DM 13,500 million. About one-third of this assistance is channelled into the industrial sector, with slightly more than 5 percent going towards mining, 2.5 percent towards promoting innovations, and just under 2 percent towards energy and raw material supply. An additional 4 percent goes towards financial assistance in shipbuilding, aircraft and steel. Finally, the transportation sector receives just over 7 percent of the total funds targeted for financial assistance by the West German government. The allocation of these funds has changed considerably since the mid-1960s. In 1966, more than one-third of the financial assistance was targeted towards the agriculture sector. By 1974, this had fallen to about one-fifth, and by the mid-1980s, to less than 10 percent of the total amount of financial assistance allocated. In the meantime, the share of financial assistance going to industry has nearly doubled from its 18.5 percent level in 1966. The financial assistance channelled to the shipbuilding, aircraft and steel industries has risen from 0.3 percent of all financial assistance in 1966 to an increase in the 1980s of more than 1000 percent.

While the total amount of financial assistance to West Germany industry grew considerably since the mid-1960s, it has levelled out somewhat within the last decade. In 1966, there was a total of DM 1,619 million ($405 million) of financial aid channelled to industries. By 1970, this amount had grown to DM 3,702 million ($1,011 million), and by 1975 to DM 5,564 million ($2,262 million). While there was DM 9,163 million ($5,035) of financial assistance granted in 1980, it was reduced somewhat to DM 8,884 million ($3,656 million) by 1982. In real terms, the amount of government assistance to West German industry has about tripled between 1966 and 1982. Thus, even after adjusting for price increases, there has been a substantial expansion of West Germany's financial assistance in the last two decades.

A third instrument for implementing industrial policy comes through the ownership of firms by the government. Frequently, nationalization enables the firm to obtain equity funds at costs substantially below that of its private counterparts. Similarly, loans are also less expensive to obtain, because the lenders typically perceive nationalized firms to be a less risky enterprise than a private firm. The government can always stand behind a nationalized firm. In general, five policy goals have been fulfilled through public ownership in West Germany. These include the acceleration of innovation and technical change, the attainment of independence and self-sufficiency for key products, the avoidance of private monopoly, the expansion of employment in chronically depressed regions and the provision of housing for low-income people. While many of the nationalized firms were sold by the government, the West German government still has much more direct ownership than does the American government. For example, nearly three-quarters of the major airline, Lufthansa, is government-owned, as is about one-third of the shipbuilding industry, more than one-quarter of the automobile industry, about one-half of the aluminium industry, and about one-tenth of the steel industry. While the government owns significant portions of important energy and chemical firms, the Länder governments[12] own portions of two different aircraft firms. While Bremen owns more than one-fourth of VFW-Fokker, Bavaria and Hamburg combine to own almost 44 percent of Messerschmitt-Boelkow-Blohm (Walters and Monsen, 1979).

The 'Kreditanstalt für Wiederaufbau', the West German Investment Bank, was founded shortly after the Second World War. The purpose of the investment bank is to provide loans for capital investment. While about four-fifths of the starting capital came from the German federal government, the remaining 20 percent was contributed by the Länder governments. The Kreditanstalt für Wiederaufbau has tended to focus its loans on small- and medium-sized enterprises. While most of the loans have been made in the agriculture, oil, housing and seaports sectors, shipbuilding has also been a major recipient of loans. Nearly 17 percent of the loan commitments went towards capital goods in 1982, including 5 percent for mechanical engineering, and nearly 5 percent for metal goods. An additional 12 percent of the 1982 loan commitments went towards consumer goods industries, including glass and ceramics wood products, paper, printing, plastics, leather and textiles and apparel. Slightly under 8 percent of the loan commitments were made in the food, beverages and tobacco sector and in the mining, fuel and power sectors.

More recently, several programs have been established to target capital into innovative funds. Under the auspices of the Economics Ministry, the First Innovation Program was established. Similarly, under the auspices of the Ministry of Research and Technology, the Technologically Oriented Firm Program was founded, with the goal of encouraging innovation by small enterprises in high-technology areas. Because smaller firms often experience difficulties in finding sources of capital, these programs attempt to supply such firms with at least part of their capital needs. Firms were eligible for interest-free loans covering up to one-half of the cost of developing a new technology under the First Innovation Program. In the case that the borrowing firm did not earn a profit on the project within the ensuing decade, the loan did not have to be repaid. The program was abandoned in 1984.

Firms are eligible for three different types of assistance under the Technologically Oriented Firms Program. These include consulting services, grants covering up to three-quarters of the development costs, and loan guarantees for up to four-fifths of the initial capital and marketing costs. In 1980, DM 30 million was targeted to providing capital for innovative firms and in 1984, DM 24 million was targeted for such use (US International Trade Commission, 1984).

Although the West German government accounted for 40 percent of the total expenditures on R&D in 1985, not all of these expenditures can be considered to represent a form of industrial policy. Not only is a significant portion of the R&D expenditures by the government not targeted towards any particular industry, but a sizeable portion is not directed towards commercial applications. By comparison, around 47 percent of the R&D expenditures in the United States came from the public sector (National Science Foundation, 1986b).

The major policymaker for technology and R&D in West Germany is the Bundesministerium für Forschung und Technologie (Federal Ministry for Research and Technology). About 55 percent of all Government R&D funds in 1985 emanated from this ministry, and three years earlier the share was nearly 90 percent of all commercial R&D (Bundesminister für Forschung und Technologie, 1985). The Bundesministerium für Verteidigung (Federal Ministry for Defense) plays as important role in allocating R&D funds. In 1985, it was responsible for nearly 20 percent of West German Federal R&D expenditures. This represented an increase of nearly five percentage points from 1981 and 1982. While the Bundesministerium für Wirtschaft (Federal Ministry of Economics) was responsible for just over 10 percent of 1985 government expenditures on R&D, the Bundesministerium für Bildung and Wissenschaft (Federal Ministry for Education and Science) controlled an additional 7.7 percent.

In 1982, the Bundesministerium für Forschung und Technologie allocated almost four-fifths of its grants to firms, slightly more than 10 percent to independent laboratories, 8 percent to universities and an additional 3 percent to other recipients in 1982. In general, not more than one-half of the funding for a R&D project is financed by the Ministry. Basic research is generally given preference over applied research, and in some cases total funding for a basic research project by the Ministry may be provided. In 1984, the total budget of the Bundesministerium für Forschung und Technologie was DM 7,126.4 million. The largest portion of this, nearly 40 percent, was allocated towards programs relating to energy R&D, and nearly 20 percent was targeted for improving industrial competitiveness. The major projects under this program include further innovation, physical and finishing technology, electronics, data processing, space and aviation. An additional 17.9 percent of the Bundesministerium für Forschung und Technologie budget went towards basic research, including 8.5 percent towards overall science promotion and 9.4 percent towards basic physical and chemical research.

Overall the government of West Germany tends to place a high priority on providing R&D funds for energy and industrial development, especially relative to that of the United States. For example, about 16 percent of West Germany's 1984 federal R&D expenditures was allocated for energy programs, while in the United States only about 8 percent went towards R&D in energy. Similarly, while the West German Government targeted around 12 percent of its R&D budget towards industrial development, there were only minimal expenditures on R&D for industrial development undertaken in the United States. On the other hand, nearly 68 percent of America's federal R&D expenditures went towards defense-related projects, while in West Germany under 10 percent of the Federal R&D budget was allocated towards defense. While both countries allocated around 5 percent of their R&D budgets toward programs involving space, in the United States nearly twice as much of the budget, 12 percent, was spent on health research than in West Germany. From the above it can be seen that the allocation of federal R&D budgets varies considerably between the two countries.

With regard to the total R&D intensity of West Germany, it can be seen that it has been growing at a somewhat faster rate than that of the United States. In 1970, 2.1 percent of gross national product (GNP) was allocated for R&D in West Germany and 2.6 percent in the United States. By 1977, the R&D intensity in the United States had fallen so that it was the same, 2.1 percent in both countries. Subsequently, R&D intensity in both countries has steadily risen. In 1985, the R&D intensity was 2.6 percent in West Germany and 2.7 percent in the United States. However, much of this US increase is due to the acceleration in defense-related R&D expenditures. The R&D intensity for non-defense programs has been greater in West Germany since the mid-1960s. While in 1970, the non-defense R&D intensity was 1.9 percent in West Germany, it was only 1.7 percent in the United States. In fact, the gap has tended to grow over time. By 1979, the non-defense R&D intensity was 2.3 percent in West Germany while it remained at 1.7 percent in the United States. By 1985, the non-defense R&D intensity of 2.5 percent in West Germany had risen to almost one-third of that in the United States, which was 1.9 percent. West Germany apparently tends to emphasize basic research more than does the United States. While 22 percent of West German R&D expenditures was allocated towards basic research, similar expenditures amounted to only 13 percent in the United States. By contrast, the United States tends to emphasize applied research. While 87 percent of US R&D was spent on applied research, the corresponding figure was only 81 percent in West Germany (National Science Foundation, 1986b).

Table 6.2 shows the 1977 composition of R&D expenditures by the West German government along with the total R&D expenditures. The most heavily financed R&D industries are chemicals, steel, mechanical engineering, vehicles, electrical engineering, precision mechanics, optics and electrical engineering. The allocation of government R&D expenditures is apparently not proportional to expenditures by the private firms. For example, while R&D expenditures in the steel, mechanical engineering and vehicles

Table 6.2 West German Federal Government Support of R&D by Industries, 1977

Industry	Total R&D expenditures		Federal Government expenditures		
	DM millions	Percentage of total	DM millions	Percentage of total	Percentage of total R&D expenditures
Energy, water and mining	739.5	4.4	257.1	9.5	34.8
Processing	16,054.9	95.4	2,442.5	90.5	15.2
Chemicals	4,644.5	27.6	165.3	6.1	3.6
Plastics, rubber, asbestos	172.4	1.0	8.8	0.3	5.1
Non-metallic minerals, glass ceramics	109.3	0.7	13.9	0.5	12.7
Iron, non-ferrous metals	393.3	2.3	62.3	2.3	15.8
Steel, mechanical engineering vehicles	5,643.9	33.6	1,265.8	46.6	22.4
Mechanical engineering	1,765.7	10.5	264.0	9.7	15.0
Road vehicles	2,053.9	12.2	—	—	—
Aircraft	1,279.7	7.6	677.1	25.0	52.9
Electrical engineering, precision mechanics, optics	4,869.1	28.9	903.2	33.3	18.5
Electrical engineering	4,461.8	26.5	870.0	32.1	19.5
Precision mechanics	280.7	1.7	32.6	1.2	11.6
Wood, paper, printing	37.5	0.2	8.3	0.3	22.1
Leather, textiles, clothing	38.4	0.2	10.7	0.4	27.9
Food	146.5	0.9	4.2	0.2	2.9
Building	35.4	0.2	13.7	0.5	38.7
Total	16,829.8	100.0	2,713.3	100.0	16.1

Source: US International Trade Commission (1984).

industries accounted for about one-third of total West German R&D expenditures, the R&D expenditures by the federal government in these industries accounted for 46.6 percent of the government's entire R&D budget. By contrast, more than one-quarter of the country's R&D expenditures were in the chemical industry, while those of the government amounted to only 6.1 percent. One-quarter of the federal government expenditures on R&D was expended in the aircraft industry, while only 7.6 percent of the total R&D expenditures went to that industry. Thus, the government accounted for more than half of the R&D expenditures in the airline industry by only 3.6 percent of the R&D expenditures in the chemical industry.

Based on an analysis of the federal budgets between 1983 and 1987, it is clear that the allocation of R&D by the West German government is undergoing a slight change in direction. In 1985, 5 percent of the federal R&D budget was allocated towards information production, representing an increase of more than 12 percent from the previous year. In the field of biotechnology, 1.1 percent of the 1985 federal R&D budget was allocated, representing an increase of more than 14 percent over the previous year. Similarly, the 1.5 percent of the budget which was devoted towards materials research was an increase of nearly 18 percent over the preceding year. At the same time, government R&D expenditures on physical technology and on chemical processes were reduced by nearly 11 and 8 percent, respectively, from the previous year. While the planned annual growth rate in West German Federal R&D expenditures between 1983 and 1987 was just over 2 percent the increase in the allocation towards R&D for production technology was nearly 37 percent. Similarly, the planned annual increase in R&D for basic research in the natural science areas was 10 percent, and in biotechnology it was 6 percent (National Science Foundation, 1986b).

In addition to the government institutions, certain non-profit research institutions play a major role in shaping the science and technology policies in West Germany. Perhaps the most important of these is the Max Planck-Gesellschaft (Max Planck Society). The Max-Planck-Gesellschaft is financed predominately through funding from the federal government as well as the Länder. In 1983, the Max-Planck-Gesellschaft had a total budget of about ⁻365.1 million, most of which was allocated towards basic research. In particular, the Max-Planck-Gesellschaft tends to emphasize cooperative research with the Universities. Also a non-profit institution, the Fraunhofer Gesellschaft tends to focus on applied research. In 1985, the Fraunhofer Gesellschaft had a budget of about DM 400 million and a staff of over 3,500. R&D is performed there cooperatively with both private firms and the federal government, and has recently been involved in programs involving microelectronics, automation, production technology, industrial robots, materials developments, and biotechnology and gene technology. The reason for this overlap with the federal government is clear. In 1983 over half of the budget of the Fraunhofer Gesellschaft came from the federal government and

Länder, while 40 percent came from private contracts. In West Germany, there are also a number of large-scale national laboratories which are financed virtually totally through government funds. In 1983, the budgets of these so-called independent research institutes totalled $1,624.2 billion (Bundesministerium für Forschung und Technologie, 1985).

The composition of total assistance and subsidies to West German manufacturing industries is shown in Table 6.3. The aircraft industry was the largest beneficiary of federal targeting, with more than 23 percent of the domestic subsidies. Printing and publishing accounted for 4.4 percent of the subsidies; non-ferrous metals accounted for an additional 2.4 percent. Among the least subsidized sectors were rubber and asbestos and leather, including leather goods and shoes.

INDUSTRIAL POLICY IN THE UNITED KINGDOM

As in West Germany, the United Kingdom's industrial policy did not really begin to enjoy a prominent place until the mid-1960s. Unlike Japan, which made the greatest use of targeting policies directly following the Second World War, such policies lay dormant in the United Kingdom for nearly two decades. Perhaps the first signs of industrial targeting appeared with the financial aid targeted by the Conservative government in the early 1960s to industries such as aircraft, cotton, ocean shipping and shipbuilding (Denton, 1976). When the Labor Government assumed power in 1964, industrial targeting continued during the government's reign through to 1970. With passage of the 1967 Industrial Expansion Bill and Industrial Reorganization Act, the Labor government established a mandate permitting it to engage in industrial targeting without the explicit permission of Parliament. The Industrial Reorganization Act was an attempt to increase economic efficiency by encouraging mergers. Between 1970 and 1974, the Conservative government sought to dismantle some of the industrial policy programs already implemented, leading to the abolition of the Industrial Reorganization Act. However, it was the same Conservative government which was responsible for saving Rolls Royce and Upper Clyde Shipbuilders from what appeared to be impending ruin. Additionally, passage of the Industry Act (1972) permitted financial assistance to be channelled to industries. While Section 7 of the Act gives the government power to provide interest relief grants and low-interest loans, Section 8 enables it to provide general investment incentives along with aid to specific industries. Sixteen industries were the recipients of subsidies under Section 8 between 1972 and 1978. These included wool, textiles, clothing, ferrous foundries, machine tools, red-meat slaughterhouses, paper and board, textile machinery, printing machinery, poultry meat processing, non-ferrous foundries, electric components, instrumen-

Table 6.3 Composition of Federal Subsidies to West German Manufacturing Industries, 1974[a]

Industry	Regional programs	Domestic Subsidies All other	Total
Stone and clay products	0.8	0.3	1.1
Basic iron and steel	0.4	0.2	0.6
Foundries	0.6	0.1	0.7
Rolling mills	0.5	0.1	0.6
Nonferrous metals	2.1	0.3	2.4
Chemicals	0.5	0.8	1.3
Saw mills	1.1	1.1	2.2
Pulp, paper, paperboard	0.7	0.2	0.9
Rubber and asbestos	0.5	0.1	0.6
Structural engineering	1.0	0.4	1.4
Machinery	0.5	0.8	1.3
Road motor vehicles	0.6	0.2	0.8
Aircraft	0.1	23.4	23.5
Electrical equipment	1.9	0.8	2.7
Precision mechanics, optics, watches	0.9	0.8	1.7
Fabricated metal products	1.1	0.2	1.3
Precision ceramics, pottery	0.9	0.2	1.1
Glass	0.6	0.3	0.9
Woodworking	0.8	0.0	0.8
Musical instruments, toys etc.	0.7	0.0	0.7
Paper products	0.6	0.2	0.8
Printing and publishing	0.6	3.8	4.4
Plastic products	1.1	0.2	1.3
Leather, leather goods, shoes	0.2	0.3	0.5
Textiles	0.7	0.6	1.3
Clothing	1.2	0.6	1.8

[a] Based on industry value added.
Source: Glismann and Weiss (1980).

tation and automation, drop-forging, footwear, energy conservation and microelectronics (US International Trade Commission, 1984).

From 1974 until 1979, the Labor government was again in power. There was an expansion of planning during this time and in 1975 the National Enterprise Board was created with the purpose of serving as a holding company for many nationalized firms. While the shipbuilding and aircraft industries became nationalized in 1977, 'working parties' – consisting of representatives from the government, the firms and labor unions – were organized in thirty-seven industries which encompassed around 40 percent of the total output in manufacturing in the United Kingdom (Grant, 1982; Davenport, 1983). With the appearance of the Conservative government under Margaret Thatcher in 1979 came a significant move towards denationalization. The amount of aid channeled to industries through targeting programs has declined substantially under the Thatcher government.

In 1976, £4,126 million of financial assistance were allocated to industries, accounting for 2 percent of gross domestic product (GDP), with such subsidies rising to £4,970 million in 1980, accounting for 2.2 percent of GDP. By 1982, the Thatcher government had been able to reduce the amount of financial assistance to £4,477 million, which accounted for 2 percent of GDP (US International Trade Commission, 1984). In 1980, 17 percent of the government financial aid was targeted towards the mechanical engineering industry, and an additional 15 percent both to the metal industry and to the electrical engineering industry. However, in terms of value added, the electrical engineering industry was nearly two-and-one-half times as large as the metal industry, while the mechanical engineering industry was nearly four times as large as the metal industry. By contrast, only 4 percent of the financial aid was targeted to the food, drink, and tobacco industry, despite the fact that it was almost as large as the mechanical engineering industry.

Unlike West Germany and Japan, the United Kingdom has not typically employed tax policy as an instrument for implementing industrial policy. While the tax system has been used to stimulate investment and R&D, these policies usually cannot be considered to constitute a type of targeting practice because they have not been industry-specific. The single major exception has been in shipbuilding, where the industry has received special tax treatment.

When the Industrial Development Act (1982) was passed, the original Section 8 of the Industry Act (1972) was preserved. Section 8 enables the government to channel funds for capital investment. Because the government sought to restrict targeting under Section 8 to firms that would not undertake the capital investment in the absence of such subsidies, a substantial part of the aid went to multinational corporations. Multinational corporations threatened to relocate their investment unless the aid was granted. Thus, to channel some of the funds under Section 8 to small- and medium-sized firms, a loan-guarantee program for small firms was established. Under the general criteria of the Industrial Development Act (1982), £257 million in grants were directed to industries. The biggest beneficiary was the mechanical engineering industry, which received nearly one-quarter of all the financial assistance. While the electrical engineering industry received an additional 20 percent of the funds, the chemical, metal and motor vehicles industries each received slightly more than 10 percent of the total outlays. The industries that enjoyed the least amount of aid included the food, drink and tobacco, metal goods, and bricks, pottery and glass industries.

The Selective Investment program, which was established to encourage capital investment, is typically limited to investments exceeding £500,000. Generally, around one-tenth of a project's costs is funded. As of 1983, more than £1,043 million in grants under the selective Investment program has been directed to private firms. Nearly 55 percent of these funds went to the chemical industry, with an additional 10 percent having been channelled into the paper, printing, and publishing industry. By contrast, clothing received just 0.5 percent of the aid, and timber and furniture just 0.1 percent. In 1981, the Loan Guarantee program for Small Business was established. Designed to aid small enterprises, the Program operates as follows: the government guarantees four-fifths of the value of a loan for a quarterly premium of 3 percent of the loans's outstanding balance. By 1983, over £300 million in loans had been guaranteed under this program.

Section 8 also provides for sector-specific targeting. These programs are shown in Table 6.4. There has been an apparent shift in the type of industry in which these programs have been undertaken. Under the Labor government, the programs tended to occur in industries in the mature and declining stages of the product life cycle. Subsequent to the Thatcher government, the programs have become more oriented towards industries in the introduction and growth stages of the product life cycle. For example, of the eight sector-specific programs initiated since 1979, one has been in the coal industry, two have been oriented towards helping chronically depressed industries with the restructuring process through capacity reduction, four have focused on encouraging innovation in high-technology sectors, and one fosters the purchases of high-technology equipment by small engineering firms.

Of particular interest are some of the more recent sectoral aid programs. The Flexible Manufacturing Systems Scheme provides grants covering up to one-third of the installation costs of flexible manufacturing systems. In addition, up to one-half of consulting fees are covered by grant money for consultants who have been approved by the Department of Trade and Industry. A similar program is the Robot Support Program in the robotics industry, which also pays for one-third of the cost of installing robots. The Small Engineering Firms Investment Scheme is oriented towards small enterprises (fewer than 200 employees) with difficulties in purchasing capital equipment. The program enables eligible firms to receive a grant of up to one-third of the cost of the project. While the first Small Engineering Firms Investment Scheme, which expired in 1983, was given only £31.3 million to allocate, the second Scheme, which lasted until 1986, was given $100 million. Similarly, the Computer-Aided Design and Test Equipment Program allocates grants of up to £60,000 where up to one-third of the costs of purchasing and installing computer-aided equipment is provided.

Of the programs for the declining sector, the Private-Sector Steel Plan, provides three types of aid to facilitate the restructuring and adjustment process. First, dislocated employees are eligible for compensation of up to 85 percent of their wages. Second, grants are awarded which cover up to one-fourth of the costs of closing or restructuring a plant. Third, grants of up to one-quarter of the industry payments are provided in a fund to pay the costs of closing plants (US International Trade Commission, 1984).

Like West Germany and the United States, the United Kingdom provides a substantial amount of public funds for R&D in following its science and

Table 6.4 Sectoral Aid Programs Under Section 8, 1972–1983

Program	Date introduced		Final date for applications		Total cost of assisted projects[a]	Aid offered[a]	Payments made
Wool textiles							
Stage 1	July	1973	December	1975	74,810	16,675	16,183
Stage 2	November	1976	December	1977	30,494	7,500	6,194
Ferrous foundry	August	1975	December	1976	284,457	61,930	47,899
Machine tools	August	1975	December	1977	168,154	34,388	22,899
Clothing	October	1975	December	1977	93,450	20,872	13,878
Paper and board	June	1976	June	1978	86,986	20,250	18,725
Non-ferrous foundry	January	1977	July	1978	101,324	21,712	11,796
Electronic components	January	1977	December	1978	59,200	15,995	11,700
Instrumentation and automation	November	1977	April	1979	50,120	8,484	6,844
Drop forging	November	1977	June	1979	24,361	5,841	4,044
Footwear	April	1978	March	1980	29,227	5,032	3,226
Printing machinery	August	1976	December	1977	73,256	14,116	8,795
Textile machinery	August	1976	December	1977	66,660	12,781	6,270
Poultry meat processing	August	1976	March	1977	42,986	8,552	7,869
Red-meat slaughterhouse	November	1976	November	1980	116,156	16,182	11,490
Microelectronic support	July	1978	March	1985	141,727	33,881	11,086
Coal firing	May	1981	December	1983	62,187	11,885	1,814
Private-sector steel	December	1981	June	1984	53,747	15,521	10,325
Small engineering firms investment	March	1982	May	1982	93,795	31,265	10,918
Flexible manufacturing systems	June	1982			4,223	1,419	0
Robotics	August	1982			3,929	1,284	0
Fiber optics	July	1981	July	1986	14,210	1,300	0
Computer-aided design and test equipment	August	1982	August	1982	26,760	6,560	389
Steel castings	December	1981			19,147	6,504	6,504

[a]In units of £ thousands.
Source: US International Trade Commission (1984).

technology policy. However, like the United States, the majority of these funds are not targeted towards particular industries and therefore cannot be considered to be part of any particular industrial policy. Still, there remains an element of industry-specific targeting within the overall technology and science policy of the British government. Most recently the government has been giving preference to the aerospace and electronics industries because of their strategic importance.

Total R&D expenditures increased from £0.68 billion in 1961 to £1.07 billion in 1969, £2.30 billion in 1975 and £6.79 billion in 1983. However, as a percentage of GNP, the R&D intensity in the United Kingdom has actually been declining since 1961. The R&D–GNP ratio of 2.47 percent in 1961 fell to 2.27 percent in 1969, 2.19 percent in 1975 and finally to 2.24 percent in 1983. This represents a R&D intensity considerably lower than that in West Germany, Japan or the United States. Similarly, while there was an average of 35.8 scientists and engineers[13] per 10,000 labor force population engaged in R&D in the United Kingdom in 1981, there were 62.7 in the United States, 46.8 in West Germany and 55.6 in Japan (National Science Board, 1985). Even when considering the non-defense R&D expenditures, the United Kingdom lags behind that of its major international competitors. While the non-defense R&D expenditures as a percentage of GNP was 1.61 in 1983 in the United Kingdom, it was 2.60 in Japan, 2.47 in West Germany and 1.91 in the United States. Further, while there were 34,223 patents granted in the United States in 1981, there were 6,188 granted in Japan, 3,967 granted in West Germany and only 1,264 granted in the United Kingdom.

Of the total United Kingdom R&D expenditures in 1981, about 50 percent were financed by the government in the electronics industry and 68 percent were government-supported in the aerospace industry. This compares to an average of about one-third of R&D coming from government sources for all of manufacturing. Further, only one percent of total R&D expenditures in the chemical and motor vehicles industries came from government institutions. Thus, the extent to which the government has been involved in financing R&D has tended to be concentrated in just a few key industries. Most of the public R&D expenditures in manufacturing industries come from the Department of Trade and Industry. In 1982, the Department had a total budget of more than £268 million. About one-fifth of this was allocated to the electronics and information technology sector. In particular, half of these funds went towards computing, communications, consumer and capital electronics, while instrumentation and control along with electronic components received smaller shares. Another fifth of the budget of the Department of Trade and Industry was allocated towards space technology; 11.6 percent was directed towards civil aircraft. While 13.1 percent of the budget was oriented towards the mechanical and electrical engineering sectors, an additional 6.8 percent went towards materials and chemicals.

Five types of subsidies are provided under the Support of Innovation Program. The first is product and process development aid, which generally consists of a grant of 33 percent of the project costs. The second is longer-term R&D aid, which is more oriented towards applied research than basic research. The third is production launch aid, which consists of grants up to 20 percent of the start-up costs. The fourth is aid for pre-production orders, in which the Department of Trade and Industry purchases a product that is being introduced, and then permits potential buyers to use the product on a trial basis. Finally, aid for market studies is also provided in a grant covering up to one-third of the costs. Under this program £280 million have recently been awarded to the information technology industry to subsidize collaborative research as well as to promote the development and production of new products and processes. Similarly, £170 million have been awarded to the microelectronics industry for applications in manufacturing, and for research, investment, launch and application. Other awards have been given recently to the robots, software, fiber optics and optoelectronics, biotechnology and flexible manufacturing systems industries (US International Trade Commission, 1984).

NATIONALIZATION IN FRANCE

The distinguishing feature about industrial policy in France, compared to the other EEC countries and Japan, is the extent to which government planning and nationalization of industry has occurred during the post-war period. During this time, the French established the system of indicative planning, which provides a framework of planning through a system of government initiatives. At the heart of this indicative system of planning are consultations made among major economic institutions encompassing the firms, labor unions, government officials and the Planning Commission (Brown, 1980). Under the first plan, between 1946 and 1951, six basic sectors for priority were targeted. These were the coal, steel, transportation, agricultural machinery, cement and electricity sectors. While the second and third plans, which lasted until 1961, did not define particular sections for priority treatment, the fourth plan identified certain investment targets. Industrial policy began to emerge during the fifth plan, which was implemented between 1966 and 1970, and in which three specific policies were emphasized to promote efficiency. The first was the active encouragement of mergers and cartelization. The second was an exemption of selected firms from regulations to induce additional capital investment, especially on R&D. Finally, there was an attempt to place a high priority on a few high-technology projects and to target resources into those projects.

The next two plans, which lasted from 1971 to 1980, continued the state's intervention in the several targeted high-technology sectors, such as computers, electronics, telecommunications, machinery and chemicals. The Concorde and Airbus were among the successful results of these projects. In 1982, the most recent plan was announced, which established the modernization of the declining industries and attainment of international competitiveness in the high-technology industries as highest priorities.

Although nationalization began immediately following the Second World War – when the electricity, gas and coal industries were put under government control, along with the Bank of France, four deposit banks, thirty-two insurance companies and the Renault automobile company – nationalization under the newly elected socialist government of Mitterrand was extended even further. Actually, at the time of the 1981 nationalizations, significant firms in the petroleum, computer, aerospace, telecommunications, electricity, gas, railroad, seaport and airport industries had already been nationalized by earlier governments. The 1981 nationalizations consisted of thirty-six banks and five major industrial groups. Subsequently, around 50 percent of all investment in manufacturing occurred in nationalized firms, and about one-quarter of the labor force worked in nationalized companies.

The formation of twelve so-called 'competitive sector groups' occurred subsequent to the 1981 nationalizations. The government arranged for much of the financing of these groups both from the federal budget and from the banks. One of the major motivations underlying the nationalizations was the chronic under-investment which had occurred in most of these sectors prior to 1981. In fact, only one of the companies in the groups, Compagnie Générale d'Electricité, was profitable in 1982. Thus, in 1983 the government arranged for FF 20.53 billion ($2.3 billion) to be channeled into these industries, of which FF 15.16 billion ($1.7 billion) was out of the federal budget and the rest from the banks. In particular, the Sacilor group in the steel industry received FF 3.51 billion from the government, and the petrochemical Kuhlman group in the aluminum industry received FF 2.40 billion from the federal budget. Similarly, the Rhone-Poulenc group in the chemicals industry received FF 1.20 billion, and Renault in the automobile industry an additional FF 1 billion from the government. Other groups to receive funds from the federal budget included Thomson-Brandt in telecommunications, CII-Bull in computers, Compagnie Générale d'Electricité in heavy electrical equipment, Saint-Gobain in glass and SNECMA in aeroengineering (US International Trade Commission, 1984).

What distinguishes industrial policy in France from that in West Germany, the United Kingdom and Japan, is that the government has undertaken means of direct assistance through nationalization rather than indirect assistance, such as subsidized, low interest rate loans, etc. That is, where industrial policy has to be implemented through indirect instruments in the other countries, in France funds can be directly allocated to the appropriate firms. Along with nationalization in 1981 has come an increased priority for targeting resources in the traditional industries, such as steel, shipbuilding, petrochemicals and non-ferrous metals. The goal of industrial policy in these sectors is to encourage an orderly restructuring through reduced capacity. For example, facing the burden of a long-term debt of approximately FF 40 billion when it was nationalized in 1978, the French steel industry has received approximately FF 30 billion to help bring about an orderly reduction of capacity. Employment was thus reduced from about 160,000 in 1975 to 97,000 in 1981, and to around 85,000 in 1986.

A second goal of French industrial policy has been to promote international competitiveness in traditional manufacturing industries such as textiles, clothing, footwear, leather and machine tools. In particular, government funds to encourage and support R&D within their industries has played an important role. For example, the government recently allocated FF 1.2 billion for the establishment of an association in the textile industry which engages in cooperative R&D. And, like its West German and UK counterparts, French industrial policy is finally concerning itself with developing the high- and new-technology industries, such as data-processing, aerospace, microelectronics, telecommunications and biotechnology. For example, the Programme Plurame en Faveur de la Filière Electronic is a plan to increase the annual growth in the telecommunications, computer, and electronics industries by between 3 and 9 percent over the next decade. To implement this policy, FF 55 billion will be targeted by the government into the electronics industry.

Certain tax policies have been used as instruments of industrial targeting. With the new government in 1981 came an investment tax deduction which enabled a firm to deduct 15 percent of its expenditures on capital goods in 1982, 10 percent in 1983 and 5 percent in 1984. However, to receive the deduction, small firms, defined as those with less than 100 employees, had to at least maintain their size, and large firms had to expand their employment. To encourage consolidation in an effort to realize scale economies, the government has provided for a special tax measure for acquisitions. Under the Interministerial Committee on Industrial Restructuring, there were around 140 mergers fostering restructuring by 1983. An example of an industry-specific tax policy is in the textile industry, where the government has granted a reduction in social security taxes by nearly one-third since 1982.

The government also tends to dominate the financial system in France. Through the Encadrement de Crédit, the government is able to influence the registered banks, virtually all of which have been owned by the government since 1981. Under the system of nationalization, the bank have played a key role in allocating resources to selected firms and industries. In 1982, the banks channeled nearly FF 6 billion to key industries, of which 50 percent were loans at favorable interest rates. The government has also established the Crédit d'Equipement des PME, which provides loans to small- and medium-sized firms for the purposes of capital investment. In 1982, nearly FF 19 billion was allocated to small- and medium-sized firms through this government agency.

The government has also used industrial policy to promote R&D expenditures in six 'industries of the future', which include bioengineering, marine industries, robotics, electronic office equipment, consumer electronics and alternative energy technologies. To promote the acceleration of innovation and technological change in these key industries, the government merged the Ministry of Research with the Ministry of Industry. With a total budget of $300 million in 1982, the new ministry was responsible for improving the technological performance of the high-technology industries. Similarly, the Technological R&D Orientation Act of 1982 called for an increase in annual R&D expenditures approaching 10 percent for the mid-1980s. In addition, the Act established Public Interest Groups in which private firms could engage in cooperative innovation projects. Finally, the 1983 Finance Act enabled firms to claim a tax credit which was the equivalent of one-quarter of the increase in the firm's R&D expenditures.

Like its counterparts in West Germany and the United Kingdom, the French government has actively promoted joint R&D enterprises. Some of these projects have extended beyond national boundaries. The Concorde, for example, was the result of a joint venture with the United Kingdom, and the Airbus, the result of a joint venture with West Germany.

CONCLUSION

To draw a conclusion concerning the effectiveness of industrial targeting in the EEC would be virtually impossible at this point. Not only are the different member nations too diverse, but their approaches to industrial policy are also too diverse to facilitate easy generalizations. While France has pursued a policy built around nationalized industries, the United Kingdom is reducing its ownership of industry. At the same time, industrial targeting shows no signs of waning in West Germany. A precise analysis concerning the advisability of such targeting practices would have to address a counterfactual question: 'How strong would the economies of the EEC countries have been in the absence of such industrial policies?' That is, while the performance of the high-technology industries in the EEC countries is apparently lagging behind its counterparts in the United States and Japan, it is not at all clear that this is the result of any industrial targeting policies. In fact, member countries have generally based their policies on the goal of achieving technological parity with the United States and Japan in these key industries. That is, in the absence of such industrial policies it is conceivable that the performance of European countries in the high-technology industries would have been weaker. Thus, it is the hope of policymakers in most of the member countries that through the constant direction of resources into key industries, technological progress can be accelerated.

One of the dangers of pursuing industrial targeting policies is the tendency to try to impose an industrial structure on either an industry or a sector that may be efficient for a different country (the United States or Japan, for example), or in a previous time-period. That is, while Servan-Schreiber (1968) called for European industrial policies as a means of meeting the challenge of US-dominated large-scale multinational corporations, it is not clear that the same type of large-scale conglomerate firm is the most efficient form of enterprise for producing the new- and high-technology products. While large enterprises which could exploit scale economies were undoubtedly the most efficient form of enterprise in the heavy industries during the 1950s and 1960s, recent empirical evidence suggests that small firms may be more efficient than their large counterparts in the high-technology industries (Acs and Audretsch, 1986c, 1987). Thus, to the extent to which European industrial policies are directed at promoting large-scale enterprises and cooperative R&D agreements, economic institutions which would have excelled in the 1960s, but may not be appropriately suited for the 1980s and 1990s, are being fostered. Perhaps the ultimate weakness of industrial targeting is that, while it can promote the achievement of a pre-determined goal through the direction of productive resources, the validity of the goal, *a priori*, can never be certain.

NOTES

1. In 1984 a European Currency Unit (ECU) was the equivalent of DM 2.239, £0.589 Sterling, 6.871 French Francs, 1.380.4000 Lira, 2.522 Guilders, 45.633 Belgian Francs, 45.633 Luxembourg Francs, 8.163 Danish Kroner, £0.727 Irish and 87.82 Drachmas (Pinder, 1986).
2. *The Economist* 18 June 1983, p. 65.
3. *Ibid.*
4. Commission of the European Communities, 1983, p. 109.
5. *Ibid.*, p. 113.
6. *Ibid.*, p. 114.
7. OJL 227, 19 August 1983.
8. OJL 137, 23 May 1982.
9. OJL 137, 26 May 1983, p. 24.
10. The case was brought under the second subparagraph of Article 93(2) EEC.
11. OJL 200, 17 August 1983.
12. State Governments.
13. Includes all scientists and engineers engaged in R&D on a full-time equivalent basis.

7· INDUSTRIAL TARGETING IN JAPAN

Of all its government policies, industrial targeting in Japan remains perhaps the most controversial. Some critics suggest that Japanese industrial targeting constitutes an 'unfair' policy which has led not only to the domination of several key markets by Japanese firms, but that the ascent to market leadership would not have otherwise occurred. For example, the US Semiconductor Industry Association (1983, p. 5) charges:

> Targeting, with all of its ramifications, has fundamentally distorted free market competition and threatens the long-term viability of many firms in the US. A number of steps should be taken by the US government to offset the impact of current and past Japanese government policies. . . . Without the Japanese government's actions to protect and support its domestic industry, it is unlikely that Japanese firms would have been as successful in challenging the US industry. The US government must now act to assure that this government assistance does not lead to further erosion of US competitiveness.

In line with this view has been the call to Western nations, such as the United States, to develop their own sets of industrial targeting. For example, Reich (1983) and Piore and Sabel (1984) suggest that only through some analgous form of directed centralized resource allocation can the United States regain its international competitiveness. Still other critics suggest that Japanese targeting practices had no decisive impact in determining the industrial structure of Japan. It is argued that those industries which gained international competitiveness would have done so without the existence of industrial targeting (Saxonhouse, 1982).

The purpose of this chapter is to examine the role of industrial targeting in Japanese manufacturing industries. In particular, the instruments for targeting which have been deployed, the reasons and rationale underlying targeting, the experience in several industries, and the impact that targeting has had will be explored. Industrial targeting is considered to be 'coordinated government actions that direct productive resources to give domestic producers in selected industries a competitive advantage.' This is the definition used by the US International Trade Commission (1983b, p. 1). The US International Trade Commission (1983b) considers four elements to be central to targeting: (1) governments must undertake the targeting; (2) targeting must involve directing productive resources; (3) only those policies which apply to specific industries and not homogeneously across all industries are considered to be targeting; and (4) the goal of targeting is to bestow the domestic producers with an international competitive advantage.

The second section of this chapter addresses the foundations of Japanese industrial targeting. The historical evolution of industrial policy in Japan is examined, along with the major institutions which implement industrial targeting. The following section examines the factors which are evaluated in determining which industries should be the recipients of targeting practices. This is followed by an examination of the major instruments used for targeting, including science and technology policies, tax policies and lending policies. In the next section, the actual targeting practices which have been implemented in certain key industries, including iron and steel, automobiles, aluminum, machine tools, aircraft, telecommunications, semiconductors, computers and robotics are explored. An empirical examination of the effect of targeting practices on the US–Japanese bilateral trade balance is then provided. There does appear to be empirical evidence consistent with the hypothesis that those industries which were targeted exhibited a more superior trade performance vis-à-vis the United States, than did those which were not. Finally, conclusions and a summary are presented in the last section.

THE FOUNDATIONS OF JAPANESE INDUSTRIAL POLICY

At the core of the motivations underlying Japanese industrial policy is the country's inherent lack of natural resources. To suggest that Japan is 'not blessed with land and resources' (Ueno, 1980, p. 375) is an understatement. In fact, it has been estimated that Japan's self-sufficiency rate for food is 75 percent, for petroleum 0.3 percent and for energy 15 percent.[1] Not only is land a scarce resource in Japan, but it is constantly exposed to the danger of earthquakes, typhoons and floods, which reduces its value and reliability that much more. The inherent scarcity of raw materials made it necessary for Japan to develop an export industry, thereby enabling the importation of essential raw materials. Through the exportation of fabricated goods, the importation of natural resources was feasible. Because a viable export industry was essential for survival, the Ministry of International Trade and Industry (MITI) argued shortly after the Second World War that it was necessary to protect and nurture key industries, starting with automobiles, to facilitate the requisite 'catching up' with the United States.[2] Thus, the principle underlying Japanese industrial policy has been described as a mandate to 'place undeveloped domestic industries with little competitive power under government's active interference and to build up a large-scale production system, while limiting entry into the domestic market of foreign enterprises with already established mass production systems and restricting the competition of foreign manufacturing in the domestic market' (Ueno, 1980, p. 396).

The post-war economic reforms introduced during the occupation period between 1945 and 1952 played a major role in providing the institutional structures required for the implementation of industrial policies.[3] Although the explicit goal of the post-war economic reforms was the 'democratization' of the Japanese economy, these reforms constituted the subsequent framework for government intervention in the private economy. Both the Anti-Monopoly Law, passed in April 1947, and the Elimination of Excessive Concentration of Economic Power Law, passed in December 1947, were aimed at the dissolution of the *zaibatsu*, the family-dominated holding companies in Japan. By separating property ownership from management control, the resulting inter-firm competition, which has been typical of post-war Japan, was assured. Similarly, the foundation for post-war labor-management negotiations was established with passage of the Trade Union Law in December 1945, the Labor Relations Adjustment Law in September 1946 and the Labor Standards Law in 1947. Finally, the Land Reform Act transferred the land rights of absentee landlords to tenant farmers, which resulted in not only tremendous gains in agricultural productivity, but also in 'an overwhelmingly conservative political stance among the farmers, which worked as the strong backbone of the conservative party governments' (Suzumura and Okuno-Fujiwara, 1986).

A major step was taken to provide a mechanism for industrial policy when the Industrial Rationalization Council[4] was established in December 1949. The mission of the Industrial Rationalization Council, set up as an advisory board under MITI, was to facilitate a consensus among the government, private firms and labor on how best to implement industrial rationalization plans. This made possible an exchange among the major economic participants in a non-adversarial framework. However, it was not until the Korean War in 1950 that Japanese industrial policy was soundly established. The Japan Development Bank, having taken over from the Reconstruction Finance Bank, made it possible for certain industries to obtain loans at low-interest rates to be used for investment in plants and equipment. Similarly, the Japan Export-Import Bank was given the responsibility of encouraging exports by channeling resources to firms with the potential for significant exports. With the enactment of the Promotion of Industry Rationalization Law, a special accelerated system for depreciated plant and equipment was instituted with the goal being to encourage investment. And, with the expiration of the Temporary Law on the Adjustment of Supply and Demand of Goods, the government lost explicit controls over the Japanese economy, resulting in 'the end of transition period from the directly controlled economy to the government-assisted competitive market economy' (Suzumura and Okuno-Fujiwara, 1986, p. 11).

Subsequently, industrial policy in Japan has been facilitated by four major institutions – the Economic Planning Agency, MITI, the Ministry of Finance and the Bank of Japan. The Economic Planning Agency falls under the direction of the office of the Prime Minister, with its Director having cabinet rank. The major task of the Economic Planning Agency is to determine the major and significant macroeconomic goals for the economy, incorporating national output, investment, trade and price levels, as well as the government's budget. While these plans generally are formulated using a five-year time horizon, they are also used to facilitate consensus-building. The nine economic plans implemented since the war have included goals such as the modernization of production facilities, the promotion of heavy industries, the reduction of dependence on imports, the promotion of exports, the improvement of infrastructure, the rectification of the dual structure of the economy, the modernization of low-productivity sectors, the stabilization of prices and the promotion of social development.[5]

Of all the government agencies implementing and formulating Japanese industrial policy, MITI stands at the center of attention. MITI has been given the responsibility or trade policy, environmental regulation, regulation of distribution systems, patent policy, energy and natural resource policy, regulation of electric power and gas utilities, small business and regional development, as well as industrial policy. MITI has typically relied upon moral suasion and voluntary compliance with their directives, a policy which has generally but not always proven successful. For example, in the 1960s MITI was unable to compel the automobile companies to consolidate, and it also failed in its attempt to force the computer industry to unite in the 1970s.

The significance of MITI's role in the Japanese economy is revealed by its budget, which totalled 791.2 billion yen ($3.6 billion) in 1982, and accounted for almost 2 percent of the General Account budget for that year (US International Trade Commission, 1983b). At the heart of MITI's policy formulation has been the Industrial Policy Bureau. The first step is deliberation by the Industrial Structure Council, which was designed to serve as an advisory body to the Industry Structure Division. The Council, which consists of representatives from government, industry, labor, universities and consumer groups, was created in 1961 and is the major source of the long-range plans central to MITI policy. While the Economic Planning Agency generally focuses upon more general macroeconomic issues, MITI plans typically identify specific sectors or even industries which should be targeted for growth.

The major function of the Ministry of Finance with respect to industrial policy is to direct the flow of capital into targeted industries by controlling both the non-governmental as well as the government financial institutions. Similarly, through its influence over the government's budget, and the Fiscal Investment and Loan Program section in particular, the Ministry of Finance has a considerable impact on Japanese industrial policy. Between 1978 and

1982, the budget of the Fiscal Investment and Loan Program ranged between 41 and 44 percent of the General Account Budget, explaining why the government has accounted for between 20 and 30 percent of gross domestic capital formation during the post-war period.

As Ueno (1980) notes, much of Japanese industrial policy is not directly based upon law. This is particularly true for the types of administrative guidance which have been directed by MITI. Thus, while some fifty-eight new laws concerning trade and industrial policy were passed between 1952 and 1965, over fifty administrative directives of significant consequence were issued by MITI. However, this is in accordance with Article 3 of the law that established MITI, which explicitly stated that 'the Ministry of International Trade and Industry shall be an administrative organ that will assume the responsibility of carrying out as one body the following national administrative affairs and activities: (1) the promotion and regulation of commerce and the supervision of foreign exchange accompanying commerce; (2) the promotion, improvement, regulation, and inspection of the production, distribution, and consumption of mineral and industrial goods'.[6] Similarly, Article 9 instructed MITI that 'The following affairs shall be administered by the Industrial Policy Bureau: (1) devising policies and plans related to the overall supply and demand of goods that are handled within the domain of the MITI as well as basic policies and plans related to commerce, mining, and manufacturing; (2) improving the industrial structure concerned with operations within the domain of MITI and, in addition, matters related to the rationalization of enterprises.' Thus, the legal statutes provided MITI with an implicit mandate for broad administrative guidance.

Once the principle of government intervention to protect and nurture developing industries was accepted, mechanisms for selecting target industries and policy instruments had to be formulated. With the goal of developing viable export industries, MITI adapted two guiding principles in selecting key industries to be the recipients of industrial policy. First, the anticipated future growth in demand had to be sufficient to facilitate mass production and mass sales. Second, the industry had to have the potential for gaining the comparative advantage, implying that it should be skilled-labor intensive. Based on these criteria, MITI selected capital-intensive and technical-intensive industries, such as iron and steel, petroleum refining, petrochemicals, automobiles and industrial machinery as key industries (Krause and Sekiguchi, 1976). In 1950, MITI issued a list of thirty-three industries that were targeted for technological improvements. With the exception of three consumer products in the pharmaceuticals industry, the industries were in heavy manufacturing. Four years later, electronics, jet aircraft and machine tools were added to the list (Peck and Tamura 1976).

Thus, Japanese industrial policy was guided by the need to develop a viable social and economic infrastructure: 'In order to promote growth, critical sectors – those that by their links to other industries can affect the entire economy – were treated as a form of industrial infrastructure, and treated as the equivalent of roads and bridges in other countries' (Zysman and Cohen, 1983, p. 1118). In fact, the Vice-Minister for MITI has defended this goal: 'In this way, like countless rivulets eventually joining together to become one large river, small amounts of capital were gathered together to be channeled, in concentration, into growth industries' (Ojimi, 1972, p. 16).

In evaluating whether or not to target an industry, MITI has tended to focus on four factors – the stage of production, the infrastructure effect, industry scale economies and the necessity of the product to the economy. Thus, MITI has typically favoured industries in the final stages of the production process, or those industries in which the ratio of value added to the value-of-shipments was relatively low. This reflected MITI's assessment that Japanese industries could never effectively compete in the world market based on raw materials or primary goods. Rather, MITI invested its hope in products utilizing relatively high-skilled labour and high levels of technological competency. Since Japan could never develop its natural resource base, MITI relied on the development of human capital and technological resources. Thus, computers, telecommunications equipment, aerospace and medical electronics are all examples of industries utilizing high levels of human capital and technological knowledge, and at the same time requiring relatively few raw materials.

Industries selected for targeting also tended to be those which contributed to the Japanese economic infrastructure. That is, MITI preferred to target intermediate producer goods over final consumer goods. Industries such as ceramics, biotechnology and microelectronics, all of which are used as inputs by other major existing industries such as chemicals, machinery, automobile, computers and consumer electronics, were preferred targets for industrial policy.

Government targeting also favored those industries in which the minimum efficient scale (MES), or the minimum level of output at which a firm attained the minimum average cost, was relatively high. These industries exhibiting large scale economies tend to be highly capital-intensive, such as steel, autos and aluminum. Finally, special status from MITI was more likely to be awarded when the industry produced a good which was essential to the economy, such as petroleum products or nuclear power.

Between 1951 and 1954, the basic heavy manufacturing industries tended to be the recipients of industrial policy, including electric power, coal mining, ocean shipping, and iron and steel. This reflected Japan's need to reconstruct the basic industries destroyed during the war. The emphasis shifted somewhat between 1955 and 1972, when industries such as steel, machinery, electronics, synthetic fibers, chemicals, fertilizers, shipping, automobiles and cotton spinning became the recipients of targeting. Industrial policy subsequent to 1970 has reflected the growing awareness of MITI that Japan's international competitiveness would have to rely in the future on high-technology and human capital intensive industries. Thus, there has been a shift in the targeted industries, away from heavy manufacturing and towards high-technology industries, such as computers, electrical machinery, precision instruments, machine tools and robotics. While these industries have been more consumer-oriented than have their predecessors, Japanese consumers have also benefited from the increased emphasis by MITI on social and environmental problems, including housing and pollution. In fact, the 'Vision for the 1970s' lists the following industries as being key industries: computers, aircraft, industrial robots, atomic-power-related industries, large-scale integrated circuits, fine chemicals, ocean development, office communication equipment, numerically controlled machine tools, pollution prevention machinery, information management services, high-quality printing, automated warehousing, high-quality furniture and clothing, electronic musical instruments, education-related industries, software and systems engineering. And, while the 'Vision for the 1980s' includes many of the same industries as being key industries, there is greater stress on energy and pollution control, as well as with the overall quality of life. Included as well are genetic engineering, cancer treatment, photosynthesis for food production, new metals, ceramics, textiles, new and alternative energy sources, coal liquefaction and gasification, additional work on computer software, microcomputers, semiconductors, aviation and systemizing of manufacturing processes through the combination of electronics and information-processing technology with machinery-related technology are included.[7]

Although the plans are formulated by MITI, it relies on cooperation throughout the economy for their implementation. A sense of the shifts in MITI's priorities can be ascertained by examining its budget allocation over time. In 1952, MITI allocated 29 percent of its budget towards medium- and small-enterprise programs, 12 percent towards trade promotion and cooperation and 8 percent towards promotion of technology. By 1960, the budget was fairly evenly allocated among trade promotion and cooperation, medium- and small-enterprise programs, promotion of technology, resource and infrastructure development, and energy development. By 1975, the percentage of the budget allocated towards trade promotion and cooperation had been cut by about 50 percent, while that of promotion of technology had almost tripled from what it had been in 1952 (US International Trade Commission, 1983b).

INDUSTRIAL POLICY INSTRUMENTS

A distinguishing feature of Japan's industrial policy has been the range and pervasiveness of instruments. Once identified as being strategic, an industry was the potential recipient of both protective and nurturing instruments. The protective instruments generally included trade tariffs, a commodity tax system biased towards home-produced goods, and the restriction of imports and foreign capital. Nurturing policies included sub-market interest rates on loans from public and private financial institutions, subsidy grants, special depreciation status and exemptions (under the Special Taxation Measures Law), exemptions from import duties on essential machinery and equipment, the authorization and provision of foreign currency to import necessary foreign technology, improving land conditions for industrial plants by means of public works and administrative guidance from MITI. Assessment of the significance of the different instruments has been varied. While Ueno (1980) emphasizes the importance of the nurturing policies of the low-interest loans and special depreciation treatment, Peck and Tamura (1976, p. 558) argue that MITI's control over access to the importation of foreign technology was decisive: 'The importation of technology is the most striking feature of postwar Japan.... The control of technology imports was a major policy instrument.'

Krause and Sekiguchi (1976) have observed that the Japanese 'have shown an extraordinary ability to organize and adopt modern technology.' This ability has not been independent of government intervention in the realm of technology. The Foreign Investment Act of 1950 enabled MITI to exercise considerable control over imported technology by requiring government approval of all transactions involving foreign currency. From 1952 to 1960, MITI administered its controls to encourage the use of foreign technology in industries producing intermediate inputs such as chemicals and iron and steel. From 1960 to 1965 the emphasis shifted towards consumer goods and from 1966 to 1972 the priority became improvements of technology previously imported (Peck and Tamura, 1976).

Although the basic allocation mechanism for R&D is the market, the government control of imported technology has had a spillover effect on the allocation and composition of R&D. By applying domestic R&D to foreign technology, Japan has promoted 'the capability to borrow technology and to absorb more advanced production methods, along with an activist role for the government in the process' (Peck and Tamura, 1976, p. 527). In particular, Japan has been most successful with expenditures on improvement technology. Because long-term research committed to developing new products and technology is assessed as being more risky, R&D has tended to be allocated towards modifying and improving existing foreign technology and products. In this way private enterprise decisions regarding R&D expenditures have been strongly influenced by the government controls over imported technology.

Table 7.1 shows that distribution in the number of Japanese technological purchases for 1968 and 1969. The greatest concentration of technological imports occurred in the chemical, primary metals, electronics and non-electrical machinery sectors. For example, in 1969 there were 243 such purchases in chemicals, 167 in primary metals, 153 in electronics and 148 in

Table 7.1 The Distribution of Japanese Technological Purchases, 1968 and 1969

Sector	Total no. 1968	Total no. 1969	No. from US 1968	No. from US 1969	No. from Europe 1968	No. from Europe 1969	No. from Japan 1968	No. from Japan 1969
Food	7	3	1	1	1	0	5	2
Tobacco	7	3	1	1	1	0	5	2
Textiles	22	28	13	18	9	10	0	0
Apparel	22	28	13	18	9	10	0	0
Lumber	0	1	0	0	0	1	0	0
Furniture	18	31	7	10	10	16	1	5
Paper	9	14	7	7	2	3	0	0
Printing	0	0	0	0	0	0	0	0
Chemicals	163	243	76	142	65	71	18	25
Petroleum	51	51	38	40	13	11	0	0
Rubber	27	29	14	13	10	13	3	3
Leather	18	31	7	10	10	16	1	5
Stone, clay and glass	13	15	6	6	5	6	2	3
Primary metals	154	167	63	69	47	47	38	43
Fabricated metal products	32	42	17	18	2	4	12	19
Machinery (non-electrical)	131	148	63	66	51	57	16	24
Electronics	145	153	58	64	30	29	56	58
Transportation equipment	52	63	21	23	24	30	7	8
Instruments	60	71	11	11	8	15	38	44
Miscellaneous manufacturing	18	31	7	10	10	16	1	5

Source: Japan, Industrial Science and Technology Agency, *Minkan Kenkyu Kaihatsu Jttai Chosa Hokoku* (1970). The data have been re-classified according to the US Standard Industrial Classification System.

non-electrical machinery. The sector with the fifth highest number of technological purchases was instruments, with just 71. It is also apparent that the majority of technological purchases emanated from the United States. The United States was the source for more purchases than was Europe in every sector except for lumber, furniture, printing, leather, stone, clay and glass and instruments. A particularly high percentage of the purchases from the United States came in the petroleum, textiles and apparel industries. Similarly, the United States was the source for more technological purchases than domestic firms in every sector except food, tobacco, lumber, printing, fabricated metal products and instruments. A relatively high share of purchases came from Europe in the transportation equipment, leather and furniture sectors. Finally, a relatively large share of purchased technology came from domestic firms in the instruments, fabricated metal products and electronics sectors. It is apparent from Table 7.1 that four sectors were the primary targets for imported and purchased technology – chemicals, primary metals, non-electrical machinery and electronics.

Thirty-three industries were targeted to be the beneficiaries of technology imports by MITI in 1950. Most of these industries were in heavy manufacturing, such as chemicals. By 1959 there were 153 agreements to purchase foreign technology, and by 1960 there were 327. After the restrictions were liberalized in 1968, the number of technology agreements jumped from 638 in 1967 to 1,061 in 1968 (Peck and Tamura, 1976). The intention of the technology controls was clearly to give priority and direction to purchases of foreign technology.

Although the government has had a long-term interest in developing the R&D capacities of the country, it would be a mistake to forget that Japan does not outspend most of its Western counterparts on R&D per dollar of sales. Similarly, in contrast to its Western counterparts, the bulk of Japanese R&D originates from private firms and not from the government. For example, in 1980, Japan spent a total of 3.9 trillion yen on R&D, while in the United States R&D expenditures were the equivalent of 5.2 trillion yen. This amounted to 2.3 percent of national income in Japan and 2.5 percent of national income in the United States. While the government accounted for about one-third of all R&D expenditures in the United States only 27 percent of the Japanese R&D emanated from the government.[8]

More recently, the Japanese government has become involved in financing R&D in high-technology industries, especially in particularly risky industries. To foster R&D in high-technology industries, the government has used tools such as tax incentives, grants and preferential financing for R&D projects, as well as regional development programs. In 1981, the Japanese government allocated $6.4 billion to major technology projects, spanning general research on the promotion of science and technology along with the general research support for space development, nuclear energy development and ocean development (US International Trade Commission, 1983b). While the government spent $1.2 billion on nuclear energy development, only $477 million was spent on space development, and $211 million on ocean development. By contrast, Toyota Motor, the leading company in private R&D expenditures, spent $650 million in 1980, while the tenth largest spender on R&D, Sony, spent $205.9 million on R&D in the same year.[9]

MITI accounted for more than 12 percent of total Japanese government expenditures on R&D in 1983. Of its R&D budget totalling $708 million, almost one-third was devoted to energy R&D. The rest was distributed among programs that include technology development for small- and medium-sized businesses, international R&D cooperation, R&D in the electronics and machinery industries and R&D on environmental problems.

Government grants and subsidies in the late 1970s averaged 0.3 percent of R&D in pharmaceuticals, 1.4 percent in machinery, 0.5 percent in precision equipment, 18 percent in agriculture, 19 percent in mining, 28 percent in transportation (including shipbuilding, aircraft and railways), and 6.5 percent in computers and semiconductors (US International Trade Commission, 1983b). In addition to the grants and subsidies, the biotechnology industry was the recipient of $35 million in direct grants in 1983; $15 million was allocated towards R&D on flexible manufacturing systems (including numerically controlled machine tools, robots, and computer-aided manufacturing), and $48 million on R&D on computers and semiconductors.

There are two methods by which the Japanese government directs R&D funds to industries. The first method is to finance completely the R&D itself and then to provide interested firms with the results. Typically, such research is conducted at the National Research Laboratories. Alternatively, private firms may carry out the government-financed research under the auspices of the government. However, MITI has legal claim to all patents resulting from the research. MITI generally allows access to the patents on a non-discriminatory basis, requiring only licensing fees.

The second method by which the Japanese government directs R&D funds to industries is indirectly, through conditional loans to private firms. The most common condition dictates that firms are not liable for repayment of the loan in the event that the R&D project proves not to be profitable within a five-year period. Typically, no interest is charged during the five-year period, and the firm retains the right to patent and license the results of the R&D program as it wishes. The purpose of these conditional loans is to alleviate some of the risk associated with long-term R&D programs.

It seems likely that the allocation and type of R&D expenditures until the 1970s was influenced by MITI. The distribution of R&D expenditures across two-digit SIC manufacturing sectors in 1969 is shown in Table 7.2. The first column compares the R&D/sales ratio across the twenty manufacturing sectors. The highest R&D intensity, 3.4 percent, occurred in the electronics sector, followed by the instruments (2.8 percent) and the chemical (2 percent) sectors. The lowest R&D intensity was in the printing (0.2 percent), paper

Table 7.2 The Distribution of R&D Expenditures Across Japanese Manufacturing Sectors, 1969*

Sector	R&D/ sales	Process innovation R&D	Product quality R&D	New products technology R&D	Technology transfer R&D	Percentage of scientists in labor force
Food	0.4	114	206	244	22	1.15
Tobacco	0.4	114	206	244	22	1.15
Textiles	0.9	110	325	141	43	0.90
Apparel	0.9	110	325	141	43	0.90
Lumber	0.4	2	5	13	1	1.21
Furniture	1.6	81	157	264	18	1.53
Paper	0.4	29	52	98	14	1.05
Printing	0.2	4	2	6	4	0.43
Chemicals	2.0	508	752	1556	146	4.48
Petroleum	0.3	125	212	86	6	1.91
Rubber	1.5	51	88	84	19	1.51
Leather	1.6	81	157	264	18	1.53
Stone, clay and glass	1.1	39	63	59	7	1.44
Primary metals	0.9	330	423	611	36	1.59
Fabricated metal products	0.6	60	92	62	7	1.61
Machinery (non-electrical)	1.6	144	618	1058	116	2.02
Electronics	3.4	362	1046	871	188	3.54
Transportation equipment	1.3	199	457	794	52	1.69
Instruments	2.8	118	192	284	4	2.82
Miscellaneous manufacturing	1.6	81	157	264	18	1.53
Total	1.2**	2661	5535	7135	784	1.70**

* All R&D figures are in units of 10 million yen.

** Mean value (unweighted) for the two-digit sectors.

Source: Japan, Industrial Science and Technology Agency, *Minkan Kenkyu Kaihatsu Jttai Chosa Hokoku* (1970). The data have been re-classified according to the US Standard Industrial Classification System.

(0.4 percent) and furniture (0.4 percent) sectors. From the ensuing columns, it is apparent that the different types of R&D expenditure were not distributed evenly across manufacturing sectors. For example, R&D expenditures allocated towards process innovation tended to play a relatively large role in the fabricated metal products and petroleum sectors. On the other hand, R&D expenditures devoted to improving the product quality of existing products tended to play a relatively important role in the electronics, textiles and apparel industries. In the textile and apparel sectors, the R&D expenditures on product quality improvement R&D were almost three times as high as similar R&D expenditures on process innovation R&D, and more than twice as great as R&D expenditures on developing new products and new technology.

In still other sectors, such as chemicals, primary metals, non-electrical machinery, transportation equipment, instruments, food and tobacco, R&D devoted towards developing new products and new technology played the largest role. Particularly in the chemical and non-electrical machinery sectors, this type of R&D was important. However, in sectors such as petroleum, rubber, stone, clay and glass, and fabricated metal products, R&D expenditures allocated towards developing new products and new technology played a much lesser role. Finally, while the absolute level of R&D expenditures on R&D oriented towards technology transfer was the greatest in the chemicals, non-electrical machinery and electronics sectors, such R&D expenditures apparently did not dominate in any one sector.

Of the different types of R&D expenditures, it is apparent that Japanese manufacturing industries tended to allocate the most resources towards R&D devoted to developing new products and technology, where 71,350 million yen was spent. This was followed by R&D expenditures allocated towards improving the quality of existing products, where 55,350 million yen was spent. While 26,610 million yen was allocated toward process innovation R&D, only 7,840 million yen was devoted to technology transfer R&D.

The last column of Table 7.2 employs a slightly different measure of R&D intensity – the mean percentage of the industry labor force composed of scientists. Using this measure, the chemical sector was the most R&D intensive, with 4.48 percent of the labor force consisting of scientists. The second most R&D intensive sector was electronics, with 3.54 percent of the labor force consisting of scientists. Other sectors with a relatively high component of scientists in the labor force were non-electrical machinery (2.02 percent), transportation equipment (1.69 percent), petroleum (1.91 percent) and primary metals (1.59 percent). On the other hand, the lowest component of scientists in the labor force occurred in the printing (0.43 percent) and apparel (0.9 percent) sectors.

Although its significance has somewhat receded, tax policy, and especially the depreciation tax, served as a major instrument for industrial policy in Japan. Three different schemes existed permitting higher depreciation allowances, each with the goal of enabling growing and profitable industries to have access to liquidity. Some companies could claim a depreciation allowance of just over 50 percent of their equipment in one year (US General Accounting Office, 1983). The Enterprise Rationalization Law (1952) enabled an increase in the depreciation rate of up to one-quarter to be applicable wherever deemed necessary by the Ministry of Finance. In the early 1970s, the following industries were some of the recipients of rationalization allowances (US General Accounting Office, 1979):[10]

> spinning, weaving, dying and finishing, industrial sharpening equipment, non-ferrous metal casting machinery, non-ferrous metal refining, non-ferrous metal rolling, electric wire and cable, wholesale and retail trade, construction machinery, power metallurgy, hydraulic machinery, industrial machinery, automobiles and parts, fertilizers, pulp, fiber board, steel forging, casting, bearings, electronics, aircraft, agriculture, petrochemicals, atomic furnaces, agriculture

Additional depreciation could also be obtained in those industries exhibiting a strong export performance. Such supplemental depreciation measures enabled firms to increase their depreciation between 30 and 60 percent.[11]

It has been estimated that the tax loss of $5.8 billion between 1967 and 1972 was a result of Japan's special tax measures. The estimated tax loss attributed to Japan's special tax measures rose to $8.7 billion between 1973 and 1977, and to $9.7 billion between 1978 and 1982. Thus, the amount of money that was channeled into the targeted industries through the special tax measures was not trivial. Almost 50 percent of tax losses were devoted to encouraging savings and investment, while just under 15 percent were aimed at technology promotion and equipment modernization (US International Trade Commission, 1983b).

The average amount of an industry's depreciation covered by a special depreciation allowance was 8 percent in manufacturing between 1962 and 1973. The industries enjoying the highest special depreciation allowance as a percentage of total depreciation between 1962 and 1973 included shipbuilding with 15 percent, autos with 13 percent, steel with 12 percent, machinery with 13 percent and textiles with 8 percent (Ogura and Yoshino, 1984). When an industry was granted such status, it signalled that MITI considered the industry to be strategic (Ito et al., 1984). According to Ueno (1980, p. 388): 'A subsidy is important in itself, but it is more important as a signal indicating that the industry or the product receiving the subsidy is publicly recognized as one under government protection'.

One of the key instruments for implementing industrial policy was the selective allocation of funds to key industries through a network of financial institutions. These included public financial institutions such as the:

Japan Development Bank
Export-Import Bank of Japan
Agriculture, Forestry, and Fisheries Financial Corporation
Small Business Finance Corporation
People's Finance Corporation
commercial banks
small-business financial institutions (such as mutual loans and saving
  banks, credit associations, Central Bank of Commerce and Industry,
  and credit unions)
agriculture, forestry, fisheries financial institutions
securities financial institutions
insurance companies.

Because the Japanese government was able to retain considerable influence over the flow of savings, it was also able to play an active role in credit allocation.

Targeted industries for the allocation of public funds in the 1960s included industries such as primary metals, metal products and machinery, along with agriculture. While there were 2,210 billion yen worth of industrial loans made by public financial institutions between 1960 and 1965, the amount nearly doubled to 4,341 billion yen during the 1966–70 period. In both of these periods, machinery received slightly more than 15 percent of those funds. While basic overhead industries such as electric power and transportation had been key industries during the 1950s, by 1970 industries such as electronic computers had become increasingly important (Ueno, 1980).

The Fiscal and Investment Loan Program, which was passed in 1953, enabled the government to influence a large share of private savings in Japan. Many of these funds were used to finance small businesses. In 1982, over 40 percent of the funds were channeled into small businesses: funds for exports, imports and overseas investments accounted for 13 percent, and loans for development an additional 10 percent.[12] While this program accounted for almost 30 percent of funds provided to industry in the early post-war period, this was reduced to just over 15 percent by the last half of the 1960s, and even further reduced to just under 15 percent by the 1970s (Noguchi, 1982).

In 1982, the chemical industry was the largest recipient of loans, from both government and non-government financial institutions. During this period, almost 6,000 billion yen were loaned to this industry. The next largest borrower was the transportation machinery industry, which borrowed almost 5,000 million yen from financial institutions. Small firms received the greatest amount of support in the fabricated metal products industry, where almost two-thirds of all loans were allocated towards small business. Similarly, the amount of funds channeled to small firms was 47 percent in the general machinery industry, 42 percent in the ceramic, stone and glass industry, and 41 percent in the precision machinery industry (US International Trade Commission, 1983b).

One of the most vital instruments of Japanese industrial policy has been the Japan Development Bank. Established in 1951, the Japan Development Bank was given the responsibility of channeling funds to encourage industrial development. Long-term investment for plant and equipment is the major focus of the Bank's loans. Such loans typically cover between 30 and 50 percent of the capital investment, including land, buildings and machinery. By law, the Japan Development Bank must be financially viable; that is, it does not regularly lose money on its loans. Less than one percent of its loans are written off because of a default. The Japan Development Bank obtains its funds from the central government, generally through the Trust Fund Bureau of the Ministry of Finance. Private firms find loans from the Japan Development Bank to be advantageous, because no compensating balances are mandatory,[13] and loans up to thirty years can be obtained (US International Trade Commission, 1983b).

In the late 1960s, the National Technology Promotion Fund was organized within the Japan Development Bank in an effort to encourage technological development. Subsequently, the Bank has allocated more than $300 million per year towards loans related to technological development. These loans have been targeted in particular towards computer leasing, manufacturing software, raising the technological level of machinery industries and general technological development.

While 50 percent of the outstanding loans in 1955 were in the electric power industry, and 32 percent in transportation, only 16 percent of the outstanding loans in 1974 were in the electrical power industry, but 37 percent were in transportation. Perhaps even more striking was the shift in the composition of new loans. In 1955, 45 percent of all new loans were directed towards the electric power industry. By 1974, only 16 percent of such loans were in this industry. Meanwhile, the allocation of loans to the chemical industry had risen from 2.2 percent in 1955 to 6 percent in 1974. In the metal manufacturing industry there was a similar increase from one percent to six percent over this same period (Ueno, 1980). More recently, the computer industry has been the target for Japan Development Bank loans. Between 1977 and 1980, almost half of the new loans for the development of technology were in the computer industry.[14]

INDUSTRIAL TARGETING IN SPECIFIC INDUSTRIES

As of 1985 there were fifty-one research associations existing in Japan. A total of 65 billion yen in 1985 was spent on R&D by these research associations, of which half was subsidized by the government (Goto and

Wakasugi, 1987). These research associations ranged from a joint research institute comprised of members of the Misui group to carry out cooperative R&D in bio-technology, formed in 1981, to the Electric Car Research Association, the Nuclear Steelmaking Research Association, and the Technical Research for Optics (Saxonhouse, 1982).

Two detailed studies (Audretsch, 1988b; forthcoming) have analyzed the cooperative R&D projects undertaken in Japan and concluded that they have contributed significantly to the international competitiveness of the targeted industries. Because cooperative R&D has not been hindered by the fair trade laws, as joint R&D in the United States was thwarted by the American antitrust laws until very recently, it has been very effective in rendering Japanese firms more competitive in global markets. These studies find that, in particular, Japanese cooperative R&D programs in the aircraft, computer, machine tool, robotic and semiconductor industries have played an important role in the overall technological progress in these industries as well as in their ascent to a leading position in the global market. The cooperative R&D programs sponsored by the Japanese government between 1966 and 1980 are summarized in Table 7.3.

Industrial targeting in the Japanese steel industry has taken form in the allocation of various financial subsidies, technological aid and credit allocation. The government played an active role in organizing the major steel producers from bidding up the prices of technology imported from other nations. This had the obvious effect of reducing the cost to Japanese steel producers of procuring essential technology. However, this policy has been abandoned since the 1970s. The industry was also the recipient of low-interest rate loans and other financial assistance, especially in the 1950s. During the first government rationalization plan between 1950 and 1955, nearly 40 percent of all of the industry's funds used for capital investment emanated from government loans, including 18 percent from the Industrial Bank of Japan and 8 percent from the Japan Development Bank. During the second rationalization, between 1956 and 1960, only about 3 percent of the steel industry's investment funds came from government loans, principally from the Export-Import Bank of Japan. Instead, nearly one-third of all investment funds came from internal financing, while one-fifth came from selling equity (Kawahito, 1972). Financial subsidies played only a minor role after 1960.

While subsidies have played a lesser role in the Japanese steel industry since 1970, government intervention in R&D support has become increasingly important. Between 1973 and 1983, over $100 million (24,450 million yen) of government funds were spent on R&D to improve the energy efficiency of the steel industry (US International Trade Commission, 1983b).

Industrial targeting in the Japanese steel industry has been quite successful, particularly when the industry was in the developing post-war stages.

Table 7.3 Cooperative R&D Projects Sponsored by the Japanese Government, 1966–1980

Project	Period	Purpose	Funding (million yen)	Companies involved
Computers	1972–76	Development of basic technology for 3rd and 5th generation computers	8,700	Fujitsu, Hitachi, Mitsubishi Electric, NEC, Oki, Toshiba
Very large scale project (VLSI)	1976–79	Development of basic technology for extra large-scale integrators of 4th generation computers	30,000	Fujitsu, Hitachi, Mitsubishi Electric, NEC, Toshiba
Development of basic software and related periphery	1979–83	Development of software for the 4th generation computers, particularly operating system software	47,000	Fujitsu, Hitachi, Matsushita Electric, Mitsubishi Electric, NEC, Oki, Sharp, Toshiba
Pattern information processing system (PIPS)	1971–80	Development of technology for an information processing system capable of understanding patterns of words, colors, voice and sounds	22,073	Hitachi, Fujitsu, Matsushita, Mitsubishi, NEC, Oki, Sanyo, Toshiba, Hoya Glass
High-speed scientific computer	1981–89	Development of technology for an information processing system	22,073	Fujitsu, Toshiba, NEC, Mitsubishi Electric, Sanyo, Matsushita, Konishiroku, Hoya Glass
Flexible manufacturing system using lasers	1977–82	Development of a complex production system which can produce various kinds of machinery components and parts in small batches	13,000	N/A
Software automation	1976–81	Develop capability for computers to write own software automatically	6,600	Over 100 software firms
Development of 5th generation computers	1979–91	Development of 1990's computers	11,375	Fujitsu, Hitachi, Mitsubishi, NEC, Oki, Toshiba
Computers-Con. Development of super-high-speed performance computers, large-scale	1966–71	Development of the newest, most powerful computer. All combine high performance software to create the largest model computer system	10,124	Fujitsu, Hitachi, Mitsubishi NEC, Toshiba, Oki
Optical measurement and System	1979–87	Develop system for remote control and monitoring of industrial processes using optical element for sensing and transmission	18,040	Fujitsu, Hitachi Furukawa, Mitsubishi, NEC, Oki, Sumitomo Electric

Aircraft	1978–82	International joint development of 200 seat aircraft resulting in the Boeing 767	16,000	Kawasaki, Fuji, Mitsubishi
Development of civil aircraft engine RJ–500	1980–87	International joint development of an engine for a 150-seat jet with Rolls Royce Ltd.	47,000	IHI, Kawasaki, Mitsubishi
Development of next generation civil aircraft	1981–87	International joint development of 150-seat jet	25,000	N/A
Aircraft-Cont. FJR–170 experimental engine	1971–81	Develop civil aircraft engine aircraft engine	20,400	IHI, Kawasaki, Mitsubishi
STOL aircraft	1978–90	Develop a commercial short take-off and landing aircraft	25,000	Kawasaki, others
Basic technologies	1981–90	Develop technologies basic to industries of the 1990s	104,000	
A. New materials: High-efficiency separation film	1981–90	Develop technologies basic to industries of the 1990s	N/A	Toray, Teijin, Asahi Chemicals, Kuraray, Toyobo
Conductive macromolecule	1981–90	Develop technologies basic to industries of the 1990s	N/A	Suminoto Denko, Daiseru Chemicals, Asahi Glass, Mitsubishi Chemicals
High crystalline macromolecule	1981–90	Develop technologies basic to industries of the 1990s	N/A	Toray, Teijin, Asahi Chemicals, Sumitomo, Denko, Sumitomo Chemicals
Fine ceramics	1981–90	Develop high strength corrosion-resistant and high-precision abrasion-resistant fine ceramic materials	14,160	Toshiba, Kyoto Ceramics, Sumitomo Denko, Kobe Steel Ishikawajima-Harima Heavy Ind., Showa Denko, Asahi Glass, Electro–Chemistry, Nippon Glass, Special Ceramics, Kurosaki Ceramics, Toyota Machine Tools, Chinagawa White Brick, Inoue Japax Research Inst, Toyota Motors
High-efficiency crystal control alloy	1981–90	Develop technologies basic to industries of the 1990s	N/A	Hitachi Works, Kobe Steel, Daido Special Steel, Mitsubishi Metals, Hitachi Metals, Sumitomo Denko, Ishikawjima Harima Heavy Ind., Mitsubishi Electric Machines, Kawasaki Heavy Ind.

Table 7.3 (cont.)

Project	Period	Purpose	Funding (million yen)	Companies involved
Processing technology for above	1981–90	Develop technologies basic to industries of the 1990s	N/A	Mitsubishi Heavy Ind., Fuji Heavy Ind., Toyota Motors, Toshiba Machines, Ishikawajima-Harima Heavy Ind., Mitsubishi Electric Machinery, Kawasaki Heavy Ind.
High molecular composite materials	1981–90	Develop technologies basic to industries of the 1990s	N/A	Toray, Teijin, Mitsubishi Chemicals, Nippon Carbon
B. Biotechnology: Technology for large-scale cultivation and utilization	1981–90	Develop technologies basic to industries of the 1990s	28,320	Asahi Chemicals, Ajinomoto, Kyowa Fermentation, Takeda Pharmaceutics, Toyo
Bio reactor	1981–80	Develop technologies basic to industries of the 1990s	28,320	Kao Soap, Daiseru Chemicals, Electro-Chemistry, Mitsui Petro-chemicals, Electro-Chemistry Mitsui Petrochemicals, Mitsubishi Gas, Mitsubishi Chemicals
Gene recombination and utilization	1981–90	Develop technologies basic to industries of the 1990s	N/A	Sumitomo Chemicals, Mitsui Toatsu, Mitsubishi Chemicals, Biological Research Inst.
New function elements-integrated circuits	1981–90	Develop technologies basic to industries of the 1990s	27,120	
Supergrid Components (ICs)	1981–90	Develop technologies basic to industries of the 1990s	8,000	Fujitsu, Hitachi, Sumitomo Denko
Three dimensional components (ICs)	1981–90	Develop technologies basic to industries of the 1990s	9,000	Nippon Electric Corp. (NEC), Oki, Toshiba, Mitsubishi Electric, Sanyo Electric, Matsushita Electric, Sharp
Elements with increased resistance to the environment	1981–88	Develop technologies basic to industries of the 1990s	8,000	Toshiba, Hitachi, Mitsubishi Electric

Source: U.S. International Trade Commission (1983b).

Under the guidance of the first rationalization plan, output of crude steel doubled over a four-year period. Under the second rationalization plan between 1955 and 1960, crude steel production nearly tripled. During this period, a considerable amount of capital investment took place, as integrated iron-steel facilities were constructed and new equipment and technology were deployed. As a result of this investment and modernization the per ton cost of pig iron decreased by $10, and labor productivity improved from 12.2 man-hours per ton in 1950, to 9.7 hours per ton in 1955 and to 6.2 hours per ton in 1960 (Kawahito, 1972). As a result of these efficiency gains, the Japanese steel industry was competitive in the world market by 1960 and had become the country's major exporter.

However, by the 1970s the growth in the steel industry had peaked. While usable capacity increased from nearly 14 million net tons in 1955 to 28 million net tons in 1960, 54 million net tons in 1965 and 114 million net tons in 1970, representing a more than 700 percentage increase over this period, capacity expanded only from 166 million net tons in 1975 to 175 million tons in 1980, representing an increase of only 6 percent. And, between 1980 and 1982, Japanese steel capacity actually decreased to 172 million net tons. Capacity utilization also began to decline in the second half of the 1970s and into the 1980s. While capacity utilization stood at 92 percent in 1972, it gradually fell to 71 percent in 1976 and 64 percent in 1982 (US International Trade Commission, 1983b).

Even into the 1970s and 1980s, the Japanese steel industry has been able to maintain its cost advantage over US producers. In 1973 the cost per ton of steel was estimated at $194 in the United States, while in Japan it was 16 percent less, at $167. This gap has narrowed somewhat over time. By 1981, steel cost $507 per ton in the United States compared with only $451 per ton in Japan, amounting to a differential of 12 percent. However, when the yen fell to a five-year low with respect to the dollar in 1982, the cost per ton of steel in the United States rose to $623, while it fell to $431 in Japan, a difference of nearly 45 percent.

As international competition in the steel market has stiffened, Japan has tended to lose its export share in the world market. While 25 percent of domestic production was exported in 1955, the export share increased to 31 percent in 1965, and then to 35 percent in 1975 before falling to 31 percent in 1981. Asia provided the greatest export markets for Japanese steel in the 1950s, accounting for more than 40 percent of Japanese steel exports. Subsequently, the Middle East has emerged as a large consumer of Japanese steel of the 1970s and 1980s.

Industrial targeting in Japan has contributed to the success of the steel industry, particularly in the formative years following the war. As a result, the steel industry in Japan has enjoyed state-of-the-art technology and has tended to be located at strategic low-cost transportation centers, two factors that have proven vital in establishing an internationally competitive industry.

In this way, Japanese steel firms were able to replace their US counterparts as the major producers in the world.

The role of targeting in the Japanese automobile industry has been of particular interest because of the industry's apparent determination to retain at least some degree of independence and not always to acquiesce to the plans inflicted upon it by MITI. Still, to recognize that the industry has not always followed the course directed by MITI is not to conclude that targeting has not played a significant role in the industry. In 1950, MITI decided to encourage development of the industry by (1) imposing trade protection in the form of tariffs, quotas and limits on foreign direct investment, in an effort to shield the domestic markets from foreign competition; (2) channeling low-interest loans, tax incentives and outright grants to facilitate capital investment; and (3) providing the mechanisms needed to develop an export market.

In fact, the one recurrent theme in MITI's plan for the Japanese automobile industry has been consolidation. Yet, the industry has consistently rejected the government's attempts at imposing such consolidation. When entry into the Japanese automobile market occurred in 1960 with the appearance of Mitsubishi, Fuji and Toyo Kogyo, MITI attempted to erect entry barriers in order to maintain the market shares of Nissan and Toyota. In one of its 1963 measures, MITI refused to allow several of the new entrants access to foreign technology. Similarly, MITI attempted to force plans on the companies which would segment the market among the various producers according to the type of car. When the producers objected strenuously to this plan, it finally had to be abandoned (Magaziner and Hout, 1980).

MITI implemented tax benefits in the industry which were aimed at encouraging exports. For example, it introduced a tax provision allowing tax-free reserves to cover the costs associated with marketing in foreign countries. And so, between 1964 and 1972, 0.5 percent of sales to foreign countries were used to pay for marketing costs of exports. However, subsequent to 1972, this tax benefit had applied only to small firms. Similarly, until 1972, the automobile industry was perhaps the principal beneficiary from the accelerated depreciation measure which was linked to exports.

More recently, MITI has provided support for R&D. For the period 1981 through 1990, $59 million (14,160 million yen) have been allocated to several companies, including Toyota Motors, to develop high-strength, corrosion-resistant and high-precision, abrasion-resistant fine ceramic materials. Still, the firms remain the major source for R&D in the automobile industry. While the four leading companies, Honda, Nissan, Toyota and Toyo Kogyo spent about $1.5 billion on R&D in 1980 alone, the government has allocated only $452 million over the next decade to be spent on R&D that could potentially benefit the auto industry.

The auto industry grew at a phenomenal rate between 1958 and 1972. In 1958, there were only 51,000 units produced. By 1963, this had increased to 408,000 units. The high rate of growth continued through 1967 when 1,376,000 units were produced, and through 1972 when 4,022,000 units were produced. Subsequent production growth, however, has occurred at a considerably slower rate. By 1977, there were only 5,431,000 units produced, and 6,887 units by 1982 (US International Trade Commission, 1983b). Still, even in the 1980s, Japan seems to hold a considerable cost advantage over the United States. It has been estimated that Mazda required nearly fifty labor hours to produce a subcompact in Japan in 1979, while in the United States Ford needed over 110 labor hours, and General Motors 130 hours to produce an analogous automobile (Tsurumi, 1984).[15]

While industrial targeting played a greater role in automobiles and steel when these industries were still in the evolving stages, industrial policy was more prominent in the aluminum industry as it reached the mature and declining stages of the product life cycle. In the 1970s, the demand for Japanese aluminum fell, as did subsequent output. In 1954, Japanese production of unwrought aluminum had been 117 million pounds, which increased to 842 million pounds in 1967 and to 2.6 billion pounds in 1976. However, after 1977, production declined until it reached 773 million pounds in 1982, below the 1967 level. Because capacity generally increased over this period, capacity utilization fell to less than 25 percent between 1977 and 1982 (US International Trade Commission, 1983b).

As a result of the industry's decline in the late 1970s and 1980s, the government intervened in an attempt to bring about an orderly adjustment process. The Industrial Structure Council of MITI recommended in 1977 that action be undertaken to reduce smelting capacity by 24 percent, to alleviate the perpetual ingot shortages by importing ingots, to set up a system of joint sales through one firm to reduce price cutting by the independent smelters, and to erect stronger tariffs and quotas. By the early 1980s, MITI had expressed the goal of reducing smelting capacity to 1.5 billion pounds. The distinguishing feature of industrial policy in the aluminum industry was the directing of a somewhat orderly decline and reduction of capacity.

While government targeting has been a permanent fixture in the machine tools industry since the mid-1950s, the actual methods used to implement that policy have varied over time. In the early post-war period, targeting practices were in the form of special tax measures and export assistance, along with trade protection and legalized cartelization. In order to transform the industry into an international competitor, the government tied tax benefits to export performance. Similarly, the purchase of foreign machine tools which were also domestically produced was not permitted. Imports of machine tools were allowed only in cases where the Japanese industry was not already producing that particular type of machine. This restriction was in effect until 1965. The Export and Import Trading Law (1952) enabled the Japan Machinery Exporters Association to exchange information, share promotional costs and arrange for single negotiations with foreign purchasers, all under supervision of MITI. Because the Association did not engage in explicit price-setting, it was not considered to be in violation of the antitrust laws.

In 1956, the Extraordinary Measures Law for the Rehabilitation of the Machinery Industry was enacted in order to develop the industrial machinery sector. Underlying the law was the desire of MITI to consolidate the industry through merging smaller firms. Not only did this law legalize rationalization cartels, but it also enabled MITI to assign specific product lines to particular producers, in an effort to promote specialization in the machine tool industry. The government also encouraged consolidation through application of preferential loans and tax rates. Under MITI's guidance, the members of the Japan Machine Tool Builder's Association agreed in 1964 to specialize in the types of machinery for which their market share exceeded 5 percent, or in products which accounted for 20 percent of the firm's production.

In the 1960s, preferential loans, mostly from the Japan Development Bank and from the Small Business Finance Corporation, became a more significant component of targeting in the machine tool industry. The Toshiba Machine Company, for example, was the recipient of a major government loan in 1965 for the purpose of developing trail production of continuous path control machines. Such loans have continued into the 1980s, when the Japan Development Bank loaned 2,500 million yen for the financing of the promotion of industrial technological development (US International Trade Commission, 1983b).

While special tax measures, including accelerated depreciation, have been successfully applied to the machine tool industry, direct government expenditures on R&D have also played a more important role. Since the 1970s, the government has been allocating between 10 and 15 billion yen annually for R&D in the machine tool industry. The government spent $54 million between 1977 and 1984 for the development of flexible manufacturing systems, with the goal of integrating computer controlled machinery with other machines.

The aircraft industry in Japan has also been the recipient of considerable targeting. A distinguishing feature of this targeting has been the lack of commercial success. It is one of the few industries that has not responded to government intervention in a positive manner. While in most targeted industries the preferential loans and special tax measures were used to spur capital investment, in the aircraft industry they have been used to reduce the costs of purchasing aircraft from foreign producers. Much of MITI's encouragement to the domestic industry has focused on the undertaking of joint ventures with foreign firms. For example, the Agency for Industrial Science and Technology recently made a grant of 20 billion yen to Kawasaki, IHI and Mitsubishi that made possible a joint enterprise with Rolls-Royce of Great Britain for pursuing the development of a fan jet engine (US General Accounting Office, 1982).

MITI has provided both loans, where repayment is conditional upon the market success of the project, and direct grants to the Society of Japanese Aerospace Companies, which is the industry's trade association, in an effort to encourage R&D in the industry. Nearly 40 percent of the cost for basic research has been paid for by direct grants from the government. Most recently, the government has supported research geared towards the implementation of microprocessors in developing a combustion control system, the use of optical fibers in data processing systems and more fuel efficient aircraft (US General Accounting Office, 1982).

Most of the targeting in the Japanese telecommunications market is facilitated through the government's firm, NTT. NTT has developed a network of more than 300 firms, many of which are relatively small suppliers. These firms are the actual manufacturers of telecommunications equipment in Japan. The major producers include Nippon Electric Co., Fujitsu, Oki Electric and Hitachi. These companies have been among the participants in numerous government programs aimed at developing electronics in Japan. The 1978 Temporary Law for the Promotion of Electronic and Machinery Industries has enabled companies producing goods such as communications-testing apparatus and instruments, electronic measuring devices and fiber optic materials, to receive grants from the Agency for Industrial Science and Technology under the auspices of MITI to facilitate R&D. An example of this is the grant Hitachi Cable received in 1982 to develop optical fiber technology (US International Trade Commission, 1983b).

Through NTT, the government also directly engages in its own R&D. Current research involves electronic switching systems, memory chips, integrated circuits, data processing, new materials, transmission systems and optoelectronics. Some fruits of this research include the VLSI semiconductor chips, and the 16K, 64K and 256K RAMs, fiber optic cable, data transmission systems and high capacity pagers.

In contrast with the targeting that has occurred in many other industries, the Japanese semiconductor industry has only recently become a recipient of targeting. In fact, most of the government's intervention occurred subsequent to 1975. During the early 1970s, the importance of the industry became increasingly clear because of, in part, the external effects on other industries such as computers, robotics, consumer electronics and machine tools. As a result, the government played an increasingly larger role. The Very Large Scale Integration Project was launched in 1976, with the goal of developing large-scale integrated circuits. These circuits were essential to the viability of the fourth generation computer development project. Hitachi, Fujitsu, Mitsubishi, Electric, NEC and Toshiba, along with MITI's Electrotechnical Laboratory, participated in the project which ultimately produced the 64K RAM chip. The total budget for the project was $325 million, with the government providing $136 million in loans which were conditional upon the success of the project (Wheeler et al., 1980).

More recently, the semiconductor industry has enjoyed support from the Next Generation Industries Project. The Project, which promotes basic research in high-technology industries such as information processing, biotechnology and alternative sources, spent $6 million of government funds in developing three-dimensional structures which facilitate a number of functions to be combined on each chip, and will be feasible for use in space, atomic reactors and automobile engines (Semiconductor Industry Association, 1983).

Between 1976 and 1982, MITI channeled more than $500 million into the semiconductor industry in the form of subsidies and loans. However, the dollar amount of the financial aid involved grossly understates the value of the MITI program to the major Japanese semiconductor companies. MITI organized joint R&D projects which reduced R&D costs per firm to a fraction of the level they would have been in the absence of such projects. MITI's selection of several large producers as the major beneficiaries of its aid effectively forced other Japanese producers to cut back or drop altogether their own semiconductor production – guaranteeing the major producers economies of scale and secure markets in Japan. The favored status enjoyed by these firms ensured easier access to private capital. The net effect of MITI's industrial 'guidance' was to organize and channel the collective resources of five of Japan's largest industrial combines towards the achievement of a relatively narrow goal – superiority in very large-scale semiconductors (Semiconductor Industry Association, 1983, pp. 19–20).

The success of targeting in the semiconductor industry seems apparent. Japanese exports increased from $449 million in 1978 to $734 million in 1979, to $1,200 million in 1982. Borrus et al. (1983, p. 143) have concluded:

> The corporate capabilities that afford a national advantage in high technology can be promoted by government policies for industry and trade. National competition in this industry is typical of the trade conflicts we may anticipate in all of the growing high-technology industries on which advanced countries depend. Indeed, the case of this one industry suggests that government policies can shape a nation's comparative advantage in trade.

While targeting has occurred in the Japanese computer industry since its incipiency in 1958, it has become increasingly important since the 1970s. A broad range of measures has been used to implement policy in the industry, including grants and subsidized loans for R&D, special tax measures, technical support and the provision of a government-financed computer-leasing company, along with protection from foreign competition in the domestic market. Although the 1957 Law Providing Temporary Measures for the Promotion of the Electronics Industry was aimed primarily at the consumer electronics industry, there was considerable spill-over into the computer industry. The Law not only erected the Electronic and Machinery Industries Deliberation Council, but also provided the computer firms with special measures for financial assistance, mainly through special depreciation measures and direct grants. The Law also enabled the industry to become exempt from the Anti-Monopoly Law (Kaplan, 1972).

Under the auspices of MITI, the Japan Electronic Computer Corp. was established in 1961 by Fujitsu, Hitachi, Mitsubishi, Oki, Toshiba, NEC and Matsushita, for the purpose of acting as a single marketing agent. Between 1961 and 1979, the Japan Electronic Computer Corp. received $2 billion in loans, largely from the Japan Development Bank (Kaplan, 1972). After MITI failed to consolidate the industry in 1969, because of the refusal of the firms involved to merge, a joint project was undertaken in 1971 to develop a fourth generation computer that used large-scale integration in a similar manner as the IBM 370 series. The major manufacturers worked together under the guidance of MITI to develop this fourth generation computer.

The US International Trade Commission (1983b) has calculated the subsidies inherent in the loans made by the Japan Development Bank to the computer industry. In 1977, this amounted to 5,602 million yen, or 0.8 percent of production. And though the subsidies rose to 6,042 million yen by 1981, this represented only 0.4 percent of total production.

More recently, government targeting has been in the form of joint R&D projects. However, government-sponsored cooperative research projects represent only between 2 and 3 percent of the total R&D expenditures in the industry. One of the most notable government-sponsored projects is for the supercomputer. This project, begun in 1981 and lasting until 1989, has the goal of developing high-calculating speeds with applications for science and defense. The actual research is being undertaken both at MITI's Electro-technical Laboratory, as well as in the laboratories of the participating firms. The Optoelectronics project is designed to promote a system for monitoring large-scale industrial processes which employ optical sensing and data transmission devices. The second phase of the Fourth Generation Computers program, which included Fujitsu, Hitachi, Matsushita, Mitsubishi, NEC, Oki, Sharp and Toshiba, was designed to develop peripheral equipment and operating system software. Between 1981 and 1985, MITI provided $102.3 million for this project, while the firms provided $111.4 million themselves. The Fifth Generation Computers project, begun in 1979 and scheduled to last until 1991, has as its target the construction of computers that will be able to apply artificial intelligence and knowledge assessment as well as process data. Finally, MITI has been involved in numerous joint R&D programs with the goal of developing computer software. For example, it allocated $30 million to a project to develop computers that can write their own applications software (US International Trade Commission, 1983b).

Perhaps the newest industry to be affected by industrial targeting has been robotics. The Japan Robot Leasing Company was organized in 1980 to proliferate the application of robots, especially in small- and medium-sized firms. The Japan Robot Leasing Company has been the recipient of low-interest Japan Development Bank loans, which have constituted around 60 percent of the Company's operating funds. Further, these loans have been at 0.3 percent below the prime interest rate. In 1980, these loans amounted to 140 million yen and 1,250 million yen in 1981. In turn, the Japan Robot Leasing Company leases robots at lower rates and at more favorable terms than the customers could otherwise obtain.

The users of robots are also entitled to subsidized government loans. In addition, those firms installing robots in manufacturing facilities are entitled to a special tax depreciation. For example in 1981, 13 percent of the initial purchase price of robots could be written off (beyond the normal depreciation allowance). The additional depreciation allowance has been calculated to reduce the costs of producing the robot by 6.2 percent (US International Trade Commission, 1983b). Of the R&D projects subsidized by the government in 1982, $3.1 billion went towards the trial utilization of industrial robots, $401 million went towards R&D to develop safety and automation technologies for deburring cast-iron application, $49 million went towards the standardization of program languages for robots and $20 million went for R&D on industrial robot applications in nuclear power plants.

EVALUATION OF INDUSTRIAL TARGETING

One measure of the success of Japanese industrial targeting is to compare certain bilateral trade measures with the United States between those industries that were the recipients of targeting and those that were not. The identification scheme used by Audretsch and Yamawaki (1986a, 1988), based on the amount of preferential depreciation allowance granted to the industry between 1962 and 1973, is adapted here to identify targeted industries. If industrial targeting is successful, then those industries subject to targeting should experience greater success in competing with the United States. Table 7.4 shows that, in fact, those industries targeted by MITI exhibited a more superior trade performance in 1977 than did those industries which were not targeted. The US–Japan trade balance is defined as $TB = (X - M)/(X + M)$, where X is Japanese exports to the United States in 1977, and M is Japanese imports from the United States in 1977. This measure weights the net exports, $X - M$, by the total amount traded between the two countries, $X + M$. This measure of comparative advantage has been used by Pugel (1978). It has the advantage of implicitly controlling for transportability, while still indicating the comparative advantage. As Pugel notes, this measure has the disadvantage of perhaps overstating the importance to the low balance of trade in industries where there is only little international trade. Thus, Table 7.4 shows that the mean US–Japanese bilateral trade balance for 233 four-digit SIC industries in 1977 was 0.227. However, in the untargeted industries, the bilateral trade balance was only 0.1861, while in the targeted industries, the mean bilateral trade balance was 0.5512. The asterik

Table 7.4 The Impact of Targeting on Trade Performance (standard deviations in parentheses)

Variable	Mean	Mean in untargeted industries	Mean in targeted industries
US bilateral	0.2270	0.1861	0.5512**
trade balance	(0.7202)	(0.7375)	(0.4526)
Import penetration	0.0129	0.0125	0.0161
in US	(0.0382)	(0.0402)	(0.0138)
US R&D/Sales	2.2360	2.1408	3.1346**
	(2.7084)	(2.7585)	(1.9859)
No. of companies introducing	11.3214	9.9625	24.1458
foreign technology	(11.0028)	(10.2894)	(9.1628)**
Exports to US	420	255	1,727*
	(2,715)	(1,261)	(7,231)
Total technology	227	187	607**
payments (10 million yen)	(357)	(334)	(351)
Process innovation	154	153	172
R&D (10 million yen)	(171)	(177)	(112)
Product quality	343	321	558**
R&D (10 million yen)	(370)	(377)	(193)
New product	442	400	840**
technology R&D	(563)	(556)	(471)

*Statistically significant at 90 percent level of confidence.
**Statistically significant at the 95 percent level of confidence.

indicates that the difference in the mean bilateral trade balance between the targeted and the untargeted industries is statistically significant at the 95 percent level of confidence. However, whether this observed statistical relationship implies that MITI's policies were actually responsible for the strong trade performance cannot be ascertained here unequivocally. For example, it is conceivable that MITI had a policy of targeting industries that were relatively strong and likely to succeed in the world market.

Similarly, while the average value of 1977 exports to the United States was $420 million, it was only $255 million in the untargeted industries, and $1,727 million in the targeted industries. That is, Japanese exports to the United States were more than three times greater in those industries which were recipients of targeting than in those industries which were untargeted. Japanese import penetration in the United States, defined as US imports from Japan divided by industry value-of-shipments, plus total imports minus total US exports, exhibits a similar pattern. While the mean Japanese import penetration rate was 1.29 percent in all industries, it was 1.25 percent in the untargeted industries and 1.61 percent in the targeted industries.

In the United States, the 1977 ratio of R&D-to-sales was 2.24 percent. However, in those industries which were targeted by MITI, the R&D intensity was 3.13 percent, while it was only 2.14 percent in the untargeted industries. This suggests that MITI was very concerned with catching up with the United States in high-technology industries. The number of companies in 1969 introducing foreign technology was nearly three times as great in the targeted industries as in the untargeted industries. This perhaps reflects the effects of MITI's control over the allocation of purchased foreign technology and its desire to channel it into high-technology industries. Similarly, the total technology payments (in yen 10 million) for 1969 were more than three times greater in the targeted industries than in the untargeted industries, again reflecting the effects of MITI's influence over purchased technology.

While the 1969 expenditures on process innovation R&D (in yen 10 million) did not significantly differ between the targeted and the untargeted industries, R&D expenditures on both product quality and the development of new products and technology were about twice as great in the targeted than in the untargeted industries. This supports the contention of Peck and Tamura (1976) and Ueno (1980), who suggest that MITI was less concerned with directing R&D for process innovation than it was with R&D for improving product quality.

In Table 7.5, the 233 industries are divided into three groups—a third of the sample exhibiting the lowest bilateral trade balance with the United States, a third of the sample exhibiting the highest bilateral trade balance with the United States, and the remaining third of the sample exhibiting the middle bilateral trade balance with the United States. The mean values of variables which were influenced by Japanese industrial targeting are then compared between the three groups. For example, while an average of about eleven companies introduced foreign technology in both the low trade balance and high trade balance industries, there was an average of thirteen companies introducing foreign technology in the medium trade balance industries. Although the F-ratio of 7.12 implies that the hypothesis stating that the number of companies introducing foreign technology is constant across low, medium and high trade balance industries is rejected at the 95 percent level of confidence, this pattern does not yield any unequivocal conclusion about the success of channeling foreign technological purchases to certain industries. However, the mean value of total technological payments was greater in the medium and high trade balance industries than in the low trade balance industries, offering some support that technological purchases improved the bilateral trade balance.

The statistically significant F-ratio combined with the higher Japanese R&D-to-sales ratios in the medium and high trade balance industries suggests that the programs increasing Japanese R&D expenditures should be beneficial to the trade performance. The effectiveness of the R&D program may, however, reflect the type of R&D undertaken. The amount of expenditures on process innovation R&D was the greatest in the low trade balance industries, although this difference is not statistically significant. Greater expenditures of R&D devoted to improving the quality of existing products are, however, associated with industries exhibiting a medium and

Table 7.5 Mean Values of Japanese Industrial Policy Instruments Compared Between Low, Medium and High US Bilateral Trade Balance Industries (standard deviations in parentheses)[a]

Variable	Low trade balance	Medium trade balance	High trade balance	F-ratio
Total technology	182	286	235	9.01**
payments (10 million yen)	(284)	(364)	(411)	
Process innovation	164	153	154	0.56
R&D (10 million yen)	(183)	(163)	(169)	
Product quality	323	378	362	2.48*
R&D (10 million yen)	(334)	(390)	398)	
New products	474	483	399	2.84**
technology R&D	(607)	(535)	(561)	
Technology transfer	49	61	52	3.60**
R&D (10 million yen)	(67)	(71)	(65)	
Japanese	1.2340	1.4792	1.3170	6.64**
R&D/Sales	(1.0006)	(0.8993)	(0.942)	
No. of companies introducing	10.8881	13.2168	10.6643	7.12**
foreign technology	(13.3095)	(11.2658)	(7.3943)	

[a]The entire sample of 233 industries has been divided into thirds on the basis of the US–Japanese bilateral trade balance.
*The hypothesis that the mean value is equal across low, medium and high trade balance industries is rejected at the 90 percent level of confidence.
**The hypothesis that the mean value is equal across low, medium and high trade balance industries is rejected at the 95 percent level of confidence.

high trade balance. On the other hand, the amount of R&D allocated towards developing new products and technology is the lowest in those industries experiencing the best bilateral trade performance. Finally, R&D devoted to the transfer of technology appears to be positively related to the trade performance, although those industries with a medium bilateral trade performance spent more on technology transfer R&D than did those industries exhibiting a high trade balance. Again, the hypothesis of Peck and Tamura (1976) is apparently supported: R&D expenditures on improving the quality of existing products and on technology transfer seem to have been more successful than R&D expenditures on process innovation or on developing new products and technology.

CONCLUSION

While the exact impact of industrial targeting in Japan would be virtually impossible to quantify, it seems indisputable that such targeting has played a decisive role in a group of selected industries. The Japanese government's role has been a permanent feature in guiding the development of more than a handful of industries. Further, this guidance transcends the implementation of a finite set of policy instruments. Rather, while certain unmistakable policies have been implemented to develop specific industries, industrial policy has also taken a more nebulous form of general government guidance and administrative suasion. While the presence of such guidance is difficult to quantify, its impact seems more obvious. Thus, the US International Trade Commission (1983, p. 49) concluded that there are

> those who believe that extensive government intervention in Japan's economy is the main reason for the success of its leading export industries, including steel and autos. Recently, some have asserted that while direct funding of industrial research by the government is often relatively low, it is aimed in particular at crucial moments and thus affords the firms in those industries important advantages not otherwise available in the free market. It is this precise, well-orchestrated government aid that is most frequently cited as the primary concern of US competitors regarding Japanese industrial targeting, particularly in rapidly growing, high-technology industries where sustained and high levels of investment can be a key element in maintaining a competitive advantage.

An important feature of Japanese industrial targeting is that it has not played a homogeneous role in every industry and has not been invariant over time. In certain industries, such as steel, machine tools and automobiles, targeting was an important feature during the formative stages of the industry and subsequently receded to a less noticeable one once the industry became established. In other industries, such as aluminum, targeting did not play such a prominent role during the industry's development, but instead became increasingly important as a mechanism for managing an orderly decline of the industry once the mature and declining stages of the product life cycle were attained. In still other industries, such as robotics and semiconductors, industrial targeting has played a decisive role in helping to develop the requisite high technology capability. And, just as industrial targeting has not always been particularly effective, as in industries such as domestic aircraft, MITI has not always succeeded in implementing its plans, as in the automobile companies' refusal to consolidate in accordance with MITI's goal. In fact, the failure of industrial policy to succeed in several industries has led Caves and Uekusa (1976, p. 152) to conclude:

> Only scant evidence is available on the effects of MITI's custodial efforts on economic welfare. There is no doubt that the ministry's policies have engendered some allocative inefficiency by strengthening collusion and some technical inefficiency by distorting incentives for additions to capacity and diverting rivalry into nonprice channels. Furthermore, our statistical evidence lends support to the doubts expressed by others over the gains flowing from MITI's preoccupation with large scale plants. On the other hand, there are probable gains that might be substantial. MITI has beaten down substantially the price that Japan pays for technology imports. Some of its efforts at standardization and rationalization have surely lowered real costs. Indeed, in oligopolistic industries with partial collusion it is logically possible that firms become

inefficiently diversified, so that an imposed rationalization limiting the items each firm produced could potentially attain scale economies without giving away a significant increase in monopolistic restriction. The favorable and unfavorable possibilities arising from ministerial guidance are strong enough to leave the net evaluation in doubt.

Despite this qualification, it does seem apparent that MITI was able to foster the development in certain industries, such as computers, semiconductors and steel. In this sense MITI, along with the entire role of government intervention, has played a decisive role in industrial development in post-war Japan. By channeling resources into what were considered to be key industries, industrial targeting seems to have been successful for a particular country within the context of a particular historical framework. And, while the full benefits and costs from implementing that policy should be considered in assessing its effectiveness, the empirical evidence does suggest that MITI selected as key industries those which subsequently exhibited a strong bilateral trade performance with the United States. Of course, whether those industries, along with the entire Japanese economy, would have developed in a similar manner in the absence of such industrial targeting is a question which will continue to be debated in the future.

NOTES

1. These estimates come from Ueno (1980. p. 377).
2. For a more detailed analysis of MITI, see Johnson (1982).
3. This point is based on Suzumura and Okuno-Fujiwara (1986).
4. The Industrial Rationalization Council was changed to the Industry Structure Council in 1964.
5. Taken from US International Trade Commission (1983b).
6. Quoted from Ueno (1980).
7. These industries are taken from US International Trade Commission (1983b). See also Shinohara (1982) and MITI (1980).
8. It should be noted that while over 20 percent of R&D is spent on defense in the United States, less than one percent of R&D in Japan is allocated towards defense.
9. *Nihon Keizai Shinbun, Sept. 11, 1981,* cited in US International Trade Commission (1983b).
10. These rationalization allowances were suspended in 1976.
11. The supplemental depreciation allowances based on export performance were abandoned in 1971 and 1972.
12. Figures are from, Japan Development Bank, *Facts and Figures About the Japan Development Bank,* 1982.
13. Compensating balances are funds which firms must have on deposit with a bank as a condition for granting the loan. Because compensating balances for long-term loans generally yield no interest, this represents a substantial opportunity cost to the borrowers.
14. From, Japan Development Bank, *Facts and Figures About the Japan Development Bank,* 1982.
15. Warren Brown, 'GM making last stab at small cars', *Washington Post,* 13 January 1985, p. 1.

PART IV

TRADE POLICY AND DOMESTIC BUSINESS

8 · THE TRADE PROTECTION QUESTION IN THE UNITED STATES

The role of trade protection in the United States resembles that of antitrust and regulation in its volatility and continual state of flux. However, an added dimension to US international trade policy, in contrast to its domestic counterpart, is the dynamics involving multilateral as well as bilateral negotiations. Trade policy, and hence its consequences for private firms in the United States, results from both domestic and foreign pressures. However, to say that US trade policy is subject to foreign influences is not to imply that it is free from domestic ones. Despite the Reagan Administration's explicit stance towards free trade, pressure from special interest groups has resulted in the erection of one trade barrier after another, leaving commentators overseas to conclude that, 'America is slouching towards protectionism.'[1]

As will be seen in the two following chapters, US trade policy differs from that in Japan and Western Europe in that there has been virtually no attempt to integrate it with competition policy and regulation. As will be clear by the end of the chapter, US trade policy is frequently in direct conflict with its antitrust and deregulation policies. Unlike the case of Japan, there has been almost no effort to coordinate these policies.

This chapter is devoted to examining the role of trade protection in the United States and its effectiveness as an instrument in promoting economic efficiency. The second section examines the contemporary trade crisis and explores the significance and dimensions of this crisis. The third section considers the major forces precipitating the decline of numerous US manufacturing sectors. The response to foreign competition – trade protection – is examined from both a historical and from a contemporary perspective in the next two sections. After examining the current institutions responsible for formulating and implementing trade policy, the actual experience and consequences of trade policy in the most significant manufacturing industries are considered. Finally, after examining the interaction between domestic competition and foreign trade policies, conclusions are presented in the last section.

FOREIGN COMPETITION AND THE TRADE CRISIS

That the United States has been experiencing an ever-increasing crisis in foreign trade is beyond doubt. In 1982, the merchandise trade deficit was about $50 billion. By 1984, the trade deficit had more than doubled, and by 1986 it was approximately $170 billion.[2] The deterioration of the trade balance reflects the erosion of America's trade advantage in manufactured goods among developed nations. While the United States accounted for 22.8 percent of the share of exports of the fifteen most important non-communist industrial countries in 1960, this share had fallen to 17.3 percent by 1975 and to 15.5 percent by 1979, representing a one-third decrease in export share over this period. Most strikingly, in the decade of the 1970s, the increase in the volume of exports was 122 percent in Japan, 110 percent in West Germany but only 79 percent in the United States (United States Department of Labor, 1980).

Along with the exponential increase in the US trade deficit has come a concern that the United States, particularly in manufacturing industries, has lost its ability to compete in global markets, leading some observers to prophesy a de-industrialization of America (Reich, 1983). In fact, in certain industries, the United States has experienced a literal invasion of imports during the first half of the 1980s. Table 8.1 lists those industries experiencing the greatest trade disadvantage and compares exports, as a percentage of value-of-shipments, imports as a percentage of value-of-shipments, and the difference between these two measures for 1984 and 1980. Thus, the kitchen articles and pottery industry apparently had the worst trade performance in both 1984 and 1980. In 1980, exports were only 8.4 percent of industry shipments compared with competing imports of 99.4 percent, resulting in a net difference of −91.0 percentage points. By 1984, this industry's trade position had deteriorated further, as exports increased to only 10 percent while imports rose to 110.7 percent of shipments, resulting in a gap of −100.7 percentage points.

The industries experiencing the greatest deterioration in trade during this period include leather products (other than industrial products and cut stock), radio and television, opthalmic goods, watches and clocks, and miscellaneous personal goods. By contrast, certain industries, such as transportation equipment (other than automobiles) and household appliances, although exhibiting weak trade performances, did not significantly deteriorate over this period. However, most of the industries included in Table 8.1 show a significantly weaker trade performance in the first half of the 1980s.

However, to say that many US industries have been losing their competitive advantage is not to say that all American industries are experiencing a deteriorating trade position. Table 8.2 lists those industries experiencing the best trade performance in the first half of the 1980s. Because exports were 30.9 percent of shipments in the steam engines and turbines industry, while

Table 8.1 The US Industries Exhibiting the Worst Trade Performance[a]

Industry	1984			1980		
	Exports	Competing imports	Exports minus competing imports	Exports	Competing imports	Exports minus competing imports
Kitchen articles, pottery	10.0	110.7	−100.7	8.4	99.4	−91.0
Other leather products	3.4	98.6	−95.4	3.2	41.2	−38.0
Radio and TV	11.0	91.6	−80.6	16.1	49.2	−33.1
Opthalmic goods, watches and clocks	12.0	76.9	−65.0	10.1	50.3	−40.2
Miscellaneous personal goods	8.6	44.4	−35.7	14.9	30.8	−15.9
Other transportation equipment	5.4	32.0	−26.7	8.3	35.7	−27.5
Apparel and related products	2.0	25.6	−23.6	3.6	14.5	−10.9
Blast furnaces, steel mills	1.9	19.8	−17.9	4.3	11.7	−7.4
Motor vehicles and parts	8.4	25.2	−16.7	12.0	23.8	−11.8
All other furniture	2.3	16.4	−14.1	2.8	11.3	−8.5
Leather industrial products and cut stock	16.6	29.1	−12.5	13.2	13.3	−0.1
Tires and tubes	3.6	16.0	−12.5	5.9	12.8	−6.9
Non-ferrous metals	7.1	18.7	−11.6	15.0	18.2	−3.3
Metalworking machinery	13.1	22.7	−9.7	17.6	15.7	1.9
Cutlery, handtools, hardware	7.5	16.2	−8.7	12.2	13.3	−1.1
Other petroleum products	2.8	11.0	−8.3	1.5	7.0	−5.5
Pulp and paperboard mills except building paper	8.4	16.2	−7.8	12.3	15.7	−3.4
Special industry machinery	12.6	19.5	−8.7	18.2	15.9	2.3
Household appliances	5.8	12.2	−6.4	9.6	17.9	1.7
Beverages	1.0	6.9	−6.0	1.4	7.0	−5.6
Electronic components	19.6	25.3	−5.7	20.9	17.7	3.2
Broad woven fabrics and other textiles	3.6	8.5	−4.9	6.8	5.6	1.2
All other wood products	5.4	9.5	−4.2	8.7	8.8	−0.1

Table 8.1 (cont.)

Industry	1984			1980		
	Exports	Competing imports	Exports minus competing imports	Exports	Competing imports	Exports minus competing imports
Communications equipment	7.0	10.9	−3.9	7.4	6.6	0.8
Other durable goods	5.2	9.0	−3.8	8.7	5.7	3.1
Floor covering mills	3.2	6.8	−3.7	5.6	5.1	0.5
Photographic goods	13.7	16.7	−3.0	15.3	10.7	4.5
Miscellaneous equipment	6.5	8.8	−2.3	6.9	6.2	0.7
Other stone, clay and glass products	3.7	5.6	−1.9	4.6	3.8	0.8
Building paper	1.7	3.0	−1.2	2.3	3.8	−1.5
Other electrical machinery	15.8	16.6	−0.8	15.7	9.5	6.2
Wood containers	0.9	1.7	−0.8	1.5	1.9	−0.3
Glass containers	1.4	2.1	−0.7	1.0	1.0	0.0
Die-cut paper and board	0.1	0.9	−0.7	0.4	0.7	−0.4
All other foods	4.0	4.6	−0.7	5.6	4.3	1.3
Other fabricated metal products	5.9	6.5	−0.6	6.7	5.0	1.7
Electrical transmission and distribution equipment	6.3	6.8	−0.5	7.1	3.6	3.5

[a] All measures are expressed as a percentage of value-of-shipments. *Source*: US Bureau of Census.

Table 8.2 The US Industries Exhibiting the Best Trade Performance[a]

Industry	1984			1980		
	Exports	Competing imports	Exports minus competing imports	Exports	Competing imports	Exports minus competing imports
Steam engines and turbines	30.9	7.0	23.8	35.2	6.6	28.7
Aircraft parts	26.4	7.3	19.1	24.5	7.2	17.3
Fats and oils	19.1	4.8	14.2	20.6	3.0	17.6
Construction, mining and material handling equipment	21.5	8.1	13.4	33.7	4.1	29.6
Ordnance	16.5	3.9	12.7	15.6	3.4	12.2
Shipbuilding and tanks	11.0	0.5	10.5	8.1	0.0	8.1
Complete aircraft	13.5	3.4	10.0	27.3	2.8	24.5
Scientific engineering products	18.8	9.4	9.5	20.1	6.6	13.5
Agricultural chemicals	13.8	4.9	8.9	21.2	4.7	16.5
Office and computing machines	26.5	18.1	8.5	26.7	7.8	18.9
Other chemical products	10.2	3.6	6.6	15.3	2.5	12.7
Tobacco manufactures	7.1	0.5	6.5	9.0	0.8	8.2
Railroad equipment	14.4	8.3	6.1	5.6	4.6	1.1
Machine shops	5.5	0.0	5.5	6.0	0.0	6.0
Service industry machinery	9.1	3.8	5.3	13.2	1.6	11.5
Industrial chemicals except pigments	14.6	9.3	5.2	15.9	7.1	8.8
General industrial machinery	27.0	23.9	3.2	28.6	13.1	15.5
Internal combustion engines	19.4	16.7	2.8	23.3	14.1	9.2
Drugs, soaps and toiletries	6.3	4.1	2.3	6.5	2.7	3.8
Electrical industrial apparatus	9.6	8.2	1.5	14.0	5.4	8.6
Household furniture	1.1	0.1	1.0	1.7	0.1	1.6
Newspaper, books and periodicals	2.1	1.3	0.8	2.1	1.2	1.0
Paperboard containers	0.9	0.4	0.5	0.9	0.1	0.8
Meat products	3.5	3.1	0.4	3.2	4.0	−0.8
Knitting mills	0.7	0.5	0.2	1.1	0.3	0.8
Iron and steel foundries	0.8	0.6	0.2	1.4	0.4	1.0
Farm machinery and equipment	17.0	16.8	0.2	14.1	11.1	3.0

Table 8.2 (cont.)

Industry	1984			1980		
	Exports	Competing imports	Exports minus competing imports	Exports	Competing imports	Exports minus competing imports
Wood building and mobile homes	0.1	0.1	0.1	2.2	0.1	2.1
Other paper products	2.5	2.4	0.1	3.0	1.6	1.4
Paints and related products	3.6	3.7	0.0	3.4	2.4	1.0
Paving and roofing materials	0.5	0.5	0.0	0.7	0.4	0.3
Metal cans, barrels and drums	1.3	1.3	0.0	1.3	0.4	0.9
Other publishing and printing	0.6	0.8	-0.1	1.1	0.7	0.4
Other rubber and plastics products	6.3	6.3	-0.1	5.6	4.2	1.4
Building materials and wire	3.0	3.1	-0.2	5.6	2.6	2.4
Dairy products	1.1	1.5	-0.4	0.8	1.4	-0.6

[a] All measures are expressed as a percentage of value-of-shipments. *Source*: US Bureau of Census.

competing imports represented only 7 percent of shipments, it is ranked as achieving the strongest trade performance in 1984. However, even this industry's trade position has deteriorated somewhat since 1980, when exports were greater and imports were fewer. Still, a number of industries in Table 8.2 exhibited a strong improvement in trade performance between 1980 and 1984. In the railroad equipment industry, for example, exports increased from 5.6 to 14.4 percent of shipments while imports rose from 4.6 to only 8.3 percent. And in the meat products and building paper industries, import penetration actually decreased over this period. Other industries exhibiting a substantial strengthening in trade performance include shipbuilding and tanks, aircraft parts, ordnance, dairy products, and paving and roofing materials. On the other hand, though still exhibiting strong trade performances in 1984, those industries that experienced some deterioration in trade performance between 1980 and 1984 include construction equipment, complete aircraft, general industrial machinery, office and computing machines, and agricultural chemicals. Most of the industries appearing in Table 8.2 experienced an increase in competing imports between 1980 and 1984. The resulting trade performance over this period tended to be determined by how successful the industry proved to be in the export market. Those industries which were able to substantially increase their export shares were also able to retain or even improve their trade performances. However, those industries which were not able to expand exports at the same rate of increase in competing imports experienced some deterioration in trade performance.

Just as the pattern of exposure to import competition and resulting trade performance has varied across industry, it has varied similarly across broader industrial sectors. Table 8.3 compares the US balance of merchandise trade, defined as exports minus imports, for the twenty major industrial sectors for the years 1975, 1980 and 1985. It can be seen that in 1975, industries in the printing and publishing, chemical and petroleum refining sectors exhibited a relatively strong trade performance, while those in the fabricated metal products, transportation equipment and instruments sectors were relatively weak. By 1985, however, the trade position of most sectors had changed, and in a generally negative direction. Three sectors which had been fairly strong – paper and allied products, furniture and fixtures, and petroleum refining – experienced considerably deteriorating trade performances. Other sectors, such as lumber and wood products, fabricated metal products, transportation equipment and instruments had weak trade performances in 1975, which only proceeded to deteriorate further over the next decade.

A third pattern is exhibited by industries in the food and kindred products, textile mill products, apparel, stone, clay and glass, primary metal products, machinery (non-electrical), and electrical and electronic equipment sectors, all of which tended to have a relatively neutral trade position in 1975 that subsequently deteriorated. The only sectors not to experience considerable

Table 8.3 The US Net Exports by Industry Sector (in billions of 1977 dollars)

Industry sector	1975	1980	1985
Food and kindred products	0.057	0.051	−2.781
Tobacco manufactures	−0.008	−0.035	−0.069
Textile mill products	−0.222	−0.390	−0.942
Apparel and other textiles	−0.128	−0.135	−0.273
Lumber and wood products	−0.568	−0.869	−3.506
Furniture and fixtures	0.150	0.212	0.187
Paper and allied products	0.309	0.470	0.126
Printing and publishing	2.603	4.333	0.510
Chemicals and allied products	1.034	2.814	1.531
Petroleum refining	0.453	0.390	−1.281
Rubber and miscellaneous plastic products	0.116	0.163	0.132
Leather and leather products	−8.162	−4.194	−6.532
Stone, clay and glass products	−0.254	−0.423	−2.510
Primary metal products	0.084	0.046	−0.117
Fabricated metal products	−1.670	−2.951	−7.000
Machinery, except electrical	0.061	0.111	−0.363
Electrical and electronic equipment	−0.335	−0.582	−1.362
Transportation equipment	−3.730	−3.848	−11.695
Instruments and related products	−1.342	−0.629	−6.955
Miscellaneous manufacturing	0.054	0.124	0.069

Source: Data Resource, Inc. Interindustry Service.

trade volatility were tobacco manufacturers, furniture and fixtures, rubber and miscellaneous manufacturing – all of which preserved a rather neutral trade balance – and the leather and leather products sector, which maintained a weak trade balance throughout the period. The single sector exhibiting a strong trade position in 1975, which subsequently became even stronger, was chemicals and allied products. However, although the trade balance in this sector increased from about $1 billion in 1975 to $2.8 billion in 1980, it subsequently fell to $1.5 billion by 1985. Thus, even the chemicals and allied products industry did not experience an unequivocal improvement in trade position over this period.

Based on Tables 8.1, 8.2 and 8.3 it is clear that, while not every industry or even sector in America has been exposed to severe market deterioration, many of the most important industries and manufacturing sectors in the United States have experienced a deteriorating trade performance in the last half of the 1970s and first half of the 1980s. While the law of comparative advantage suggests that certain industries will almost inevitably experience a trade disadvantage, the rapid deterioration of US trade, and especially penetration of domestic markets by foreign rivals, has apparently caught most economists as well as businessmen by surprise.

The advent of foreign competition resulted from the interaction of two factors – the gradual recovery from the Second World War by Western

Europe and Japan, and the evolution of US manufacturing industries towards the mature and declining stages of the product life cycle. Since the United States emerged as the only nation that was economically stronger after the war than preceding it, and given the devastation suffered by both the Allies and former enemies, post-war US dominance is not surprising. Because both Japan and West Germany achieved their economic miracles through assimilating US technology (Peck and Tamura, 1976), American preeminence was rarely questioned. The capital intensity, which was a prerequisite for success in the post-war economy of mass production, when combined with the relative capital abundance in the United States, seemed to ensure continued American dominance (Hartland-Thunberg, 1981). Even as the Marshall Plan and other US assistance projects contributed to the restoration of Western Europe and Japan, only 8 percent of American manufacturing was exposed to foreign competition in the early 1960s.[3] But, as Nye (1983) argues, growth of European and Japanese industry relative to the United States was inevitable since these countries started from a base of virtually zero. Thus US industrial predominance could only be a temporary phenomenon as the rest of the developed world gradually recovered. The failure of capital intensity to protect the comparative advantage previously enjoyed by many US industries came as even more of a surprise than the relative decline of US manufacturing. In fact, as Japan, Western Europe and the newly developing countries evolved, capital intensity proved to be a liability for US firms trying to maintain an international competitive advantage. The explanation for this paradox lies in the theory of the product life cycle (Vernon, 1966; Wells, 1966).

Decades earlier, industries had been manufacturing products in the infant and growth stages of the life cycle.[4] When the product concept was new, no singular product design dominated the industry. Typically, management would experiment with design in short production runs, and gauge the reaction and needs of consumers. In the early stages, market survival depended upon developing the technology best adapted to meeting consumer demand. Because of the typically short production runs required by constantly changing product design, a skilled labor force was superior to an unskilled one, not only in order to operate fairly general-purpose machinery, but also to help in improving the product design and production process. Thus, the country with the most skilled labor force and highest level of technology tended to capture the competitive advantage (Audretsch and Yamawaki, 1986a, 1988a).

As the product became well defined and standardized, it evolved from the growth to the mature and declining phases of the product life cycle. In the mature stage, the rate of technological change slowed, and a fixed set of product design concepts became entrenched. The system of American scientific management was at its zenith in the late growth and early maturity stages.

In these stages, success in the industry was more easily attained through decreasing unit cost by extending the scale of output to the level of MES[5] than through altering the basic product design.

Prior to 1970, US manufacturing generally enjoyed a competitive advantage for two reasons. First, many industries still had enough elements of the growth phase so that relatively high levels of skilled labor and technological knowledge were still required. Second, during the immediate post-war years, US manufacturing faced no credible foreign competition. But, as manufactured products became sufficiently standardized and evolved towards the latter life cycle stages, a skilled labor force and high level of technology no longer guaranteed the competitive advantage. Rather, with product standardization and the increased use of specialized machinery, unskilled labor could be economically substituted for skilled workers. And, as the production process became established and standardized, it could be easily copied. Thus, the competitive advantage shifted away from many US manufacturing industries to countries with lower input prices. While US labor had previously been able to attain relatively high wages – due to the absence of international competition – it was now the same high wages, along with other input costs, that rendered US manufacturing a competitive disadvantage (Maskus, 1983; Stern and Maskus, 1981).

In fact, many of America's trade problems may be the result of the inevitable equalization process following the near annihilation of trading partners in the Second World War. This is evident from the shifts in both capital intensity and human capital of the American economy with respect to its trading partners over time. For example, in 1963 the United States had the most capital intensive economy in the world, with $9,204 (in 1966 dollars) of capital-per worker,[6] while the third-ranking country, Sweden, had a capital-labor ratio of $7,710. More strikingly, the capital-labor ratio was only $2,459 in Japan and $5,665 in West Germany. Although capital intensity grew in the United States between 1963 and 1975, the rate of growth was insufficient for it to retain its superiority. By 1975, the capital-per-worker of $11,270 in the United States was ranked only as the sixth largest in the West. The most capital-intensive economy was Norway, with $13,314 of capital-per-worker. While the growth rate in capital intensity over this period in the United States was 22.45 percent, it was 235.18 percent in Japan and 66.32 percent in West Germany. Perhaps the most striking increase in capital intensity occurred in countries such as Korea, which experienced a 316.18 percent increase in capital-per-worker over this period. Thus, between 1963 and 1975, America's share of the capital stock in the non-communist countries fell from 41.93 to 33.43 percent, while it increased in Japan from 7.09 to 14.74 percent.

Similarly, in 1963, the United States had the second most skill-intensive labor force, with 12.32 percent of its work force accounted for by skilled labor. Although the component of skilled labor in the work force had grown to 14.35 percent in 1975, the United States was only ranked seventh, following countries such as Sweden, Norway and Denmark. The share of skilled labor in non-communist countries accounted for by the United States thus fell from 29.36 percent in 1963 to 26.33 percent in 1975.

America's virtual dominance in high-technology trade also receded as trading partners were able to expand their investment of R&D at a rate exceeding that in the United States. For example, based on an index of comparative advantage in high technology trade, where the OECD average is defined as unity, the index was 1.27 for the United States, 0.72 for Japan, 1.20 for West Germany and 1.02 for the United Kingdom in 1963 (Cardiff, 1986).[7] By 1970, the index had fallen in the United States to 1.18, in West Germany to 1.00 and in the United Kingdom to 0.94, while it had risen in Japan to 1.07. By 1985, the comparative advantage had evolved to 1.42 in Japan, 1.25 in the United States, 0.94 in West Germany and 0.89 in the United Kingdom. America's predominance in high-technology goods had ended by the 1980s.

The protected and stable market structures of the post-war period enabled input costs, particularly labor costs, to capture a share of the economic rents generated by monopolistic pricing (Weston and Lustgarten, 1974). As a result, wages and, most importantly, unit labor costs rose gradually relative to the rest of the world. By 1970, the average hourly compensation of production workers in manufacturing industries was $3.84 in the United States, $2.50 in West Germany, $0.47 in Mexico and $0.54 in Brazil. Average hourly compensation in Mexico and Brazil was only 12 and 14 percent, respectively, of US compensation (US Congress, 1973).

Even by 1970, the United States still maintained a large productivity advantage over its international competitors – but not one large enough to compensate for the large wage differentials. This is reflected by the large gap in unit labor costs – labor cost per unit of output – between the United States and its trading partners. For example, the US unit labor cost of $0.09 in the chemicals industry in 1970 was about double that in Mexico ($0.04) and in Brazil ($0.05). Similarly, in the electrical machinery industry, the US unit labor cost was $0.17 compared to $0.07 in Mexico and $0.11 in Brazil (US Congress, 1973).

Even after adjusting for productivity differences, these input cost differentials caused US corporations to locate more and more production facilities in lower cost countries through foreign direct investment (see Kindleberger and Audretsch, 1983). US foreign direct investment was only $0.6 billion in 1897 and $7.75 billion by 1929. Following the Second World War, multinationalization had still not grown appreciably – in 1945 there were only $8.4 billion of foreign direct investment and $11.8 billion in 1950. But as the unit labor cost gap grew, and the US comparative advantage in manufactured goods eroded, foreign direct investment virtually exploded, nearly doubling from $56.6 billion in 1967 to $101.3 billion in 1973. By 1978, foreign direct investment had grown to $168.1 billion, and to $213.5 billion by 1980

(Fayerweather, 1982). By shifting manufacturing from domestic plants to plants abroad, US corporations attempted to salvage the competitive advantage by the application of the same strategy that had always constituted the kernel of mass production: employ low-wage, unskilled labor to perform repetitive tasks in producing low-cost, standardized products.

Confronted by such deterioration in their competitive advantage, American manufacturing firms have increasingly focused on one particular solution – trade protection. Essentially, with the advent of foreign competition, it has seemed less costly for American firms to invest in political resources with the goal of winning trade protection than to undertake the necessary steps to regain global competitiveness. The most recent trend towards protectionism is evidenced by the increased number of investigations completed by the US International Trade Commission in the first half of the 1980s. While there were only 41 investigations undertaken considering some sort of trade protection in 1977, there were 232 such investigations completed in 1982 and 184 completed in 1984.[8] The explanation underlying this increased trend towards protectionism lies perhaps with the theory of collective action (Olson, 1965, 1982) along with the theory of rent-seeking (see Buchanon et al., 1980; Colander, 1984).

The theory of collective action suggests that if the number of sellers in the market is sufficiently small, and if information is widespread among those firms, then the organizational costs of obtaining a restrictive policy will be relatively small. And if a few parties stand to gain from the transfer of a large amount of wealth, the value to each member of seeking restrictive policies is high. The parties losing from that policy, on the other hand, especially consumers, tend to suffer from high organizational costs and a deficient distribution of information (Krueger, 1974). Thus, it may be rational and profitable in instances of small coalitions with recognizable gains and low organizational costs to invest collectively in institutional change via the political process.[9] In connecting the political process with the economic interest groups, Stigler (1971) predicts that legislatures will respond to special interest group pressure and supply the legal structures necessary to protect industries from competition. Because many manufacturing industries are relatively well-organized and can form a political coalition at a relatively low cost, while consumers of the products remain dispersed and face a relatively high cost of organizing into an effective political coalition, the procurement of trade protectionism has proved to be an economical investment in a number of American industries.

Hufbauer and Rosen, of the Institute for International Economics, estimated that the total cost of import protection in nineteen manufacturing industries to American consumers was $56 billion in 1984.[10] While the greatest absolute cost to consumers, $27 billion, occurred in the textiles and apparel industry, the greatest cost per job saved was $1 million in the specialty steel and benzenoid chemicals industries. Similarly, the total cost to consumers of trade protection in the carbon steel industry was $6.8 billion, which amounted to $750,000 per job saved. Other industries incurring a high cost of protection include automobiles, dairy products, orange juice, motorcycles, canned tuna and rubber footwear. Despite the fact that 'protectionism costs money and consumers foot the bill',[11] the protectionist movement has gained the support of both major political parties in the United States. In May 1986, fifty-eight Republicans in the House of Representatives abandoned the President's commitment to free trade in order to support the Democratic-sponsored trade protection bill, which was overwhelmingly passed, 295–112.[12] It seems reasonable to conclude that the greater the threat of foreign competition, the greater the incentive to the domestic industry for investing in political resources to achieve protectionist policies.

THE EVOLUTION OF AMERICAN TRADE POLICY

At the heart of American trade policy is the tension between autonomous nationally determined policy and multilaterally negotiated policy. Contemporary US trade policy arises from principles established between 1922 and 1934. Following the First World War agriculture prices were subject to a declining spiral. After President Warren Harding advocated tariff protection for the explicit benefit of the agricultural sector, Congress voiced its approval with passage of the Emergency Tariff Act (1921). Shortly thereafter, manufacturing industries, which had greatly expanded to replace the loss of imports during the war, similarly pressed for protection which was granted under the Tariff Act (1922). This resulted in an 'average rate on free and dutiable products' which was 'more than 50 percent higher than under the 1913 Underwood–Simmons Tariff' (Kelly, 1963, p. 7).

The determinator of tariff protection was placed on the Tariff Commission, which had been established by Congress in 1966 for the purpose of divorcing or at least mitigating the political process from trade protection.[13] The underlying principle which Congress instructed the Tariff Commission to implement when considering protection was the equalization of production costs between foreign and domestic producers. However, the Congress further raised tariff levels with passage of the Smoot–Hawley Tariff in 1930. According to Vernon (1954, p. 2), 'this statute has attracted superlative abuse not alone because it set American tariffs so high, but also because the rates were set with such a single-minded concern for the wishes of specific producer groups as to shock the sense of fitness and propriety of many of those who were exposed to the process .... The rates in the act were, in effect, largely an expression of the relative power of lobby groups.' Further, Schattschneider (1963, p. 99) observed that the Smoot–Hawley Tariff was a 'revision of a protectionist law by protectionists for people whom they sought to make more and more protectionist.'

The Smoot-Hawley Tariff accomplished at least one thing unequivocally – the reduction of US exports. The trading partners of the United States did not passively accept the heightened tariff barriers; rather, they responded by erecting their own versions of the Smoot–Hawley Tariff. US exports declined from an average of $5 billion between 1925 and 1929 to about $1.7 billion between 1933 and 1934 (Beckett, 1941). The failure of the Smoot–Hawley Tariff to provide an antidote to the Great Depression, and in fact its apparent exacerbation of America's economic condition in the 1930s, led to the abandonment of the purely unilateral trade policy approach. With the election of President Franklin D. Roosevelt came the passage of the Trade Agreements Act in 1934, which constituted the kernel of Roosevelt's Reciprocal Trade Agreements Program. The purpose of the Act as well as the program was to undo as much of the damage as possible which had been done through the enactment of the Smoot–Hawley Tariff, thereby promoting international trade and the economic recovery of the United States as well as that of its trading partners. The four essential components of the Trade Agreements Act were: (1) authority granted by the Congress to the President to enter into negotiations with the purpose of reaching agreements with trading partners to explicitly reduce domestic and foreign tariffs; (2) tariff concessions by the United States had to be simultaneously matched by equivalent tariff concessions of trading partners; (3) all tariff concessions, either bilateral or multilateral, were required to be stipulated through formal trade agreements; and (4) each trade agreement was to follow the principle of most favored nation status (Monroe, 1975). The significance of the Reciprocal Trade Agreements Act was that it marked the reversal of the spiral of increased tariff protection. While there were few actual reductions in tariff rates throughout the 1930s, at least their rise had been limited.

Beginning in 1947, American trade policy took on a new dimension with the establishment of the General Agreement on Tariffs and Trade (GATT). The twenty-two countries which signed the Act agreed to enter into multilateral tariff negotiations. The principle forum for these negotiations has been the eight tariff conferences held since 1947, which have been called 'rounds' by the popular press. The focal point of the rounds are concessions, which constitute either a reduction in the tariff associated with a given commodity or else a promise not to increase the rate of duty. Prior to each round, nations typically assemble lists of commodities in which they have a special interest in procuring concessions. During the multilateral negotiating sessions, countries usually grant a concession only in the presence of reciprocity. However, the United States also established a procedure to institute an escape clause if the Tariff Commission determined through an investigation that 'as the result of unforeseen developments, the concession granted by the United States on any article in the trade agreement is imported in increased quantities and under conditions which cause or threaten injury to domestic producers of the same or similar articles' (Hawkins and Norwood, 1963). The 1958 Trade Renewal Act enabled the Tariff Commission to find injury with even less evidence of damage to the domestic industry. And, once having determined injury, an industry was able to receive a tariff increase of up to 50 percent of the 1934 tariff rates. Between 1947 and 1961, there were over 130 petitions filed for relief under the escape clause. The Tariff Commission determined that the domestic industry had been injured in 40 of these cases.[14] The President raised the tariffs in 13 cases and rejected the Commission's recommendation in the remaining ones (Lenway, 1985).

When the Reciprocal Trade Agreements Act was due to expire in 1962, following its eleven renewals subsequent to its original legislation in 1934, President John F. Kennedy replaced it with the Trade Expansion Act (1962). The particular distinction of the new Act enabled the President to abandon the particular commodity negotiating approach for the 'across-the-board' approach. The Act also enabled firms and workers injured by imports to petition the Tariff Commission for an investigation to determine whether they were eligible for adjustment assistance. After a determination of either serious injury or the threat of serious injury, the petitioning firm could submit a proposal outlining adjustment assistance to the Secretary of Commerce. The firm would then be qualified to benefit from adjustment assistance in the form of loans and tax concessions. Similarly, workers, once identified by the Secretary of Labor, were qualified to receive adjustment assistance in the form of retraining and relocation allowances along with extended unemployment compensation coverage.

The 1962 Act also established the Office of the Special Trade Representative, which was designated to be the chief representative of the United States in negotiating trade agreements. Finally, the Trade Expansion Act authorized the United States to participate in what has become known as the 'Kennedy Round' of the GATT negotiations. The stated goal of the Kennedy Round was 'a target of 50 percent across-the-board reductions on a wide variety of goods'.[15] As a result of the Kennedy Round, tariff reductions of an average of about 35 percent of the existing rates prior to the negotiations were achieved for non-agricultural goods. And for the United States, tariffs were reduced around an average of 65 percent (Evans, 1971). For example, before the Kennedy Round, the average tariff on dutiable imports in the chemical industry, which applied to 59 percent of total imports, was 17.8 percent. Subsequent to the Kennedy Round, the average tariff fell to 9.3 percent, representing a 48 percent reduction in the average tariff rate. Other manufacturing industries subject to similar substantial tariff reductions included wood (natural cork), raw hides, transportation equipment, non-electrical machinery and paper products (Meier, 1973). Other industries were subject to substantially smaller tariff reductions, such as yarn and basic fibers, apparel, footwear and headwear, and natural fibre and waste, all of which experienced average tariff reductions of less than 25 percent. As a result of the negotiations transpiring in the Kennedy Round, the average tariff rate fell from 14.3 to 9.9 percent (Meier, 1973).

A world-wide system of relatively free trade did not emerge following the Kennedy Round due to the proliferation of non-tariff barriers which served to offset at least some of the effects of the tariff reductions. That the Kennedy Round had failed to substantially liberalize trade was evident by the end of the 1960s (Evans, 1971, p. 263):

> Many of us like to think that the decades since the war have been marked by a continuing movement toward freer world trade and payments. The Kennedy Round in this vision is seen by shortsighted persons as the crowning achievement of the drive forward for freer trade, but they have ignored the fact that as tariffs have been dismantled . . . quotas, licenses, embargoes, and other rigid and restrictive trade barriers have been created.

A good example of this is the American textile industry. In response to the rising import penetration of the American textile market, and the declining domestic market shares of American manufacturers, the United States persuaded Japan, Korea, Taiwan and Hong Kong to enter bilateral textile quota agreements in 1971. Similarly, in 1974 Congress passed the Trade Reform Act, authorizing the United States to enter into trade negotiations in the Tokyo Round of the GATT. Equally important, the Trade Reform Act enabled the President to negotiate over non-tariff barriers with US trading partners.

While the Kennedy Round had focused on the reduction of tariff rates, the Tokyo Round was concerned primarily with alleviating non-tariff barriers. Although some additional reductions in tariff rates resulted from the Tokyo Round, the major focus was on non-tariff barriers.[16] In order to procedurally accommodate agreements dealing with the problem of non-tariff measures which were negotiated in the Tokyo Round, a number of dispute settlement provisions were agreed upon. These codes include the Agreement on Technical Barriers to Trade (Standards Code, dealing with product standards), the Agreement on Government Procurement,[17] the Subsidies Code (dealing with countervailing duties and subsidies), the International Dairy Arrangement, the Customs Valuation Agreement, the Agreement on Import Licensing Procedures, the Agreement on Trade in Civil Aircraft and the Antidumping Code (US International Trade Commission, 1985). Between 1975 and 1985, there were sixteen cases filed by the United States disputing trade measures by a trading partner.[18] While only one case represented a tariff measure, three cases represented a subsidy, four cases involved quotas, two cases involved tax benefits and six cases represented other types of non-tariff barriers, such as import licensing and standards. During this same period, there were eight cases filed against the United States, including three cases regarding tariff measures, none involving subsidies, three cases involving quotas and two cases concerned with other types of non-tariff barriers (US International Trade Commission, 1985b). In over half of these complaints, some type of remedy was established.

Perhaps the most significant aspect of the Tokyo Round involved the counterveiling duty code, which allowed the imposition of countervailing duties equal to the amount of the subsidy in those circumstances where it could be demonstrated that the imports being considered had benefited from a subsidy and resulted in 'material injury' to the domestic industry.

US INSTITUTIONS IMPLEMENTING TRADE POLICY

The focal points for contemporary US trade policy are the ITC, the Office of the Special Trade Representative and the Commerce Department. Although it is not a policy making institution, the ITC is an independent, bipartisan, quasi-judicial agency assigned by Congress the responsibility of investigating 'all factors relating to the effect of US foreign trade on domestic production, employment, and consumption' in order to contribute 'substantially to the development of sound, equitable international trade policy' (US International Trade Commission, 1985f, p. ix). The Commission, which includes six commissioners,[19] who are assigned voting powers and a staff of almost 500, including numerous attorneys and economists, is charged with: (1) making recommendations for relief to the President in cases where a domestic industry has been seriously injured by increasing imports; (2) determining whether a petitioning US industry has been materially injured by imports and whether those imports benefited from subsidization of charged dumping prices; (3) directing action against unfair trade practices; (4) advising the President whether agricultural imports conflict with the goals of the US Department of Agriculture's price-support programs; (5) undertaking studies investigating trade and tariff issues and monitoring trade relationships, especially US import levels; and (6) developing uniform statistical trade data and establishing an international harmonized commodity code (US International Trade Commission, 1985f).

Section 201 of the Trade Act (1974)[20] provides an administrative procedure enabling domestic industries to petition for import relief in the form of either a tariff or else a quota. Under Section 201, an industry is not required to demonstrate that an unfair trade practice by a trading partner exists; rather, a petitioning industry must demonstrate that the industry has sustained 'serious' injury and that the substantial cause of injury, meaning the greatest source, is the result of import penetration.[21] Section 201 is based on Article XIX of GATT, which is referred to as the escape clause, because it enables the signatory a temporary release from its obligations under GATT. In 1985, the Commission made two Section 201 determinations. In Potassium Permanganate,[22] the Commission ruled that the potassium permanganate industry was neither a substantial cause of serious injury nor threat of substantial injury and thus no recommendation for import relief was made to the President. In Nonrubber Footwear,[23] the Commission ruled that the imports of non-rubber footwear were a substantial cause of serious injury. Of the fifty-five cases Section 201 completed by the International Trade Commission under the Trade Act of 1974, thirty-two resulted in an affirmative decision (i.e., in favor of the petitioning industry) and twenty-three resulted in a negative determination (i.e., against the petitioning industry). Subsequent to a determination of serious injury by the Commission along with the recommendation for appropriate relief, the President is given a period of sixty days within which to decide whether or not to act upon the Commission's recommendations. Measures of relief typically include tariff increases, the imposition of quotas, the negotiation of orderly marketing agreements or some combination of these measures. The President also has the option of requiring the Secretary of Labor to administer trade adjustment assistance. In fact, the President has granted relief in 18 of the 32 cases in which the Commission recommended relief. In eight of those cases, the President applied the exact measures of relief advocated by the Commission; in ten other cases the President modified the relief. For example, in the Nonrubber Footwear case, while four commissioners recommended quotas, President Reagan ended by implementing trade adjustment assistance. Similarly, in the 1984 Carbon and Alloy Steel Products case,[24] the Commission recommended an increase in the tariff along with the implementation of quotas; President Reagan decided against imposing any relief measures. However, in the Heavyweight Motor-Cycles case,[25] President Reagan approved the tariff increase recommended to him by the Commission. The other industries in which the President implemented the Commission's recommendation without some modification include nonelectric cookware, bolts, nuts and large screws, clothespins, high-carbon ferrochrome, citizens band receivers, color televisions, and footwear, shrimp, mushrooms, and stainless and alloy tool steel.[26]

The ITC also is charged by Section 731 and Section 751 of the Tariff Act (1930)[27] with undertaking antidumping investigations. In 1985, 129 antidumping investigations were completed, with 56 involving steel products, including hot-rolled carbon steel plate, carbon steel wire rod, stainless steel sheet and strip, welded carbon steel pipes and tubes, and carbon steel sheets. In accordance with the Tokyo Round agreements, the Department of Commerce first determines whether an import has been directly or indirectly subsidized by a trading partner of the United States. If the Department of Commerce determines that US imports have benefited from subsidies, the ITC then undertakes an investigation to determine whether the domestic industry had, in fact, been harmed or threatened with material injury. For the Commission to make a positive determination requires that there must have been a decrease in sales in the domestic industry, with the decline having been the result of the subsidized imports.[28]

TRADE POLICY IN VITAL INDUSTRIES

A substantial source of the tension in American trade policy emanates from the spectrum of different stages of the product life cycle within which affected industries operate. That is, the trade concerns of mature and declining industries such as textiles, apparel and steel are very different from and often conflict with those concerning industries in the introduction and growth stages, such as high-technology products. Meier (1973, p. 93) frames this 'fundamental question' as: 'What policy measures, if any, should be taken to protect a large domestic industry that faces keen competition from a sharp and substantial increase of imports? Should potential imports be foreclosed through quotas? Or should the economic, social, and political costs of dislocation of local production be endured?'

Even by the end of the 1950s the textile industry was experiencing pressure from foreign competition. Following President Kennedy's promise to the cotton textile industry to provide some form of relief from the encroaching wave of imports from Asia, the Long-Term Arrangement regarding International Trade in Cotton Textiles was signed in 1962 by thirty-three countries, including virtually every major cotton textile importing and exporting country.[29] However, the agreement did not mitigate the rise of imports in the United States. Between 1979 and 1981, there was a loss of almost 90,000 workers from the American textile and apparel industries, which GATT (1973) attributed to 'low-cost imports which forced an increasing number of United States plants to shut down'. However, the decline in employment during this period was certainly exacerbated by the substantial increases in labor productivity resulting from capital substitution for labor (Lenway, 1985). Whatever the major causes of decline in the American Textile and apparel industries, the Nixon Administration was sufficiently impressed that it moved to negotiate bilateral agreements limiting US imports with Japan and four other Asian countries between 1969 and 1971. This protection was largely a response to the flat growth in the textile industry's sales between 1968 and 1971 combined with the large rise in textile and apparel imports, which increased by 42 percent between 1970 and 1971.[30] Not surprisingly the profitability of the major companies suffered, with profits of $109 million in 1970 (first quarter) declining to $93 million in 1971 (first quarter). Thus, between 1970 and 1971 it was estimated that 150,000 jobs were lost.[31]

Following the wave of US bilateral of agreements, negotiations between fifty countries resulted in the GATT 1973 Multifiber Agreement (US International Trade Commission, 1981). The trade agreements covered around 90 percent of cotton, 60 percent of wool, 75 percent of man-made fiber and about 80 percent of total (including cotton, wool and man-made fiber) US imports.[32] As of 1 April 1985, thirty-two countries had agreed upon quantitive limitations on US imports of textiles under the Multifiber Agreement, ranging from a ceiling of 0.6 million square yard equivalents from Panama,

0.8 from the Maldives and 1.0 from Yugoslavia, to 1,883.8 from Taiwan, 987.5 from Korea, 928.1 from Hong Kong and 841.7 from China (US International Trade Commission, 1985g).

Despite the success of the US industry in obtaining such a pervasive net of protection, domestic firms have still been unable to prevent the erosion of the domestic market or to make significant gain through the export of textile products. Figure 8.1 shows the trends in US total textile shipments (including cotton, wool and man-made fibers), US imports of textiles and US exports of textiles between 1974 and 1984. Over this period the quantity of shipments actually decreased slightly from 11,101 million pounds in 1974 to 10,881 million pounds in 1984. During the 1982 recession, shipments fell even lower to 9,379 million pounds. Imports, however, rose substantially during the same period. While there were only 948 million pounds of textile imports in 1974, imports had more than tripled by 1984, when 3,018 million pounds of textiles were purchased from foreign producers. Man-made fibers constituted the greatest source of this rise in imports, increasing from 371 million pounds in 1974 to 1,343 million pounds in 1984, compared with increases in cotton imports of 503 to 1,465 million pounds and in wool imports of 74 to 210 million pounds in this same period. Thus, US total domestic consumption of textile products rose by 17.3 percent, from 11,240 million pounds in 1974 to 13,186 million pounds in 1984. The failure of domestic production to keep up with the continual increased presence of imports is reflected by the steady erosion of market share by foreign producers. In 1974 the import penetration ratio was 8.4 percent.[33] Subsequently, the import penetration ratio has gradually risen, reaching 22.8 percent in 1984. At the same time, US exports have declined from 809 million pounds in 1974 to 713 million pounds in 1984 (US International Trade Commission, 1985g).

The biggest source of US imports of cotton textiles in 1984 was Hong Kong, which sold $1,449.8 million (661.4 millions of equivalent square yards) to the United States. While the People's Republic of China sold $554.2 million (640.9 millions of equivalent square yards), and Taiwan sold $478.2 million (403.5 millions of equivalent square yards) of cotton textiles to the United States in 1984, Japan contributed $408.2 (167.7 millions of equivalent square yards) to US imports (US International Trade Commission, 1985g).

On the other hand, the largest source of US imports of wool textiles in 1984 was Italy, which sold $350.9 (42.3 millions of equivalent square yards) of wool textiles to the United States. And, the biggest sources of US imports of man-made fibers were Taiwan, which sold $1,651.1 (926.7 millions of equivalent square yards) and the Republic of Korea, which sold $1,442.6 (778.6 millions of equivalent square yards) to the United States in 1984. Thus, while Taiwan accounted for 31 percent and the Republic of Korea for 26 percent of the US man-made fiber textile imports, Italy accounted for 18 percent and Hong Kong for 26 percent of the US cotton textile imports in 1984.

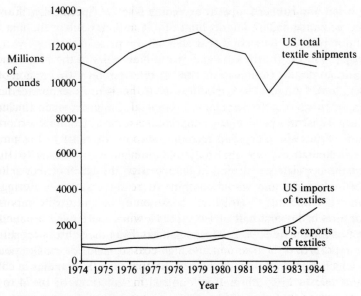

Note: US Total textile shipments = Mill Consumption.
Source: US International Trade Commission, 1985g.

Fig. 8.1 Performance of the US Textile Industry Subsequent to the Multifiber Agreement

As a result of the Multifiber Agreement's failure to prevent a further erosion of the domestic textile market, US manufacturers have been lobbying for a more restrictive new version of the Multifiber Agreement to preserve its $100 billion-a-year industry. While the industry was able to pressure the Congress into passing the 1986 Jenkins Bill, which would have constrained textile imports from developing countries at their level of 1984 imports, it was not able to prevent President Reagan from vetoing the bill. Since 1980 it has been estimated that over 260,000 jobs have been lost due to imports (12 percent of the 1980 labor force in the industry), 250 mills have been closed, and the net profits of the largest eleven publicly quoted cloth companies declined by more than 33 percent. In 1985, Burlington Industries, the industry leader with $2,802 million of sales, listed a profit of just $13 million, while the second largest firm, J. P. Stevens, with sales of $1,698 million, actually posted a loss of $16 million. The response of the American textile industry is 'that the Reagan administration is too tardy in acting against predatory pricing and dumping.'[34]

On 1 July 1985 the ITC determined that the non-rubber footwear industry in the United States had sustained serious injury due to imports and therefore, under Section 201 of the Trade Act of 1974, recommended that President Reagan impose quantitative restrictions for a five-year period on all imported non-rubber footwear exceeding $2.50.[35] Specifically, the Commission recommended an import limit of 474 million pairs in the first year, 474 million pairs in the second year, 488 million parts in the third year, 517 million pairs in the fourth year and 564 million pairs in the fifth year (US International Trade Commission, 1985a).[36] After reviewing the case the President, on 28 August 1985, modified the Commission's recommendations and elected to instruct the Secretary of Labor to administer trade adjustment assistance. What was particularly remarkable about the Commission's determination of serious injury and recommendation for relief in the form of quantitive limitations, was that only one year before the Commission had reached the opposite conclusion in finding that 'the US footwear industry had been successful and would continue to be successful in meeting competition from abroad'.[37] However, because of the industry's very rapid deterioration in the first half of 1985, the Commission moved to reverse its decision of the previous year. Most significant was the substantial penetration of imports into the medium- and high-cost segments of the shoe market areas, which had traditionally been a bastion of US dominance. Those Commissioners voting affirmative[38] noted that all three of the necessary conditions stated by Section 201 to determine serious injury and recommend relief – (1) imports are increasing either in actual terms or relative to domestic production, (2) the domestic industry is seriously injured or threatened with serious injury, and (3) such increased imports are a substantial cause of the serious injury or threat thereof – were met in the case of the US non-rubber industry.

The industry has experienced continual increases in imports since 1980. Imports rose to 376 million pairs in 1981 from 366 million pairs in the previous year, representing an import penetration ratio of 50 percent (US International Trade Commission, 1985c). However, following 1981, imports rose to 480 million pairs in 1982, 582 million pairs in 1983, 726 million pairs in 1984 and 820 million pairs in 1985. The import penetration ratio rose from 58 percent in 1982 to 63 percent in 1983, to 71 percent in 1984 and 83 percent in 1985. Thus, the first condition, that imports have increased (in this case in both absolute and relative numbers), has clearly occurred in the shoe industry.

The second condition under Section 201 requires that the domestic industry be seriously injured or threatened with serious injury. In the shoe industry, capacity rose from 412 million pairs in 1980 to 428 million pairs in 1982, but then fell drastically to 388 million pairs in 1984. In 1980, there were only 3 plant closures, but in both 1981 and 1982 there were 11, 14 in 1983 and 84 in 1984. Even though capacity dropped over this period, it did not fall fast enough to prevent a concomitant decline in capacity utilization, which dropped from 78 percent in 1980 to 70.1 percent in 1984. Not surprisingly, operating income for domestic footwear manufacturers' operations producing non-rubber footwear fell from $375 million (10.1 percent of net sales) in

1981 to $204 million (5.8 percent of net sales) in 1984. In 1982, 22 firms reported operating losses and 23 firms reported net losses before taxes; by 1984, 36 firms (27 percent of the total number of reporting firms) suffered operating losses, while 43 firms had net losses before taxes. The decline in capacity, sales, capacity utilization and profitability all substantiate that the domestic industry has suffered injury. This is also supported by the substantial decline in the average number of production and related workers producing footwear. While there were 104,000 workers in 1980, the number declined to 87,000 by 1984, representing almost a 20 percent drop between 1981 and 1984 and a 10 percent drop between 1983 and 1984.Thus, in 1980, there were 16,000 unemployed footwear workers comprising an unemployment rate of almost 8 percent. The following year, there were 27,000 unemployed workers as the unemployment rate rose to 12.5 percent, and 41,000 unemployed workers in 1982, constituting an unemployment rate of nearly 20 percent. By 1984, a sufficient number of people had exited from the industry so that the number of unemployed fell to 27,000, constituting an unemployment rate of 16.6 percent (US International Trade Commission, 1985c).

The final criterion for reaching the determination of serious injury and recommending to the President some form of trade relief is that imports constitute the largest cause of the injury incurred by the domestic industry. That is, other sources of the industry's economic problems, such as dislocation caused by the abundance of suboptimal plants,[39] and the shift in consumer tastes from non-rubber footwear towards athletic, woven and 'soft' shoes have not been responsible for more of the industry's decline than has the rise in imports (US International Trade Commission, 1985c). Thus, because the non-rubber footwear industry in the United States met the three criteria required to determine serious injury and recommend relief, the industry subsequently received government assistance.

That the US steel industry is also experiencing economic decline is apparent from Figure 8.2, which lists US total steel mill shipments, US imports of steel mill products and US exports of steel mill products between 1976 and 1985. While US shipments of total steel mill products rose from 89.4 millions of net tons in 1976 to 100.3 in 1979, shipments subsequently declined to 61.6 in 1982 before again rising to 73.0 in 1985. Thus, between 1976 and 1985, US shipments of total steel mill products fell by almost one-fifth. Over this same period, US exports of all steel mill products fell from 2.7 million net tons in 1976 to 0.93 in 1985. However, US imports rose by nearly 70 percent between 1976 and 1985. In 1976, 14.3 million net tons of steel were imported into the United States. By 1985, steel imports had risen to 24.3 millions of net tons. Thus, the import penetration ratio in the domestic steel market also rose, from 14.1 percent in 1976 to 25.2 percent in 1985.

While almost one-third of US steel imports came from Japan in 1981, Japan's share of total imports fell to just over one-quarter by 1984 (US

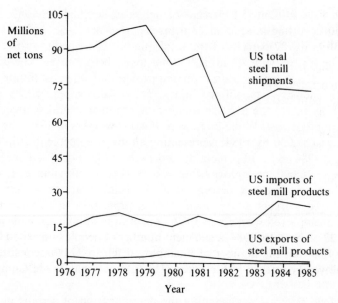

Source: American Iron and Steel Institute (1986).

Fig. 8.2 Performance in the US Steel Industry

International Trade Commission, 1985d). Similarly, while the members of the EEC accounted for almost one-third of US steel imports in 1981, their share also declined to about one-quarter by 1984. Together, Japan and the EEC accounted for almost two-thirds of all US steel imports in 1981 and about half of those imports in 1984. The Republic of Korea increased its share of US steel imports, from 6.12 percent in 1981 to 8.54 percent in 1984, as did Brazil, from 2.75 percent in 1981 to 5.58 percent. Within the EEC, West Germany, France and Belgium/Luxembourg have captured the largest shares of the US import market. While West Germany accounted for nearly 11 percent of all US steel imports in 1981 and almost 13 percent in 1982, its share fell to 8.1 percent in 1983 before recovering to 9.7 percent in 1984. France's share of US imports fell from 6.5 percent in 1981 to 4.3 percent in 1984, while Belgium/Luxembourg's share has fallen from 5.6 percent in 1981 to 3.5 percent in 1984.

While there is a long, complex post-war history of steel protection in the United States (see Borrus, 1983), one of the most recent mechanisms for protection went into effect on 21 October 1982. The Arrangement Concerning Trade in Certain Steel Products between the European Coal and Steel Community (ECSC) and the US limited the US imports of most steel products from the EEC between 1 November 1982 and 31 December 1985.[40] The Arrangement explicitly placed a ceiling on the import penetration of certain steel products from the EEC 'as a share of apparent US consumption'. The fifteen steel products and the relevant ceilings which were covered by the Arrangement include:

hot-rolled sheet and strip, both carbon and alloy	(6.81%)
coated-rolled sheet, both carbon and alloy	(5.11%)
plate, both carbon and alloy	(5.36%)
structural steel, both carbon and alloy	(9.91%)
carbon wire rod	(4.29%)
hot-rolled bar, both carbon and alloy	(2.38%)
carbon and alloy coated sheet and plate	(3.27%)
tin plate	(2.20%)
carbon and alloy rails	(8.90%)
and carbon and alloy sheet piling	(21.85%)

Similarly, US imports from the EEC were restricted for eleven products including an export ceiling of 780 short tons for concrete reinforcing bars, 32,275 short tons for cold finished and other bars, and 73,090 short tons for round and flat wire products.[41]

Subsequent to the aforementioned EEC Arrangement, the Pipe and Tube Accord was negotiated,[42] restricting EEC exports of steel pipe and tube products to 7.6 percent of the American market. The Arrangement has been extended through 30 September 1989, and will restrict US imports of finished steel mill products from the EEC to around 5.5 percent of domestic consumption (US International Trade Commission, 1985d).

President Reagan in September 1984 requested that the US Trade Representative negotiate agreements with the major exporters of steel to the United States. Agreements had been negotiated with fourteen steel-exporting nations by August 1985. These agreements set limits on the import penetration allowed each country through September 1989.[43] Under these negotiations, Japan agreed to limit its import penetration of the US steel market to 5.80 percent, although it had attained a 6.94 percent penetration ratio in 1984. In particular, Japan's market share will not exceed 5.57 percent for steel sheets and strips, 0.60 percent for steel plates, 13.26 percent for steel pipe and tubing, 1.50 percent for steel bars, 8.52 percent for structural steel, and 6.71 percent for wire and wire products. Similarly, Korea agreed to reduce its import penetration rate from 2.48 percent on all steel products in 1984 to 1.9 percent. Korea's most substantial market penetration occurs for pipe and tubing, where it had a market penetration ratio of 9.56 percent in 1984 and wire and wire products, and achieved a market penetration ratio of 4.04 percent. As a result of these restrictions in US steel imports, President Reagan predicted the emergence of 'a more normal level of steel imports, or approximately 18.5 percent (of domestic consumption), excluding semi-finished steel',[44] which would represent a decrease in the import penetration of about six percentage points.

One-quarter of a century ago, the automobile industry was centered principally in the United States and in Western Europe. With the sole exception of the Volkswagen Beetle, automobile sales were limited to General Motors, Ford and Chrysler. While Japanese production of automobiles remained below 100,000 units until 1960, it had reached 3.2 million units by 1970. US imports of automobiles from Japan rose from 942 units of 1960 to 232,671 units in 1970.[45] Thus, in the 1970s and first half of the 1980s, the American automobile industry underwent a drastic structural shift. While factory sales increased by 25 percent, from 5.3 million units in 1951 to 6.7 million units in 1960, and by 49 percent, from 5.5 million units in 1961 to 8.2 million units in 1969, sales actually decreased by 22 percent during the subsequent decade, as they fell to 6.4 million in 1980. By 1984, production had somewhat recovered, with factory sales having increased to 7.6 million units.

While there were only 1,453 units imported into the United States in 1947, representing an import penetration ratio of just 0.04 percent, imports had grown to 259,434 units, or 4.16 percent of the market by 1956. By 1966 imports constituted almost 10 percent of the domestic market, as just under 900,000 foreign units were sold in the United States. In the early 1960s, as previously mentioned, nearly two-thirds of the imported automobiles came from West Germany, with an additional 15 percent coming from the United Kingdom. Meanwhile, US exports had declined from 216,973 units in 1951 to 177,703 units by 1966. Between 1967 and 1970 the important penetration rate doubled to 24.33 percent, as imports rose from just over 1 million units in 1967 to just over 2 million units in 1970. Thus, while there was a 100 percent growth in US imports of automobiles, domestic production contracted by 12 percent, as US factory sales fell from 7.4 million units in 1967 to 6.5 million units in 1970. Whereas Japan had captured just under 3 percent of the US import market in 1964, with sales of 8,533 units, its import market share jumped to 10.48 percent (112,606 units) in 1966, and to just under 19 percent (312,649 units) in 1970.

During the same period, West Germany's import market share fell from 67.94 percent in 1964 to 33.53 percent by 1970. While US production in the 1970s and 1980s has generally not exceeded the 1960s levels, US imports have grown nearly 80 percent between 1970 and 1984, from just over 2 million units in 1970 to just over 3.5 million units in 1984. During this period, Japan's share of the import market rose continually until it peaked at almost 24 percent in 1982, before subsiding to 18.44 percent in 1984. The number of Japanese manufactured units sold in the United States increased from 703,672 units in 1971 to 1.1 million units in 1976, and then reached a peak of 1.99 million units in 1980 before subsiding slightly to 1.95 million units in 1984.

In the meantime, West Germany's sales in the United States actually decreased from 676,967 units in 1972 to 349,804 units in 1976, reaching their lowest at 234,052 units in 1981, before rebounding to 335,032 units in 1984.

West Germany's share of US imports fell from 7.15 percent in 1971 to 3.38 percent in 1976, and reached a low in 1983 of 2.57 percent before rebounding to a 3.17 percent share of the market in 1984 (US International Trade Commission, 1985i). Throughout the 1970s, the import penetration remained around 25 percent until it jumped from 28.2 percent in 1979 to 35 percent in 1980. In 1984, almost 34 percent of the US automobile market was accounted for by imports.

As a result of the loss in domestic market share, total employment of the domestic producers[46] declined from 929,214 employees in 1979, 83.8 percent of whom were production workers, to 622,885 employees in 1982, before rebounding to 720,448 employees in 1984. While the number of hours worked decreased from 1,781 million in 1979 to 1,279 million in 1984, the average hourly wage rose over this period from $10.52 to $15.33 (US International Trade Commission, 1985h). Similarly, profitability in the industry was dismal in the late 1970s and early 1980s. In 1979, the domestic producers of automobiles reported a net loss on US operations of $400 million. In the following year, the loss had risen to $4.6 billion, and in 1981 the industry suffered a loss of $2.3 billion. However, in 1982 the domestic industry began to recover, reporting a loss of only $553 million, which was followed by a net profit of $5.3 billion in 1983, and $10.4 billion in 1984 (US International Trade Commission 1985i). The dramatic reversal of the US automobile industry is attributable to several factors, one of which was trade protection which has enabled the domestic industry to expand output. Because capital costs are very high, once fixed costs are covered, the profitability in the industry increases at a rapid rate.

Explicit trade protection in the US automobile industry began in June 1980 when the Ford Motor Co. and the United Auto Workers jointly filed a petition with the US International Trade Commission requesting relief from imports under Section 201 of the Trade Act of 1974. Shortly after assuming office, President Reagan recognized that sustaining a veto of the impending Congressional legislation, which would restrict the importation of autos from Japan to 1.6 million units, would be a political hazard.[47] MITI, perhaps also perceiving the inevitability of such Congressional legisalation, attempted to preempt legal action by Congress by proposing a voluntary restraint of between 1.6 million and 1.7 million units imported form Japan to the United States, which would be enforced by MITI.[48] MITI's proposal for voluntary restraints was met with resistance not only from the Japanese automobile manufacturers, who argued that the high demand for small cars combined with the relatively high level of American compensation to labor were the catalysts for the domestic decline, but also from the EEC, who demanded the same status for Japanese voluntary restraints which the United States would enjoy.[49]

Despite such formidable opposition, especially from the Japanese auto manufacturers, the threat of Congressional legislation loomed even more ominously, leading MITI to announce on 1 May 1981, a voluntary restraint agreement limiting the sales of Japanese manufactured automobiles to the United States. Under the Automobile Voluntary Restraint Agreement (VRA), MITI agreed to reduce exports to the United States by 7.7 percent between 1981 and 1982. In the next two years, Japanese sales of automobiles in the United States were constrained to 1,832, 500 units (US International Trade Commission, 1985e). The VRA was further extended in November of 1983. However, MITI raised the restraint to 1.85 million units for 1984. The VRA has been in effect since that time.[50]

Adoption of the Agreement has certainly made an impact on the US automobile market. Without it, US imported automobiles from Japan would have meant fewer domestic sales, lower output and probably lower prices. The US International Trade Commission (1985e) has estimated that in the absence of the VRA, US imports of Japanese automobiles would have been greater by 5.6 percent in 1981, 11.0 percent in 1982, 30.8 percent in 1983 and 51.2 percent in 1984. Similarly, as a result of the VRA, sales of domestic autos have increased by 1.2 percent in 1981, 2.2 percent in 1982, 5.3 percent in 1983 and 7.8 percent in 1984. For Japan, it resulted in 1984 exports of almost 2 million fewer autos to the United States and American manufacturers sold slightly more than 600,000 additional autos in the domestic market. Because of the VRA, the total sales of autos in the United States were 0.3 percent less in 1981, 0.7 percent less in 1982, 2.1 percent less in 1983 and 3.3 percent less in 1984. Finally, the US International Trade Commission (1985e) calculated that due to the VRA, the average price of an imported Japanese automobile rose by 2.5 percent in 1981, 4.8 percent in 1982, 10.0 percent in 1983 and 14.4 percent in 1984. That is, the average price of an imported automobile form Japan in 1984 was $9,300. In the absence of the Agreement, the average price of an imported automobile from Japan would have been approximately $7,962.

Similarly, the effect of the Agreement on the price of domestic automobiles was estimated to be an additional $426 in 1983 and an additional $659 in 1984, based on the actual average domestic automobile prices in $10,504 in 1983 and $10,998 in 1984. Thus, because of the VRA, US consumers paid an additional $351 million for Japanese automobiles in 1981 and an additional $3.3 billion in 1984. And, when the additional cost of domestic automobiles is included, the increased costs of all automobiles purchased by US consumers as a result of the VRA amounted to $835 million in 1981, $1.7 billion in 1982, $4.7 billion in 1983 and $8.5 billion in 1984 (US International Trade Commission, 1985e).

It was also calculated that the VRA saved 5,400 jobs in the domestic industry in 1981, 9,100 jobs in 1982, 25,600 jobs in 1983 and 44,100 jobs in 1984. Thus, it can easily be determined that the VRA was responsible for US consumers paying $155,000 per job saved in 1981, $181,000 per job saved in 1982, $183,000 per job saved in 1983 and $193,000 per job saved in 1984.

In 1977 West Germany was the world's largest producer of machine tools,[51] accounting for 17.4 percent of the world market, with the United States following with 16.1 percent of the market and the USSR with 14.6 percent of the market. By 1979, the United States had become the world leader of the $22.9 billion machine tool industry, capturing 18 percent of the market, followed closely by West Germany. Most significantly, however, Japan's market share had increased from 10.6 percent in 1977 to 12.6 percent in 1979. This trend continued, so that by 1981 Japan had a market share of 18.2 percent, second only to that of the United States, which was 19.3 percent. And, by 1982 Japan became the industry leader, with a 17.1 percent share of the world market. Thus, within six years, Japan's market share had risen by almost seven percentage points, from 10.6 percent in 1977 to 17.1 percent in 1982, while the market share of the United States actually declined by 0.2 percentage points over the same period, from 16.1 percent in 1977 to 15.9 percent in 1982, and the market share of West Germany declined by two percentage points, from 17.4 percent in 1977 to 15.4 percent in 1982 (US International Trade Commission, 1983a).

Imports of machine tools now constitute an increasing share of the US market. In 1977, $400 million of metal working machine tools were imported into the United States. In just one year, imports increased by nearly three-quarters as $715.3 million of foreign-produced machine tools were sold to the United States in 1978. Although the rate of growth slowed somewhat after this time, imports rose to just over $1 billion in 1979 and $1.3 billion in 1980. By 1981, imports had risen to $1.4 billion, before falling to $1.3 billion in 1982. Thus, between 1977 and 1982, US imports of machine tools more than tripled. By comparison, imports in West Germany rose only by 60 percent. Similarly, US exports have not been growing as rapidly as have exports in competing countries. With $640 million of exports in 1982, the United States ranked as the sixth largest exporter of machine tools. However, this reflected a drop of more than one-third from the almost $1 billion of exports in 1981.

Despite the increase in output in the industry between 1977 and 1982, from $1.4 billion to $2.3 billion (after peaking at $3.0 billion in 1981), employment fell from 36,950 workers in 1977 to 34,541 workers in 1982 (US International Trade Commission, 1983a). But despite the drop in employment, wages earned in the machine tool industry rose from an average of $6.33 per hour in January 1977 to about $10.00 per hour in October 1982.[52] Although the average wage in the American machine tool industry has generally been below its counterpart in the automobile, transportation equipment and aircraft industries, it has typically exceeded that in most other durable-goods industries. In fact, while employment fell by only 7 percent between 1977 and 1982, the number of man-hours fell by almost 18 percent (US International Trade Commission, 1983a). This seeming discrepancy between the trends in US output, employment and man-hours is explained by the substantial increases in productivity made in recent years. While production per employee was $29,000 in 1977, productivity rose continually to a peak of $53,000 of output per employee in 1981 before declining to $41,000 in 1982. Thus, between 1977 and 1982, the value of production per employee rose by 41 percent.

Between 1975 and 1983 there were nine certifications affecting 1,711 workers, and forty-one denials for trade adjustment assistance in the machine tool industry. In March 1981, South Bend Lathe, Inc. petitioned for loan assistance under the Department of Commerce's trade adjustment assistance program. Between 1981 and 1983, there were thirteen subsequent petitions requesting similar loan assistance.

The domestic machine tool industry has launched several major campaigns to restrict imports. The National Machine Tool Builders' Association charged European and Japanese manufacturers with dumping and 'predatory' practices. However, when the US Department of Justice began an investigation of suspected price-fixing between US firms and Japanese manufacturers, the case was dropped (US International Trade Commission, 1985f).

In 1983, the Reagan Administration initiated a joint US–Japan machine tool industry task force involving the Office of the US Trade Representative and MITI. This was in part a response to a petition filed with the US Trade Representative by Houdaille Industries, Inc. in 1982, requesting that President Reagan deny the investment tax credit to purchasers of certain machine tools produced by Japanese firms on the grounds that the Japanese industry was the beneficiary of a government-sponsored cartel in the 1950s and 1960s.

The domestic machine tool industry also filed a petition with the US Department of Commerce in 1983, in which import quotas were regulated under Section 232 of the Trade Expansion Act of 1962. The Act empowers the President with the right to impose trade protection in the event that imports are a threat to national security. Accordingly, the industry petitioned that 'imports of machine tools of one or more of the foregoing types would be permitted at levels between 17.5 and 20 percent of domestic consumption, provided that the sales-weighted average value of imports did not exceed 17.5 percent of domestic consumption in either the metal-cutting or metal-forming sector.'[53]

However, despite its accusations of governmental assistance to foreign competitors, the American machine tool industry has benefited considerably from the US government. Funds have been channeled to the industry through the Department of Defense, the National Aeronautics and Space Administration, the National Bureau of Standards' Center for Manufacturing Engineering, the National Science Foundation and the Department of Commerce and Export-Import Bank. In 1982, the Department of Defense, through its three major branches, purchased approximately $564 million of machine tools (US International Trade Commission, 1983a). In conjunction with its purchases and requirements, the Department of Defense funds extensive research oriented towards manufacturing technology, which amounted to $209 million in 1982. In 1980, the Export-Import Bank of the United States subsidized the domestic industry with $230,000 in short-term insurance, $3.7 million in medium-term insurance, $849,000 under the Co-operative Financing Facility Program, $6.7 million in bank guarantees, $5 million in discount loans and $5.1 million in financial guarantees.[54]

As early as 1968, firms in the American color television industry attempted to procure governmental protection from foreign competition. In 1971, the three major labor unions in the industry filed a petition requesting import relief. Claiming that import penetration of television receivers had caused serious injury to the domestic industry, the petitioners requested a restoration of the original 1930 rate of duty at 35 percent *ad valorem* under Section 301 of the Trade Expansion Act of 1962. While none of the major producers supported the petitioners in 1967, RCA, GE, Admiral, Motorola, Magnavox, Sylvania and Zenith all had substantial offshore production facilities by 1972 (Millstein, 1983). When the Tariff Commission reached a negative determination, the labor unions responded by filing eleven additional petitions before the Commission between 1970 and 1973. None of these petitions received an affirmative determination from the Commission. However, in 1971, responding to a petition from several domestic producers, including Zenith, the Tariff Commission voted affirmative on a dumping case, but the countervailing duty was not actually imposed by the Treasury Department until 1978 (Millstein, 1983).

After formation of the Committee to Preserve American Color Television (COMPACT), which consisted of a coalition between producers and labor, COMPACT filed a petition with the ITC[55] under Section 201 of the Trade Act (1974), alleging that 'the color television segment of the industry cannot survive as a viable domestic industry unless immediate relief from imports is afforded. Petitioners have no desire to see their plants and jobs relocated to foreign shores.'[56] On 8 March 1977, the Commission reached the decision that a 'serious injury' had been inflicted upon the domestic industry and that increased quantities of imports were a substantial cause of this injury. While the Commission had recommended the imposition of an increased tariff rate of up to 25 percent *ad valorem*, which would gradually be reduced to 10 percent over a subsequent five-year period, the President instead opted for quantitative limitations. Thus, on 20 May 1977, President Carter signed an Orderly Marketing Agreement (OMA) with the government of Japan. Under this agreement, Japan agreed to limit the number of color television receivers shipped to the United States for the period 1977 to 1980. The terms of the agreement restricted imports from Japan to 1.75 million units per year.

That the OMA has failed to reverse the industry's decline has slowly become apparent. Between the first quarter of 1981 and the first quarter of 1982, US production of color television receivers declined by almost one fifth, while shipments decreased by more than 11 percent. During the same period imports rose by more than 15 percent, while US exports fell by 30 percent. And, the total number of employees in the industry fell by nearly 13 percent over this period (US International Trade Commission, 1982). As Millstein (1983, p. 140) determined for the color television industry, 'The OMA have encouraged an offshore production strategy by US firms trying to adjust to the competitive conditions in the color market, but they have in no way helped reconstruct the domestic sector so as to assure it as a competitive position.'

Under the Trade and Tariff Act 1984, the President was authorized to 'continue, modify, or eliminate duties on certain high-technology products in order to carry out agreements concluded pursuant to section 104A(c) of the Trade Act of 1974' (US International Trade Commission, 1985f).[57] Surprisingly, a number of domestic producers constituted a political interest group supporting the elimination of tariffs on high-technology products. At the public hearing of the ITC, the Semiconductor Industry Association testified that eliminating the tariff would be beneficial for four major reasons. First, domestic producers accounted for around three-quarters of the US imports, through offshore production. These firms would save approximately $100 million on the cost of the duty as well as make additional gains from the subsequent decrease in administrative costs. Second, the cost savings could be used to supplement existing R&D. Third, Japan would be expected to eliminate its tariffs in a reciprocal move, opening up Japanese markets to American producers. Finally, the increase in market share would allow American manufacturers to expand output significantly, enabling them to reduce average costs.

Between 1979 and 1983, American production of high-technology goods increased from $18.3 billion to $36.1 billion, representing nearly a 100 percent expansion. During the same period, US exports also increased, from $4.7 billion to $0.2 billion, as did US imports, from $2.8 billion to $7.3 billion. The greater rate of growth in imports versus domestic production is reflected in the increase in the import penetration ratio, from 17 percent in 1979 to 21.3 percent in 1983. The greatest sources for US exports of high-technology products included Malaysia, Canada, and the United Kingdom. On the other hand, US imports in 1983 tended to emanate from the foreign subsidiaries of US firms and from Japan, Malaysia and Singapore (US International Trade Commission. 1985f, 1985j).

The US International Trade Commission calculated the effect that the duty-free treatment of certain high-technology products would have had in 1983 to be $215 million. Similarly, in 1984, the duty savings by US importers would have been $331 million. Because the majority of imports were from US manufacturers' offshore facilities, domestic producers of semiconductors estimated potential savings of $100 million, while Japanese firms would have saved $80 million.

However, the trend in the semiconductor industry has not emerged quite as the Commission predicted. While US consumption of semiconductors and parts grew from $6.5 billion in 1979 to over $13 billion in 1983, and to more than $15 billion in 1984, US imports increased by more than 100 percent between 1979 and 1983, from $2.4 billion to $5.0 billion. Between 1979 and 1983, imports from Japan grew at a faster rate than those originating from any other source. While Japan accounted for just 10 percent of all US imports in 1979, its market share of US imports climbed to just under 25 percent by 1984. However, the domestic industry entered a painful slump beginning in 1985. Because 'an enormous glut of capacity still hangs over the industry',[58] prices plunged, leading the American producers to accuse their Japanese counterparts of dumping. In response to the $1 billion loss of American chipmakers in 1985,[59] domestic producers won an anti-dumping suit in October, 1986.[60] In its investigation, the Commerce Department ruled that Japanese producers had been dumping several types of memory chips by selling them well below costs. However, under a trade agreement reached on 30 July 1986, between the United States and Japan, MITI agreed to prevent such dumping practices. Perhaps, equally important, 'other industries battered by Japanese competition may cite chips as proof that Japan routinely uses predatory pricing. The question now is whether those industries will eye the semiconductor arrangement as a model for similar deals, touching off a wave of government meddling in more markets.'[61]

THE EFFECTS OF TRADE PROTECTION

While trade protection may have preserved jobs in the protected American manufacturing industries, it has also had deleterious effects on other US industries. For example, the US International Trade Commission (1985d) estimated that, as a result of the US–EEC Arrangement on the sales of EEC-produced steel to the United States, the EEC's share of the US market would have been 8.73 percent instead of the actual 5.49 percent in 1983 and 12.3 percent instead of the actual 4.79 percent in 1984. As a result, the total import penetration of steel mill products in the United States would have been 22.32 percent in 1983 instead of the actual 20.72 percent, and 29.94 percent in 1984 instead of the actual 26.45 percent. The lower import penetration achieved by the steel restraints also resulted in a higher price – 0.73 percent higher in 1983 and 1.62 percent higher in 1984. Because a number of US industries require steel products as an important input in the production process, their prices were subsequently raised, reflecting the higher cost of obtaining steel products. And, along with the increase in prices throughout American industries, especially in manufacturing, exports were adversely affected. Thus, as a result of the steel export restraint program, US exports in the motor vehicles and equipment industry were calculated to have been reduced by almost $43 million in 1983 and by $100 million in 1984. Similarly, exports in the aircraft and parts industry were reduced by $23 million in 1983 and $42 million in 1984. And, while the office, computing and computing machines industry experienced reduced exports of $13 million in 1983 and $31 million in 1984, the metal working machinery and equipment industry faced reduced exports of almost $8 million in 1983, and of over $15 million in 1984. Other industries suffering from reduced exports because of US protection in the steel industry include the engines and turbines, general machinery and equipment, and electric industrial equipment and apparatus industries (US International Trade Commission, 1985d).

CONCLUSION

It appears that the recent wave of protectionism in the United States has not served to provide an adequate solution to America's trade problems. In November of 1986, the US trade deficit widened to $19.22 billion from $14.71 billion in the previous month.[62] In fact, beginning in December of 1986, the United States imposed a 'user fee' on most imported products. The fee was set at 22 cents for each $100 of import value and applies to virtually all countries except those in the Caribbean.

Similarly, America's response to its trade problems has been the erection of further trade barriers. In January 1987, the Reagan Administration eliminated duty-free status for $3 billion in imports from Taiwan, South Korea and other developing countries along with the duty-free eligibility of Nicaragua, Paraguay and Romania.[63] Affected by the elimination of duty-free status were 290 products which subsequently received tariffs of between 5 and 9 percent. And, the Reagan Administration also announced the imposition of 200 percent tariffs on some imports from the EEC in a dispute over feed grain sales.

Thus, despite the evidence that trade protection in America is an inefficient method for assisting otherwise dislocated workers that also results in higher prices to consumers, it still remains a central aspect of US industrial policy. In this sense, the effects, and perhaps even the underlying intentions, of trade protection are contrary to those of antitrust and deregulation.

NOTES

1. 'Routing protectionists', *The Economist*, 9 August 1986, pp. 15–16.
2. *1987 Economic Report of the President*.
3. This observation is taken from the 1960–63 editions of the US Department of Commerce, Bureau of the Census, *US Commodity Exports and Imports as Related to Output* (US Government Printing Office, Washington DC).

4. For a more detailed description of the industry lifecycle, see Audretsch (1986, 1987a).
5. The minimum efficient scale (MES) is defined as the minimum level of output where minimum average cost is attained (see Scherer, 1980).
6. The values for capital intensity are taken from Bowen (1983).
7. The index of comparative advantage (specialization) is calculated as $(X_{ij}/X_j)/(X_i/X)$, where

   X_{ij} is the exports of product j by country i,
   X_j is the total world exports of product j,
   X_i is the total exports of manufactured products by country i, and
   X is the total world exports of manufactured goods (Cardiff, 1986, p. 7).

8. Office of the Secretary, United States International Trade Commission.
9. For a more formal analytical presentation of rent-seeking, see Audretsch and Woolf (1987).
10. 'Protection: making it pay for itself', *Business Week*, 7 April 1986, p. 12.
11. 'Soaked by protectionists', *The Economist*, 13 September 1986, pp. 17–18.
12. 'Trade has Reagan hemmed in', *Business Week*, 9 June 1986, pp. 18–19.
13. The United States Tariff Commission was renamed the United States International Trade Commission in the 1970s.
14. For the Tariff Commission to reach a determination of injury, a majority of the six Commissioners must find injury.
15. *The Economist*, 13 April 1963, p. 55.
16. Actually, the Tokyo Round resulted in an average reduction of tariff rate on manufactured goods of about 25 percent (Krasner, 1979).
17. The Agreement on Government Procurement established a framework for equalizing the treatment of both domestic and foreign suppliers by making information available through foreign sources on the rules of bidding, allowing for a sufficient pre-bid preparation period for foreign supplies, and publishing both the magnitude and recipients of the winning bids (US International Trade Commission, 1985b).
18. This represented 38 percent of the total number of cases (World Bank, 1984).
19. As of 1 January 1987, the six Commissioners included Chairwoman Paula Stern, Democrat, Vice Chairman Susan W. Liebler, Independent, Alfred E. Eckes, Republican, Seeley G. Lodwick, Republican, David B. Rohr, Democrat, and Anne E. Brunsdale, Republican.
20. 19 U.S.C. 2251, 1974.
21. Prior to the 1974 Trade Act, imports had to constitute the majority cause (exceeding 50 percent) of the injury to enable the Commission to reach a determination of injury.
22. TA–201–54.
23. TA–201–55.
24. TA–201–51.
25. TA–201–47.
26. Office of the Secretary, US International Trade Commission, 1986.
27. 19 U.S.C. 1671, 1930.
28. Trade Agreements Act of 1974, amendment to the Tariff Act of 1930.
29. *Long-Term Arrangement Regarding International Trade in Cotton Textiles*, GATT, Geneva, 1963.
30. *New York Times*, 4 July 1971.
31. *Wall Street Journal*, 18 October 1971.

32. Based on 1976–84 imports (US International Trade Commission, 1985g).
33. The import penetration ratio is defined as US imports divided by US shipments minus US exports plus US imports.
34. 'Holding its salvation in its hands', *The Economist*, 5 April 1986, pp. 69–72.
35. TA–201–55.
36. The actual decision of the US International Trade Commission reads: 'On the basis of information developed during the course of investigation No. TA–201–55, the Commission determines that footwear, provided for in . . . the Tariff Schedules of the United States . . . is being imported into the United States in such increased quantities as to be a substantial cause of serious injury, or the threat thereof, to the domestic industry producing articles like or directly competitive with the imported articles' (US International Trade Commission, 1985a, p. 1).
37. Statement of Chairwoman Paula Stern (US International Trade Commission, 1985a, p. 5), referring to case TA–201–50.
38. Chairwoman Stern and Commissioners Eckes, Lodwick, and Rohr voted affirmative, while Vice Chairman Liebler voted negative.
39. The number of plants producing less than 500,000 pairs has decreased more than any other plant size group.
40. *Council Regulation (EEC) No. 2869/82 of 21 October 1982*, 25 O. J. Ew. Comm. (No. L307) 1 (1982).
41. *Complementary Arrangement in the Form of an Exchange of Letters to the 1982 Arrangement Concerning Trade in Certain Steel Products between the European Communities and the United States of America*, 28 O. J. Eur. Comm. (No. L 215) 2 (1985).
42. *Arrangement in the Form of an Exchange of Letters between the European Communities and the United States Concerning Trade in Steel Pipes and Tubes*, 28, O. J. Eur. Comm. (No. L 9) 2 (1985).
43. 'Steel import determination', Memorandum for the United States Trade Representative, *Federal Register*, 49, 20 September 1984.
44. Quoted from US International Trade Commission, 1985d, p. 22.
45. Statistics taken from *Japan Automobile Manufacturers Association, Motor Vehicle Statistics of Japan*, 1984, and Motor Vehicle Manufacturers Association of the United States, *World Motor Vehicle Data*, 1980 Edition.
46. The six US manufacturers are General Motors, Ford, Chrysler, American Motors, Honda, and Volkswagen. A seventh manufacturer, New United Motors Manufacturing, Inc., which is a joint venture between General Motors and Toyota Motors, produced only twenty automobiles in 1984 (US International Trade Commission, 1985e).
47. 'Japan links auto cut to concessions', *Washington Post*, 18 April 1981.
48. 'Japanese car exports stir conflicting views', *Automotive News*, 5 April 1981, p. 27.
49. 'Tokyo said to ask 7 percent auto-export cut', *Washington Post*, 22 April, 1981.
50. 'Japan sets new limits on car exports', *Washington Post*, 1 November 1983.
51. *The Tariff Schedules of the United States Annotated* defines metal working machine tools as machines use for shaping or surface-working metals, including metallic carbides, 'whether by cutting away or otherwise removing the material or by changing its shape or form without removing any of it'. Rolling mills and hand-directed or hand-controlled tools are excluded from the definition.
52. Statistics from US Department of Labor, Bureau of Labor Statistics, 'Employment and Earnings', various editions.
53. Petition under the National Security Clause, Sec. 232 of the Trade Expansion Act of 1962 (19 USC. 1862), For Adjustments of Imports of Machine Tools, sub-

mitted to the Department of Commerce by the National Machine Tool Builders' Association, p. 4.

54. Export-Import Bank of the United States.

55. TA–201–19.

56. 'Petition for import relief' by COMPACT, submitted to the International Trade Commission, September 1976, p. 11, quoted from Millstein (1983), p. 128.

57. High-technology products were generally considered to consist of certain parts of automatic data-processing machines and certain semiconductors and parts.

58. 'The chips may not be down much longer', *Business Week*, 16 December 1985, p. 16.

59. 'Rigged chips', *The Economist*, 26 July 1986, p. 12.

60. 'US chip makers accuse Japan of continued dumping', *Wall Street Journal*, 29 October 1986, p. 5.

61. 'The chip market goes haywire', *Business Week*, 1 September 1986, pp. 24–5.

62. 'November US trade gap widened to $19.22 billion', *Wall Street Journal*, 2 January 1987, p. 1.

63. 'US imposes tariffs on 8 nations' imports', *International Herald Tribune*, 3–4 January 1987, p. 1. The reason given by the United States for imposition of the tariffs was 'their poor records on worker rights'.

9 · THE COMMUNITY
EXPERIMENT IN EUROPE

On 25 March 1987 the EEC celebrated its thirtieth birthday. Since the Treaty of Rome was signed in 1957, the Community has been an experiment in unifying remarkably diverse cultures and economies into an entity based on mutual interest and cooperation. In particular, the EEC has successfully established a customs union, an external trade policy common among all members, a common competition policy, a unified agricultural policy, a coherent monetary system, and a reduction in the barriers facing labor and capital in mobility between the different member countries. Further, the Community has grown from the original six members in 1957 to twelve. However, to conclude that the EEC has been successful in some matters is not to assert that it has been successful in all. One relatively pessimistic assessment of the Community on its thirtieth birthday found that

> it is easy to be gloomy about the EEC's present predicament. Financially, the Community is almost bankrupt, yet member governments are reluctant to pay more. It is falling behind America and Japan in the high-tech race, yet France, West Germany and Britain are blocking a move to raise spending on joint research-and-development projects. It is groaning under huge and unsellable food surpluses, yet West Germany has made its opposition to a two-percent cut in farm prices a matter of national dignity.[1]

Like its counterparts in Japan and the United States, the governments in the EEC-member countries have followed an exceedingly interventionist foreign trade policy of protection during the last four decades. What makes the EEC experience particularly interesting is that these policies have been coordinated among the member nations through its governing body. In particular, just as tariffs across member countries have been eliminated, a common external tariff applied to non-member countries has been implemented. However, the effects of commercial policy have varied considerably across EEC-member countries. The purpose of this chapter is to examine the approach to foreign trade policy that has been adapted by the EEC and to analyze it within the framework of industrial policy.

The second section of this chapter examines the historical evolution of Community policy and the major institutions shaping commercial policy in the EEC. The third section considers several studies which have provided empirical evidence on the benefits and costs of economic integration. While the fourth section focuses on the trade policy of West Germany, the fifth section is concerned with commercial policy in the United Kingdom. The problems of policy towards development and trade in the new- and high-technology industries are examined in the sixth section. Finally, after considering in the seventh section the inherent conflict between trade policy, industrial targeting and competition policy in the EEC, conclusions are drawn in the final section.

THE EUROPEAN ECONOMIC COMMUNITY

While it was always obvious that the European Economic Community would not become a complete economic union functioning under a single political authority, Meier (1973) notes that there are three different directions in which the EEC could have traveled. The first involves the formation of a common market, in which a customs union and the elimination of barriers to the mobility of capital and labor would be instituted. This would involve the free mobility of factors between member nations. The second involves the creation of a customs union, which would require that participating countries eliminate or at least reduce tariffs for the nations within the union, and simultaneously agree to a common tariff level for nations outside the union. Finally, the third focuses on the formation of a free trade area, which involves a concerted commercial policy within the group, but autonomous policies exercised by each member country for nations outside the group. This distinction is important, because while the United Kingdom advocated the third direction – the formation of a free trade area – the other six major countries (West Germany, France, Italy, Belgium, the Netherlands and Luxembourg) advocated the second approach, namely the establishment of a customs union. According to Meier (1973), it was exactly this tension in the desired direction for European unity that led to the retreat of the United Kingdom from the European Economic Community. Because the United Kingdom did not want to relinquish the right to determine commercial policy autonomously, it was not until 1971 that a reconciliation could finally be reached.

Article 2 of Part One of the Treaty Establishing the European Economic Community asserts that

> It shall be the task of the Community, by establishing a Common Market and gradually approximating the economic policies of Member States, to promote throughout the Community a harmonious development of economic activities, a continuous and balanced expansion, an increased stability, an accelerated raising of the standard of living and closer relations between its Member States.

In particular, Article 3 called for: (1) the elimination of customs duties and quantitative restrictions for exports and imports between all member states;

(2) the implementation of a singular customs tariff and a common commercial policy towards countries outside the Community; (3) the increase in mobility of persons, services and capital between member states; (4) the foundation of a common agricultural policy; (5) the foundation of a common transportation policy; (6) the promotion of competition policy, 'ensuring that competition in the Common Market shall not be distorted'; (7) the establishment of the means to coordinate economic policies of member states and to correct any resulting balance-of-payments disequilibria; (8) the creation of a European Social Fund which would be aimed at raising the standard of living for workers; (9) the establishment of a European Investment Bank, which was oriented towards promoting economic growth; (10) the promotion of trade with non-member countries in such a way that would improve the economic well-being of all member countries. While Section 1 of Chapter One called for the establishment of a customs union through elimination of customs duties between all member states, Section 2 provided for the establishment of a common customs tariff.

In fact, by 1968 all tariffs applying to member countries within the EEC had been removed, signaling the establishment of an effective European customs union. Similarly, the autonomous commercial policy of each of the six member nations had been replaced by a policy of a common tariff, known as the Common External Tariff. As set out in Article 19 of the Treaty of Rome, the Common External Tariff was based on the mean tariff applied by each member nation for any particular commodity. Consequently, West Germany, Belgium, the Netherlands and Luxembourg ended up with a higher tariff than before the establishment of the Common External Tariff, while France and Italy ended up with generally lower tariffs (Meier, 1973).

Great Britain, Denmark and Ireland joined the EEC in 1973, Greece in 1981, with Spain and Portugal becoming members on 1 January 1986. *The Economist* observed:

> The European co-ordination of national policies has grown appreciably. Instead of putting up trade barriers against each other, the 12 are at least in theory committed to dismantling non-tariff trade obstacles within the common market by the early 1990s. The habit of foreign-policy consultation is growing. A squeeze on the Community's outdated and over-grown farm policy has at last started, it is to be hoped, in earnest.[2]

BENEFITS OF INTEGRATION

To assess the benefits of economic integration in the EEC is at best difficult. In general, most studies trying to measure the benefits of the EEC to the member countries have not been able to provide directly an assessment of integration on each member's real per capita income. One study (Mendes, 1984) does, however, consider the impact of formation of the EEC on the annual growth rate of the individual member countries. Mendes notes, for example, that between 1961 and 1972 the annual growth rate in per capital real output was 4.39 percent. Of this, he calculated that − 0.02 percent was attributable to the EEC. In other words, West Germany's growth rate would have been 4.41 percent in the absence of European integration during this period. This counterfactual calculation was based on the negative change in the trade balance position of West Germany, net EEC budget payments and foreign investment, which were attributable to economic integration. Similarly, while France had the highest annual growth rate of 5.4 percent between 1961 and 1972, Mendes calculated that it would have been greater by 2.71 percentage points in the absence of the EEC's integration. While West Germany and France apparently did not experience greater economic growth as a result of economic integration during the ten years subsequent to the formation of the EEC, Italy, the Netherlands, Belgium and Luxembourg were positively affected by economic integration. In particular, the EEC accounted for over one-half of the annual growth rate of 5.17 percent for the Netherlands and 4.56 percent growth rate for Belgium and Luxembourg. The major source of benefits accrued from the expansion in the volume of exports, presumably due to the removal of trade barriers within the EEC.

While the smaller member countries apparently enjoyed more benefits from economic unity than did their larger counterparts during the period 1961–72, this situation was reversed between 1974 and 1981. During this latter period the larger EEC members, such as West Germany and France, benefited more greatly from the EEC than did their smaller counterparts. For example, the annual growth rate for West Germany was 2.65 percent during this period. However, in the absence of the EEC, the annual growth rate would have been only 1.74 percent. In particular, West Germany benefited from an increase in the exports of food products and beverages as well as a gain in foreign direct investment. While France had virtually the same growth rate during this period as West Germany, 1.57 percent of the annual growth was attributable to economic integration. By contrast, Denmark's average annual growth rate of 1.98 percent would have been substantially higher at 2.62 percent had it not joined the EEC. Although Ireland and the Netherlands benefited from EC participation, the gains were considerably smaller than for their larger counterparts (Mendes, 1984).

Other studies have analyzed the impact of economic integration on international trade flows. In general, such studies have estimated trade creation and trade diversion and have concluded that the trade creation effect substantially exceeded the trade diversion effect from formation of the Common Market (Kreinin, 1974, and Mayer, 1978). Similarly, it has commonly been found that along with the formation of the EEC came a significant increase in the volume of intra-industry trade among the Common Market countries (Swann, 1984). Other benefits, which have received less scrutiny, include the effect of the establishment of the EEC on market structure as well as performance within the various member countries.

Such effects on the industrial organization of markets find form in the alteration of the extent of specialization in production, the scale of production, the recognition of mutual dependence across national boundaries and the effects of trade flows on competition. Yamawaki *et al.* (1986) examined the effect that creation of the EEC had on market structure and market performance. Because domestic sellers in member countries were more likely than before to recognize their interdependence on foreign producers in other EEC member countries following the establishment of economic integration, the market performance of each country would presumably be altered. In particular, they tested the hypothesis that the EEC-wide seller concentration became more relevant to determine the market performance of member countries than the domestic seller concentration subsequent to the formation of the EEC. The market performance effects might not be expected to be trivial, since the EEC-wide concentration is presumably less than that for the individual member countries. In fact, Yamawaki *et al.* (1986) found that while the average 1978 four-firm concentration ratio for 47 three-digit manufacturing industries was 0.231 in West Germany, 0.305 in France, 0.283 in Italy, 0.397 in the Netherlands and 0.418 in Belgium, it was only 0.185 for the EEC taken as an entire market.[3] What is perhaps the most relevant is that all five of these countries experienced a significant rise in average domestic market concentration between 1963 and 1978. However, to the extent that the entire EEC became the relevant market, rather than just the domestic market for each country, the effective extent of concentration experienced by each member country actually fell. This would suggest a significant improvement in the market performance beyond what otherwise would have occurred.

In particular, some markets may have been considerably affected by the expansion of the relevant market from a domestic towards a European-wide geographic market. For example, while the 1978 four-firm concentration ratio in the iron and steel industry was 0.54 in West Germany, 0.58 in France, 0.55 in Italy, 1.00 in the Netherlands and 0.64 in Belgium, it was only 0.38 for the entire EEC market. Similarly, the 1978 four-firm concentration ratio in the radio, television, and electric components industry was 0.51 in West Germany, 0.37 in France, 0.30 in Italy, 0.83 in the Netherlands and 0.87 in Belgium, while for the entire EEC it was only 0.3. Finally, the largest four firms in the household electric appliances market controlled 0.47 percent of the market in West Germany, 0.53 percent in France, 0.65 percent in Italy, 0.83 percent in the Netherlands and 0.75 percent in Belgium, compared to an EEC-wide concentration ratio of just 0.38 percent in 1978 (Yamawaki *et al.*, 1986).

Using regression analysis, Yamawaki *et al.* (1986) found that the EEC-wide concentration ratios serve as a better explanatory variable for predicting 1978 national market price-cost margins than do domestic concentration ratios for the larger EEC countries, including West Germany, France and Italy. The results suggest that an additional benefit in economic integration within the EEC has been an increased extent of competition, extending beyond national boundaries, resulting in a superior economic performance in manufacturing markets throughout the EEC. To the extent that the EEC has replaced the domestic markets of the member states as the relevant geographic market, an additional and not insignificant effect of European integration has been an improvement in market performance.

TRADE POLICY IN WEST GERMANY

While the common external tariff applies equally to all EEC member nations, the effective rates of protection, which incorporate all trade restrictions as a group, vary considerably. This is largely due to varying extents of non-tariff barriers and subsidies which have been applied to any given industry among the EEC states. In West Germany, there have been five major changes or periods dominating commercial policy. The first period covered the pre-EEC regime, when substantial differentials in commercial policy still existed among the European countries. In 1958, the average nominal tariff rate in manufacturing[4] for those countries which subsequently formed the European Community was 8.5 percent, while it was 9 percent for non-members. The effective rate of protection[5] was 10.4 percent for member countries compared with 11.8 percent for non-members. The industry with the highest tariff protection was paper and paperboard products, which had a 15 percent nominal tariff rate for both members and non-members. This amounted to a 24.4 percent effective tariff rate. Other industries with high rates of protection during this early period included glass and glass products, shoes, rubber and asbestos goods, chemical products and coal derivatives, and motor vehicles. Several industries, such as steel, wood products, and clocks and watches, actually had a higher rate of tariff protection for the subsequent EEC countries than for other non-members (Hiemenz and von Rabenau, 1976).

The second significant period for commercial policy in West Germany began in 1959, which was the year when the EEC member nations first started to jointly reduce tariffs. While substantial progress was made towards unification of EEC tariffs by 1964, complete reductions were made by 1968. Thus, the average nominal tariff rate for goods purchased from other EEC countries decreased from around 9 percent in 1958 to 1.4 percent in 1964. This represented a decline in the effective rate of tariff from 10.4 percent to 1.9 percent. By 1964, the differential between tariff protection applying to EEC countries and that applying to non-EEC countries had widened significantly. The second highest effective tariff rate for imports from member countries was 5.7 percent in the non-ferrous metal foundaries industry. By comparison, non-member countries faced an effective tariff rate of 47.1 percent. The highest effective tariff was in the pulp, paper and paperboard industry, where EEC member nations faced an effective tariff rate of 6.3 percent. However, an effective tariff rate of 41.3 percent was imposed on non-member countries. An effective tariff rate of 4.5 percent applied to EEC member nations for textile products, while their non-EEC counterparts faced an effective tariff rate of 24 percent.

The third important phase of West German commercial policy involved the adjustment of tariffs for non-member countries with those mandated by the EEC. This synchronization of tariffs for non-member countries established the common external tariff. In order to facilitate the adjustment in tariffs necessary to bring into harmony West German commercial policy towards non-member countries with that of the EEC-wide policy, West Germany raised its nominal external tariff rates by an average of about 20 percent between 1958 and 1964. This coincided with an increase in the effective tariff rate on non-member imports of three percentage points.

The fourth important period for West German commercial policy involved the adjustment for the external tariff to the principles achieved during the Kennedy Round negotiations. The agreements established in the Kennedy Round resulted in a reduction of West German tariff rates for non-EEC nations, so that by 1970 the nominal tariffs for non-member countries were roughly the equivalent of the 1958 levels. And by 1972, the tariff rates for non-member countries were actually somewhat lower than the 1958 levels. Table 9.1, which shows the tariff rates in West German manufacturing industries for 1972 and 1982, indicates that the industries with the greatest tariff protection in 1972 were coal mining, plastic products, motor vehicles, paper products, textiles and clothing. The last two columns include the amount of effective subsidization in calculating the amount of total protection. Incorporating the effective subsidization into the calculations suggests that the industries experiencing the greatest amount of protection in West Germany in 1972 were coal mining, aircraft, clothing, textiles and paper products. By contrast industries experiencing relatively low nominal and effective tariff rates included oil refining, mechanical engineering, printing and steel construction (Weiss, 1987). It is perhaps significant that the structure of nominal and effective tariff rates did not greatly change between 1958 and 1972, despite the interruptions of the EEC formation and Kennedy Round. That is, the relative tariff levels have remained fairly consistent over a long time period, even if the absolute levels have not.

The fifth significant phase for West German commercial policy involved the response of the government to fulfilling the agreements reached by GATT. Many of these responses involved the elimination or at least the reduction in non-tariff barriers.[6] For example, the West German government used to engage in preferential procurement practices. However, beginning in

Table 9.1 Trade Protection in West German Manufacturing

	Nominal tariff rates		Effective tariff rates		Total protection	
	1972	1982	1972	1982	1972	1982
Coal mining	—	—	—	—	96.1	265.5
Chemicals	10.7	6.5	16.2	9.8	18.1	12.5
Oil refining	3.1	3.1	10.7	10.7	12.2	11.3
Plastic products	11.7	6.1	15.8	7.1	18.1	8.5
Rubber	9.6	6.3	12.7	8.0	13.3	7.5
Stone goods	5.6	4.2	8.7	6.1	9.0	6.4
Ceramic products	7.2	5.1	7.3	5.6	9.1	8.0
Glass	8.5	5.9	10.6	7.8	11.8	9.1
Iron and steel	6.5	4.7	9.9	9.7	−4.4	53.9
Non-ferrous metals	6.4	5.3	12.1	11.2	14.3	13.1
Foundries	7.5	5.2	11.6	7.6	11.9	5.4
Rolling mills	7.4	5.2	7.7	6.1	8.2	−1.3
Steel construction	5.5	4.1	4.8	3.1	7.1	0.4
Mechanical engineering	6.2	4.1	2.6	1.6	5.3	3.3
Data processing equipment	8.1	5.9	8.1	9.8	14.9	11.8
Road vehicles	11.0	10.0	10.3	12.7	11.8	11.6
Shipbuilding	2.6	2.6	−7.1	−1.2	5.8	15.0
Aircraft	8.0	6.5	15.6	14.1	86.4	40.8
Electrical engineering	8.4	5.5	8.6	5.1	12.1	7.8
Precision mechanics, optics	9.4	5.6	7.2	5.2	8.8	7.0
Metal products	7.8	5.6	7.9	5.7	9.1	4.3
Musical instruments, toys, etc.	8.3	7.2	8.3	8.9	8.9	8.5
Wood	6.7	5.1	21.7	16.1	23.6	18.3
Wood products	9.0	5.4	12.7	6.5	13.5	7.2
Pulp, paper	8.0	5.9	19.3	14.2	21.6	15.0
Paper products	12.2	8.9	27.9	19.8	30.3	23.9
Printing	4.2	2.7	2.0	0.9	6.3	0.7
Leather, leather goods	7.7	6.1	9.2	7.2	9.1	7.5
Textiles	13.0	9.7	18.9	13.3	57.3	49.9
Clothing	16.1	12.5	31.4	23.2	82.2	73.5

Source: Weiss (1987).

1981, West Germany has adhered to the GATT Agreement on Government Procurement. Subsequently the West German government has abandoned its policy of directing the purchases of government-owned firms, such as the equipment purchases of Lufthansa. The firm has engaged in its procurement practices independent of government policy. Similarly, the state-owned telecommunications firm has become increasingly open to foreign firms since 1981 (US International Trade Commission, 1984).

Table 9.1 shows that the nominal and effective tariff rates in 1982 were generally, but not always, below their 1972 levels. For example, while the effective nominal tariff rate for plastic products was reduced from 11.7 percent in 1972 to 6.1 percent in 1982, the effective tariff rate fell from 15.8 to 7.1 percent during this period. However, while the nominal tariff rate in the musical instruments and toys industry fell from 8.3 percent in 1972 to 7.2

percent in 1982, the effective tariff rate actually rose during this period, from 8.3 to 8.9 percent. The industries with the highest effective tariff rates in 1982 were clothing, paper products, motor vehicles and wood (Weiss, 1987). In general, although again not in every case, the amount of total protection also decreased in most industries between 1972 and 1982. The total protection rate, which includes effective subsidization and non-tariff barriers, decreased from 18.1 to 8.5 percent between 1972 and 1982 in the plastic products industry, and from 9.1 to 4.3 percent in the metal products industry. It increased from 96.1 percent to 265.5 percent for coal mining over the same period. Similarly, in the iron and steel industry the effective rate of total protection increased from −4.4 percent in 1972 to 53.9 percent in 1982.

In general, West Germany's commercial policy has applied itself to two different types of industry. The first has involved the application of tariffs and quotas in industries which are primarily labor-intensive and raw-material intensive.[7] These industries are the recipients of protection measures that compensate for their inherent comparative disadvantage in West Germany. Textiles, apparel, coal, wood products and agricultural products are all in this category. By contrast, industries in the early stages of the product life cycle have not been the recipients of tariffs and quotas in West Germany. However, this is not to say that the high-technology industries have been free from protection. Rather, non-tariff barriers have been applied more generally in the high-technology industries. Unlike Japan, West Germany has not had a statutory requirement forcing all state-owned enterprises to purchase domestically manufactured products when possible, but in general there has been a tendency to engage in preferential procurement practices where possible.

COMMERCIAL POLICY IN THE UNITED KINGDOM

Like most other Western countries, trade protection in the United Kingdom was a response to the Great Depression of the 1930s. The national government, facing an economic crisis when it took power in 1931, put into effect two emergency Acts which imposed prohibitively high tariffs on a broad spectrum of industries. The purpose of these Acts, of course, was to discourage imports and to encourage the expansion of domestic aggregate demand. These moves culminated in the passage of the Import Duties Act (1932), which approved the imposition of an across-the-board *ad valorem* tariff of 10 percent on all goods, with the exception of products emanating from the Empire, food products and raw materials. The Act also established the Import Duties Advisory Committee, which was instructed to suggest additional trade protection measures in appropriate cases (Oulton, 1976). This resulted in the approval by the Committee of numerous tariff increases, also for a broad spectrum of products. It was not until the beginning of the

Kennedy Round in 1968 that significant reductions in the extent of protection in British manufacturing began in earnest.

By 1968, the highest nominal tariff rates were 23.4 percent on chemical products, 23.9 percent on iron castings, 22.6 percent on electrical machinery and 21.9 percent on textile machinery. However, the highest effective rates of tariff were 171.2 percent for imports of grain milling products, 217.2 percent for insulated wires and cables, 75.7 percent for chemical products and 57.3 percent for iron castings. By contrast, other products, such as cans and metal boxes, cereal foodstuffs and paint actually had negative effective rates of tariffs on imports in 1968. In general, both the nominal and effective tariff rates tended to rise with the processing stage. That is, consumer goods tended to be the most heavily protected, while raw materials and foodstuffs tended to be the least protected. However, as Oulton (1976) observes, the incidence of non-tariff barriers seemed to be applied much more evenly across manufacturing industries, with little regard for the stage of production.

Within four years, however, the levels of tariffs in the United Kingdom had been considerably reduced. This, of course, came about as a result of the Kennedy Round agreements. By 1972, the highest nominal tariff rate was placed on the imports of iron castings, where a 15.3 percent tariff rate was charged. Similarly, the tariff rate was 14.9 percent in grain milling, 12.3 percent in textile machinery, 13.7 percent in electrical machinery, 11.9 percent in packaging products of paper and board, and 10.4 percent for other paper and board products. Most industries, however, had nominal tariff rates of less than 5 percent by 1972. The highest effective rates of tariff protection were 172.4 percent for imports of grain milling, 131.2 percent for imports of insulated wires and cables, and 38.2 percent for chemical products. Other industries, including wire and wire manufactured products, bolts, nuts and screws, and mechanical engineering products actually had negative effective rates of tariff protection by 1972.

A number of industries in the United Kingdom have played particularly prominent roles in Britain's commercial policy. One of these, the textile industry, has been subjected to substantial protection during the post-war period. Even by the 1950s, the domestic industry was suffering from chronic excess capacity. Between 1957 and 1959, for example, less than two-thirds of the spindles for cotton were in operation, as employment drastically fell from 333,000 in 1951 to 241,000 by the end of the decade (Miles, 1976). The response of the government was the 1959 Adjustment Programme, initiated with passage of the 1959 Cotton Industry Act. The Act called for voluntary restrictions on exports of textile goods from the Commonwealth countries to Britain. The goal of the Act was 'to bring about a reorganised and re-equipped industry which could compete with success in the markets of the world with the types of cloth that are wanted wherever living standards are high' (Miles, 1976, p.189). In implementing this goal, the Act called for a reduction in capacity by 50 percent in the spinning section and 40 percent in weaving and finishing. As it became apparent that the Act was not succeeding in promoting industrial restructuring, the government gradually engaged in a series of protectionist moves between 1959 and 1965. Then, beginning in 1966, the government complied with the global quota system for textiles, which quantitatively restricted imports between 1966 and 1972. In 1973, specific quotas for cotton products were implemented according to EEC standards. Even fifteen years later, the industry continues to suffer from chronic excess capacity and disintegration. It is doubtful that the commercial policy applied in the British textiles industry contributed significantly to reversing the fate of a declining industry.

A second industry in the United Kingdom that has been the subject of substantial interventionist commercial policy is footwear. The application of non-tariff barriers, in particular, has played a significant role in the non-leather footwear industry in the United Kingdom (Greenway, 1983). The most predominant instrument of protection used has been the voluntary export restraint. According to Greenway (1986, p. 1065), the reason for the use of voluntary export restraints is obvious:

> From the standpoint of the policy maker, voluntary export restraints are attractive because they serve to transfer income from domestic consumers to domestic and foreign producers in a well disguised manner. The invisibility of the instrument to consumers ensures that potential votes foregone are minimized, whilst the high profile to producers ensures that potential gains in votes are maximized. Furthermore, since some of the rents generated by the instrument are transferred overseas, the instrument may be more acceptable to trading partners than a tariff.

The essential problem has been a decline in domestic production since the mid-1960s, as shown in Table 9.2. The figures refer to the number of pairs sold domestically. While 156.8 million pairs of shoes were sold domestically in 1950, and 169.2 million sold by 1960, domestic shoes sales peaked in 1965 with total sales of 185.5 million pairs. Subsequently, domestic sales fell to 169.7 million pairs in 1970, 146.4 million pairs in 1975 , 117.6 million pairs in 1980, and finally to 108.6 million pairs in 1982.

At the same time, exports have remained remarkably constant over this thirty-year period, increasing only from 13.2 million pairs in 1950 to 15.8 million pairs in 1982. There has, however, been a dramatic rise in imports. In 1950, there were only 7.3 million pairs of shoes imported. While the number doubled by 1955, imports reached 36.1 million pairs in 1960, 65.1 million pairs in 1970, 105.6 million pairs in 1980 and finally 135.0 million pairs by 1982. Thus, while domestic consumption has risen by around 50 percent over this thirty-year period, the import penetration ratio has risen from 4.4 percent in 1950 to 27.7 percent in 1970, and finally to 55.4 percent in 1982. Not surprisingly, employment has been cut in half, from 112,000 employees in 1950, to 93,000 employees in 1970 and to 52,000 employees in 1982.

Table 9.2 Shoe Production in the United Kingdom, 1950–1982

156.8 million		1950
169.2 million		1960
185.5 million	(peak)	1965
169.7 million		1970
146.4 million		1975
117.6 million		1980
108.6 million		1982

The performance of the shoe industry in the United Kingdom reflects its stage in the product life cycle. Because the technology is fairly standardized, low-wage competitors in developing countries such as Hong Kong, South Korea, Taiwan and the Philippines are able to produce shoes at less cost by relying on less expensive inputs. In response to this loss in competitive advantage, the footwear industry has been able to maintain a relatively high level of tariff protection. The current average tariff rates range from 8 percent for imports of leather shoes to more than two-and-a-half times that for imports of non-leather shoes. However, the most important and significant response has been the imposition of 'voluntary' quotas. The first of these was with Taiwan, beginning in 1977, when the country agreed not to ship more than 5.5 million pairs to the United Kingdom. During the previous three years, imports from Taiwan had increased from less than 3 million pairs in 1975 to more than 14 million pairs in 1977. The voluntary export restraint remained at 5.5 million pairs, until it was raised to 7.9 million pairs in 1981 and to 9.26 million pairs in 1982. In 1980 nearly 8 million of these shoes were either textile footwear or plastic footwear, while only 60,000 pairs of rubber footwear and 530,000 pairs of slippers were permitted.

South Korea also adhered to a voluntary export restraint scheme, which limited the sales of all shoes to the United Kingdom to 14.57 million pairs in 1979, 15.32 million pairs in 1980, 16.825 million pairs in 1981 and 17.86 million pairs in 1982. The 1982 quota was made up of 11.5 million pairs of textile footwear, 2.3 million pairs of plastic foowear, 2.8 million of slippers, 810,000 pairs of leather footwear and 450,000 pairs of rubber footwear. Greenway (1986) has estimated for 1982 the costs of footwear protection, including both the effect of the tariff and the voluntary export restraints. While he calculated the deadweight loss to consumers to be £1.4 million, the calculated deadweight loss in production is £2.5 million. Adding on the income transfer to the foreign producers, this amounted in 1982 to a net loss to the United Kingdom of £43.4 million. Similarly, the cost per job saved from the tariff is estimated to be £17,000 for a single year. Thus, Greenway concludes that the system of voluntary export restraints is clearly less efficient, or rather more inefficient, than the application of tariffs. Like the application of commercial policy in the textile industry, trade policy in the United Kingdom does not seem to have generated an increase in the welfare of consumers.

TRADE POLICY AND HIGH TECHNOLOGY INDUSTRIES

In general, trade policy towards industries which are typically characterized as 'high-technology' varies considerably from that applied to depressed industries. Frequently, industries in the depressed sectors are the recipients of not only significant government funding programs involving direct and indirect subsidies, but also of extensive protectionist measures involving both tariff and non-tariff barriers. While the depressed industries, such as steel, coal, shipbuilding, and to some extent automobiles, have been protected from foreign competition in the EEC countries, the new- and high-technology industries generally have not been subjected to such extensive protectionist measures. However, commercial policy is controversial in these industries in the birth and growing stages of the product life cycle because many Europeans argue that the key to the economic well-being of the EEC lies in achieving parity with the United States and Japan in these industries, if not in achieving some degree of technological leadership (Cardiff, 1986). However, up to the mid 1980s, the major form of government intervention in these industries within the EEC has been through industrial targeting. While there is a persuasive view within Europe that technology is lagging behind that of their competitors to the East as well as to the West, typically the response has been to provide tax incentives for R&D and for direct government expenditures on R&D. Still, these types of industrial policy in Europe do not yet seem to have provided a satisfactory solution to the perceived technological lag. Business executives in Europe were asked recently in a survey to rank a list of countries according to their sophistication of technology. While 84 percent considered the United States as one of the technological leaders, 63 percent of the executives included Japan. By contrast, scarcely one-third included West Germany, and slightly less than one-fifth included the United Kingdom as being among the technological leaders. And France was identified as a technological leader by only 15 percent of the surveyed executives. Perhaps most revealing was that a majority of the executives felt that the technological gap between the EEC countries and the United States and Japan had been increasing and not decreasing in recent years.[8]

In fact, as Table 9.3 indicates, the trade performance for the high-technology products has not taken the same path in France, West Germany and the United Kingdom, as it has in the United States and Japan. Technology-intensive products are defined as products for which the R&D

Table 9.3 EEC Trade in Technology-Intensive Products,[a] 1970–1982

	Total		US		Japan		France		West Germany		United Kingdom	
	Imports[b]	Exports[b]	Imports	Exports	Imports	Exports	Imports	Exports	Imports	Exports	Imports	Exports
1970	21,338	35,243	5,861	12,527	2,017	5,088	3,304	3,276	4,140	7,774	3,043	4,499
1971	22,749	37,699	6,371	13,012	2,026	5,793	3,441	3,511	4,538	8,200	3,288	5,068
1972	26,983	42,110	7,917	13,299	2,193	7,180	4,222	4,134	5,105	9,537	3,948	5,586
1973	34,363	53,089	9,570	16,803	2,861	8,876	5,567	5,425	6,665	13,030	5,374	6,484
1974	38,984	64,311	10,298	21,246	3,618	10,525	6,510	6,534	7,475	15,748	6,127	7,631
1975	36,293	62,735	9,219	20,810	2,889	9,870	6,198	7,124	7,791	14,294	5,671	8,141
1976	42,366	69,366	12,199	21,808	3,185	12,733	7,171	7,830	9,127	16,021	5,879	7,990
1977	46,167	74,628	13,299	21,990	3,297	14,520	7,532	8,386	10,359	17,652	6,755	9,069
1978	56,277	87,237	16,744	25,475	3,927	17,359	8,770	9,693	12,427	20,297	8,908	11,025
1979	64,484	97,316	17,271	29,161	4,801	17,420	10,504	11,902	14,860	22,428	10,883	12,581
1980	70,321	107,508	18,728	33,468	5,378	20,156	11,878	11,926	15,843	22,847	12,077	15,056
1981	66,593	101,594	20,169	33,364	5,284	22,684	9,947	10,239	13,962	19,207	10,209	11,694
1982	63,177	94,487	19,787	30,663	4,888	19,642	9,220	10,080	13,267	18,736	10,049	11,315

[a]Technology-intensive products are defined as those for which R&D expenditures exceed 2.36% of value-added.
[b]In units of million constant 1972 dollars.
Source: National Science Board (1985).

expenditures exceed 2.36 percent of the industry value-added. These product groups include (National Science Foundation, 1986a):

industrial inorganic chemicals,
plastic materials and synthetics
office and computing machines
electrical machinery and equipment
radio and tv receiving equipment
engineering and scientific instruments
agricultural chemicals
drugs
communications equipment
engines and turbines
aircraft and parts

In particular, by comparing trends in imports and exports, measured in real terms, the technological gap between the EEC-member countries and the United States and Japan is seen to be widening. For example, while exports of technology-intensive products increased by 141 percent for West Germany between 1970 and 1982, imports of high-technology goods rose by even more, namely 220 percent, over this same period. Similarly, while imports of high-technology products grew more than did exports of the same goods in the United Kingdom between 1970 and 1982, by the end of this twelve-year period, the United Kingdom barely had a trade surplus for technology-intensive products. By contrast, the trade surplus in technology-intensive products in the United States increased from $6,666 million in 1970 to $10,876 million in 1982. And in Japan, the trade surplus of high-technology goods rose from $3,071 million in 1970 to $14,754 million in 1982.

These trends are substantiated by Cardiff (1986), who calculated the evolution of comparative advantage for high-technology goods for the OECD countries over the period 1963–85. The index of comparative advantage was measured by dividing each country's export share in the world for the technology-intensive goods by the export share of the country in all manufactured goods in the world market.[9] As Table 9.4 shows, the evolution of comparative advantage in high-technology goods has varied somewhat among the EEC-member countries. For example, in 1963, Ireland possessed a comparative disadvantage in technology-intensive goods. However, its competitive position continually improved so that by 1985, Ireland actually experienced a comparative advantage in the trade of high-technology products. By contrast, the index decreased from 1.20 in 1963 to 0.94 in 1985 for West Germany, while it fell from 1.02 in 1963 to 0.89 for the United Kingdom over the same period. For the EEC as a whole, the index declined from 1.01 in 1963 to 0.80 in 1985, indicating a significant transition from a

Table 9.4 Evolution of Comparative Advantage in High Technology Trade, 1963–1983 (OECD average = 1.00)

Country	1963	1970	1978	1983	1985
Belgium/Luxembourg	0.65	0.72	0.81	0.80	0.74
Denmark	0.65	0.70	0.63	0.58	0.64
France	0.93	1.00	0.96	0.84	0.83
Germany (West)	1.20	1.06	0.99	0.97	0.94
Greece	0.07	0.07	0.16	0.13	0.14
Ireland	0.42	0.61	0.92	1.14	1.16
Italy	0.83	0.87	0.65	0.56	0.52
Netherlands	1.10	0.85	0.68	0.61	0.60
United Kingdom	1.02	0.94	0.92	0.91	0.89
EEC 10[a]	1.01	0.94	0.88	0.82	—
Portugal	—	—	—	—	0.50
Spain	0.33	0.44	—	0.68	0.72
EEC 12[b]	—	—	—	—	0.80
USA	1.27	1.18	1.27	1.26	1.25
Japan	0.72	1.07	1.27	1.36	1.42

[a]Refers to the ten member countries of the EEC prior to 1985.
[b]Refers to the twelve member countries of the EEC after 1985.
Source: Cardiff (1986).

slight comparative advantage in the trade of technology-intensive goods to a substantial comparative disadvantage in high-technology products over this time period, By contrast, the index for the United States remained quite stable over the entire period, indicating a continued comparative advantage in the trade of high-technology goods during the entire post-war period. The index for Japan virtually doubled between 1963 and 1985, suggesting that while Japan experienced a comparative disadvantage in high-technology trade in the early 1960s, this position reversed itself by the 1970s. By the 1980s, Japan had the strongest position for trade in high-technology products.

Another area which presents a challenge to trade policy within the EEC involves industries in the mature and declining stages of the product life cycle (i.e. those industries currently undergoing a technological revitalization). In these industries, the existing firms are faced with a dilemma: they must either learn to adapt to the new technology or else exit the industry. A good example within the EEC of such a market is the machine tool industry. According to Harrop (1985, p. 61):

> The dilemma facing the Community is that some of its most potent policy instruments, such as its common commercial policy, may be severely constrained. This is because the machine tool industry has a high degree of trade dependence, and protectionism would both reduce choice and place additional costs on user industries, making manufacturing industry in the Community even less efficient. Whilst the machine tool industry itself might welcome some selective protection, it would be singularly inappropriate for use industries.

While the traditional mechanical engineering aspects of the industry represent a mature industry, other aspects, such as those regarding electronic control systems, represent the early stage of the product life cycle. Although numerical control enables flexibility in manufacturing, improved quality control, lower inventory, and less floor space, its implementation demands significantly greater capital costs, higher maintenance costs, and the use of more highly skilled labor. In 1976, the EEC (including the ten member nations) accounted for one-quarter of the consumption of all numerically controlled machine tools, while the United States accounted for an additional one-third and Japan one-fifth. By 1980, EEC consumption had risen to 30 percent, while that of the United States had fallen somewhat to 28 percent, and Japan's consumption had also fallen to 15 percent. In 1976, the EEC member countries accounted for 41 percent of all of the production of numerically controlled machines, while 38 percent came from the United States, and an additional 13 percent from Japan. By 1980, this situation had changed considerably. The EEC accounted for 35 percent of production, the United States 24 percent and Japan 30 percent. Thus, while the share of world consumption accounted for by the EEC countries had risen within this five-year period, the share of world production emanating from the EEC had fallen (Harrop, 1985).

The EEC countries have also fallen behind in the production of robots. In 1984, Japan had 64,600 robots, compared to 13,000 in the United States, 6,600 in West Germany, 3,380 in France, 2,700 in Italy and only 2,623 in the United Kingdom.[10] As a result of the deteriorating performance by the EEC countries in the machine tools a number of academics and policymakers called for a well-formulated industrial policy from the EEC. Early in his tenure, President Mitterrand was quoted as emphasizing the value of the machine tool sector and committing the government not to watch passively its continued erosion.[11]

While there is a growing pressure to erect trade barriers preventing the further penetration of European markets by Japanese machine tools, Harrop (1985, p. 73) argues that the appropriate policy is not further trade barriers but rather industrial targeting: 'Machine tools are too important technologically not to be supported by appropriate policies. At a Community level, only a limited amount can be achieved through the common commercial policy. . . . A more effective Community policy to strengthen the machine tool industry may emanate from a fuller use of Community institutions.'

TRADE POLICY, INDUSTRIAL TARGETING AND COMPETITION POLICY

The interrelationships between trade policy, industrial targeting and competition policy are complex. At times, such policies are complementary and mutually reinforcing. In other instances, they are contradictory in nature and exist only in conjunction with a certain degree of tension. There are two major areas of overlap between competition policy and international trade policy. The fundamental goal of competition policy in the EEC is to advance the efficient functioning of markets through promoting the market structure of competition. The presence of foreign competition promotes economic efficiency in domestic markets.[12] International trade increases the degree of competition in domestic markets, thereby contributing to the maximum quality, minimum price and greatest rate of technological progress possible for consumers. This is consistent with the findings of Shepherd (1982), who notes that one of the major sources of increased competition in US manufacturing industries has been the intensified presence of foreign competition.

The second area of overlap between competition policy and international trade policy involves the impact which the instruments of commercial policy, such as tariff and non-tariff barriers, can have on the market performance of domestic industries. That is, while the superficial goal of such trade policies is, typically, to allow the domestic industry sufficient time and breathing space to restructure itself into a viable entity in the global market, by insulating the market from foreign competition, the result may in fact be paradoxically the opposite. According to the OECD (1984, p. 84):

> Most member countries believe that in the long run, managed international trade and inward-oriented trade policies will frustrate the effective implementation of competition policy by favouring market structures that are unresponsive to competitive pressures. In sheltered economies, benefits accruing to specific national producers are generally accompanied by an overall reduction in efficiency and substantial welfare losses to be borne by consumers, taxpayers and/or other sectors of domestic production.

At the heart of the tension between trade policy and competition policy is a difference in the perception of the relevant time horizon. Competition policy generally has a much shorter time perspective. That is, a substantial increase in competition will typically result in an improvement in economic efficiency through the erosion of monopoly rents within a relatively short time span. If a domestic industry, which is either inefficient or else dominated by market power, is subjected to the removal of trade barriers, consumers would be expected to enjoy the benefits of foreign imports, presumably of higher quality and lower price, quite rapidly. Experience has shown that, with the possession of either a superior product or else a more efficient means of production, foreign markets can be penetrated remarkably rapidly in the absence of trade barriers. So, the competitive effects of dismantling trade barriers are relatively quick to take place. By contrast, the presumed gains from restructuring, which are hoped to be achieved by insulating the domestic industry from foreign competition, are frequently of a much longer-term nature. It may take years for an industry to transform itself through the process of industrial restructuring. This is supported by the experience of the coal, shipbuilding and steel industries in the EEC.

In balancing the trade-off between competition policy and trade policy there are eight essential considerations. The first involves the expected direct economic gains to the domestic market, in terms of producers' surplus and in terms of job creation. The second involves the expected direct increase expected in government revenues from tariffs, import licenses and tax receipts, or the expected direct increase in government costs in the form of export promotion, government subsidies and lost tax revenues. The third is the direct cost burden which the consumers must bear as a result of higher prices and a reduced level of consumption, or the loss in consumers' surplus. The fourth involves the decrease in competition and the impact on the market structure resulting from the implementation of commercial policy. The fifth involves the likely impact that protection will have on technological innovation and whether the technological gap will subsequently be closed or widened. Investment by the existing firms, entry by new firms and foreign direct investment are all likely to be affected by commercial policy. Sixth, the spillover effects into other markets should be considered. This involves firms and markets in both the upstream and downstream markets. Seventh, the reaction of foreign governments and firms to any commercial policy must be considered. That is, just as foreign governments may respond to the imposition of trade barriers by retaliating and erecting trade barriers of their own, foreign firms may also alter their R&D policies to match those of the domestic industry (Yamawaki and Audretsch, 1988).

CONCLUSION

During the 1960s and 1970s much of the focus of EEC trade policy was towards reversing the technology gap considered to exist with respect to the United States. While this concern still exists, to some extent the focal point of European commercial policy has moved towards the question of imports from Japan. Not only has the EEC's trade deficit with Japan virtually doubled in eight years, reaching $13.7 billion in 1985, but Japanese exports to the Community increased by 53 percent in dollar terms between 1985 and 1986. As *Business Week* reports: 'When someone drives a new car out of a showroom in West Germany these days, odds are good that it's a Toyota or Mazda. In France, electronics stores are most likely to have Sony videocassette recorders on the shelves. More and more, Japanese companies are pushing products through the pipeline to Europe – and European consumers are snapping them up in record volume.'[13] Most recently, industries such as photocopiers, semiconductors and electronic components have been threatened by competition from Japanese firms. A common reaction to the rising import penetration of Japanese firms, especially in high-technology markets, has been protectionism. However, despite a 19.5 percent import duty throughout the EEC on compact-disk players, the sales of compact-disks from Japan increased by 400 percent between 1985 and 1986.

In fact, the EEC's experience with protectionist policies suggests that trade barriers are not an effective instrument for rising to the challenge presented by foreign competition. The World Bank has estimated that the cost of saving a job in the non-leather shoe industry in Britain is approximately twelve times as great as the cost of adjusting to free trade. The cost of maintaining domestic production and employment in the shoe industry is estimated as £2.35 billion ($3.5 billion), or about £117 per British household.[14] Similarly, the voluntary export restraints concerning shipments by Japan of automobiles to Great Britain has been estimated to raise the cost of cars by around 15 percent. And, while the Multifiber Arrangement has been estimated to raise the cost of clothing in the United Kingdom by 10 percent, the cost of protecting clothing producers in the EEC as a whole has been estimated at $1.4 billion in 1980 alone.[15]

In perhaps one of the most crucial markets, semiconductors, it is apparent that a protectionist policy alone will not help the EEC countries to close the technology gap. In 1986, less than one-half of the sales of semiconductors in Europe were produced by European firms. Even in the market for gate array chips, a custom chip that was once considered to be a specialty of European firms, the share accounted for by European firms declined from one-third in 1980 to 10 percent in 1986. While there is a strong temptation to resort to protectionist measures to preserve or restore the market share of the EEC firms in the semiconductor market, *The Economist* admonishes such an approach in favor of a simultaneous opening of markets and cooperation with rivals in Japan and the United States: 'Mistakenly, the Europeans are spending much of their remaining cash, energy and design skills in efforts to take on the Americans and Japanese where they are strongest. Philips and Siemens, for example, are trying to break back into memory chips. Instead of battling the Japanese head on, perhaps the Europeans should instead try to enlist them as allies – before the Americans beat them to it.'[16]

NOTES

1. 'The European Community: happy birthday', *The Economist*, 21 March 1987, pp. 65–6.
2. 'Bienvenido Iberia', *The Economist*, 4 January 1986.
3. Only five countries – West Germany, France, Italy, the Netherlands, and Belgium – were included in the estimates of EEC concentration ratios.
4. Also includes mining products.
5. For a complete treatment of the measurement of the effective rate of protection see Grubel (1971), Corden (1971), and Ethier (1971).
6. For a more extensive discussion of the effect of the GATT agreements on West German trade policy, see Fels (1976).

7. For a definition and list of those industries see Audretsch (1986).
8. 'Europeans offer reasons for their research lag', *Wall Street Journal*, 1 February 1984, p. 28.
9. The index of comparative advantage (CA) is calculated as follows:

$$CA_i = \left(XHT_i / \sum_{i=1}^{n} XHT_i \right) \Big/ \left(X_i / \sum_{i=1}^{n} X_i \right)$$

where i represents the country, XHT_i is the exports of high-technology products by country i, n is the number of countries, and X_i is the total exports by country i.
10. *Production Engineer*, March 1985, p. 4 (quoted from Harrop, 1985, p. 67).
11. Taken from Harrop (1985).
12. The presence of imports has been found to exert a negative impact on price-cost margins by Koo and Martin (1984), Caves *et al.* (1980), Pagoulatos and Sorenson (1976), and White (1974).
13. 'Hooked on Japanese imports', *Business Week*, 21 July 1986, pp. 52–3.
14. 'Soaked by protectionists', *The Economist*, 13 September 1986.
15. *Ibid.*
16. 'Semiconductors: leaving Europe in the cold', *The Economist*, 21 March 1987, pp. 65–6.

10 · EXPORT POLICIES IN JAPAN

While commercial policy, or trade protection, in Japan has been the focus of recent coverage in the popular press, more attention is often given to the perceptions of the significant participants involved, including both Japan's major corporate and government officials as well as its trading partners, than to the actual record and effects of trade protection in the country itself. The popular perception in at least Western Europe and United States is clear. As Staiger *et al.* (1985a, p. 1) observe: 'Japan is often singled out as a country whose trade policies substantially distort its trade away from that [which] would emerge as a result of its natural comparative advantage. In view of the tensions which have developed between Japan and its major trading partners, it seems important to determine whether this allegation is well founded.'

One of the more difficult aspects in evaluating Japan's commercial policy is that it has not remained stable over time. That is, the strategy which Japan pursued during the immediate post-war period had long been abandoned by the 1970s, and today a considerably different policy is being followed. The role of trade protection during the immediate post-war period was strictly adhered to – apply tariff and non-tariff barriers to shield the emerging domestic industries from the crippling exposure to competition from viable, well-established firms. This enabled these industries, guided by an arsenal of domestic targeting policies, the opportunity to develop into internationally competitive industries. Thus, Borrus (1983, p. 61) notes that, 'The Japanese economic miracle was not achieved simply by companies competing with one another in burgeoning domestic markets. The "high-growth" system was fostered by a variety of coordinated government policies.... The government played a powerful role in preventing the domestic market from being over-run by foreign competition and in assuring the resources needed for companies to expand.'

The purpose of this chapter is twofold. First, the extent of trade protection in Japan during the post-war period is examined. After considering the relationship between commercial policy and industrial targeting in the second section, the most significant instruments of protection are examined in the third section. Those tools which have been most widely applied include the allocation of foreign exchange, tariffs, quotas, non-tariff barriers and legal sanctions restricting the extent of foreign direct investment. The second major focus of this chapter involves the role of Japanese trade protection in its major trading relationships. This is accomplished chiefly through an extensive examination of US–Japanese bilateral trade, with a special consideration of the effects of trade protection policies in both countries. In the fourth section, the recent patterns of US–Japanese bilateral trade are examined, along with the role of tariff and non-tariff barriers. In the fifth section, we present an econometric analysis that tests the hypothesis that the interactions between endowments of factors of production, market structure characteristics and the United States, and US trade policies are a significant determinant of bilateral trade between the United States and Japan. By combining standard international trade models with industrial organization concepts, a cross-section regression model is estimated for the balance of US–Japanese trade for 230 four-digit SIC industries. Finally, a summary and conclusion is presented in the last section.

INDUSTRIAL TARGETING AND TRADE PROTECTION

Trade protection has often been treated in the international economics literature as if it has neither an effect upon, nor is affected by, industrial policies targeted at developing specific industries. However, viewed within the context of industrial targeting, trade protection, and certainly commercial policy in Japan, can be seen to be an essential instrument for industrial promotion. By assuring a domestic market through the imposition of a wide range of protectionist tools, the Japanese government has been able to facilitate the development of newly emerging industries, enable existing firms to retain their international competitiveness once they have reached the mature stage in the life cycle and promote a relatively smooth exit from declining industries. Thus, trade protection has emerged as one of Japan's most significant tools of industrial policy.

Under the economic plans of the 1950s and 1960s, MITI decided to promote those industries which were significant for production and employment and in which demand was anticipated to grow at a greater rate than income, those industries which would provide externalities in the form of technological progress, leading to a high-technology infrastructure, and those industries which were likely to become export-oriented. Trade protection played an essential role in this development policy, because it was only through government intervention limiting foreign entry into domestic markets that the requisite large-scale production could effectively be attained. Because foreign competitors, principally the United States, had already established large-scale production facilities enabling mass production, protectionist policies were considered by MITI to be essential for promoting the domestic industry. Thus, trade protection was an especially essential ingredient of industrial policy until the mid-1960s.

The protective and nurturing trade policies generally involved some form of protective tariffs, a tax system which provided incentives for purchasing domestic goods, the allocation of foreign exchange to inhibit the purchase of foreign goods and specific regulations concerning the use of foreign exchange. For example, certain items were not permitted to be purchased from a foreign producer unless the product was not made available by domestic manufacturers. Such laws lasted into the 1970s. Similarly, high quotas and high tariffs on particular goods extended into the mid-1970s. Foreign direct investment by foreigners in Japan was also restricted until 1973, and foreign firms were not able to participate in bidding for government contracts until 1981. Most recently, MITI has tried to bring about the elimination of residual import restrictions, abolition or at least relaxation of tariff and non-tariff barriers, and the simplification of customs procedures and import standards. For example, MITI has encouraged the Japanese semiconductor industry to restrain from dumping semiconductors, or selling them at prices below costs, in foreign markets, and to constrain sales to United States.[1]

THE INSTRUMENTS OF PROTECTION

The most significant instruments of protection for Japan have been the allocation of foreign exchange, tariffs, quotas, constraints on foreign direct investment in Japan, policies discouraging purchases of goods produced abroad in favor of domestically produced ones and exclusion of foreigners from the process of government procurement. The allocation of foreign exchange for the purchase of imports was perhaps the most significant instrument of protection in the immediate post-war period. Enacted in 1950, the Foreign Exchange and Foreign Trade Control Act enabled the Japanese government to regulate both the nature and the quantity of commodities and technology that were imported. Through the control of foreign exchange, MITI directed resources towards those key industries which had been selected for targeting. The actual mechanics of the foreign-exchange allocation were implemented through the foreign-exchange budget of the Ministry of Finance. The budget set the levels of imports permitted for specific commodities along with the source of those imports, and the corresponding foreign exchange that would be required for payment. After MITI made public those commodities which had been approved for importation, potential importers had to apply for import licences. They also had to make a deposit of a fixed proportion of the value of the proposed imports. Thus, MITI was not only able to make speculation in imports more difficult, but was also able to discourage the overall consumption of imports (US General Accounting Office, 1982). With the achievement of a trade surplus by the 1960s, the importance of foreign-exchange allocation greatly subsided. However, when lifting the controls, MITI was always conscious of the implications for global competitiveness on the domestic industry. Thus, in targeted industries, such as semiconductors, measures such as licensing agreements served as a barrier to foreign entry, even after the import quotas were lifted (Borrus *et al.*, 1983).

Much has been made in the Western press about the 'unreasonably high and intolerable levels of import tariffs in Japan'.[2] In fact, more recently the evidence is to the contrary. Since at least the early 1980s, the average level of tariffs in Japan has fallen below the average level of its major trading partners, including the United States and the EEC. Bergsten and Cline (1985) found that import restrictions in Japan were no greater than those in the United States, and that, even if those existing restrictions were completely removed, the bilateral trade deficit between the United States and Japan would decrease by at most $10 billion per year, leaving still around three-quarters of the $36 billion 1984 deficit untouched.

It is true that tariff levels in Japan were extremely high during the immediate post-war period. Even by 1963 the average tariff rate (percentage *ad valorem*) was nearly 21 percent on dutiable imports and 7.3 percent on all imports.[3] Subsequently, however, the tariff levels were gradually reduced, to an average of 10.2 percent on dutiable imports and 5 percent on all imports in 1973. This was largely a consequence of the Kennedy Round, which took place in 1971. The average tariff level for mining and manufactured goods fell to just under 10 percent in Japan, which was only slightly higher than the corresponding average tariffs on similar goods of 8.2 percent in the United States and 9.7 percent in the EEC.

As in virtually all of the industrialized nations, the post-Kennedy Round but pre-Tokyo Round weighted average tariff rates[4] in Japan were not very evenly distributed across different sectors. The 1976 pre-Tokyo Round tariffs in Japan by sector are listed and compared to their equivalents in both the United States and in all major industrialized countries in Table 10.1. For example, the highest weighted average tariffs were in the industries comprising the food, beverages and tobacco sector, where the average rate of duty was 25.4 percent. By contrast, the analogous weighted average tariff was only 6.3 percent in the United States and 12.5 percent in all the major industrialized countries. Similarly, Japan tended to impose high tariff rates, both in an absolute and relative sense, on products in the agriculture, forestry and fish sector, as well as in the footwear sector. However, the average weighted tariffs in Japan tended to be relatively smaller than their counterparts in the United States and the EEC in the apparel, non-metal mineral products and leather sectors.

The Tokyo Round tariff negotiations reduced average tariff levels even further. While the average duty rate in Japan had been lowered to 4.3 percent on dutiable imports and 2.5 percent on all imports by 1981, the average tariff on manufactured goods in Japan was scheduled to be reduced to around 5.5 percent by 1987, largely resulting from negotiations undertaken in the Tokyo

Table 10.1 Pre-Tokyo Round (1976) Tariffs by Sector in Japan and the United States[a]

Sector	Japan	United States	All major industrialized countries
Agriculture, forestry, & fish	18.4	2.2	7.8
Food, beverages, & tobacco	25.4	6.3	12.5
Textiles	3.3	14.4	10.8
Apparel	13.8	27.8	20.7
Leather	3.0	5.6	4.4
Footwear	16.4	8.8	12.4
Wood products	0.3	3.6	2.7
Furniture	7.8	8.1	10.0
Paper	2.1	0.5	5.9
Printing	0.2	1.1	2.9
Chemicals	6.2	3.8	9.1
Petroleum	2.8	1.4	1.5
Rubber products	1.5	3.6	5.8
Non-metallic mineral products	0.6	9.1	5.8
Glass & glass products	7.5	10.7	10.5
Iron & steel	3.3	4.7	5.7
Non-ferrous metals	1.1	1.2	2.0
Metal products	6.9	7.5	9.0
Non-electric machinery	9.1	5.0	6.7
Electric machinery	7.4	6.6	9.6
Transport equipment	6.0	3.3	7.5
Miscellaneous manufacturing	6.0	7.8	7.7
All industries	6.3	4.5	6.6

[a]Tariffs are given in percentages and are weighted by the own-country imports.
Source: Office of the US Trade Representative (from Staiger *et al.*, 1985c).

Round. Since the United States reduced tariffs on manufactured goods only to 6 percent, and the EEC only to 7 percent, by 1987 the trade weighted average tariff level in Japan was lower than that of its two major Western trading partners (Saxonhouse, 1982).

To find that the average level of weighted average tariff levels in Japan has been significantly reduced during the last twenty years does not imply that the extent of tariff reductions has been similar across all industries. That is, there has been considerable variance in the tariff reductions across manufacturing industries. The US International Trade Commission (1983b) has found that the tariff reductions have generally been tied to the success of Japanese industries achieving international competitiveness. For example, while the tariff on small cars was 40 percent in 1968, it was reduced to just over 6 percent in November 1972, and was completely abandoned in 1980. By contrast, in 1983 the rate of tariff on imported automobiles was nearly 3 percent in the United States and between 10 and 21 percent in the EEC. Similarly, in the computer mainframe market, the 13.5 percent duty on imports in Japan was relatively high in 1972. The tariff was reduced to just under 10 percent in 1980, and to just under 5 percent in 1983. While the corresponding tariff stood at 4.7 percent in the United States it was nearly 6 percent in the EEC in 1983.

A similar pattern has also occurred in the computer peripherals market, where Japan imposed a tariff rate of 22.5 percent in 1972. By 1978 the tariff had been reduced to 17.5 percent, and by 1983 it had been reduced to 6 percent. This was slightly more than one percentage point greater than the corresponding 1983 tariff in the United States, but nearly half of that imposed in the EEC countries. And, by 1983 the tariff rate of 4.2 percent on imports of semiconductors in Japan was identical to that imposed in the United States, but only one-quarter of the equivalent tariff imposed in the EEC countries. Further, the tariff rate of 8.1 percent on imported optic cables was about one percentage point less than that imposed in the United States and about one-half of the analogous tariff imposed by the EEC. Finally, while 1983 tariff rates on machine tools ranged between 5 and 6 percent in the United States and between 2 and 9 percent in the EEC countries, they had been completely removed in Japan.

A third instrument of trade protection which was used in Japan to develop its industrial prowess was quota restrictions. In 1962 there were over 460 such restrictions on imported goods.[5] However, the number of import quotas in Japan has been subsequently reduced by a significant amount. While there were still 122 import quota restrictions in 1965, this number was reduced to 118 in 1969, 33 in 1972 and finally to 27 in 1975. Since then, the number of quotas has remained fairly constant. In particular, the quotas on steel were removed in 1961, those on color televisions in 1964. Import quotas on passenger cars were eliminated in 1965, and those on restricting machine tools, printing machines, film and typewriters in 1971. Of the remaining import quotas at the present time, twenty two of them are on agricultural products, livestock and leather products. In 1983, by contrast, the United States had only seven remaining import quotas, namely one on agricultural products and six on manufactured goods while the United Kingdom had only three – one on agricultural products and two on manufactured goods.

While the tariff rates and formal quotas in Japan have been significantly reduced in recent years, the trading partners' attention has shifted towards non-tariff barriers. A number of these take the form of 'demands for excessive documentation and rigid adherence to regulations by Japanese Customs officials' (US International Trade Commission, 1983b, p. 68), while others are in the form of standards and certification. Other non-tariff barriers take on a more cultural form: 'Many Japanese and Western businessmen believe that the prinicipal problem in selling foreign products in Japan lies in the cultural differences between East and West, rather than in economic protective measures.... History, language, customs and current living conditions affect what people buy.'[6] Similarly, Drucker notes that cultural factors pose a significant barrier to foreign companies attempting to market their products in Japan, because, 'To buy foreign brands made domestically is what the Japanese have long preferred – they feel they're getting the best of both worlds.... The Japanese surely will continue to prefer most of their "foreign" goods to be made domestically.'[7]

Product standards imposed by the Japanese government and product certification have posed a particularly difficult barrier to foreign competitors. According to Lecraw (1986), such product standards represent a particularly onerous non-tariff barrier in Japan because the mandatory standards are imposed on a far wider range of products than on those by its trading partners. The Japanese Standards System has had four stated goals: (1) the increased efficiency and technological progress of Japanese industry through heightened product compatibility, interchangeability, simplification and up-grading of products and processes; (2) the promotion of exports through the assurance of high quality associated with Japanese products, along with the minimization of 'destructive' competition; (3) quality control; and (4) health, safety and environmental protection, along with energy conservation (Japanese Standards Association, 1985).

While it is not explicitly stated as a goal, an implicit purpose of the standards was to discourage imports. This was made possible by Article 26 of the Industrial Standards Law, which states that 'Whenever the State or any local public body intends to decide on technical standards with respect to the mineral and manufacturing industry or specifications of mineral or industrial products to be purchased or in carrying out other business in connection with the determination of certain standards set forth in each item of Article 2, it shall carry them out by having respect of Japanese Industrial Standards.'[8] This Law effectively required the government to purchase only those goods conforming to the Japanese Industrial Standard (JIS) and which carried the JIS mark. Only those goods actually produced domestically could be tested and were eligible to receive the JIS mark. As Lecraw (1986) notes, even those products manufactured by Japanese multinational subsidiaries operating overseas were not eligible for the JIS mark. Through this mechanism, the government was legally prevented from purchasing foreign produced goods if the equivalent product was domestically produced and carried the JIS mark. These are administered through the Japanese Industrial Standards Committee, which reports directly to MITI through the Standards Department of the Agency of Industrial Science and Technology.

The system of standards also serves to inhibit the purchase of products not branded with the JIS mark. Since the Japanese Standards Association, a non-profit organization receiving support from both the government and from industry, actively promotes the 'public awareness and acceptance of their marks' (Lecraw, 1986, p. 9), the public has responded with a very high recognition and acceptance of the JIS marks. This, of course, presents a considerable barrier to any foreign producer wishing to market his products in Japan. The extent and range of the standards are apparently not trivial. In 1985 there were nearly 8,000 such JIS standards. Each standard is reviewed every three years, with around 500 standards being revised annually (Lecraw, 1986). Additionally, there were about 250 group standards, consisting of a total of 4,100 standards, which were written and administered by industry associations in 1985.

Not surprisingly, the Japanese system of standards has posed numerous problems for foreign producers. As Lecraw (1986) notes, all testing to meet the standards must be done in Japan. For complex products, up to thirty standards might apply, but the foreign producers could not easily determine which specific standards might be applicable to the particular product. Upon shipping the product to Japan, 'Each lot of the imported product was inspected to determine compliance to the standard – a cumbersome and lengthy process. If the product did not meet the standard, it was refused entry into Japan' (Lecraw, 1986, p. 13). Thus, not only were the procedures for meeting the standards expensive and time-consuming, but involved considerable risk, since a foreign producer could not be certain whether the product would pass inspection until it was on the docks in Japan.

As a result of the Japanese system of standards, the Japan External Trade Organization has determined that, 'large headaches are experienced by foreign business men who would like to export their products to Japan but cannot determine what compulsory specifications their products must comply with.' However, solutions are difficult to obtain, because 'It must be pointed out that standards and certification systems are inherently comprised of highly specialized and technical matters and it is not always possible to simplify the same and explain in an easily understandable fashion.'[9]

A comparison of non-tariff barriers between Japan and the United States is provided in Table 10.2. The non-tariff barriers are expressed as approximations of selected ad valorem tariff equivalents, ranging over the period from 1973 to the early 1980s.

Thus, the highest non-tariff barriers tended to be in industries comprising the agriculture, forestry and fish sector, where the non-tariff barriers in Japan ranged from a tariff equivalent of 27.2 to 97 percent. Within manufacturing, the sectors with the most stringent non-tariff barriers have been in food, beverages, and tobacco, petroleum and wood products. By contrast, the highest non-tariff barriers in the United States have tended to be in industries comprising the food, beverages, tobacco, apparel and footwear sectors.

Another instrument of protection in Japan has been the pre-emption of government procurement. That is, the 115 public corporations in Japan have explicitly pursued a policy of purchasing from Japanese companies rather than from foreign firms.[10] Under the Government Procurement Code, which went into effect in 1981, small- and medium-sized businesses are eligible for special consideration in the government's system of procurement. Thus, in 1980, about 36 percent of all government procurement came from small- and medium-sized firms, and by 1982 this figure had increased to 37 percent (US International Trade Commission, 1983b).

Table 10.2 Non-Tariff Barriers in Japan and the United States

Sector	Japan		United States	
	High	Low	High	Low
Agriculture, forestry, & fish	97.0	27.2	—	—
Food, beverages, & tobacco	75.0	16.5	31.9	15.9
Textiles	15.0	15.0	17.3	15.0
Apparel	18.0	15.0	28.0	15.0
Leather	11.0	3.0	—	—
Footwear	11.0	3.0	27.0	—
Wood products	25.0	22.0	—	—
Furniture	—	—	—	—
Paper	—	—	—	—
Printing	—	—	17.2	17.2
Chemicals	17.9	8.1	10.0	5.0
Petroleum	65.6	27.3	—	—
Rubber products	—	—	5.0	—
Non-metallic mineral products	10.0	7.5	10.0	5.0
Glass & glass products	—	—	—	—
Iron & steel	—	—	10.0	5.0
Non-ferrous metals	10.0	—	—	—
Metal products	—	—	—	—
Non-electric machinery	9.0	3.0	—	—
Electric machinery	9.0	9.0	5.0	—
Transport equipment	10.0	—	—	—
Miscellaneous manufacturing	—	—	—	—

Source: Staiger *et al.* (1985b).

A particular source of friction between the Japanese government and its trading partners has been the procurement system of the Japanese telecommunication monopoly, Nippon Telephone and Telegraph (NTT). NTT has continually demonstrated loyalty by purchasing from its network of suppliers, dominated by Hitachi, Fujitsu, Nippon Electric Corporation and Oki. While nearly half of NTT's purchases emanate from these supplying firms, purchases from foreign manufacturers have accounted for just one percent of the annual orders amounting to around $3 billion during the early 1980s (Curran, 1982). However, between 1981 and 1983, about thirty foreign companies were designated to become suppliers of specified equipment to NTT, including Northern Telecom, Rolm, ITT, Memorex, General Electric and Motorola. And, in 1983, NTT agreed to: (1) accept applications in English; (2) accept applications in its New York office; (3) extend the application period by three months for expensive equipment; (4) use more flexibility in formulating specifications for the products in its procurement practices; (5) extend the duration of contracts; and (6) make procurement announcements simultaneously in both Japan and the United States (US International Trade Commission, 1983b).

Finally, the last significant instrument of trade protection in Japan has been the restrictions on foreign direct investment. Although the phenomenon of foreign direct investment was becoming increasingly apparent in other industrialized nations (see Kindleberger and Audretsch, 1983), foreign firms were sharply restricted in their efforts to invest in Japanese assets. Under the Foreign Investment Law of 1950, the Japanese government was able to restrict foreign direct investment into Japan. These restrictions remained in effect until 1967. In 1967, automatic approval for up to 50 percent of foreign ownership was granted in thirty-three industries. And, in seventeen industries, foreign firms were allowed to fully own a subsidiary in Japan. The major qualification was that the liberalized rules towards foreign direct investment applied only to newly established enterprises. This trend towards liberalization continued. By 1970, over 500 industries were granted similar conditions (US International Trade Commission, 1983b).

More recently the restrictions on foreign direct investment in Japan have been significantly relaxed. Starting in 1975, most applications by foreign companies were approved within a ninety-day review period. And, under the 1980 amendments to the Foreign Exchange and Foreign Trade Control Law, restrictions applied only to agriculture, mining, petroleum and leather. As a result of these relaxations, foreign direct investment in Japan has become a significant feature. In 1981 there were 1,224 establishments in Japan involved in foreign direct investment, with slightly more than 500 of them in the manufacturing sector. Of these firms, 621 were American, with 339 in the manufacturing sector. Thus, the United States accounted for just over half of the number of total direct foreign investments in Japan.

PROTECTION AND TRADE IN JAPAN

The relationship between trade protection and its impact and relationship to actual trade flows is complex and difficult to disentangle. Since the focal point of Japanese trade has been on the United States, we will concentrate on the US–Japanese bilateral trade patterns. Table 10.3 shows the major components comprising the US–Japanese trade structure, aggregated to the two-digit SIC sector for 1977 to facilitate presentation. While the second column lists the number of four-digit industries comprising the two-digit sector, the third column reveals the average four-digit industry value of US imports from Japan for 1977 within the two-digit sector. The average value of industry imports from Japan ranged from $2,000 in the tobacco sector, to over $2.5 billion in the transportation equipment sector. Sectors with the greatest average value of industry imports from Japan were transportation equipment, primary metal products, electronics and instruments. Industries in the tobacco, lumber, furniture and paper sectors tended to experience the lowest value of Japanese imports.

The fourth column lists the average four-digit industry value of US exports to Japan in 1977 within each two-digit sector. The average value of industry

Table 10.3 The Structure of US–Japanese Trade, by Two-Digit SIC Sector, 1977 (Industry Weighted Average Value for Sector)

Sector	Number of industries	Japanese exports to US ($100,000)	Japanese imports from US ($100,000)	Japanese import penetration in US (%)	US export share (%)
Food	33	20.53	791.83	0.07	0.41
Tobacco	3	0.02	282.69	0.00	0.45
Textiles	26	369.67	28.37	0.94	0.10
Apparel	31	101.10	11.04	0.94	0.10
Lumber	7	14.76	3,279.34	0.04	4.46
Furniture	12	15.51	1.78	0.08	0.01
Paper	16	16.23	162.71	0.06	0.47
Printing	12	41.36	33.78	0.09	0.06
Chemicals	23	130.50	549.65	0.35	0.91
Petroleum	5	256.75	938.89	0.03	0.12
Rubber	5	990.64	336.17	0.72	0.17
Leather	6	94.41	6.19	1.54	0.12
Stone, clay, glass	26	56.31	22.91	0.79	0.14
Primary metals	19	8,586.49	100.35	2.13	0.06
Fabricated metal products	19	409.88	61.08	1.13	0.13
Machinery (non-electrical)	35	801.57	545.17	1.59	0.71
Electronics	29	3,250.49	241.96	3.80	0.44
Transportation equipment	9	25,580.68	711.97	3.43	0.18
Instruments	7	3,069.39	842.94	3.64	1.26
Miscellaneous manufacturing	16	371.15	111.81	2.22	0.63

exports to Japan ranged from $178,000 in the furniture sector, to over $327 million in the lumber sector. While industries in the lumber, petroleum, instruments and food sectors tended to have the highest value of exports to Japan, the average value of industry exports was lowest in the furniture, leather, apparel, and stone, clay and glass sectors.

The fifth column in Table 10.3 shows the industry average Japanese import penetration ratio in the United States, defined as US imports from Japan divided by industry value of shipments, plus total imports minus total US exports. Although the industries in the transportation equipment sector experienced the greatest absolute level of imports from Japan, the average import penetration ratio of 3.43 percent was slightly lower than in the electronics and instruments sectors. Other industries with a high Japanese import penetration ratio tended to be in the primary metals, non-electrical machinery, and leather sectors. Despite relatively high levels of imports from Japan, the import penetration ratio was not particularly high in the rubber and textile sectors, presumably due to the relatively large size of the markets in the United States.

Finally, the last column lists the industry average US export share, defined as the value of US exports to Japan as a percentage of domestic production in the United States. The US export share tended to be the largest in the industries in the lumber sector, where an average of 4.46 percent of US production was exported to Japan. Despite relatively high levels of the absolute value of exports in industries in the petroleum, transportation equipment, food and non-electrical machinery sectors, the US export shares are not particularly large, presumably due to the relatively large size of the domestic markets.

Table 10.3 suggests that neither US imports from nor US exports to Japan are evenly distributed across manufacturing industries. The US trade performance is apparently the strongest in the lumber, food, petroleum, chemicals and paper sectors. The Japanese trade performance is similarly the strongest in industries in the transportation equipment, electronics, primary metal products and textiles sectors. In several sectors, both the industry average value of US exports to and imports from Japan is relatively large. Such sectors represent the existence of substantial intra-industry trade. For example, while the United States had an average value of $54.5 million of exports to Japan in the industries in the non-electrical machinery sector, there was simultaneously an average of $80.2 million imports in the same industries from Japan. Thus, the Japanese average import penetration ratio in the United States was 1.59 percent, while the United States exported 0.71 percent of its total domestic production in Japan. Other sectors comprised of industries experiencing similar levels of intra-industry trade include instruments, miscellaneous manufacturing and printing.

The relationship between Japanese imports from the United States and the corresponding trade barriers in Japan is shown for those Japanese industries with the largest value of US imports in Table 10.4. In the first column, industries are ranked according to the absolute dollar value of Japanese imports from the United States. The largest export industry was logging contractors, which imported over $831 million of products from the United States. The second largest, meatpacking plants, imported only $350 million worth of goods from the US. The tenth largest import industry, aircraft, had $119 million of imports from the United States. Thus, the size distribution of Japanese imports from the United States is skewed towards a relatively select group of industries.

The second column in Table 10.4 shows how large the value of the Japanese imports from the United States was relative to US production – or the US export share. For example, in the logging contractors industry, 13.34 percent of the value of US shipments was sold to Japan. This industry had the highest export share to Japan. While some industries, such as petroleum refining and motor vehicles, export a relatively large value of goods to Japan, the percentage of total production in the United States – 0.11 and 0.12 percent, respectively – is relatively small. In other industries, such as measuring and controlling devices, and jewelers' materials, the value of US

Table 10.4 The Japanese Industries with the Largest Value of Imports from the United States, and Corresponding Trade Barriers in Japan, 1977

Industry	Japanese imports from US ($100,000)	Percentage of US output	Japanese non-tariff barriers	Japanese weighted tariffs (%)
Logging contractors	8,311.87	13.34	Low	0.3
Meatpacking plants	3,498.68	1.12	Moderate	25.4
Electronic computing equipment	2,794.64	2.16	Moderate	9.1
Sawmills	2,744.83	2.53	Low	0.3
Industrial inorganic chemicals	2,274.13	2.62	Low	6.2
Pulpmills	1,717.83	8.21	Low	2.1
Photographic equipment	1,461.11	1.47	Low	7.4
Industrial organic chemicals	1,408.05	0.58	Moderate	6.2
Medicinals & botanicals	1,227.34	6.49	Low	6.2
Aircraft	1,194.68	0.81	Low	6.0
Aircraft equipment	1,013.23	2.13	Low	6.0
Petroleum refining	996.72	0.11	Moderate	2.8
Motor vehicles	902.56	0.12	Moderate	6.0
Special industry machinery	787.94	2.17	Low	9.1
Canned seafoods	775.57	5.38	Moderate	25.4
Semiconductors	751.21	1.41	Moderate	7.4
Plastics materials & resins	746.40	0.69	Low	6.2
Chemical preparations	722.24	1.83	Low	6.2
Instruments to measure electricity	627.67	2.27	Moderate	7.4
Polishes & sanitation goods	615.22	1.95	Low	6.2
Measuring & controlling devices	607.86	5.44	Moderate	7.4
Radio & TV communication equipment	603.74	0.41	Moderate	7.4
Aircraft engines	580.79	0.93	Low	6.0
Soybean oil mills	560.24	0.74	Low	25.4
Paperboard mills	525.35	0.74	Low	2.1
Pharmaceutical preparations	511.89	0.45	Low	6.2
Plastics products	498.66	0.21	Moderate	2.8
Condensed milk	487.12	1.53	High	25.4
Cyclic crudes	472.11	0.84	Low	6.2
Secondary non-ferrous metals	439.47	1.24	Low	1.1
Surgical instruments	416.24	2.27	Low	7.4
Animal fats & oils	415.44	2.51	Low	25.4
Sporting goods	407.33	1.68	Low	6.0
Jewelers' materials	391.22	5.71	Moderate	6.0
Construction machinery	384.54	0.30	Low	9.1

Source: Audretsch and Yamawaki (1986b).

sales to Japan is relatively large compared to the value of domestic production.

The third column in Table 10.4 lists a qualitative assessment of the non-tariff barriers in Japan during the 1970s. The non-tariff barrier rankings are based on evaluations from the US International Trade Commission, which have been used by and described by Ray (1981a, 1981b), Audretsch and Yamawaki (1986a), and from the evaluations of Staiger *et al.* (1985c). The last column lists the weighted average of tariff protection in Japan. Just as there is no apparent relationship between the extent of Japanese non-tariff barriers and Japanese imports from the United States, there does not appear to be any strong relationship between the level of tariff protection and US shipments to Japan.

Table 10.5 lists the 35 four-digit SIC industries in Japan with the greatest value of exports to the United States in 1977. Thus, the automobile industry, with slightly more than $4.6 billion of Japanese exports to the United States, was by far the largest exporter of Japanese goods. By contrast, the blast furnace and steel mills as well as the radio and television sets industries had less than half the dollar value of exports. Each of the next three largest exporting industries – radio and television communication equipment, motorcycles and bicycles, and photographic equipment – exported a considerably smaller value of Japanese goods, between $586 million and $788 million. Thus, the size distribution of exports to the United States is skewed towards a select group of industries.

The second column in Table 10.5 shows the Japanese import penetration ratio in the United States, defined as US imports from Japan divided by industry value-of-shipments plus total imports minus total US exports. It should be observed that there is not always a close relationship between the absolute value of Japanese exports to the United States and the penetration ratio in the US market. For example, although the motor vehicles industry experienced the larger value of exports to the United States, measured in absolute dollars, the Japanese import penetration ratio in the US market ranked only nineteenth at 5.48 percent. In some industries, such as motor vehicle parts and accessories, industrial organic chemicals and plastic products, the ranking of the Japanese import penetration ratio is relatively low compared to the absolute dollar value of imports from Japan. In other industries, such as sewing machines, fine earthenware, food utensils and medicinals and botanicals, the ranking of the Japanese import penetration ratio is relatively high compared to the absolute dollar value of sales from Japan. Several industries, such as radio and television sets, motorcycles and bicycles, and optical instruments, have both a high absolute dollar value of Japanese exports as well as a high import penetration ratio in the US market. Finally, the last two columns suggest, as with the imports from the United States, that there is no obvious relationship between Japanese non-tariff and tariff barriers and exports to the United States. Nor does any drastic difference in Japanese commercial policy appear between those industries which have the highest value of exports to the United States and those industries which have the highest value of imports from the United States.

Several industries appear both in Table 10.4 and Table 10.5. Such industries represent the existence of substantial intra-industry trade. For

Table 10.5 The Japanese Industries with the Largest Value of Exports to the United States, and Corresponding Trade Barriers in Japan

Industry	Japanese exports to US ($100,000)	Penetration in US (%)	Japanese non-tariff barriers	Japanese weighted tariffs (%)
Motor vehicles	46,031.25	5.48	Moderate	6.0
Steel mills	21,659.47	4.70	Low	3.3
Radio & TV sets	20,926.13	23.93	Moderate	7.4
Radio & TV communication equipment	7,875.33	5.30	Moderate	7.4
Motorcycles & bicycles	6,868.50	37.01	Low	6.0
Photographic equipment	5,859.96	6.18	Low	7.4
Bolts, nuts, rivets & washers	2,527.75	7.09	Low	6.9
Motor vehicle parts	2,090.54	0.62	Low	6.0
Optical instruments	2,055.67	14.06	Low	7.4
Electronic computing equipment	2,046.47	1.97	Moderate	9.1
Construction machinery	1,778.73	1.86	Low	9.1
Calculating machines	1,739.76	18.79	Low	9.1
Tires and inner tubes	1,645.09	1.73	Low	2.8
Ball and roller bearing	1,518.00	5.72	Low	9.1
Watches & clocks	1,454.93	6.87	Low	7.4
Weaving mills	1,316.37	2.09	Low	3.3
Electronic components	1,241.14	2.40	Low	7.4
Steel wire	1,220.61	4.83	Low	3.3
Internal combustion engines	1,097.30	1.47	Low	9.1
Hand & edge tools	1,049.30	4.72	Low	6.9
Sporting & athletic goods	1,045.62	3.80	Low	6.0
Electric housewares & fans	1,012.77	3.92	Low	7.4
Industrial organic chemicals	996.00	0.44	Low	6.2
Machine tools (metal cutting)	959.41	3.33	Low	9.1
Sewing machines	949.97	22.02	Low	7.4
Fine earthenware food utensils	947.29	44.11	Low	0.6
Plastics products	920.32	0.39	Low	2.8
Cyclic crudes	853.25	1.61	Low	6.2
Medicinals & botanicals	837.78	5.89	Low	6.2
Semiconductors	815.37	1.58	High	7.4
Valves & pipe fittings	723.96	1.33	Low	6.9
Musical instruments	685.38	7.27	Low	6.0
Office machines	685.67	2.49	Moderate	9.1
Games & toys	680.56	2.29	Low	6.0
Vitreous china food utensils	675.98	24.96	Low	0.6

Source: Audretsch and Yamawaki (1986b).

example, while Japan exported $205 million of electronic computing equipment to the United States, it simultaneously imported from the US $279 million in the same industry. Thus, the Japanese import penetration ratio in the US market was 1.97 percent, while the United States exported 2.16 percent of its total domestic production to Japan. Other industries experiencing similar levels of intra-industry include photographic equipment, medicinals and botanicals, semiconductors and crylic crudes.

ECONOMETRIC ANALYSIS OF US–JAPANESE TRADE

Although only a few studies have attempted to identify the determinants of bilateral trade between the United States and Japan, a number of studies examining aggregate US trade have generally reached the same conclusion, namely, none of the international trade hypotheses fully explains variations in the trade structure (Baldwin, 1971; Stern, 1975; Stern and Maskus, 1981). Rather, as Baldwin found, 'it is necessary to discard the simple single factor trade theories in favor of multifactor trade models' (1971, p. 143). Hufbauer (1970), Baldwin (1971, 1979), and Stern and Maskus (1981) found that the standard Heckscher–Ohlin theory, human skills hypothesis, and neo-technology theories, combine to provide the fullest and most complete explanation of actual trade behavior. According to the Heckscher–Ohlin theory, the proportion of productive factors determines the trade structure. If there exists an abundance of physical capital relative to labor, a country will tend towards export of capital-intensive goods; an abundance of labor relative to physical capital leads to the export of labor-intensive goods (Lowinger, 1971). The human skills hypothesis extends the Heckscher–Ohlin theory by including human capital as a third factor. In the presence of a relative abundance of a highly trained labor force and professional personnel, a country is predicted to export skill-intensive goods. Conversely, the abundance of skilled labor tends to promote the importation of skill-intensive goods (Keesing, 1966).

The neo-technology theories focus on R&D and the stage of an industry in the product life cycle. Gruber et al. (1967) suggest that R&D expenditures reflect a temporary comparative advantage resulting from products and production techniques that have not yet been adapted by foreign competitors. Thus, industries with a relatively high R&D component are considered to be in the early stages of the product life cycle and are expected to be net exporters (Vernon, 1966).

Just as the theory of international trade in the context of monopolistic competition has recently emerged, recent empirical work has sought to incorporate industrial organization concepts in explaining trade behavior. White (1974), Pagoulatos and Sorenson (1976), Pugel (1978) and Caves et al. (1980) show that market structure significantly affects the trade structure, largely through creating barriers to entry.

In trying to identify the effect of Japanese commercial policy and R&D on US–Japanese trade, we have included variables representing each of the major theories and influences discussed above. Specifically, we use:

Dependent variable
TB: The US–Japanese trade balance, defined as $TB = (X - M)/(X + M)$, where X is US exports to Japan in 1977, and M is US imports from Japan in 1977. Thus, this measure weights net exports, $X - M$, by the total amount traded between the two countries, $X + M$. The identical variable was used by Pugel (1978), and Audretsch and Yamawaki (1988). It has the advantage of implicitly controlling for transportability, while still indicating the comparative advantage. As Pugel notes, this measure has the disadvantage of perhaps overstating the importance to the low balance of trade of industries in which there is only little international trade.

Independent variables
K/L: The capital-labor ratio; K/L has been found to be negatively related to US net exports in most empirical studies, giving rise to the famous 'Leontieff Paradox' (Baldwin, 1971; Stern and Maskus, 1981). In his study, which excluded trade barriers and industrial policy, Baldwin found a negative, but statistically insignificant relationship between K/L and net exports between the United States and Japan.

HUMK: A measure of human capital and skilled labor, measured as the difference between the annual average industry wage per employee and the annual wage for persons with less than eight years' education, capitalized at 10 percent, for 1970. This measure is identical to the one described by Kenen (1970) and used by Baldwin (1971). As Stern (1975, p. 12) reports after surveying the empirical literature, 'There seems to be little question now that US exports are relatively more human-capital intensive than imports.' Thus, most studies have found HUMK and other measures of the level of labor skills (see Keesing, 1966) to have a positive and significant coefficient.

RD: R&D intensity: To test the robustness of the results with respect to different measures of R&D intensity, we use four separate R&D measures – (1) the percentage of total employment consisting of scientists and engineers who are engaged in R&D, RDSE/N; (2) expenditures on R&D as a percentage of sales, RD/S; (3) the percentage of total employment consisting of scientists and engineers, S/N; and (4) the percentage of scientists and engineers who are engaged in R&D, RDSE/SE. These measures have been used by Ray (1981a, and 1981b), Baldwin (1971), Gruber et al. (1967), Keesing (1967) and Lowinger (1975). They all found a positive relationship between R&D intensity and US exports.

CR: The four-firm concentration ratio, 1977. White (1974) demonstrated that market concentration is conducive to imports through the incentive of elevated price-cost margins. Accordingly, Koo and Martin (1984) found a negative and statistically significant relationship between CR and net exports.

ADCON: Advertising intensity in those consumer industries which were classified by Porter (1976) and Pugel (1978) as being convenience goods, for 1977. ADCON = AD/VS C, where AD is the 1977 advertising expenditures, VS is the 1977 industry value of shipments, and C is a dummy variable equalling one for consumer goods industries that are also convenience products and zero otherwise. According to Caves (1974) and Pagoulatos and Sorenson (1976), the mainstream view in industrial organization is that advertising creates an entry barrier and therefore should be negatively related to imports.

TARIF: The ratio of average US tariff rates in 1970 divided by the average tariff rates in Japan in 1970. Ray (1981a, 1981b) argues that tariff barriers should not have a strong effect on exports and imports. Although, as Ray finds, tariff rates are certainly endogenous to trade performance, the seven-year lag between the relative tariff values and the dependent variable suggests that we can consider TARIF as a predetermined variable.

NTBUS: An index of non-tariff barriers in the United States for 1970 divided by an index of non-tariff barriers in Japan for 1970. Ray (1981a, 1981b) argues that non-tariff barriers should have a larger effect on trade than do tariff barriers. While non-tariff barriers may also be endogenous to the contemporary trade structure, the seven-year lag between NTBUS and TB is sufficient to classify NTBUS as a pre-deternmined variable.

Using the balance of trade between the United States and Japan (TB) in 1977 as the dependent variable, the cross-section regression results for 230 four-digit SIC manufacturing industries are shown in Table 10.6. Equation 1 includes the R&D measure of the number of scientists and engineers who are engaged in R&D as a percentage of the total employment, RDSE/N. The positive and statistically significant coefficient of K/L implies that the United States tends to import goods from Japan in industries that are relatively labor-intensive and export goods to Japan in industries that are relatively capital-intensive. Apparently, the general finding that capital-intensive industries are associated with a relatively high level of US imports – the Leontief paradox – dose not hold for the case of bilateral trade between the United States and Japan.

The negative and statistically significant coefficient of HUMK implies that US imports from Japan tend to occur in industries requiring a relatively high component of skilled labor while US exports to Japan tend to occur in industries utilizing relatively low levels of skilled labor. Again, the US–Japanese bilateral trade structure in 1977 is apparently contradictory to the general pattern of US trade, where net export industries have been found

Table 10.6 Regressions of the Balance of Trade Between the United States and Japan (standard error in parentheses)[a]

	Regressions			
	(1)	(2)	(3)	(4)
K/L	0.0106	0.0109	0.0100	0.0112
	(0.0024)***	(0.0025)***	(0.0024)***	(0.0024)***
HUMK	−0.1683	−0.1739	−0.1737	−0.1409
	(0.0671)***	(0.0689)***	(0.0068)***	(0.0659)***
CR	−0.0055	−0.0053	−0.0053	−0.0055
	(0.0022)***	(0.0023)***	(0.0022)***	(0.0022)***
ADCON	55.6310	57.9650	55.7940	56.5770
	(36.0970)*	(36.2230)*	(36.1380)*	(36.0240)*
TARIF	0.0258	0.0250	0.0245	0.0233
	(0.0455)	(0.0458)	(0.0455)	(0.0452)
NTBUS	0.0674	0.0673	0.0691	0.0609
	(0.0238)***	(0.0241)***	(0.0240)***	(0.0236)***
RDSE/N	0.0787	—	—	—
	(0.0359)***			
RD/S	—	0.0321	—	—
		(0.0187)*		
SE/N	—	—	3.7354	—
			(1.8043)***	
RDSE/SE	—	—	—	1.0744
				(0.4568)***
Intercept	0.1487	0.1651	0.1417	−0.1959
	(0.2483)	(0.2501)	(0.2484)	(0.2830)
Sample Size	230	230	230	230
$\bar{R}^2$	0.160	0.153	0.158	0.163
F	7.222	6.903	7.134	7.348

[a]The dependent variable is the balance of trade between the United States and Japan.
*Statistically significant at the 90 percent level of confidence, one-tailed test.
**Statistically significant at the 95 percent level of confidence, one-tailed test.
***Statistically significant at the 99 percent level of confidence, one-tailed test.

to be skilled labor-intensive and net import industries have been found to be unskilled labor-intensive. These results are apparently robust with respect to the four different measures of R&D intensity.

The negative and statistically significant sign of CR supports the findings of Koo and Martin (1984) that, *ceteris paribus*, foreign competitors have a bigger incentive to enter concentrated markets. Similarly, the positive and significant coefficient (90 percent level of confidence) of ADCON supports the contention by Caves (1974) that advertising intensity, particularly in those industries producing convenience goods, serves as a barrier to foreign entry.

The measure of relative tariff barriers, TARIF, has a positive coefficient, but, as Ray (1981b) predicted, this effect is sufficiently small to be statistically negligible. The positive and statistically significant coefficient of NTBUS implies that US non-tariff barriers are effective at impeding Japanese imports.

Thus, as Ray found, non-tariff barriers are a more effective instrument for altering the trade balance than are tariff barriers.

The positive and statistically significant coefficient of RDSE/N implies that the United States tends to hold the comparative advantage in industries where R&D intensity plays a relatively significant role. That R&D-intensive industries are associated with a relatively high US trade balance is consistent with the findings of the previous literature towards the general US trade structure.

The measure of R&D expenditures as a percentage of sales, RD/S, is substituted in Equation 2. While its effect on the bilateral trade balance is somewhat weaker, based on the significance of the coefficient, the implication remains unchanged: the United States tends to hold the comparative advantage in R&D-intensive industries. Using a substitute R&D measure has little effect on the regression results of the other variables. The third R&D measure, the percentage of employment consisting of scientists and engineers, SE/N, is used in Equation 3. Again, the results remain essentially unaffected from substituting the different R&D measure. Finally, in Equation 4 the percentage of scientists and engineers who are actually engaged in R&D is used. As in the previous three regressions, R&D intensity exerts a positive influence on US exports relative to US imports with respect to US–Japanese trade.

Thus, the results from Table 10.6 suggest that high levels of capital intensity, non-tariff barriers, and R&D, tend to promote US comparative advantage vis-a-vis Japan. By contrast, the United States tends not to hold the comparative advantage in industries which use relatively high levels of human capital. Further, Japanese firms tend to enter highly concentrated industries but are deterred in markets where advertising is important.

CONCLUSIONS

While several patterns regarding the US general trade structure have emerged in the literature, these patterns may not hold in the case of bilateral trade, at least between the United States and Japan. A positive association has consistently been found between the level of skilled-labor content in an industry and US exports. The United States has been considered to hold the comparative advantage in high-skill industries. However, in the case of bilateral trade between the United States and Japan, we find the reverse. The United States tends to import more from Japan in industries requiring skilled labor and export more to Japan in industries utilizing less skilled labor.

Similarly, the United States has consistently been found to have a greater value of imports in capital-intensive industries, and a greater value of exports in labor-intensive industries – the Leontieff paradox. Again, in the case of US–Japanese bilateral trade, this finding is apparently reversed. The United

States tends to export goods in capital-intensive industries to Japan and import goods in labor-intensive industries from Japan.

NOTES

1. 'US, EC to act on Japan trade', *International Herald Tribune*, 21/22 February 1987, p. 1.
2. 'Japan's surplus in trade widens to $3.94 billion', *International Herald Tribune*, 1 April 1986, p. 13.
3. The tariff data are from the US International Trade Commission (1983b).
4. Weighted average tariffs are tariff rates which have been weighted by the value of imports of the importing country. For a further explanation, see Staiger *et al.* (1985b).
5. The data on quota restrictions are from the US International Trade Commission (1983b).
6. 'Barriers to business remain cultural, rarely economic', *International Herald Tribune*, 10 October 1986, p. 9.
7. 'Beyond the Japanese export boom', *The Wall Street Journal*, 8 January 1987.
8. Quoted from Lecraw (1986, p. 8).
9. Quoted from Lecraw (1986, p. 24).
10. *The Economist*, 6 August 1983, p. 57.

REFERENCES

Abernathy, W.J., K.B. Clark and A.M. Kantrow (1983), *Industrial Renaissance*, New York: Basic Books.

Abrams, R.M. (ed.) (1970), *The Issues of the Populist and Progressive Eras, 1892–1912* (2nd edn), Columbia: The University of South Carolina Press, 1970.

Acs, Z.J. (1984), *The Changing Structure of the US Economy*, New York: Praeger.

Acs, Z.J. and D.B. Audretsch (1986a), 'The determinants of innovation in large and small firms', Wissenschaftszentrum Berlin, Discussion Paper IIM/IP 86–18.

Acs, Z.J. and D.B. Audretsch (1986b), 'Accounting for the differences between large- and small-firm innovation', Wissenschaftszentrum Berlin. Discussion Paper IIM/IP 86–19.

Acs, Z.J. and D.B. Audretsch (1986c), 'The restructuring of US markets', Wissenschaftszentrum Berlin, Working Paper.

Acs, Z.J. and D.B. Audretsch (1987a), 'Innovation in large and small firms', *Economics Letters* 23.

Acs, Z.J. and D.B. Audretsch (1987b), 'The determinants of small-firm entry in US manufacturing', Wissenschaftszentrum Berlin, Discussion Paper IIM/IP 87–6.

Acs, Z.J. and D.B. Audretsch (1987c), 'The determinants of small-firm growth in US manufacturing', Wissenschaftszentrum Berlin, Discussion Paper IIM/IP 87–10.

Acs, Z.J. and D.B. Audretsch (1987d), 'Innovation, market structure, and firm size', *Review of Economics and Statistics* 69.

Acs, Z.J. and D.B. Audretsch (1987e), 'An empirical examination of small firm growth', *Economics Letters*, 25.

Acs, Z.J. and D.B. Audretsch (1988), 'Innovation in large and small firms: an empirical analysis', *American Economic Review* 78.

Acs, Z.J. and D.B. Audretsch (forthcoming), 'Small-firm entry in U.S. manufacturing', *Economica*.

Acs, Z.J., D.B. Audretsch and R.J. Judd (1987), 'Economic development and public policy: the growth of new/small business', Center for Policy Studies, Springfield, IL.

Adams, W. (1958), 'The role of competition in the regulated industries', *American Economic Review* 48.

American Iron and Steel Institute (1986), *Annual Report on the US Steel Industry*, Washington DC.

Anderson, A. & Co. (1979), *Cost of Government Regulation Study for the Business Round Table*, Boston, MA.

Areeda, P. (1974), *Antitrust Analysis* (2nd edn), Boston, MA: Little, Brown.

Armentano, D.T. (1982), *Antitrust and Monopoly: Anatomy of a Failure*, New York: John Wiley.

Audretsch, D.B. (1983a), *The Effectiveness of Antitrust Policy Towards Horizontal Mergers*, Ann Arbor, MI: UMI Press.

Audretsch, D.B. (1983b), 'An evaluation of horizontal merger enforcement', in J.V. Craven (ed.). *Industrial Organisation, Antitrust, and Public Policy*, Boston, MA: Kluwer–Nijhoff.

Audretsch, D.B. (1985a), 'US antitrust enforcement and the deterrent effect', Wissenschaftszentrum Berlin, Discussion Paper IIM/IP 85–38.

Audretsch, D.B. (1985b), 'The four schools of thought in antitrust economics' Wissenschaftszentrum Berlin, Discussion Paper IIM–IP 85–32.

Audretsch, D.B. (1986), 'The effect of technology and the industry life-cycle on the concentration-profits relationship', Wissenschaftszentrum Berlin, Discussion Paper IIM–IP 86–5.

Audretsch, D.B. (1987a), 'An empirical test of the industry life-cycle', *Weltwirtschaftliches Archiv* 123.

Audretsch, D.B. (1987b), 'The Celler-Kefauver Act and the deterrent effect', *Review of Industrial Organization* 2.

Audretsch, D.B. (1988a), 'Divergent views in antitrust economics', *Antitrust Bulletin* 33.

Audretsch, D.B. (1988b), 'An evaluation of Japanese R&D and Industrial Policies', *Aussenwirtschaft* 43, reprinted in H. Hauser (ed.) *Technology and Public Policy*, Grüsch, Switzerland: Verlag Rügger.

Audretsch, D.B. (forthcoming a), 'Legalized cartels in West Germany', *Antitrust Bulletin*.

Audretsch, D.B. (forthcoming b), 'Joint R&D and industrial policy', in A. Link and G. Tassey (eds), *Cooperative Research: A New Strategy for Competitiveness*, Norwell, MA: Kluwer Academic Publishers.

Audretsch, D.B., L. Sleuwaegen and H. Yamawaki (1989a), 'The dynamics of export competition', in D.B. Audretsch, L. Sleuwaegen and H. Yamawaki (eds), *The Convergence of International and Domestic Markets*, Amsterdam: North-Holland.

Audretsch, D.B., L. Sleuwaegen and H. Yamawaki (eds) (1989b), *The Convergence of International and Domestic Markets*, Amsterdam: North-Holland.

Audretsch, D.B. and A.G. Woolf (1986), 'The product life cycle and the concentration-profits relationship', *American Economist*, Fall.

Audretsch, D.B. and A.G. Woolf (1987), 'Regulatory reform in the 1980s: an anti rent-seeking movement?' *European Journal of Political Economy* 3.

Audretsch, D.B. and H. Yamawaki (1986a), 'Industrial policy, R&D, and US–Japanese Trade', Wissenschaftszentrum Berlin, Discussion Paper IIM/IP 86–13.

Audretsch, D.B. and H. Yamawaki (1986b), 'The determinants of US–Japanese bilateral trade', Wissenschaftszentrum Berlin, Working Paper.

Audretsch, D.B. and H. Yamawaki (1987), 'Industrial policy and US–Japanese Trade', *Economics Letters* 23.

Audretsch, D.B. and H. Yamawaki (1988), 'R&D rivalry, industrial policy and US–Japanese trade', *Review of Economics and Statistics* 70.

Bailey, E. (1985), 'Economic Deregulation: transportation and communication', survey for OECD.

Bailey, E., D.R. Graham and D.P. Kaplan (1985), *Deregulating the Airlines*, Cambridge, MA: MIT Press.

Baldwin, R.E. (1971), 'The determinants of the commodity structure of U.S. trade', *American Economic Review* 61.

Baldwin, R.E. (1988), 'Evaluating strategic trade policies', *Aussenwirtschaft* 43, reprinted in H. Hauser (ed.) *Technology and Public Policy*, Grüsch, Switzerland: Verlag Rügger.

Baldwin, R.E. and T.S. Thompson (1984), 'Responding to trade-distorting policies of other countries', *American Economic Review* 74.

Bardach, E. (1984), 'Implementing industrial policy', in J. Chalmers (ed.), *The Industrial Policy Debate*, San Francisco, CA: Institute for Contemporary Studies.

Baxter, W.F. (1970), 'NYSE fixed commission rates: a private cartel goes public', *Stanford Law Review* 22.

Beckett, G. (1941), *The Reciprocal Trade Agreements Program*, New York: Columbia University Press.

Benisch, Werner (1968), '10 Jahre Praxis des Bundeskartellamtes', in Arbeitskreis Kartellgesetz im Ausschuß für Wettbewerbsordnung des Bundesverbandes der Deutschen Industrie (ed.), *10 Jahre Kartellgesetz, 1958–1968: Eine Würdigung aus der Sicht der deutschen Industrie*, Bergisch Gladbach: Heider Verlag.

Bergsten, F. and W. Cline (1985), *The US–Japan Economic Problem*, Cambridge, MA: MIT Press.

Bittlingmayer, G. (1985), 'Did antitrust policy cause the great merger wave?' *Journal of Law and Economics* 28.

Bittlingmayer, G. (1986), 'Monopoly and competition Chicago-style', Wissenschaftszentrum Berlin, Working Paper.

Blair, R.D., D.L. Kaserman and J.T. McClave (1986), 'Motor carrier deregulation: the Florida experiment', *Review of Economics and Statistics* 18.

Böbel, I. (1984), *Wettbewerb und Industriestruktur – Industrial-Organization-Forschung im Überblick*, Berlin: Springer-Verlag.

Böbel, I. (1987), 'Marktmacht versus Effizienz: Ein wirtschaftspolitisches Dilemma?' *List Forum* 1.

Boltho, A. and C. Allsopp (1987), 'The assessment: trade and trade policy', *Oxford Review of Economic Policy* 3.

Bork, R.H. (1966), 'Legislative intent and the policy of the Sherman Act', *Journal of Law and Economics* 60.

Bork, R.H. (1978), *The Antitrust Paradox: a Policy At War with Itself*, New York: Basic Books.

Borrus, M. (1983), 'The politics of erosion in the US steel industry', in J. Zysman and L. Tyson (eds), *American Industry in International Competition: Government Policies and Corporate Strategies*, Ithaca, NY: Cornell University Press.

Borrus, M., J.E. Millstein and J. Zysman (1983), 'Trade and development in the semiconductor industry: Japanese challenges and American response', in J. Zysman and L. Tyson (eds), *American Industry in International Competition: Government Policies and Corporate Strategies*, Ithaca, NY: Cornell University Press.

Borrus, M., L. Tyson and J. Zysman (1986), 'Creating advantage – how government policies shape international trade in the semiconductor industry', in P. Krugman (ed.), *Strategic Trade Policy and the New International Economics*, Cambridge, MA: MIT Press.

Bowen, H. P. (1983), 'Changes in the international distribution of resources and their impact on US comparative advantage', *Review of Economics and Statistics* 65.

Braeutigam, R.R. (1981), 'The deregulation of natural gas', in L.W. Weiss and M.W. Klass (eds), *Case Studies in Regulation: Revolution and Reform*, Boston, MA: Little, Brown.

Brander, J.A. and B.J. Spencer (1983), 'International R&D rivalry and industrial strategy', *Review of Economic Studies* 50.

Brander, J.A. and B.J. Spencer (1985), 'Export subsidies and international market share rivalry', *Journal of International Economics* 18.

Breyer, S. (1982), *Regulation and its Reform*, Cambridge, MA: Harvard University Press.

Brown, C.J.F. (1980), 'Industrial policy and economic planning in Japan and France', *National Institute Economic Review*.

Buchanon, J.M., R.D. Tollison and G. Tullock (eds) (1980), *Toward a Theory of the Rent-Seeking Society*, College Station, TX: Texas A&M University Press.

Bundeskartellamt (1968), *Zehn Jahre Bundeskartellamt*, Berlin: Carl Heymanns Verlag, KG.

Bundesminister für Wirtschaft (1985), 'Bericht des Bundeskartellamtes über seine Tätigkeit in den Jahren 1983/1984 sowie über Lage und Entwicklung auf seinem Aufgabengebiet', Bonn.

Bundesminister für Forschung und Technologie (1985), *Statistische Informationen*, Bonn.

Cable, V. (1982), *Protection and Industrial Decline*, London: Hodder and Stoughton.

Cairncross, A. (1974), *Economic Policy for the European Community*, London: Macmillan.

Calvani, T. (1985), 'The FTC's role in ensuring free trade', *Economic Review of the Federal Reserve Bank of Atlanta*, December.

Cardiff, B. (1986), 'Community competitiveness in high technology', paper presented at the University Association for Contemporary European Studies: The United States, The European Community and Japan – Trade and the World Economy, Reading University, September.

Caves, R.E. (1962), *Air Transport and its Regulators: An Industry Study*, Cambridge, MA: Harvard University Press.

Caves, R.E. (1974), *International Trade, International Investment and Imperfect Markets*, Special Papers in International Economics, No. 10., Princeton, NJ: Princeton University.

Caves, R.E. (1985), 'International trade and industrial organization: problems solved and unsolved', *European Economic Review* 28.

Caves, R.E. and J. Khalilzadeh-Shirazi (1977), 'International trade and industrial organization: some statistical evidence', in A.P. Jacquemin and H.W. de Jong (eds), *Welfare Aspects of Industrial Markets*, vol. 2, Leiden, Netherlands: Martinus Nijhoff.

Caves, R.E., M.E. Porter, and A.M. Spence with J.T. Scott (1980), *Competition in the Open Economy*, Cambridge, MA: Harvard University Press.

Caves, R.E. and M. Uekusa (1975), *Industrial Organization in Japan*, Washington DC: The Brookings Institution.

Caves, R.E. and M. Uekusa (1976), 'Industrial Organization', in H. Patrick and H. Rosovsky (eds), *Asia's New Giant: How the Japanese Economy Works*, Washington DC: The Brookings Institution.

Caves, R.E. and M. Uekusa (1978), *Industrial Organization in Japan*, Washington DC: Brookings Institution.

Chang, C.S. (1981), *The Japanese Auto Industry and the US Market*, New York: Praeger.

Cicchetti, C.J. and J. Jurewitz (eds), (1975) *Studies in Utility Regulation*, Cambridge, MA: Ballinger.

Colander, D.C. (ed.) (1984), *Neoclassical Political Economy: The Analysis of Rent-Seeking and DUP Activities*, Cambridge, MA: Ballinger.

Comanor, W. (1968),'Vertical territorial and customer restrictions: white motor and its aftermath', *Harvard Law Review* 81.

Commission of the European Communities (1966), 'Concentration of enterprises in the Common Market, December 1965', Memorandum, *CCH Common Market Reports* 26.

Commission of the European Communities (1972), *Report on Competition Policy*, Brussels.

Commission of the European Communities (1982), *Communication to the Council on Laying the Fundamentals for a European Strategic Program in Research and Development in Information Technology: The Pilot Phase*, Com (82) 486, Brussels.

Commission of the European Communities (1983a), *Report from the Commission to the Council and the European Parliament on the Borrowing and Lending Activities of the Community in 1982*, Com (83) 527, Brussels.

Commission of the European Communities (1983b), *Twelfth Report on Competition Policy*, Brussels.

Commission of the European Communities (1984), *Thirteenth Report on Competition Policy*, European Economic Commission, Brussels.

Corden, W.M. (1971), *The Theory of Protection*, Oxford: Clarendon Press.

Corder, W.M. and Gerhard Fels (1976), 'Public assistance to industry in Britain and Germany', in W.M. Corder and G. Fels (eds), *Public Assistance to Industry*, Boulder, CO: Westview Press.

Corsten, H. (1987), 'Using the results of research financed and conducted by public bodies – a comparative review of the situation in the member states of the European Community', *Technovation* 6.

Crombrugghe, D. de (1987), 'Beyond comparative advantage: interim progress report', unpublished manuscript, EIASM, Brussels.

Curran, T.J. (1982), 'Politics and high technology: The NIT case', in I.M. Destler and Hideo Sato (eds), *Coping With US–Japanese Economic Conflicts*, Lexington, MA: Lexington Books.

Davenport, M. (1983),'Industrial policy in the United Kingdom', in F.G. Adams and B.R. Klein (eds), *Industrial Policies for Growth and Competitiveness*, Lexington, MA: Lexington Books.

Denton, G. (1976), 'Financial assistance to British industry', in W.M. Corden and G. Fels (eds), *Public Assistance to Industry*, London: Macmillan.

Dixit, A. and V. Norman (1980), *Theory of International Trade*, Cambridge, MA: Nisbet.

Dixit, A. and J.E. Stiglitz (1977), 'Monopolistic competition and optimum product diversity', *American Economic Review* 67.

Dorges, J.B. (1980), 'Industrial policies in West Germany's not so market-oriented economy', *World Economy* 3.

Denzau, A.T. (1987),'Can trade protection save jobs?' Center for the Study of American Business, Washington University, Discussion Paper OP62.

Douglas, G. and J. Miller (1974), *Economic Regulation of Domestic Air Transport: Theory and Policy*, Washington DC: The Brookings Institution.

Eads, G. (1975), 'Competition in the domestic trunk airline industry: too much or too little?' in A. Phillips (ed.), *Promoting Competition in Regulated Markets*, Washington, DC: The Brookings Institution.

Eaton, J. and G.M. Grossman (1986), 'Optimal trade and industrial policy under oligopoly', *Quarterly Journal of Economics* 101.

Eddy, A.J. (1912), *The New Competition*, Chicago, MI: McClury.

Edwards, C.D. (1978), 'American and German policy toward conduct by powerful enterprises : a comparison', *Antitrust Bulletin* 23.

Elzinga, K.G. (1969), 'The antimerger law: pyrric victories', *Journal of Law and Economics* 12.

Enke, H. (1972), *Kartelltheorie*, Tübingen: J.C.B. Mohr (Paul Siebeck).

Ethier, E.J. (1971), 'General equilibrium theory and the concept of the effective rate of protection', in H.G. Grubel and H.G. Johnson (eds), *Effective Trade Protection*, Geneva: GATT Secretariat and Graduate Institute of International Studies.

Evans, D.S. (ed.) (1983), *Breaking Up Bell: Essays on Industrial Organization and Regulation*, New York: North-Holland.

Evans, J.W. (1971), *The Kennedy Round in American Trade Policy: The Twilight of the GATT?*, Cambridge, MA: Harvard University Press.

Fair Trade Commission (1971), *Nihon no Kigyo Shuchu* (Corporate Concentration in Japan), Tokyo: Printing Office of the Ministry of Finance.

Fayerweather, J. (1982), *International Business Strategy and Administration*, Cambridge, MA: Ballinger.

Federal Republic of Germany, Ministry of Finance (1986). *Ninth Subsidy Report*.

Feinberg, R.M. (1986), 'The effects of European competition policy on pricing and profit margins', *Kyklos*.

Fels, G. (1976), 'Overall assistance to German industry', in W.M. Corder and G. Fels (eds), *Public Assistance to Industry*, Boulder, CO: Westview Press.

First, H. (1986), 'Japan's antitrust policy: impact on import competition', in T.A. Pugel (ed.), *Fragile Interdependence: Economic Issues in US–Japanese Trade and Investment*, Lexington, MA: Lexington Books.

Fisher, F.M. (1985), 'The financial interest and syndication rules in network television: regulatory fantasy and reality', in F.M. Fisher (ed.), *Antitrust and Regulation: Essays in Memory of John J. McGowan*, Cambridge, MA: MIT Press.

Fisher, F.M. (1987), 'Horizontal mergers: triage and treatment', *Journal of Economic Perspectives* 1.

Fisher, F.M. and V.E. Ferrall, Jr. (1966), 'Community antenna television stations and local television station audience', *The Quarterly Journal of Economics* 80.

Fisher, F.M., J.J. McGowan and J.F. Greenwood (1983), *Folded, Spindled and Mutilated*, Cambridge, MA: MIT Press.

Fisher, F.M., J.W. McKie and R.B. Mancke (1983), *IBM and the U.S. Data Processing : An Economic History*, New York: Praeger.

Fox, E.M. (1982), 'The new merger guidelines – a blueprint for microeconomic analysis', *Antitrust Bulletin* 27.

Franko, L.G. (1980), 'Current trends in protectionism in industrialized countries: focus on Western Europe', in *Protection or Industrial Adjustment?*, Paris: The Atlantic Institute for International Affairs.

Friedlaender, A.F. (1971), 'The social costs of regulating the railroads', *American Economic Review* 61.

Friedlaender, A.F., R.H. Spady and J.S. Wang Chiang (1980), 'Regulation and the Structure of Technology in the Regulated Trucking Industry', in T. Cowling and R. Stevenson (eds), *Productivity Measurement in Regulated Industries*, New York: Academic Press.

Friedman, D. (1983), 'Beyond the age of Ford: the strategic basis of the Japanese success in automobiles', in J. Zysman and L. Tyson (eds), *American Industry in International Competition*, Ithaca, NY: Cornell University Press.

Friend, I. and M.E. Blume (1972), *The Consequence of Competitive Commissions on the New York Stock Exchange*, Philadelphia, PA: The University of Pennsylvania.

Fruhan, W.E., Jr. (1978), *The Fight for Competitive Advantage: A Study of the United States Domestic Trunk Air Carriers*, Cambridge, MA: Harvard University, Graduate School of Business Administration.

Gabriel, S.L. (1971), 'Der Begriff "Rationalisierung" unter wettbewerbspolitischem Aspekt', in Erich Hoppman (ed.), *Rationalisierung durch Kartelle?*, Berlin: Duncker und Humblot.

Galbraith, J.K. (1967), *The New Industrial State*, Boston, MA: Houghton Mifflin.

Gallo, J.C. and S.C. Bush (1983), 'A statistical analysis of antitrust enforcement for the period 1963–1983', unpublished manuscript, University of Cincinnati.

Gallo, J.C., J.L. Craycraft and S.C. Bush (1985), 'Guess who came to dinner: an empirical study of federal antitrust enforcement for the period 1963–1984', unpublished manuscript, University of Cincinatti.

Geimer, H. and R. Geimer (1981), *Research Organization and Science Promotion in the Federal Republic of Germany*, Munich: K.G. Saur.

General Agreement on Tariffs and Trade (1973), *GATT Study on the Textile and Apparel Industry*, Geneva: GATT.

George, K.D. and C. Joll (1975), 'The legal framework', in K.D. George and C. Joll (eds), *Competition Policy in the UK and EEC*, Cambridge: Cambridge University Press.

Geroski, P. and A. Jacquemin (1985), 'Industrial change, barriers to mobility, and European industrial policy', *Economic Policy* 1.

Glismann, H.H. and F.D. Weiss (1980), 'On the political economy of protection in West Germany', World Bank Staff Working Paper 427.

Gold, B. (1982), *Productivity, Technology and Capital: Economic Analysis, Managerial Strategies and Government Policies*, Lexington, MA: Lexington Books.

Gold, B. (1986), 'Some international differences in approaches to industrial policy', *Contemporary Policy Issues* 4.

Goto, A. and R. Wakasugi (1984), 'Gijutsu Seisaku' (Technology Policy), in R. Komiya, M. Okuno and K. Suzumura (eds), *Nihon no Sangyo Seisaku* (Industrial Policy in Japan), Tokyo: University of Tokyo Press.

Graham, D.R., D.P. Kaplan and D.S. Sibley (1983), 'Efficiency and competition in the airline industry', *The Bell Journal of Economics and Management Science* 14.

Grant, W. (1982), *The Political Economy of Industrial Policy*, London: Butterworths.

Greenway, D. (ed.) (1983), *International Trade Policy: From Tariffs to the New Protectionism*, London: Macmillan.

Greenway, D. (1986), 'Estimating the welfare effects of voluntary export restraints and tariffs: an application to non-leather footwear in the UK', *Applied Economics* 18.

Griliches, Z. (1986), 'Productivity, R&D, and basic research at the firm level in the 1970s', *American Economic Review*, 76.

Grubel, H.G. (1971), 'Effective tariff protection: a non-specialist guide to the theory, policy implications and controversies', in H.G. Grubel and H.G. Johnson (eds), *Effective Trade Protection*, Geneva: GATT Secretariat and Graduate Institute of International Studies.

Gruber, W.H., D. Mehta and R. Vernon (1967), 'The R&D factor in international trade and international investment of the United States', *Journal of Political Economy* 75.

Günther, E. (1968), 'Zehn Jahre Bundeskartellamt: Rückblick und Ausblick', in Arbeitskreis Kartellgesetz (ed.) *Zehn Jahre Bundeskartellamt*, Berlin: Carl Heymanns Verlag KG.

Hadley, E.M. (1970), *Antitrust in Japan*, Princeton, NJ: Princeton University Press.

Harbeson, R.W. (1971), 'Towards better resource allocation in transport', *Journal of Law and Economics* 61.

Harrop, J. (1985), 'Crisis in the machine tool industry: a policy dilemma for the European Community', *Journal of Common Market Studies* 24.

Hartland-Thunberg, P. (1981), 'The political and strategic importance of exports' in Center for Strategic and International Studies (ed.), *The Export Performance of the United States*, New York: Praeger.

Hawkins, H. and J. Norwood (1963), 'The legislative basis of United States commercial policy', in W.B. Kelly, Jr. (ed.). *Studies in United States Commercial Policy*, Chapel Hill, NC: University of North Carolina Press.

Hiemenz, U. and K. von Rabenau (1976), 'Effective protection of German industry', in W.M. Corden and G. Fels (eds), *Public Assistance to Industry*, London: Macmillan.

High, J. (1984–85), 'Bork's paradox: static v. dynamic efficiency in antitrust analysis', *Contemporary Policy Issues* 21.

Hölzer, H. and W.D. Braun (1982), 'Antitrust control over "pure" export cartels: the new German approach', *The Antitrust Bulletin* 27.

Hoppmann, E. (1971), *Rationalisierung durch Kartelle?*, Berlin: Duncker und Humblot.

Hufbauer, G.C. (1970), 'The impact of national characteristics and technology on the commodity composition of trade in manufactured goods', in Raymond Vernon (ed.), *The Technology Factor in International Trade*, New York: Columbia University Press.

Hughes, K.S. (1986), 'Exports and innovation: a simultaneous model', *European Economic Review* 20.

Imai, K. (1980), 'Japan's industrial organization', in K. Sato (ed.), *Industry and Business in Japan*, White Plains, NY: M.E. Sharpe.

Ito, M., M. Okuno, K. Kiyono and K. Suzumura (1984), 'Sijo no shippai to hoseitekisangyoseisaku' (Market Failure and Industrial Policy), in R. Komiya, M. Okuno and K. Suzumura (eds), *Nihon no Sangyo Seisaku* (Industrial Policy in Japan), Tokyo: University of Tokyo Press.

Jacquemin, A.P. (1975), 'Abuse of dominant position and changing European industrial structure', in K.D. George and C. Joll (eds), *Competition Policy in the UK and EEC*, Cambridge: Cambridge University Press.

Jacquemin, A.P. (1987), 'Collusive behavior, R&D, and European competition policy', paper presented at Arbeitstagung Industrieökonomik, Wissenschaftszentrum Berlin für Sozialforschung.

Jacquemin, A.P. and H.W. de Jong (1977), *European Industrial Organization*, London: Macmillan.

Jacquemin, A.P., T. Nanbu and I. Dewez (1981), 'A dynamic analysis of export cartels: the Japanese case', *The Economic Journal* 91.

James, G.W. (1985), 'Airline deregulation: has it worked?' *Business Economics* 20.

Japanese Standards Association (1985), *JIS Yearbook 1985*, Tokyo: JSA.

Johnson, C. (1982), *MITI and the Japanese Miracle*, Cambridge, MA: Harvard University Press.

Johnson, C. (1984), 'The idea of industrial policy', in C. Johnson (ed.), *The Industrial Policy Debate*, San Francisco, CA: Institute for Contemporary Studies.

Jordan, W. (1970), *Airline Regulation in America*, Baltimore: Johns Hopkins University Press.

Kallfass, H.H. (1980), 'Die Chicago-School – Eine Skizze des "Neuen" amerikanischen Ansatzes für die Wettbewerbspolitik', *Wirtschaft und Wettbewerb* 30.

Kaplan, E.J. (1972), 'The government-business relationship', Washington DC: US Department of Commerce.

Kawahito, K. (1972), *The Japanese Steel Industry*, New York: Praeger.

Kaysen, C. and D.F. Turner (1959), *Antitrust Policy: An Economic and Legal Analysis*, Cambridge, MA: Harvard University Press.

Keeler, T.E. (1972), 'Airline regulation and market performance', *The Bell Journal of Economic and Management Science* 2.

Keeler, T.E. (1981), 'The revolution in airline regulation', in L.W. Weiss and M. Klass (eds), *Case Studies in Regulation: Revolution and Reform*, Boston, MA: Little, Brown.

Keeler, T.E. (1983), *Railroads, Freight and Public Policy*, Washington DC: The Brookings Institution.

Keeler, T.E. (1986), 'Public policy and productivity in the trucking industry: some evidence on the effects of highway investments, deregulation and the 55 mph speed limit', *American Economic Review* 76.

Keeler, T.E. and A. Abrahams (1981), 'Market structure, pricing, and service quality in the airline industry under deregulation', in W. Sichel and T.G. Gies (eds), *Applications of Economic Principles in Public Utilities Industries*, Boston, MA: Ballinger.

Keesing, D.B. (1966), 'Labor skills and comparative advantage', *American Economic Review* 56.

Keesing, D.B. (1967), 'The impact of research and development on United States trade', *Journal of Political Economy* 75.

Kenen, P.B. (1970), 'Skills, human capital, and comparative advantage', in W.L. Hansen (ed.), *Education, Income, and Human Capital*, Conference on Research in Income and Wealth, Studies in Income and Wealth, Volume 35, New York: Columbia University Press for National Bureau of Economic Research.

Kellermann, A. (1968), 'Fairer Wettbewerb durch Wettbewerbsregeln', in Arbeitskreis Kartellgesetz, *Zehn Jahre Bundeskartellamt*, Berlin: Carl Heymanns Verlag KG.

Kelly, W.B., Jr. (1963), 'Antecedents of present commercial policy, 1922–1934', in W.B. Kelly, Jr. (ed.), *Studies in United States Commercial Policy*, Chapel Hill, NC: University of North Carolina Press.

Kindleberger, C.P. and D.B. Audretsch (eds) (1983), *The Multinational Corporation in the 1980s*, Cambridge, MA: MIT Press.

Klein, B. and L.F. Saft (1985), 'The law and economics of franchise tying contracts', *Journal of Law and Economics* 78.

Klein, D.J. (1987), 'Collusion and the *per se* debate: evidence from the United Kingdom', paper presented at the American Association Annual Meeting, December.

Klodt, H. (1987), 'R&D subsidies and export performance of manufacturing industries', *Technovation* 7.

Kolko, G. (1963), *The Triumph of Conservativism*, New York: Macmillan.

Kolko, G. (1965), *Railroads and Regulation*, Princeton, NJ: Princeton University Press.

Koo, A.Y.C. and S. Martin (1984), 'Market structure and U.S. trade flows', *International Journal of Industrial Organization* 2.

Kramny, L. (1968), 'Das Wirken des BDI in der Wettbewerbs politik', in Arbeitskreis Kartellgesetz im Ausschuß für Wettbewerbsordnung des Bundesverbandes der Deutschen Industrie (ed.), *10 Jahre Kartellgesetz, 1958–1968: Eine Würdigung aus der Sicht der deutschen Industrie*, Bergisch Gladbach: Heider Verlag.

Krasner, S. (1979), 'The Tokyo Round: particular interests and prospects in the global trading system', *International Studies Quarterly* 23.

Krause, L.B. and S. Sekiguchi (1976), 'Japan and the World Economy', in H. Patrick and H. Rosovsky (eds), *Asia's New Giant: How The Japanese Economy Works*, Washington, DC: The Brookings Institution.

Kreinin, M.E. (1974), *Trade Relations of the EEC: An Empirical Investigation*, New York: Praeger.

Krueger, A.O. (1974), 'The political economy of the rent-seeking society', *American Economic Review* 64.

Krugman, P.R. (1979), 'Increasing returns, monopolistic competition, and international trade', *Journal of International Economics* 9.

Krugman, P.R. (1984), 'Import protection as export promotion: international competition in the presence of oligopoly and economies of scale', in H.

Kierzkowski (ed.). *Monopolistic Competition in International Trade*, Oxford: Oxford University Press.

Krugman, P.R. (1987), 'Is free trade passé?', *Journal of International Perspectives* 1.

Lancaster, K. (1980), 'Intra-industry trade under perfect monopolistic competition', *Journal of International Economics* 10.

Langenfeld, J. and D. Scheffman (1988), 'Innovation and U.S. competition policy', *Aussenwirtschaft* 43, 1988, reprinted in H. Hauser (ed.). *Technology and Public Policy*, Grüsch, Switzerland: Verlag Rügger (forthcoming).

Lecraw, D. (1986), 'Japanese standards: a barrier to trade?' paper presented at Symposium on Product Standardization as a Tool of Competitive Strategy, INSEAD, Fontainbleau, France, June.

Lee, D.R. and D. Orr (1980), 'Two laws of survival for ascriptive government policies', in J.M. Buchanon, R.D. Tollison and G. Tullock (eds), *Toward a Theory of the Rent-Seeking Society*, College Station, TX: Texas A&M University Press.

Lenel, H.O. (1971), 'Zur Problematik der Rationalisierungskartelle', in E. Hoppmann (ed.), *Rationalisierung durch Kartelle?*, Berlin: Duncker und Humblot.

Lenway, S.A. (1985), *The Politics of US International Trade: Protection, Expansion and Escape*, Marshfield, MA: Pitman.

Levine, M.E. (1965), 'Is regulation necessary: California air transportation and national regulatory policy', *Yale Law Journal* 75.

Leonard, W.N. (1983), 'Airline deregulation: grand design or gross debacle?' *Journal of Economic Issues* 42.

Link, A.N. and L.L. Bauer (1984), 'An economic analysis of cooperative research', *Technovation*.

Lipsky, A.B. (1982), 'Current antitrust division views on patent licensing practices', *Antitrust Law Journal* 50.

Lowinger, T.C. (1971), 'The neo-factor proportions theory of international trade: an empirical investigation', *American Economic Review* 61.

Lowinger, T.C. (1975), 'Technology factor and the export performance of U. S. manufacturing industries', *Economic Inquiry* 13.

MacAvoy, P.W. (1971), 'The regulation-induced shortage of natural gas', *Journal of Law and Economics* 14.

MacAvoy, P.W. (ed.) (1977), *Deregulation of Cable Television*, Washington DC: American Enterprise Institute.

MacAvoy, P.W. (1979), *The Present Condition of the Regulated Industries*, New York: W.W. Norton.

MacAvoy, P.W. and R.S. Pindyck (1973), 'Alternative regulatory policies for dealing with the natural gas shortage', *The Bell Journal of Economics and Management Science* 4.

MacAvoy, P.W. and R.S. Pindyck (1975), *Price Controls and the Natural Gas Shortage*, Washington DC: American Enterprise Institute.

Magaziner, I. and T. Hout (1980), *Japanese Industrial Policy*, Berkeley, CA: Institute of International Studies.

Mann, M.H. (1975), 'The New York Stock Exchange: a cartel at the end of its reign', in A. Phillips (ed.), *Promoting Competition in Regulated Markets*, Washington DC: The Brookings Institution.

Market, K. (1975), 'EEC competition policy towards mergers', in K. D. George and C. Joll (eds), *Competition Policy in the UK and EEC*, Cambridge: Cambridge University Press.

Markham, J.W. (1965), 'Mergers: the adequacy of the new section 7', in A. Phillips (ed.), *Perspectives on Antitrust Policy*, Princeton, NJ: Princeton University Press.

Martin, F.D. (1959), *Mergers and the Clayton Act*, Berkeley, CA: University of California Press.

Maskus, K.E. (1983), *The Changing Structure of Comparative Advantage in American Manufacturing*, Ann Arbor, MI: UMI Press.

Matsushita, M. (1979), 'Export control and export cartels in Japan', *Harvard International Law Journal* 20.

Mayer, D.G. (1978), 'The effects of economic integration on trade', *Journal of Common Market Studies* 17.

McGee, J.S. (1958), 'Predatory price cutting: the Standard Oil (N.J.) case', *Journal of Law and Economics* 1.

McMillan, C.J. (1984), *The Japanese Industrial System*, New York, NY: Walter de Gruyter.

Meier, G.M. (1973), *Problems of Trade Policy*, Oxford: Oxford University Press.

Mendes, A.J.M. (1984), 'Contribution of the European Community to economic growth', *Journal of Common Market Studies* 24.

Meyer, J.R., C.V. Oster, I.P. Morgan, B.A. Berman and D.L. Strassman (1981), *Airline Deregulation: The Early Experience*, Boston, MA: Auburn House.

Miles, C. (1976), 'Protection of the British textile industry', in W.M. Corden and G. Fels (eds), *Public Assistance to Industry*, London: Macmillan.

Millstein, J.E. (1983), 'Decline in an expanding industry: Japanese competition in color television', in J. Zysman and L. Tyson (eds), *American Industry in International Competition: Government Policies and Corporate Strategies*, Ithaca, NY: Cornell University Press.

Mitnick, B. (1980), *The Political Economy of Regulation*, New York: Columbia University Press.

Miyazaki, Y. (1980), 'Excessive competition and the formation of keiretsu', in K. Sato (ed.) *Industry and Business in Japan*, White Plains, NY: M.E. Sharpe.

Monopolkommission (1976), *Mehr Wettbewerb ist möglich*, Baden-Baden: Nomos Verlagsgesellschaft.

Monopolkommission (1983), *Anhang zum Hauptgutachten 1982/1983 gemäß § 24b Abs. 3 und 5 Satz 1 GWB.*

Monroe, W.F. (1975), *International Trade Policy in Transition*, Lexington, MA: Lexington Books.

Montgomery, W.D. (1981), 'Decontrol of oil prices', in L.W. Weiss and M.W. Klass (eds), *Case Studies in Regulation: Revolution and Reform*, Boston, MA: Little, Brown.

Moore, T.G. (1974), 'Deregulating surface freight transportation', in A. Phillips (ed.), *Promoting Competition in Regulated Markets*, Washington DC: The Brookings Institution.

Moore, T.G. (1976), *Trucking Regulation*, AEI-Hoover Policy Study 18, Palo Alto, CA.

Moore, T.G. (1978), 'The beneficiaries of trucking regulation', *Journal of Law and Economics* 21.

Moore, T.G. (1985), 'US airline deregulation: its effects on passengers, capital and labor', unpublished working paper, May.

Motoshige, I., M. Okuno, K. Kiyono and K. Suzumura (1984), 'Sijo no shippai to hoseiteki san-gyo seisaku' (market failure and industrial policy), in R. Komiya, M. Okuno and K. Suzumura (eds), *Nihon no Sanyo Seisaku* (Industrial Policy in Japan), Tokyo: University of Tokyo Press.

Mueller, D.C. (1985), 'United States antitrust: at the crossroads', Wissenschaftszentrum Berlin, Discussion Paper IIM/IP 85–17.

Mueller, W.F. (1978), *The Celler–Kefauver Act: The First 27 Years*, A Staff Report to the Subcommittee on Monopolies and Commercial Law, 95th Congress, 2nd Session, December.

Mueller, W.F. (1983), 'The anti-antitrust movement', in John V. Craven (ed.),

Industrial Organization, Antitrust, and Public Policy, Boston, MA: Kluwer-Nijhoff.

Müller, J. (1986), 'Competition in the British telecommunications market: the impact of recent privatization/deregulation decisions', Symposium of the Max-Planck-Institut on 'The Law and Economics of Transborder Telecommunications'.

Nakazawa, T. and L.W. Weiss (1988), 'The legal cartels of Japan', Wissenschaftszentrum Berlin, Discussion Paper.

National Science Board (1985), *Science Indicators*, US Government Printing Office, Washington DC.

National Science Foundation (1986a), *National Patterns of Science and Technology Resources*, NSF 86–309, Washington DC.

National Science Foundation (1986b), *The Science and Technology Resources of West Germany: A Comparison with the United States*, NSF 86–310, Washington DC.

Neale, A.D. (1970), *The Antitrust Laws of the USA*, Cambridge: Cambridge University Press.

Nelson, F. and R. Noll (1985), 'Policymakers' preferences for alternative allocations of the broadcast spectrum', in F.M. Fisher (ed.), *Antitrust and Regulation: Essays in Memory of John J. McGowan*, Cambridge, MA: MIT Press.

Nelson, R.L. (1959), *Merger Movements in American Industry 1895–1956*, National Bureau of Economic Research, General Studies No. 66, Princeton, NJ: Princeton University Press.

Nicholls, W.H. (1949), 'The tobacco case of 1946', *American Economic Review* 39.

Nichols, A. and R. Zeckhauser (1981), 'OSHA after a decade: a time for reason', in L.W. Weiss and M.W. Klass (eds), *Case Studies in Regulation: Revolution and Reform*, Boston, MA: Little, Brown.

Noguchi, Y. (1982), 'The government business relationship in Japan', in K. Yanamura (ed.), *Policy and Trade Issues of the Japanese Economy*, Seattle, WA: University of Washington Press.

Noll, R.G. (1983), 'The future of telecommunications regulation', in E. Noam (ed.), *Telecommunications Today and Tomorrow*, San Diego, CA: Harcourt Brace Jovanovich.

Noll, R.G., M.J. Peck and J.J. McGowan (1973), *Economic Aspects of Television Regulation*, Washington DC: The Brookings Institution.

Nye, J.S., Jr. (1983), 'The multinational corporation in the 1980s', in C.P. Kindleberger and D.B. Audretsch (eds.), *The Multinational Corporation in the 1980s*, Cambridge, MA: MIT Press.

Odagiri, H. (1985), 'Industrial policy in theory and reality', Wissenschaftszentrum Berlin, Discussion Paper IIM/IP 85–16.

Ogura, S. and N. Yoshino (1984), 'Zeisei to zaisei toyushi' (The tax system and public finance), R. Komiya, M. Okuno and K. Suzumura (eds), in *Nihon no Sangyo Seisaku* (Industrial Policy in Japan), Tokyo: University of Tokyo Press.

Ojimi, Y. (1972), 'Basic philosophy and objectives of Japanese industrial policy', in *The Industrial Policy of Japan*, Paris: OECD.

Olson, M, (1965), *The Logic of Collective Action*, Cambridge, MA: Harvard University Press.

Olson, M, (1982), *The Rise and Decline of Nations*, New Haven, CT: Yale University Press.

Organization for Economic Cooperation and Development (1972), *The Industrial Policy in Japan*, Paris: OECD.

Organization for Economic Cooperation and Development (1982), *Annual Reports on Competition Policy in OECD Member Countries*, Paris: OECD.

Organization for Economic Co-Operation and Development (1983), *Annual Reports on Competition Policy in OECD Member Countries*, Paris: OECD.

Organization for Economic Cooperation and Development (1984), *Competition and Trade Policies: Their Interaction*, Paris: OECD.

Organization for Economic Cooperation and Development (1987), *Annual Reports on Competition Policy in OECD Member Countries*, Paris: OECD.

Oulton, N. (1976), 'Effective protection of British industry', in W.M. Corden and G. Fels (eds), *Public Assistance to Industry*, London: Macmillan.

Owen, B.M., J. Beebe and W.G. Manning (1974), *Television Economics*, Lexington, MA: Lexington Books.

Owen, B.M. and R. Braeutigam (1978), *The Regulation Game*, Cambridge, MA: Ballinger.

Owen, B.M. (1981), 'The rise and fall of cable television regulation' in L.W. Weiss and M.W. Klass (eds), *Case Studies in Regulation: Revolution and Reform*, Boston, MA: Little, Brown.

Owen, B.M. (1986), 'The evolution of Clayton Section 7 enforcement and the beginnings of US industrial policy', *Antitrust Bulletin* 31.

Owen, N. (1983), *Economies of Scale, Competitiveness and Trade Patterns within the European Community*, Oxford: Oxford University Press.

Ozaki, R.S. (1984), 'How Japanese industrial policy works', in C. Johnson (ed.), *The Industrial Policy Debate*, San Francisco, CA: Institute for Contemporary Studies.

Page, S. (1987), 'The rise in protection since 1974', *Oxford Review of Economic Policy* 3.

Pagoulatos, E. and R. Sorenson (1976), 'Domestic market structure and international trade: an empirical analysis', *Quarterly Review of Economics and Business* 16.

Parsons, D.O. and E.J. Ray (1975), 'The United States Steel Corporation: the creation of market control', *Journal of Law and Economics* 18.

Peck, M, and S. Tamura (1976), 'Technology', in H. Patrick and H. Rosovsky (eds), *Asia's New Giant: How the Japanese Economy Works*, Washington, DC: The Brookings Institution.

Pepper, T. (1986), 'Comment on industrial policy in Japan', in T.A. Pugel (ed.), *Fragile Interdependence: Economic Issues in US–Japanese Trade and Interdependence*, Lexington, MA: Lexington Books.

Pinder, D.A. (1986), 'Regional development and the European Investment Bank', *Journal of Common Market Studies* 24.

Piore, M.J. and C.F. Sabel (1984), *The Second Industrial Divide*, New York, NY: Basic Books.

Porges, A. (1979), 'On import cartels and industrial organization in Japan', Office of the US Trade Representative, Memorandum.

Porter, M.E. (1976), Interbrand Choice, *Strategy and Bilateral Market Power*, Cambridge, MA: Harvard University Press.

Porter, M.E. (1979), 'How competitive forces shape strategy', *Harvard Business Review* 79.

Posner, R.A. (1976), *Antitrust Law: An Economic Perspective*, Chicago, IL: University of Chicago Press.

Posner, R.A. (1979), 'The Chicago School of antitrust analysis', *University of Pennsylvania Law Review* 127.

Pugel, T.A. (1978), *International Market Linkages and US Manufacturing: Prices, Profits, and Patterns*, Cambridge, MA: Ballinger.

Pugel, T.A. (1986), 'Industrial policy in Japan: implications for technological catchup and leadership', in T.A. Pugel (ed.), *Fragile Interdependence: Economic Issues in US–Japanese Trade and Investment*, Lexington, MA: Lexington Books.

Rapp, W.V. (1986), 'Japan's invisible barriers to trade', in T.A. Pugel (ed.), *Fragile*

Interdependence: Economic Issues in US–Japanese Trade and Invesment, Lexington, MA: Lexington Books.

Ray, E.J. (1981a), 'The determinants of tariffs and nontariff trade restrictions in the US', *Journal of Policial Economy* 89.

Ray, E.J. (1981b), 'Tariff and Nontariff Barriers to Trade in the United States and Abroad', *The Review of Economics and Statistics* 63.

Reich, R.B. (1983), *The Next American Frontier*, New York: Times Books.

Richmond, S.B. (1961), *Regulation and Competition in Air Transportation*, New York: Columbia University Press.

Riesenkampff, A. (1977), *Gesetz gegen Wettbewerbsbeschränkungen*, Köln: Dr. Otto Schmidt.

Riffel, P. (1968), '10 Jahre deutsche Wettbewerbspolitik', in Arbeitskreis Kartellgesetz im Ausschuß für Wettbewerbsordnung des Bundesverbandes der Deutschen Industrie (ed.), *10 Jahre Kartellgesetz, 1958–1968: Eine Würdigung aus der Sicht der deutschen Industrie*, Bergisch Gladbach: Heider Verlag.

Robertson, T.S. and S. Ward (1983), 'Management lessons from airline deregulation', *Harvard Business Review* 61.

Rose, N. (1985), 'The incidence of regulatory rents in the motor carrier industry', *The Rand Journal of Economics* 16.

Rule, C.F. (1986), 'The administration's views: antitrust analysis after the nine no-no's', *Antitrust Law Journal* 54.

Sato, R. (1986), 'Japan's challenge to technological competition and its limitations', in T.A. Pugel (ed.), *Fragile Interdependence: Economic Issues in US–Japanese Trade and Investment*, Lexington, MA: Lexington Books.

Saxonhouse, G.R. (1982), 'Evolving comparative advantage and Japan's import of manufactures', in K.O. Yamura (ed.), *Policy and Trade Issues of the Japanese Economy*, Seattle, WA: University of Washington Press.

Saxonhouse, G.R. (1984), 'The micro- and macroeconomics of foreign sales to Japan', in W.R. Cline (ed.), *Trade Policy in the 1980s*, Cambridge, MA: MIT Press.

Scharrer, H.E. (1986), 'EG-Protektionismus als Preis für die Verwirklichung des europäischen Binnenmarktes', *Wirtschaftsdienst* 12.

Schattschneider, E.E. (1963), *Politics, Pressures, and the Tariff*, Hander, CT: Archon Books.

Scheffman, D. and P. Spiller (1987), 'Geographic market definition under the department of justice merger guidelines', *Journal of Law and Economics* 30.

Scherer, F.M. (1973), 'The determinants of industrial plant sizes in six nations', *Review of Economics and Statistics* 34.

Scherer, F.M. (1977), 'The posnerian harvest: separating wheat from chaff', *Yale Law Review* 86.

Scherer, F.M. (1979), 'The causes and consequences of rising industrial concentration', *Journal of Law and Economics* 22.

Scherer, F.M. (1980), *Industrial Market Structure and Economic Performance* (2nd edn), Chicago, IL: Rand McNally.

Schlögl, H. (1971), 'Bericht über die Diskussion des Steinzeugfalles', in E. Hoppmann (ed.), *Rationalisierung durch Kartelle?* Berlin: Duncker und Humblot.

Schmalensee, R. (1979), *The Control of Natural Monopolies*, Lexington, MA: Lexington Books.

Schmalensee, R. (1982), 'Antitrust and the new industrial economics', *American Economic Review* 72.

Schmalensee, R. (1987), 'Horizontal merger policy: problems and changes', *Journal of Economic Perspectives* 1.

Schmidt, I. and U. Kirschner (1985), 'Darstellung und wettbewerbspolitische würdigung der US Vertical Restraints Guidelines', *Wirtschaft und Wettbewerb* 35.

Schmidt, J. and B. Rittaler (1986), *Die Chicago-School of Antitrust Analysis: Wettbe- werbstheoretische und-politische Analyse eines Credos*, Baden-Baden: Nomos Verlagsgesellschaft.

Segelmann, F. (1968), 'Wettbewerb und Rationalisierung unter Berücksichtigung der Syndikate und Spezialisierungskartelle', in Karl Schiller (ed.), *Zehn Jahre Bundes- kartellamt: Beiträge zu Fragen und Entwicklungen auf dem Gebiet des Kartellrechts*, Berlin: Carl Heymanns Verlag KG.

Semiconductor Industry Association (1983), *The Effect of Government Targeting on World Semiconductor Competition: A Case History of Japanese Industrial Strategy and its Costs on America*, Washington DC.

Servan-Schreiber, J.-J. (1968), *The American Challenge*, London: Hamish Hamilton.

Sharp, M. (1987), 'Europe: collaboration in the high technology sectors', *Oxford Review of Economic Policy* 3.

Shepherd, W.G. (1979), *The Economics of Industrial Organization*, Englewood Cliffs, NJ: Prentice Hall.

Shepherd, W.G. (1982), 'Causes of increased competition in the US Economy, 1939–1980', *Review of Economics and Statistics* 64.

Shepherd, W.G. (1983), 'Price structures in electricity', in A.P. Danielson and D.R. Kamerschen (eds), *Current Issues in Public-Utility Economics*, Lexington, MA: Lexington Books.

Shepherd, W.G. (1985), *Public Policies Toward Business* (7th edn), Homewood, IL: Richard D. Irwin.

Shinohara, M. (1982), *Industrial Growth, Trade, and Dynamic Patterns in the Japanese Economy*, Tokyo: University of Tokyo Press.

Sirbu, M.A. (1982), 'A review of common carrier deregulation in the United States', MIT Paper Research Program on Communications Policy.

Solow, R. (1984), 'Industrial policy', *Journal of Economic Issues* 18.

Spence, M.A. (1976), 'Product selection, fixed costs and monopolistic competition', *Review of Economic Studies* 43.

Staiger, R.W., A.V. Deardorff and R.M. Stern (1985a), 'An evaluation of factor endowments and protection as determinants of Japanese and American foreign trade', University of Michigan, Ann Arbor, Research Seminar in International Economics, Discussion Paper 158.

Staiger, R.W., A.V. Deardorff and R.M. Stern (1985b), 'The effects of protection of the factor content of Japanese and American foreign trade', University of Michigan, Ann Arbor, Research Seminar in International Economics, Discussion Paper 159.

Staiger, R.W., A.V. Deardorff and R.M. Stern (1985c), 'The employment effects of Japanese and American protection', University of Michigan, Ann Arbor, Research Seminar in International Economics, Discussion Paper 165.

Steckmeister, M. (1986), 'Die gegenwärtige Zusammenschlußwelle in den Vereinigten Staaten und ihre Ursachen', *Wirtschaft und Wettbewerb* 36.

Stern, L.W., T.W. Dunfee and E.F. Zelek, Jr. (1982), 'A rule of reason analysis of territorial restrictions in the soft drink industry', *Antitrust Bulletin* 27.

Stern, R.M. (1975), 'Testing trade theories', in P.B. Kenen (ed.), *International Trade and Finance: Frontiers of Research*, New York: Cambridge University Press.

Stern, R.M. and K.E. Maskus (1981), 'Determinants of the Structure of US Foreign Trade, 1958–76', *Journal of International Economics* 11.

Stigler, G.J. (1950), 'Monopoly and oligopoly by merger', *American Economic Review* 40.

Stigler, G.J. (1971), 'The theory of economic regulation', *Bell Journal of Economics and Management Science* 2.

Stigler, G.J. (1982), 'The economists and the problem of monopoly', *American Economic Review* 72.

Stocking, G.W. and M.W. Watkins (1946), *Cartels in Action*, New York: The Twentieth Century Fund.

Stoll, H.R. (1979), *Regulation of Securities Markets: An Examination of the Effects of Increased Competition*, New York: New York University Graduate School of Business Administration.

Stoll, H.R. (1981), 'Revolution in the regulation of securities markets: an examination of the effects of increase competition', in L.W. Weiss and M.W. Klass (eds), *Case Studies in Regulation: Revolution and Reform*, Boston, MA: Little, Brown.

Streit, M.E. (1984), 'Innovationspolitik zwischen Unwissenheit und Anmaßung von Wissen', *Hamburger Jahrbuch für Wirtschafts- und Gesellschaftspolitik* 29.

Streit, M.E. (1985), 'Industrial policies for technological change: the case of West Germany', unpublished manuscript, University of Mannheim.

Suzumura, K. and M. Okuno-Fujiwara (1986), 'Industrial policy in Japan: brief overview and evaluation', paper presented at the Conference on Trade Friction and Economic Policy, at the Graduate School of Business Administration, New York University, April.

Sveikauskas, L. (1983), 'Science and technology in United States foreign trade', *The Economic Journal* 93.

Swann, D. (1984), *The Economies of the Common Market* (5th edn), Harmondsworth: Penguin Books.

Thurow, L.C. (1980), *The Zero Sum Society*, New York: Basic Books.

Thurow, L.C. (1985), 'Healing with a thousand bandages', *Challenge* 28.

Toepke, U.P. (1982), *EEC Competition Law*, New York: John Wiley.

Trebbing, H.M. (1976), *New Dimensions in Public Utility Pricing*, East Lansing, MI: Michigan State University.

Trezise, H. and Y. Suzuki (1976), 'Politics, government, and economic growth in Japan', in H. Patrick and H. Rosovsky (eds), *Asia's New Giant: How The Japanese Economy Works*, Washington DC: The Brookings Institution.

Tsurumi, Y. (1976), *The Japanese Are Coming: A Multinational Interaction of Firms and Politics*, Cambridge, MA: Ballinger.

Tsurumi, Y. (1984), *Multinational Management*, Cambridge, MA: Ballinger.

Tumlir, J. (1978), 'Salvation through cartels? on the revival of a myth', *The World Economy* 1.

Tyson, L. and J. Zysman (1983), 'American industry in international competition', in J. Zysman and L. Tyson (eds), *American Industry in International Competition: Government Policies and Corporate Strategies*, Ithaca, NY: Cornell University Press.

Ueno, H. (1980), 'The conception and evaluation of Japanese industrial policy', in K. Sato (ed.). *Industry and Business in Japan*, White Plains, NY: M.E. Sharpe.

United States Civil Aeronautics Board (1974), *Domestic Passenger Fare Investigation*, CAB Reports, Special Volume, Washington DC: US Government Printing Office.

United States Congress (1973), 93rd, first session, *Implications of Multinational Firms for World Trade and Investment for US Trade and Labor*, Report to the Committee on Finance of the United States Senate and Its Subcommittee on International Trade on Investigation No. 332–64, Under Section 332 of the Tariff Act of 1930, Washington DC: US Government Printing Office.

United States Department of Labor (1980), Office of Foreign Economic Research. *Report of the President on US Competitiveness*, Washington DC: US Government Printing Office.

United States Federal Communications Commission (1979), *Report on the Inquiry into the Economic Relationship Between Television Broadcasting and Cable Television*, Washington DC: US Government Printing Office.

United States Federal Energy Administration (1975), *The Natural Gas Shortage: A Preliminary Report*, Washington DC: US Government Printing Office.

United States Federal Power Commission (1975), *National Gas Survey*, Washington DC: US Government Printing Office.

United States General Accounting Office (1979), *US–Japan Trade: Issues and Problems*, Washington DC: US Government Printing Office.

United States General Accounting Office (1982), *Industrial Policy: Case Studies in the Japanese Experience*, Washington DC: US Government Printing Office.

United States General Accounting Office (1983), *Industrial Policy: Japan's Flexible Approach*, Washington DC: US Government Printing Office.

United States International Trade Commission (1981), *Multifiber Arrangement, 1973 to 1980*, Washington DC: US International Trade Commission.

United States International Trade Commission (1982), *Color Television Receivers: US Production, Shipments, Inventories, Exports, Employment, Manhours and Prices, First Calendar Quarter 1982*, Report to the President on Investigation No. 332–112 under Section 332 of the Tariff Act of 1930, Washington DC: US International Trade Commission.

United States International Trade Commission (1983a), *Competitive Assessment of the US Metalworking Machine Tool Industry*, Report to the United States International Trade Commission on Investigation No. 332–149, Under Section 332 of the Tariff Act of 1930, Washington DC: US International Trade Commission.

United States International Trade Commission (1983b), *Foreign Industrial Targeting and its Effects on US Industries, Phase I: Japan*, Washington DC: US International Trade Commission.

United States International Trade Commission (1984), *Foreign Industrial Targeting and its Effects on US Industries, Phase II: The European Community and Member States*, Report to the Subcommittee on Trade, Committee on Ways and Means, US House of Representatives on Investigation No. 332–162 Under Section 332 (6) of the Tariff Act of 1930, Washington DC: US International Trade Commission.

United States International Trade Commission (1985a), *Non Rubber Footwear*, Report to the President on Investigation No. TA-201–55 Under Section 201 of the Trade Act of 1974, Washington DC: US International Trade Commission.

United States International Trade Commission (1985b), *Review of the Effectiveness of Trade Dispute Settlement under the GATT and the Tokyo Round Agreements*, Report to the Committee on Finance, US Senate, on Investigation No. 332–212 Under Section 332(g) of the Tariff Act of 1930, Washington DC: US International Trade Commission.

United States International Trade Commission (1985c), *Non Rubber Footwear*, Quarterly Statistical Report, Washington DC: US International Trade Commission.

United States International Trade Commission (1985d), *The Effects of Restraining US Steel Imports on the Exports of Selected Steel Consuming Industries*, Washington DC: US International Trade Commission.

United States International Trade Commission (1985e), *A Review of Recent Developments in the US Automobile Industry Including An Assessment of the Japanese Voluntary Restraint Agreements*, Preliminary Report to the Subcommittee on Trade, Committee on Ways and Means of the US House of Representatives in Connection with Investigation No. 332–188, Washington DC: US International Trade Commission.

United States International Trade Commission (1985f), *Annual Report '85*,

Washington DC: US International Trade Commission.

United States International Trade Commission (1985g), *US Imports of Textile and Apparel Products Under the Multifiber Arrangement, 1981–1984*, Washington DC: US International Trade Commission.

United States International Trade Commission (1985h), *The Internationalization of the Automobile Industry and its Effects on the US Automobile Industry*, Report on Investigation No. 332–188 Under Section 332 of the Tariff Act of 1930, Washington DC: US International Trade Commission.

United States International Trade Commission (1985i), *The US Automotive Industry: US Factory Sales, Retail Sales, Imports, Exports, Apparent Consumption, Suggested Retail Prices, and Trade Balances with Selected Countries for Motor Vehicles, 1964–84*, Washington DC: US International Trade Commission.

United States International Trade Commission (1985j), *Probable Economic Effect on Providing Duty-Free Treatment for US Imports of Certain High-Technology Products*, Report to the President on Investigation No. TA-13, (6)–9 Under Section 131(b) of the Trade Act of 1974, Washington DC: US International Trade Commission.

United States Tariff Commission (1974), *Trade Barriers*, Report to the Committee on Finance of the United States Senate, Washington DC: US Tariff Commission.

Valden, T. (1976), 'Truckers fear continued deregulation drive', *Congressional Quarterly* 34.

Vernon, R. (1954), 'American foreign trade policy and the GATT', *Essays in International Finance* 21, Princeton, NJ: Princeton University Press.

Vernon, R. (1966), 'International investment and international trade in the product life cycle', *Quarterly Journal of Economics* 80.

Wada, M. (1986), 'Selling in Japan: consumer behavior and distribution as barriers to imports', in T.A. Pugel (ed.), *Fragile Interdependence: Economic Issues in US–Japanese Trade and Investment*, Lexington, MA: Lexington Books.

Wallace, A. and J. Penoyer (1978), 'Directory of Federal Regulated Agencies', Washington University Center for the Study of American Business, Working Paper 36.

Walsh, A.E. and J. Paxton (1975), *Competition Policy*, London: Macmillan.

Walters, K.D. and R.J. Monsen (1979), 'State-owned business abroad: new competitive threat', *Harvard Business Review*, 75.

Weiss, F.D. (1987), 'A political economy of European Community trade policy against the less developed countries?' *European Economic Review* 31.

Weiss, L.W. (1974a), 'An analysis of the allocation of antitrust division resources', in J.A. Dalton and S.L. Levin (eds), *The Antitrust Dilemma*, Lexington, MA: Lexington Books.

Weiss, L.W. (1974b), 'The concentration-profits relationship and antitrust', in Harvey J. Goldschmid, H.M. Mann and J.F. Weston (eds), *Industrial Concentration: The New Learning*, Boston, MA: Little, Brown.

Weiss, L.W. (1979), 'The structure-conduct-performance paradigm and antitrust', *University of Pennsylvania Law Review* 127.

Weiss, L.W. (1981), 'State regulation of public utilities and marginal-cost pricing', in L.W. Weiss and M.W. Klass (eds), *Case Studies in Regulation: Revolution and Reform*, Boston, MA: Little, Brown.

Weiss, L.W. (forthcoming), 'Cartel', in *The New Palgrave*.

Weiss, L.W. and G. Pascoe (1984), 'The extent and permanence of market dominance', Wissenschaftszentrum Berlin, Discussion Paper IIM/IP 84–23.

Wells, L.T. (1966), *The Product Life Cycle and International Trade*, Cambridge, MA: Harvard University Press.

West, R. and S. Tinic (1971), 'Minimum commission rates on New York Stock Exchange transactions', *Bell Journal of Economics and Management Science* 2.

Weston, F.J. and S.H. Lustgarten (1974), 'Concentration and wage-price changes', in H.J. Goldschmid, M. Mann and J.F. Weston (eds), *Industrial Concentration: The New Learning*, Boston, MA: Little, Brown.

Wheeler, J.W., M.E. Janow and T. Pepper (1980), *Japanese Industrial Development Policies in the 1980s: Implications for US Trade and Investment*, New York: Hudson Institute.

Wheelwright, S.C. (1985), 'Restoring competitiveness in US manufacturing', *California Management Review* 27.

White, L.J. (1987), 'Antitrust and merger policy: review and critique', *Journal of Economic Perspectives* 1.

White, L.J. (1974), 'Industrial organization and international trade: some theoretical considerations', *American Economic Review*, 64.

Windblicher, C. (1980), 'Informal practices to avoid merger control litigation in the US and West Germany: a comparison', *Antitrust Bulletin* 25.

Wildavsky. A. (1984), 'Squaring the political circle', in C. Johnson (ed.), *The Industrial Policy Debate*, San Francisco, CA: Institute for Contemporary Studies.

Winston, C. (1985), 'Conceptual developments in the economics of transportation: an interpretative survey', *Journal of Economic Literature* 23.

World Bank (1984), *World Development Report*, Washington DC: World Bank.

Wyckoff, D.D. and D. Maister (1975), *The Motor Carrier Industry*, Lexington, MA: Lexington Books.

Wheeler, J.W., M.E. Janow and T. Pepper (1980), *Japanese Industrial Development Policies in the 1980s: Implications for US Trade and Investment*, New York: Hudson Institute.

Yamamura, K. (1982), 'Guidance and cartels', in K. Yanamura (ed.), *Policy and Trade Issues of the Japanese Economy*, Seattle, WA: University of Washington Press.

Yamawaki, H. and D.B. Audretsch (1988), 'Import share under international oligopoly with differentiated products', *Review of Economics and Statistics* 70.

Yamawaki, H., L.W. Weiss and L. Sleuwaegen (1986), 'Industry competition and the formation of the European Common Market', Wissenschaftszentrum Berlin, Discussion Paper IIM/IP 86–14.

Zysman, J. and S.S. Cohen (1983), 'Double or nothing: open trade and competitive industry', *Foreign Affairs* 64.

INDEX

INDEX OF CASES